MW00745315

"The approach is unique—scholarly thoughts for the preachers and teachers, and practical for every believer. That's the kind of balance I like! I especially appreciate the way the authors have handled the symbolism in John's Gospel. John was a poet-theologian-evangelist, and they've done a splendid job bringing out all three aspects of his writing. Commentators who approach John's Gospel only as a theological treatise miss so many of the beautiful 'asides' that John has put there.

The new believer and the most seasoned saint will both find enlightenment and nourishment in the book. Best of all, they won't have to struggle through a lot of academic obstacles to get to the treasures. I'm recommending this book."

Warren W. Wiersbe, D.D.
Bible Teacher

"The unique format will prove highly useful to scholars, students, under-scholars, and Sunday school teachers alike! I enthusiastically recommend it!"

Harold L. Willmington, D.Min.
Dean, Liberty Home Bible Institute

"An excellent and insightful work. It opens the Gospel of John to the student in a fresh and helpful manner."

R. C. Sproul, Ph.D.
Professor of Systematic Theology

"C. S. Lewis observed, 'Any fool can write learned language, the vernacular is the real test.' This commentary passes the 'test,' for its authors have opened profound treasures of John with laser accuracy and brilliance. A book for those sharing the 'light of life.' I am enthused about this book."

R. Kent Hughes, D.Min.
Senior Pastor Emeritus, College Church, Wheaton, IL

"This is a splendid and very helpful book on John's Gospel. Combining percep-tive historical background materials, keen exegetical insights, practical life applications, pertinent illustrations, and suggested preaching helps, the authors have produced a rich and valuable study for serious Bible scholarship, both textual and interpretive. The authors do not dodge the problem of difficult passages, but deal fairly with them and their interpretations. Presentation of varying views are carefully drawn. Any time spent in studying this volume will be fully repaid. This is a book that pastors and Bible students will want to own."

William F. Kerr, Th.D.†
Former Dean, PAC RIM Bible College & Seminary

"Here is a solid truckload of top-class expository material. Preachers and teachers, rejoice!—and buy your copy at once! You will not regret the investment."

J. I. Packer, D.Phil.
Professor of Theology, Regent College

"Even though I've read the Gospel of John many times, it took on a new freshness as I read *Opening the Gospel of John*. This will be a 'must book' for everyone who wants to teach or preach the Gospel of John."

Bernie May
Wycliffe Bible Translators

"Every teacher looks for a commentary that provides historical background, textual insights, and practical applications in a form easily grasped. This excellent resource does all of it beautifully."

J. Allan Petersen[†]
Family Concern

"The authors have produced a valuable study of John's Gospel that should be of great value for ministers preparing sermons on John or for laypeople preparing Bible studies. *Opening the Gospel of John* tackles the Gospel in significant sections, highlights the theme of each section, lists the major points, discusses key terms, and provides a running commentary on the verses. The whole is very practical. Readers will find many useful applications to today's evangelical church."

James M. Boice, Th.D.[†]
Former Pastor, Tenth Presbyterian Church, Philadelphia, PA

[†]Deceased

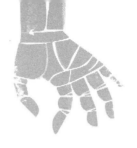

Opening John's Gospel and Epistles

Pastoral Reflections on Love, Light, and Logos

Philip W. Comfort
Wendell C. Hawley

TYNDALE HOUSE PUBLISHERS, INC. | CAROL STREAM, ILLINOIS

Visit Tyndale's exciting Web sites at www.newlivingtranslation.com and www.tyndale.com

TYNDALE, New Living Translation, NLT, and the New Living Translation logo are registered trademarks of Tyndale House Publishers, Inc.

Opening John's Gospel and Epistles

Library of Congress Cataloging-in-Publication Data

Comfort, Philip Wesley.
  [Opening the Gospel of John]
  Opening John's Gospel and Epistles / Philip W. Comfort and Wendell C. Hawley.
    p. cm.
  First work originally published: Opening the Gospel of John. Wheaton, Ill. : Tyndale House, c1994. 2nd work originally published: Cornerstone biblical commentary. Carol Stream, Ill. : Tyndale House Publishers, c2005- <c2009>.
  Includes bibliographical references.
  ISBN 978-1-4143-3153-9 (sc)
  1. Bible. N.T. John—Commentaries. 2. Bible. N.T. Epistles of John—Commentaries. I. Hawley, Wendell C., date. II. Title. III. Title: Cornerstone biblical commentary.
  BS2615.53.C66 2009
  226.5'07—dc22   2009021515

Printed in the United States of America

15   14   13   12   11   10   09
7   6   5   4   3   2   1

Contents

Dedication vii
Preface ix

JOHN'S GOSPEL

DEDICATION

*The authors are very appreciative
of the insightful suggestions
of Mrs. Beth Bergman,
whose editorial touch enhanced
this work immeasurably;
and the support of Phil's wife,
Georgia, and
Wendell's wife, Nancy, whose
encouragement and affirmation
never ceased.*

Preface

For six years, early on Wednesday mornings, we laid the Gospel of John open before us to study it verse by verse. We asked God to open our spiritual eyes to see Jesus afresh, and he was faithful time and again to reveal living truth to us. As the years went on, we decided to expand our studies to include John's epistles and to share our thoughts with others—especially those who teach and preach from them.

One of the authors, Philip Comfort, has taught this Gospel at various colleges and churches during the past twenty years. The other author, Wendell Hawley, has preached this Gospel in many churches and army services as a pastor and a chaplain. Our goal in writing this book was to combine our efforts in producing a book on John's writings that would provide the teacher and preacher with exegetical and homiletical insights. To this end, each section has an introduction and/or exposition, a preaching focus (not a fully developed sermon, but a "seed starter" or "pump primer" devotional suggestion), a section on key words and phrases, exegetical comments on every verse, and textual notes. It is our prayer that our readers will use this fresh resource, together with the text of the Bible itself, to strengthen the believers' living faith in Jesus Christ, the Son of God.

The Gospel of John

Introduction

THE AUTHORSHIP OF JOHN'S GOSPEL

In a day when John's authorship of the fourth Gospel is routinely challenged, it is important for teachers and preachers to know how to make a case for the well-founded premise that the fourth Gospel was written by John the son of Zebedee, for he was both an eyewitness of Jesus and an apostle. We must be able to affirm for our listeners and students that this Gospel is an eyewitness account with apostolic authority.

Though John's authorship is not explicitly stated anywhere in the Gospel, the text itself points to his authorship. The writer of this Gospel, one of Jesus' twelve disciples, calls himself "the one whom Jesus loved" (13:23; 19:26; 20:2; 21:7, 20). From the synoptic Gospels we realize that three disciples were especially close to Jesus: Peter, James, and John. Peter could not have been the author of this Gospel because the one who identified himself as "the one whom Jesus loved" communicated with Peter at the Last Supper (13:23-25), raced Peter to the empty tomb on the morning of the Resurrection (20:2-4), and walked with Jesus and Peter along the shore of Galilee after Jesus' resurrection (21:20-23). Thus, someone other than Peter authored this Gospel. And that someone could not have been James, for he was martyred many years before this Gospel was written (see Acts 12:2). That someone must have been John, who shared a deep friendship with Jesus. Most likely, it was also John who was "one of the two"—the one who, with Andrew (Peter's brother), was the first to follow Jesus (1:35-40). Furthermore it seems probable that he was the one whose acquaintance with the high priest later gained him access along with Peter into the courtyard of the place where Jesus was on trial (18:15-16). This eyewitness, "the disciple whom Jesus loved," stood by Jesus during his crucifixion (19:25-26) and walked with Jesus after his resurrection (21:20). This is that same disciple who wrote the Gospel that bears his name (21:24-25). (See Westcott, who follows a similar line of reasoning to prove John's authorship.)

The question remains, Why didn't John identify himself directly? Why, instead, would he call himself "the disciple whom Jesus loved" or "the/that other disciple"? The former expression seems a bit arrogant—after all, didn't Jesus love the other disciples? Of course. But John wanted his readers to know that he had a special relationship with Jesus—not for the sake of boasting, but for the sake of affirming the trustworthiness of his testimony. As the Son "in the bosom of the Father" (1:18, NKJV) was the one qualified to explain the Father to mankind because of his special relationship with the Father, so John, who reclined on Jesus' chest (13:23, see NLT mg), was qualified to explain Jesus and his message to readers because of his special relationship with Jesus. In this Gospel "the beloved disciple" or "the other disciple" is given a certain kind of preeminence: He is the first to follow Jesus (1:35-37); he is the closest to Jesus during the Last Supper (13:22-25); he follows Jesus to his trial (18:15); he alone of all the disciples goes to Jesus' cross and is given a direct command from Jesus to care for Jesus' mother (19:26-27); he outruns Peter to the empty tomb and is the first to believe in Jesus' resurrection (20:1-8); and he is the first to recognize that it is Jesus appearing to them in his Galilean visitation (21:7). If John had named himself in all these instances, he would have appeared quite arrogant. Rather, he attempted to retain some humility by referring to himself in the third person; at the same time, he probably expected the immediate circle of readers to clearly identify him as the apostle John and to believe in the validity of his written account.

We also gather from early church history that this Gospel was attributed to John. Several of the early church fathers stated so with great conviction. Irenaeus, writing around AD 200, said, "John, the disciple of the Lord, he who had leaned on his breast, also published the Gospel, while living at Ephesus in Asia" (*Heresies* 3.1.1). Irenaeus indicated that he had obtained his information from Polycarp (c. 70–155), who was a disciple of John (and even quoted 1 John in his own epistle around 120). Furthermore, Irenaeus cited Papias, a contemporary of Polycarp, as giving witness to the fact that John was the author of the fourth Gospel (ibid., 5.33.4). Other early (second- and early third-century) church fathers attributed the fourth Gospel to John: Heracleon (the first known commentator on John, repeatedly quoted by Origen), Theophilus, Clement of Alexandria, Tertullian, Hippolytus, and Origen. And several second-century sources (whether orthodox, heterodox, or heretical) provide evidence for the existence of John's Gospel: the Gnostic Basilides, *The Gospel of Truth* by Valentinus, Tatian's *Diatessaron, The Apocryphon of John,* and *The Gospel of Thomas.* These sources show that John's Gospel, written at the end of the first century, was prevalent throughout the Greco-Roman world in the early second century.

Since the time of Irenaeus, the church has given constant witness to the tradition that John wrote the Gospel while residing in Ephesus. Not until the past century or so has the apostle John's authorship been challenged. The gravest problem with some of these challenges is that they undermine the eyewitness account found in the Gospel; for in declaring that someone other than John the apostle, the son of Zebedee, wrote this Gospel, they take away the apostolic testimony. The writer of the Gospel clearly claims to have seen the Word incarnate (1:14), to have witnessed the Crucifixion (19:35), and, in fact, to have witnessed all the events recorded in the Gospel (21:24). The apostle John's eyewitness account is what authenticates this Gospel and gives us ground for believing its testimony about Jesus Christ, the Son of God (see 20:31; cf. 1 Jn 1:1-4).

Some scholars affirm the eyewitness account of the Gospel writer, but then do not identify him as John the apostle. Who else could the eyewitness be? All attempts at naming another person are unconvincing. Therefore, many of the same scholars who reject the apostle John's authorship feel compelled to name him as the authority behind the Gospel but not the writer of it. (For more on this, see J. A. T. Robinson's *Redating the New Testament,* pp. 254–311, which aptly defends the apostle's authorship.)

John's eyewitness authorship of the fourth Gospel is repeatedly affirmed by the historical and geographical accuracy of the text. For example, archaeological and related historical studies have verified John's description of (1) the Samaritans—their theology, worship at Mount Gerizim, and the location of Jacob's well; (2) the pool of Bethesda and accompanying details; (3) the theological themes associated with the Jewish feasts and ceremonies current in Jesus' day; and (4) details about Jerusalem itself—the pool of Siloam, Solomon's portico (a shelter in winter), and the stone pavement of Pilate's praetorium. John's descriptions reflect an accurate knowledge of Jerusalem prior to its destruction in AD 70. The same reporting accuracy was at work when John provided an eyewitness account of Jesus' words, feelings, and miraculous signs.

PLACE OF WRITING

Readers and students of John's Gospel usually want to know the historical setting for its writing. In order to provide this background, one may look at the earliest accounts of church history. Eusebius, the first church historian (after Luke), wrote *Ecclesiastical History* around 325, and he gives us a great deal of information about the composition of the fourth Gospel.

Irenaeus said that John, the disciple associated with this Gospel, lived in Ephesus (*Heresies* 3.1.1). Polycrates (bishop of Ephesus around 190) also said that John had lived in Ephesus (Eusebius's *History* 3.31.3). Another tradition (provided by the Muratorian Canon) tells us that John wrote this Gospel at the request of some of his fellow disciples and the elders of the church residing with him in Ephesus. Clement of Alexandria affirmed the same: "Last of all John, . . . being urged by his friends, and inspired by the Spirit, composed a spiritual gospel" (ibid., 6.14.7). Most likely these "elders" or "friends" at Ephesus were the men who, at the conclusion of the Gospel, bore witness to the authenticity of John's narrative. We read in John 21:24 (NRSV), "This is the disciple who is testifying to these things and has written them." To these words, the elders at Ephesus appended their testimony, "And we know that his testimony is true."

The final composition of John's Gospel—including the epilogue (ch 21) and other editorial adjustments—could have taken place anywhere between AD 80 and 100. Very likely the initial work—i.e., John's preaching about Jesus' life and teachings—began as early as AD 70, followed sometime later by an initial draft of the Gospel.

THE WRITING AND PUBLICATION OF JOHN'S GOSPEL

According to Irenaeus, John "published" his Gospel, which most likely means he wrote it and had it reproduced into multiple copies for distribution to various churches. The Greek word *exedōke,* appearing in Irenaeus's account (*Heresies* 3.1.1), was used in ancient times to mean this kind of publication. Many portions of the Gospel were probably first uttered by John through oral discourse, in homilies or teachings to the early believers about the life and sayings of Jesus Christ. In the first-century church, most of the Christians learned of the life and teachings of Jesus through oral transmission and catechisms; the written Gospels were a later development, created to affirm and/or clarify the oral tradition (Luke 1:1-4).

When the occasion arose for John to put his "sermons" into writing, he evidently composed a series of vignettes, each saturated with Jesus' discourse, woven into a sequential narrative. The entire Gospel focuses on "the Word"— God's expression to men, God's explicator. First, Jesus, as the Word, came to explain God to men; then John expounded on this exposition and formed it into a series of teachings for the church. Thus, each passage in the Gospel of John is not only a historical narrative but a homily packed with spiritual instruction for the believers of John's time, as well as for believers throughout all time. The author's intention was to produce a document not of history, but of faith (see 20:30-31). Yet John is very historical—historical in the sense in which history is concerned not only with what happened but also with the deepest meaning of what happened (Brown 1966).

John must have also participated in publishing its final form. The anti-Marcionite prologue to John says, "According to Papias, the dear disciple of John, in his five exegetical books, his Gospel was published and sent to the churches by John himself during his lifetime." In John's day it was the customary practice for an author to dictate his words to a scribe and then read over the manuscript to make editorial adjustments.

At that time it was common for books to be published in multiple copies. Prior to the first century, most books were published in the form of a papyrus roll. From the first century onward, more and more books, especially those containing Scripture, were published in the form of a papyrus codex. (The term *codex* designates a book having a spine to which folded pages were stitched.) Christians used the codex almost exclusively for preparing copies of both Old and New Testament books. Very likely, John's Gospel was first published in several codices. Perhaps John (or the Johannine community) employed the use of professional scribes in the great library at Pergamum (a city not far from Ephesus, where John wrote his Gospel) in making the publication. If he did not, then he would have relied on the church community to make the publication.

Very likely, John published a first edition of his Gospel and then another with an appended chapter at the end. Chapter 20 provides the first conclusion with an excellent colophon telling the reader why this book was written. Chapter 21 is clearly an addendum. It is possible that John added this chapter shortly after he wrote the Gospel and then published all twenty-one chapters in the first publication, but it is likely that John added chapter 21 some time after the first publication, in a second edition. There seems to be evidence that the Gospel of John circulated as a twenty-chapter Gospel and also as a twenty-one-chapter Gospel even as late as AD 200 because two early papyrus manuscripts, 𝔓5 and 𝔓75, very likely had only twenty chapters (see discussion at the end of ch 20). If, in fact, 𝔓5 and 𝔓75 originally contained a Gospel of only twenty chapters, this would confirm the view that the Gospel of John was first published and circulated without the epilogue. Sometime after the first publication, John added the epilogue and sent forth another publication. This publication superseded the first one—as is attested to by all other extant manuscripts. (See the appendix to Comfort's *Quest for the Original Text of the New Testament.*)

As was previously mentioned, tradition tells us that John wrote his Gospel at the request of some of the elders of the church residing with him in Ephesus. Most likely these are the men who, at the conclusion of the Gospel, bore witness to the authenticity of John's narrative.

THE CIRCULATION OF JOHN'S GOSPEL THROUGHOUT THE MEDITERRANEAN WORLD

As was noted earlier, John's written Gospel was probably reproduced into multiple copies by the Johannine community (perhaps with the help of professional scribes at Pergamum) and sent out to the churches in Asia Minor and beyond. This Gospel, as with the other three Gospels, usually circulated as a book of its own, unattached to any of the other Gospels. It wasn't until the third century that the four Gospels began to be collected into one volume.

The fourth Gospel had widespread distribution in the second century and was generally regarded as the work of John the apostle. The second-century church fathers who read this Gospel and referred to it were Papias, Polycarp, Irenaeus, and Theophilus (of Antioch); the third-century church fathers who read John's Gospel and quoted it were Origen, Clement of Alexandria, Tertullian, Hippolytus, and Melito (bishop of Sardis).

The Gospel of John was also popular among those who professed the orthodox Christian faith. Braun (*Jean Theol I*) shows that John's Gospel was accepted in orthodox circles in Egypt, Rome, Syria, and Asia Minor from the early years of the second century. John was also popular among early Egyptian Gnostics. In the second century several Egyptian Gnostics, such as Basilides (who quoted John 1:9, according to Hippolytus), Valentinus (who wrote *The Gospel of Truth*), Ptolemaeus (who wrote a commentary on John's prologue), and Heracleon (who is the first one known to write a commentary on John's Gospel), misused the Gospel of John to support their views. This misuse involved flawed exegesis and prooftexting, more than textual tampering.

The Gospel of John was also very popular in the second and third centuries among the Egyptian Christians. Several papyri containing portions of John have been discovered in Egypt, and many of these have been dated to the second or early third centuries. The John Rylands Papyri, 𝔓52, containing portions of John 18, has been dated from 110–125; Papyrus Edgerton 2, containing portions drawn from John, has been dated around 150; the Bodmer Papyrus II, 𝔓66, preserving almost all of John, has been dated around 175; the Bodmer Papyrus XV, 𝔓75, displaying John 1–15, has been dated around 200; the Oxyrhynchus Papyrus, 𝔓90, containing portions of John 18 and 19, has also been dated around 200. Some other Oxyrhynchus Papyri, such as 𝔓5 and 𝔓22, are early-third-century manuscripts, as is the Chester Beatty Papyrus, 𝔓45.

John's Gospel enjoyed widespread distribution because of its universal appeal. It seems directed to the universal church composed of Jewish and Gentile believers. John had served the Jewish Christians in Jerusalem for many years (AD 30–70) and then later in life (probably after AD 70) ministered to the Gentile churches in Asia Minor. Thus John ministered to both Jewish and Gentile churches and would have been well received by both. Unlike Paul, whose commission took him to the Gentiles and away from the Jews, John had served both communities. Furthermore, so far as we know, John had not taken sides during the Jew/Gentile controversies described in Acts 15. His Gospel manifests a Jewish orientation, for most scholars readily point out that this Gospel was written by a Palestinian Jew. Nonetheless, it retains a universal appeal. The Jewish Christians reading this Gospel would immediately see all the connections with the Old Testament; the Gentiles would read this Gospel and immediately recognize that Jesus had come to give life, light, and truth to the whole world.

JOHN'S PRIMARY PURPOSE FOR WRITING HIS GOSPEL

At the time John wrote this Gospel (anywhere from AD 70 to 100), the early Christians needed written documentation from Jesus' eyewitnesses to confirm and clarify what they had been taught orally. Most likely, the immediate recipients of John's Gospel were the churches in Asia Minor (seven of which are also addressed in the book of Revelation), because John labored among these churches in the latter part of his ministry. As with all the New Testament writings, the audience has extended far beyond those to whom the writings were originally directed. Nevertheless, it is important to put each book in its historical context.

When John wrote his Gospel narrative, his aim was for the readers to keep on believing in Jesus as the Christ, the Son of God, and to keep on having life in his name (20:31). His Gospel was written primarily to those who already believed yet needed their faith infused with a fresh breath of life and strengthened by a clear presentation of Jesus Christ, the Son of God. (The verb tense for *believe*, a present subjunctive in the earliest manuscripts containing John 20:31, indicates that John wrote this Gospel to encourage ongoing faith, more than to produce initial faith, though it can certainly do the latter quite well. The other verbal expressions in John 20:31—"believing" and "have life"—are also in the present tense, emphasizing continual action.) John wrote his Gospel to encourage ongoing faith and ongoing participation in Christ's life. As Raymond Brown put it, "The evangelist wants the believer to realize that he already possesses eternal life, that he is already a son of God, and has already met his judge. . . . The major purpose of the Gospel, then, is to make the believer see existentially what this Jesus in whom he believes means in terms of life" (lxxviii).

OTHER PURPOSES FOR WRITING

When John wrote this Gospel, he was attempting to meet several needs, some of which are introduced below:

1. *To provide a polemic against Docetism.* Early in church history, heresies plaguing the believers distorted the true presentation of Jesus, the God-man. Thus another Gospel account (in addition to the synoptic Gospels)—from the pen of an eyewitness—was needed to paint a clear picture of Jesus as the one who was fully God and fully man. In particular, John was doing battle with the heresy that later became known as Docetism (from the Greek word *dokeō,* which means "it seems to be so"). The Docetists taught that Jesus only seemed to be man; his humanity, they said, was actually just a guise. John confronted this heresy in its early stages by asserting that the Word, who was very much God, became flesh; God became a real man with flesh and bones. This was Jesus. However, it should be noted that it was John's first and second epistles, more than his Gospel, that were aimed at confronting this heresy directly. In these epistles he made it very clear that anyone who would not confess that Jesus had come in the flesh was a person who did not belong to God and was united with the spirit of the antichrist (see 1 Jn 4:1-3; 2 Jn 1:7).

2. *To encourage Jewish Christians to leave Judaism.* Another reason John may have written this Gospel was to encourage believing Jews to leave Judaism and openly follow Jesus Christ. As was noted earlier, Jesus is presented as the spiritual fulfillment and reality of all the major themes in the Jewish economy. As with the book of Hebrews, John's Gospel encourages the Jewish Christians to forsake Judaism and pursue a living relationship with Jesus. John presented the Jewish leaders (whom he often simply calls "the Jews") as people who were opposed to Jesus and to the followers of Jesus—to the extent that all those who openly confessed Jesus as the Messiah were thrown out of the synagogues. His expression "be put out of the synagogue" (12:42; 16:2) literally means "become de-synagogued"—similar to our idea of excommunication.

According to Jewish regulations, there were two kinds of excommunication:

one that would last for thirty days until the offender was reconciled, and one that was a permanent ban accompanied by a curse. Many Jews in John's day had been "de-synagogued" or permanently banned because they confessed Jesus to be the Christ. (This was predicted by Jesus in 16:2.) An ancient document found in the Cairo Genizah (c. 80–90) contains a curse against the Nazarenes, banning them from participating in the synagogue. In Jesus' day there was also a kind of informal prohibition against any Jew who confessed Jesus to be the Christ.

"The Jews" in John's day were the Pharisees who still persecuted Jewish Christians after the destruction of Jerusalem. John wrote his Gospel to encourage true Jewish believers in the diaspora synagogues to suffer the excommunication and become part of Jesus' flock. His Gospel should have been a help to those Jews who became believers but were afraid to openly confess Jesus as their Messiah (see 12:42).

3. *To encourage unity among Jewish and Gentile believers.* Since John did not take sides during the Jew/Gentile and law/grace controversies that shook the church in its beginning days and that occupied Paul's energies, he was well received by all the church. His Gospel was aimed at promoting unity in the church. He alludes in John 10:16 to the Jewish and Gentile believers as two groups of sheep becoming one flock under the care of one shepherd, Jesus. (The imagery parallels Paul's analogy of Jewish and Gentile believers becoming one body under Christ's headship.) John 11:52 also speaks of the gathering together of all God's people into one entity, and John 17 is a plea for a unity among all the believers based upon their spiritual oneness with the triune God. Furthermore, this Gospel shows Jesus proclaiming the Good News to the Jews (Nicodemus), the Samaritans (the Samaritan woman and the others of Sychar), and Gentiles (the royal official in Cana and the Greeks in Jerusalem). These are the same groups to whom the gospel was proclaimed in successive order when the church first began (Acts 1:8). All believers—whether Jews, Samaritans, or Gentiles—would have seen in this Gospel that it was Jesus' intention to have one church (even though the word *church* doesn't appear in this Gospel) united to himself, just as many branches are united with one another by virtue of their union with the vine (John 15).

4. *To clarify the relationship between John the Baptist's followers and Jesus' followers.* The reader of John's Gospel will notice that John the Evangelist refers to John the Baptist and his followers on several occasions (see 1:6-8, 15, 19-37; 3:22-36; 4:1-2; 10:40). John had a special interest in John the Baptist and his disciples, as the apostle himself had originally been a disciple of the Baptist before becoming a disciple of Jesus. Thus John the Evangelist had the advantage of participating in both discipleships. It is clear from the Gospel that only some of the Baptist's disciples followed Jesus, while many stayed on with the Baptist and continued his ministry. Eventually, two baptisms were going on concurrently: John the Baptist's and Jesus' (3:22-23; 4:1-2). This led to a competitive spirit aroused by the jealousy of John's disciples over the success of Jesus' disciples (3:26). John the Baptist himself had no such spirit—as is clearly proven by his speech in 3:27-36. In fact, the Baptist pointed all men to Jesus Christ. However, even after his death,

John the Baptist still had a following. This sect perpetuated John's baptism and John's teachings. Among some of his early followers may have been Apollos and the group of men at Ephesus (Acts 18:24-25; 19:1-6).

John used the prologue, the remainder of the first chapter, the latter part of the third chapter, and the end of the fourth chapter to show the Baptist's role in introducing the Messiah and his own avowed inferiority to the Christ. The Gospel writer would hope that the words of the Baptist himself would convince his followers to go to the Bridegroom, for all the increase belongs to him (3:29-30). John the Gospel writer was among the first to make the move; his Gospel was written to motivate the others.

OPENING JOHN AS A PORTRAIT OF JESUS

The Gospel of John is not event-oriented; it is person-oriented. There are events, but the events function as a platform for exhibiting Jesus. While Gospel writers like Mark narrate action upon action, John mainly selects those stories that will manifest some specific aspect of Christ's person. The scene at the well in Samaria serves as a good backdrop for portraying Jesus as the fountain of living waters; the multiplication of the loaves gives a good setting for showing Jesus as the Bread of Life; and the raising of Lazarus from the dead is a marvelous stage for presenting Jesus as the resurrection and the life.

No other book of the New Testament reveals as much about Christ's person as does the Gospel of John. The prologue alone contains more descriptions about Jesus than any other passage in the Bible of equivalent size. Jesus is presented as the Word, the one who was face-to-face with God, God himself, the one in the beginning, the Creator, the life, the light of men, the rejected one, the received one, the incarnate Word, the tabernacle of God, the one and only Son of the Father, the one full of grace and truth, and God's interpreter. What a Christ!

John does not present Jesus in an objective way—as if he were providing a list or positing a creed. John's record is warm and personal, as one would find in a memoir. With fond recollection, John recounts the awe with which he (and the other disciples) gazed upon Jesus' special glory (1:14). The entire Gospel is delightfully enhanced by John's firsthand experience and personal interaction with Jesus. He had been with Jesus. John and Jesus shared a special love—so much so that John named himself "the disciple whom Jesus loved." This is the disciple who gives us a penetrating look at Jesus as both God and man.

John wrote this Gospel to present Jesus as the Christ, the Son of God (20:31). If we miss Jesus as we read this Gospel, we miss the author's intent. The Gospel of John is not preeminently a theological treatise; it is a portrait (or a series of portraits), a biography containing narrative "snapshots" of Jesus' life and person. With each scene and each picture, John reveals another aspect of Jesus Christ, the Son of God. John told us that there were so many things that Jesus did that even the world itself could not contain the books that could be written about them (21:25). John, therefore, selected certain events and put them in a kind of photo album. Scene after scene presents another view of Jesus. It is the preachers' and teachers' task to make these scenes come alive for the modern imagination. This book is dedicated to that task.

The structure of this book will basically follow this motif, as well as give special attention to the spiritual journey motif and to the unveiling of the triune God. The outline for this book (as seen in the table of contents) follows the "portrait of Jesus" approach.

MAPS TO OPENING JOHN

Word studies

In addition to looking for major thematic movements in John's Gospel, it is important to present the key words and phrases used in John's Gospel. These will be thoroughly explained for each passage in the commentary notes. Some of the terms that appear more frequently throughout the entire book are as follows:

Believe: This word indicates belief and trust. In John it is usually followed by the preposition *eis* with the accusative: *pisteuō eis auton* (I believe in him). Sometimes it is not followed by a prepositional phrase or an object; in such cases it usually means that the people believed that Jesus was the Christ. However, it should be noted that there are different levels of belief in the Gospel of John. Some believe Jesus is the Christ when he performs some miraculous sign and then don't believe him when he speaks of having come from heaven or of going to the cross. This kind of belief fluctuates. Others put their trust in Jesus, and their faith remains firm. When John speaks of believing in Jesus' name (see 1:12), he means that people have believed in Jesus' person completely—in all that he is. This constitutes true faith.

Eternal: This word is often used with "life" to indicate everlasting life. The expression is both quantitative (illimitable time) and qualitative (eternal in nature, as is the nature of God).

I am: This expression is often used by Jesus in identifying himself as deity and in describing his divine realities. This expression, without a predicate nominative, can mean "I am that I am" (see John 8:58) or "I am the one" (i.e., "I am the Christ"—see John 8:29; cf. 4:26). This expression, followed by a predicate nominative, is often used by Jesus to describe what he is—such as: "I am the bread of life" (6:48), "I am the light of the world" (8:12), "I am the resurrection and the life" (11:25), and "I am the way, the truth, and the life" (14:6, NRSV).

Life (*zōē*): The only word for "life" that is used with "eternal." The word *zōē* is used to describe the eternal life, the divine life—present in Jesus and available as a gift to all who believe in Jesus. To receive *zōē* is to have God's life now and to be guaranteed of eternal life in the future.

Light and darkness: These two words are often used to contrast the realm of God in Christ versus the realm of Satan in the world (i.e., fallen humanity). God through Christ gives light to a world in darkness.

Signs (*sēmeia*): John consistently uses this word to speak of the miraculous signs that Jesus performed. Every miracle is a sign pointing to the sign-giver, the Son of God, Jesus Christ. John has often been called the book of signs because the Gospel is structured around the giving of a sign followed by a discourse.

Truth: This means reality, veracity—especially spiritual reality as opposed to religious falsehood.

World: This is the world system in which every human being lives. The word is used to describe this system (as it stands in opposition to God) and the people in this system.

Narrative structure

Finally, the teacher and preacher should have a good handle on the narrative structure of John's Gospel. John's Gospel begins with a prologue and John the Baptist's testimony, as follows:

1:1-18	Prologue
1:19-28	John the Baptist's testimony—He provides a link between Jesus and Jesus' first followers, including John, the Gospel writer.

Then the narrative commences, in which there is a historical and geographical sequence, as follows:

1:29	The next day—after John the Baptist's initial testimony
1:35	The next day—the first day for John the Gospel writer (initially a disciple of John the Baptist) to follow Jesus
1:43	The next day—the second day in Galilee
2:1	The third day of the disciples' following Jesus
2:12	After this, Jesus went to Capernaum but didn't stay there long.
2:13	The first Passover—Jesus went to Jerusalem.
3:22	After these things (that occurred in Jerusalem), Jesus went to Judea, where Jesus' disciples baptized people.
4:1-3	Jesus left Judea to go to Galilee because the Pharisees heard about how many people were being baptized.
4:4	Jesus went through Samaria.
4:46	Jesus went to Cana of Galilee.
5:1	Jesus went to Jerusalem to participate in a Jewish feast (probably Pentecost).
6:1	After these things, Jesus went beyond the Sea of Galilee, near Capernaum (6:16-17, 24, 59).

6:4	It was near the time of Passover, but Jesus stayed in Galilee.
7:1	After these things, Jesus stayed in Galilee.
7:2, 14	The Feast of Tabernacles—Jesus went to Jerusalem during the middle of the feast.
8:12-59	Jesus spoke in the treasury area of the Temple in Jerusalem.
9:1–10:21	Jesus remained in Jerusalem.
10:22	There was a feast of dedication—referring to the Festival of Lights (Hanukkah)—and it was winter.
10:23	During this festival Jesus taught at Solomon's court.
10:40	Jesus left Jerusalem and went beyond the Jordan to the place where John was first baptizing (cf. 1:28).
11:1, 17ff	Jesus went to Bethany, where he raised Lazarus from the dead.
11:54	Jesus left Judea.
11:55	Passover was about to begin.
12:1	Six days before the Passover Jesus went to Bethany.
12:12	The next day—Jesus made his triumphal entry into Jerusalem.
13:1–14:31; 15:1–17:26	Before the Passover feast—Jesus celebrated the Last Supper with his disciples. (All that follows until 17:26 could have taken place during this time together. But according to 14:31 ["Rise, let us be on our way" (NRSV)], it is more likely that what follows [15:1–17:26] is a compilation of Jesus' speeches between the time of the Passover meal [which, according to John, was not on the evening before his crucifixion] and his arrest in the Garden of Gethsemane.)
18:1	Jesus went to the Garden of Gethsemane.
18:13	After Jesus was arrested, he was taken to Annas, the high priest.
18:28	Jesus was taken to the praetorium to be interrogated by Pilate.
19:17	Jesus went to Golgotha, where he was crucified.
19:42	Jesus was buried in a garden cemetery near Golgotha.
20:1	Early on the first day of the week—Jesus rose from the dead.
20:19	Early evening that same day—Jesus appeared to his disciples in a room in Jerusalem. (Thomas was absent.)
20:26	After eight days—Jesus appeared to his disciples again in Jerusalem. (This time Thomas was present.)
21:1-25	Jesus appeared to some of his disciples as they were fishing on the Sea of Galilee.

The Prologue: Jesus, the Word Become Flesh

INTRODUCTION

A prologue is an introduction to a literary work. Its purpose is to set the tone for the work, introduce major characters and significant themes that will be developed later in the narrative, and provide background information necessary to the narrative. Greek readers were familiar with prologues. Homer's *Iliad* and *Odyssey*, two very popular works in John's day, begin with well-crafted prologues.

John's prologue is a masterpiece in its own right. It is the first of two true prologues found in the New Testament. Hebrews 1 is the only other portion that could be called a true prologue, and it, too, is a masterpiece. Luke's small introduction (Luke 1:1-4) is more like a preface than a prologue in that it states why he wrote his Gospel but does not really introduce it. First John 1:1-4 and Revelation 1:1-8, both written by John, could also be called prologues, but neither one is as rich and full as the prologue John wrote for his Gospel.

When teaching or preaching the prologue, the teacher would do well to read the entire passage out loud—slowly and with feeling. Try doing this with the *New Jerusalem Bible,* the *New English Bible,* the *New American Standard Bible,* or the *New Living Translation* because they have the prologue set in poetic lines. Nearly everyone present will then recognize that the prologue is very poetic.

The prologue has been considered by many commentators to be a poem or at least rhythmical prose. Some commentators have thought that verses 1-5, 10-12, and 14-18 may have been parts of one or several early Christian hymns.[1] Others have thought that verses 14-18 may have come from a kind of church confessional or corporate testimonial.[2] Whatever John's sources, he crafted a beautiful poem—sublime in its simplicity, yet profound in its complexity. Readers and commentators have seen allusions to Old Testament passages and many associations with the rest of the Gospel. Verses 1-5 seem to have a great affinity with the Wisdom Literature, and verses 14-18 with the Old Testament books covering Israel's exodus and years in the wilderness.

Furthermore, the prologue is itself a kind of miniature Gospel of John. Almost every major item that one reads in the rest of the Gospel is found in the prologue. We are introduced to key terms—such as *the Word, God, life, light, darkness, witness, the world, rejection/reception, belief, regeneration* (becoming a child of God), *incarnation* (the Word become flesh), *the one and only Son of the Father, glory, grace, truth,* and *fullness*—that are expanded upon and illustrated in the rest of the Gospel. Throughout the Gospel narrative Christ is presented as the one who expresses God (the Word); as God himself; as the giver of eternal life to those who believe; as the bringer of light into a dark world that rejected him against the witness of John the Baptist, the Old Testament Scriptures, and Jesus' miraculous signs; as the giver of grace to those who receive him; as the unique Son sharing an intimate relationship with his Father; as the bearer of heavenly truth; and as the expression of God's glory and fullness. It is important to grasp the significance of the key words and phrases in the prologue in order to unlock the rich meaning of the narrative that follows.

The structure of the prologue is fascinating. The first five verses form a kind of mini-prologue. Containing most of the key elements found in the rest of the prologue, these five verses span the time frame from eternity, to Creation, to Christ's ministry, to the present (note the present tense verb in 1:5—"the light shines"). The prologue begins and ends on the same theme; John 1:1 and 1:18, in effect, mirror each other. In both verses the Son is called God, the Son is depicted as the expression ("the Word") and explainer of God, and the Son is shown in intimate fellowship with the Father—face-to-face with God and "in the bosom of the Father." In the third verse of the prologue we read how the Word was the instrument of Creation but was rejected by his own creatures (1:10-11). The struggle between light and darkness is elaborated in the following verses. Those who reject Jesus are in darkness; those who receive him become children of God.

EXPOSITION

1:1-18/The Uniqueness of Jesus

Those preaching this passage should emphasize how unique Jesus Christ is. In a single sentence the personality, eternity, and deity of Christ are all affirmed: "In the beginning was the Word, and the Word was with God, and the Word was God" (NRSV). John proclaims, right at the start, what the rest of the Scriptures teach: that the Son has always existed, even from eternity, and the Son has always lived in the closest possible fellowship and communion with the Father. This delightful relationship is more than we can adequately comprehend.

The Son left the glories of that eternal relationship with the Father to bring life and light to earth by becoming a man among men. What a pitiful commentary on this world that mankind was so engrossed in darkness that the Light was neither recognized nor received when he appeared. Who needs to be told the sun is shining? The blind! Light penetrates the darkness and accurately reveals man's fallen condition. Jesus alone illumines every man who hears the gospel. There is no other Light for man than Christ Jesus. The reception of that Light brings about the new birth that comes not by heredity or inheritance, not by natural instinct, and not by human volition or desire. The new birth comes from God through his Son, who as the Word is the perfect revelation of God to men.

God's desire is to be known by people—by you and me. Apart from Christ, such knowledge would be impossible. Christ is the unique expression of God to us. In him and through him we can see God and know God personally and experientially. As we begin our journey through the rest of John's Gospel, let us look for him, and let us seek to know him. In this prologue we have been introduced to the most extraordinary person alive—Jesus Christ, who is God, the Word, Creator, life, light, grace, truth, the one and only Son, and God's explainer. In John's first epistle he declared that he (with the other disciples) had seen, heard, and touched the Word of life (who had been face-to-face with God and then was manifest in the flesh to them); and then John declared that he (with the other disciples) had entered into fellowship with the Son and the Father. But this fellowship is not exclusive; John extended an invitation for participation to all who believe in Jesus Christ (see 1 Jn 1:1-3). God the Father through his Son has opened the way for us to have fellowship with him. May we accept the invitation and enjoy this divine privilege.

KEY WORDS AND PHRASES

- » The Word (1:1-2, 14)
- » The Word was God (1:1, 18)
- » Life (1:4-5)
- » Light (1:4-5, 7-9)
- » Believe (1:7, 12)
- » Born of God (1:13)
- » The Word became flesh (1:14)
- » Full of grace and truth (1:14, 16)
- » He [Jesus] has explained God (1:18)

NOTES

1:1 *In the beginning.* When John speaks of the beginning, he might have been thinking of the beginning of creation. If so, his point is that the Word already existed at the time of creation (as is translated in the NEB). But it is more likely that John was thinking of a beginning before "the beginning" in Genesis 1:1, a kind of timeless beginning. Thus, we could translate the first part of the verse as "in eternity the Word existed," or "the Word existed in perpetuity," or "as to a beginning, the Word already was." John takes us back as far as our minds can go, for our finite minds cannot conceive of eternity—only of beginnings and endings. And yet God never began; he always was and will be. He is eternal.

the Word. As the Word, the Son of God fully conveys and communicates God. The Greek term is *logos;* it was used in two ways by the Greeks. "The word might be thought of as remaining within a man, when it denoted his thought or reason. Or it might refer to the word going forth from the man, when it denoted the expression of his thought—i.e., his speech. The Logos, a philosophical term, depended on the former use" (Morris). As a philosophical term, the *logos* denoted the principle of the universe, even the creative energy that generated the universe. The term *logos* may also have some connection with the Old Testament presentation of wisdom as a personification or attribute of God (Prov 8). In both the Jewish conception and the Greek, the *logos* was associated with the idea of beginnings—the world began through the origination and instrumentality of the Word (Gen 1:3ff, where the expression "God said" is used again and again). John may have had these ideas in mind, but most likely he originated a new term to identify the Son of God as the divine expression. He is the image of the invisible God (Col 1:15), the express image of God's substance (Heb 1:3). In the Godhead, the Son functions as the revealer of God and the reality of God. This is a central theme throughout the Gospel of John. How grateful we are that the Son of God has expressed the Father to us and made him real to us. Otherwise, we could not know God intimately and personally.

the Word was with God. This simply means that the Son knew the Father intimately from eternity, enjoying fellowship in the very richest sense. The preposition in Greek is *pros,* associated with the Greek expression *prosōpon pros prosō pon,* meaning "face-to-face with." The expression was commonly used in Greek language to indicate a personal relationship (Matt 13:56; 26:18; Mark 6:3; 14:49; 1 Cor 16:10; 2 Cor 5:8; Gal 1:18). By using this expression, John was intimating that the Word (the Son) and God (the Father) enjoyed an intimate, personal relationship from the beginning. The last verse of the prologue (1:18) tells us that the Son was in the bosom of the Father, and in Jesus' intercessory prayer of John 17 he revealed that the Father loved him before the foundation of the world. We cannot imagine the extent of their union and communion. Yet what is even more astounding is the truth that God has extended this fellowship to include us. What a blessed privilege!

the Word was God. Not only was the Son with God, he was himself God. This phrase suggests relationship. In the previous clause ("the Word was with God"), there is an article before God (*ton theon*)—pointing to God the Father. In this clause, there is no article before God. The distinction may indicate that John did not want the reader to think that the Son was the Father—but the same as the Father; that is, both are God (*theos*). The NEB reads, "And what God was, the Word was," and TEV reads, "And he was the same as God." John's Gospel, more than most books in the New Testament, asserts Jesus' deity. He is called God in 1:1, 18; 20:28. Jesus said that he existed before Abraham even came into being (8:58), and he asserted that he and the Father are one (10:30)—an assertion the Jews understood as a claim to deity (10:31-33).

1:2 *He was in the beginning with God* (NRSV). This underscores the truth that the Word coexisted with the Father from the beginning. A heresy developed in the days of the early church that stated the Son was created by the Father at some point in time, meaning that the Son is not eternal. This heresy, known as the Arian heresy, still exists today in several religious cults. The orthodox Christian position affirms the truth that the Son of God is coeternal with the Father; that is to say that he always existed.

1:3 *Through him all things were made.* The New Testament reveals that the Son of God was the agent of creation, for all things were created through him (see 1 Cor 8:6; Col 1:16; Heb 1:2). All the things created by God came into being through Christ's instrumentality.

1:4 *In him was life.* The word *zōē* in classical Greek was used for life in general. There are a few examples of this meaning in the New Testament (see Acts 17:25; Jas 4:14; Rev 16:3), but in all other instances the word was used to designate the divine, eternal life—the life of God (Eph 4:18). This life resided in Christ, and he made it available to all who believe in him. Human beings are born with natural life—called *psuchē* in Greek (translated "soul," "personality," or "life"); they do not possess eternal life. This life can be received only by believing in the one who possesses the *zōē* life, namely, Jesus Christ.

that life was the light of men. The divine life in Christ illuminates the inner lives of men. It reaches and penetrates people, illumining them to the divine truth and exposing them to their sin. Wherever Christ was present, he gave light—light to reveal his identity and light to expose sin (3:21; 8:12). No one can come into contact with Christ without being enlightened. His light either exposes or illumines or both. In his presence we see our sin and we see his glory. Of course, a person can refuse to come to the light and remain in darkness. But whoever comes to the light will receive Christ's enlightening. In the Gospel of John this enlightening is usually gradual rather than instantaneous. This was true for the disciples, Nicodemus, the Samaritan woman (ch 4), and the blind man whom Jesus healed (ch 9).[3]

1:5 *The light shines in the darkness.* Although John said that Jesus *was* the Light of the World, John thinks of him as still being the Light of the World, for John shifts to present tense: "the light is shining in darkness." Christ's life and message are still effective even after his ministry on earth. First John 2:8 says that the darkness is passing away, and the true light is now shining. As the light shines, the darkness is expelled. And darkness is a metaphor for unregenerate humanity (12:40; Eph 5:8) blinded by the god of this world (2 Cor 4:4).

darkness has not understood it. Christ shone in the midst of a hardened, darkened humanity—and he continues to shine. The darkness did not grasp or comprehend the light, and yet it could not "extinguish it" (TLB). The NEB uses the word *mastered* to convey both ideas. This statement indicates that there has been a struggle between the darkness and the light. The darkness—unregenerate humanity under the influence of Satan, the prince of darkness—has not accepted the light and even resists the light. But the light prevails!

1:6 *There came a man who was sent from God; his name was John.* The reader is now introduced to Jesus' forerunner and herald, John the Baptist. He was sent from God to prepare the way for the Messiah, and his ministry ushered in the long-awaited messianic age. No wonder he is given such a prominent position as this Gospel begins. He was instrumental in pointing the people to Jesus the Messiah. In fact, John the Gospel writer was a disciple of John the Baptist but then left him after John the Baptist pointed his disciples to the Lamb of God (1:36ff).

1:7-8 *he came as a witness to testify to the light* (NEB). John the Baptist's function was to bear testimony to Christ. The greatest man ever born (John the Baptist; see Matt 11:11) had the highest privilege: He was a witness to Christ, an emissary through whom people could come to belief in Christ. John himself was **not the light**, therefore no one should believe in him. In 5:35 (Greek text) John is called a lamp. Thus, Jesus was the light, and John was a lamp through which the light shined. Though we are not as great as John the Baptist, and our testimony will not be as profound, we also have the privilege of being witnesses to Christ. People can come to believe in Christ through us. According to Philippians 2:15, we are called upon to be luminaries in the midst of a crooked and perverse generation.

1:9 *coming into the world.* According to the Greek grammar, this phrase can modify "the light" (see RSV, NASB, NIV) or "every man" (KJV, TLB). According to the context, John was probably speaking about the light coming into the world, not every person coming into the world. Either way, the verse states that the light enlightened every person. This is a bold assertion. Has Christ enlightened everyone? And if so, in what ways? His presence and divinity are manifest in creation (1:3; Rom 1:19-20), and his truth should be operative in any conscience that has heard the gospel.

1:10 *the world did not recognize him.* This indeed is one of the greatest of all tragedies: The world—humankind—did not recognize its own Creator.

1:11 *He came to His own* (NKJV). Gr., "He came to his own things"—i.e., he came to that which belonged to him. This could refer to all the people of his creation or to his own native place, Israel.

His own did not receive Him (NKJV). According to the Greek, his own people did not receive him. The Greek word for "receive," *paralambanō,* means "to welcome," literally, "to receive alongside." The Jews did not welcome Jesus. This is one of the saddest statements in the Bible. How tragic that Jesus was neither recognized nor welcomed by his very own people. As a nation, they rejected their Messiah. This rejection is further described at the end of Jesus' ministry in 12:37-41.

1:12 all who received him. That is, accepted him into their lives. The Greek word for "receive" is used in 1:5 in the sense of grasping (*katalambanō*), in 1:11 in the sense of welcoming (*paralambanō*), and here (*lambanō*) in the sense of accepting.

to those who believed in his name. The new birth comes by believing in Jesus Christ. To believe in his name is to believe in his person—who he is and what he represents. Many believed in Jesus' ability when they saw his miracles, but they did not believe in Jesus himself. They believed in him when he fulfilled their expectations of what the Messiah should be, but they did not believe in him when he defied their preconceived notions (see comments on 2:23-25). We must believe in Jesus as Jesus, the Son of God; we must be careful to believe in him according to the biblical presentation of his person, not according to our own concepts. Some today believe in Jesus as a great teacher, a great moralist, a great humanitarian, but not as the great reconciler to God.

right. Gr., "authority." In this context, it speaks of God's granting the right or giving the privilege for the new birth. No one can attain this new birth by his or her own power; it is granted by God.

children of God. The Greek word for "children" emphasizes the idea of birth: *tekna* from *tiktō* (to give birth).

1:13 natural descent. Lit., "bloods," suggesting bloodline.

human decision. Or "human volition."

a husband's will. Or "a man's decision."

of God. God is the unique progenitor, the source of the new birth. The new birth is divinely given. It cannot be attained because one is a Jew by natural birth (or even born into a Christian family); it cannot be attained by an act of human will; and it has absolutely nothing to do with human planning. It is a gift of God.[4]

1:14 The Word. This continues the theme of the prologue; it is logically connected with 1:1ff, not with 1:13.

became flesh. Many modern translators have rendered this phrase "became a man." Of course, this is what the text means. But John purposely used the word *flesh* because he was combating a heresy called Docetism, which denied the actuality of Jesus Christ's human body. The Docetists claimed that the Son of God merely assumed the guise of humanity but was not truly human. In his first epistle, John said that any person who did not confess that Jesus Christ had come in flesh was a person who did not belong to God (1 Jn 4:3). God became what he never was before—a man, a human being. Yet when he became a man he did not cease being God. He was both God and man, the God-man. This is a mystery. How could God become a man? How could he limit himself to the human life process? He became a fetus, a child, a son, and a man. He became flesh the same way all men become flesh, and yet his flesh was without sin (2 Cor 5:1).

made his dwelling. The Greek word means "tabernacled" or "pitched [his] tent." To the reader familiar with the Old Testament, this easily would have brought to mind the Old Testament Tabernacle. The next words ("We have seen his glory") would have especially emphasized this association, for the Tabernacle was filled with the shekinah glory of God (Exod 40:34). The Tabernacle in the wilderness was temporary and outwardly unattractive. It was nevertheless God's dwelling place among men, where God met man and man met God. Jesus was God's new Tabernacle among men. God in Jesus dwelt among men. What a thought! This man living with the disciples was God incarnate!

We have seen [gazed upon] **his glory.** John, speaking on behalf of the apostles, with fond recollection affirms that they had seen his glory. No doubt John was thinking of the time he and two other disciples saw Jesus' transfiguration. (Peter spoke of it specifically in 2 Pet 1:16-18.) But John was also probably speaking of that glory they beheld in Jesus at any and all times. Within that veil of his flesh, underneath the appearance of an ordinary Jewish carpenter, was the indwelling glory of God. To the outsider, he was nobody special; to those in the inner circle, he was the unique Son of God filled with the shekinah glory. Although we have not been granted the privilege of seeing this, we have been given the testimony of those who did. Through their eyes and their testimony, we can imagine the one who was so glorious to gaze upon, and in spirit we can gaze upon him and see the glory of God in the face of Jesus Christ (2 Cor 4:6).

the glory of the One and Only. The Greek word for "only begotten" (*monogenous*) suggests a one and only son; it does not necessarily convey the idea of a birth. For example, Isaac is called Abraham's *monogenous* in the Septuagint (Gen 22:2, 12, 16), when actually Abraham had two begotten sons: Ishmael and Isaac. But Isaac was his one and only son (Heb 11:17). The Son of God was the Father's one and only, his unique Son. Although the Father has begotten many sons (1:12-13), none of these sons are exactly like Jesus Christ, the unique Son of God. His sonship is from eternity. As the unique Son of God, he has had a special glory and an unrivaled place of honor.

who came from the Father. Lit., "came from a father." The phrase could be connected with glory (i.e., the glory given to the Son came from the Father), or the phrase could simply indicate that the Son came to us from the Father. The second alternative is preferable.

full of grace and truth. This phrase should be connected with "the Word" who dwelt among men. The Greek word for "full" (*plērēs*) should probably be connected with "the Word," not with "glory" or with "Father." According to John, the Word was full of grace and truth. The Greek word for "grace" (*charis*) is probably equivalent to a Hebrew word meaning "loving-kindness" (see TLB, Exod 34:6, a verse that describes God in relationship to the declaration of the covenant on Mount Sinai); the word in Greek also means "that which gives joy" and "that which is a free gift."

The Greek word for "truth" (*alētheia*) means "reality" and "verity"; in John it is usually connected with the idea of divine revelation (8:32; 17:17; 18:37). Those who have been enlightened by God realize that Christ is the divine reality (see comments on 14:6). Christ is full of loving-kindness and full of divine reality.

We might have loving-kindness and we might express truth, but none of us are continually full of grace toward others or are consistently true. With Christ, there is always grace and always verity. He is constantly full (see comments on 1:16).

1:15 This verse seems to interrupt the flow of the narrative because 1:16 naturally follows the end of 1:14 ("full of grace and truth . . . and of his fullness have we all received, and grace for grace" [NRSV]). Nevertheless, the writer must have had a reason for placing this testimony from John the Baptist here, a testimony which is repeated in its logical, chronological order in 1:30. John probably decided to insert the testimony here to underscore a major theme in the prologue: Christ's eternal existence. John the Baptist declares that Christ *has surpassed me because he was before me.* Another way to render this is, "He takes precedence over me because he was prior to me." Although Jesus was actually born three months after his cousin John the Baptist, Jesus existed from eternity. John the Baptist's witness to Christ, here specified for the first time, is expanded upon in 1:19-36.

1:16 *of His fullness* (NKJV). Or "out from his plenitude." The Greek word for "fullness" is *plērōma;* it indicates plenitude and totality. The Gnostics used the word to describe the totality of all deities. Both John and Paul used the word to describe Christ—he is the fullness, the plenitude of God, for all the fullness of the Godhead dwells in him bodily (Col 1:19; 2:9). Since all of God's fullness dwells in Christ, every spiritual reality is found in Christ. In Christ, we lack nothing.

   we have all received (NRSV). At this point, John includes all the believers, not just himself and the apostles. No single believer could receive all that Christ is; it takes the body of Christ to appropriate Christ's fullness and to express it (Eph 1:23). Nevertheless, each believer receives in measure the same content of that fullness. Christ is continually full; he never is depleted—no matter how much the believers receive of him, he keeps on giving. Believers do not need to seek any other source but Christ. Paul said, "For in Him dwells all the fullness of the Godhead bodily; and you are complete [or *made full*] in Him" (Col 2:9-10a, NKJV).

   grace upon grace (NRSV). The Greek text literally says, "grace instead of grace," meaning "grace replenishing grace," a continual supply of grace (unmerited favor). Just as one measure of grace is used up, another replaces it. This grace keeps on coming like a spring-fed well that never runs dry. Christ's dispensation of grace to every believer can never be exhausted because he is full of grace. In our Christian life, we often get weary and discouraged, wondering if we can make it another day, another week, and so on. But just as we are about to give up, Christ gives us a fresh supply of grace to revive us and sustain us.

1:17 *For the law was given through Moses; grace and truth came* [lit., "came into being"] *through Jesus Christ.* This statement presents a contrast between the law given through Moses and the grace and truth coming into being through Jesus Christ. According to the divine economy, the two dispensations (law via Moses and grace via Christ) are complementary and not contradictory. The

Law, as an expression of God's character, was intended to show humankind that they should live lives reflecting God's nature. Because of their fallen nature and indwelling sin, they cannot. But God incarnate—that is, Jesus Christ—lived a life fulfilling all the righteous requirements of the law. In addition, Christ provided something Moses could not provide: grace and truth.

Christ did not set himself in opposition to Moses; rather, he presented Moses as one who wrote about him (5:45-47) and as one who gave the moral law for men to keep (7:19-23). However, Jewish religionists were obsessed with keeping the minute legalities of the ceremonial laws. They opposed Jesus because he did not precisely keep the ceremonial laws (e.g., he broke their rules on how one should observe the Sabbath). The moral law—that which pertains to relationships between God and men and those between men and men (the Ten Commandments in Exod 20)—was upheld by Jesus, but not the ceremonial law (the law pertaining to conduct in worship and religious practice). The tension between Jesus and the Jews centered on their interpretation of the Mosaic law, which missed the purpose of the law (7:19-24).

1:18 No one has ever seen God. This statement recalls what God said to Moses in Exodus 33:20. Moses wanted to see God's glory, but he was not allowed to gaze directly upon God's glory—for God told him that no man could see God and live. This, therefore, continues the contrast between Moses and Jesus. Moses, a man, was among those mortals who could not see God. Jesus, God's Son—himself God—lived in the presence of the Father. In 6:46 Jesus said that no one has seen the Father except he who is of God—this one has seen the Father. Only the Son, who is himself God, has seen God and can communicate his glory to men.

God the One and Only. More precisely rendered, "an only one, God." This reading is supported by all the earliest manuscripts; later manuscripts read, "the only begotten Son." The first reading is clearly the preferred reading because it is the more difficult of the two and best explains the origin of the variation. Scribes would not be inclined to change a common wording ("only begotten Son") to an uncommon wording ("an only begotten God"—which is a literal translation) Whatever the rendering, the reading in all the earliest manuscripts indicates that Jesus is here called "God," as well as "the one and only."[5] This perfectly corresponds to the first verse of the prologue, where the Word is called God and is shown as the Son living in intimate fellowship with the Father.

who is at the Father's side. Lit., "who is in the bosom of the Father." This picturesque language portrays the Son as a child in close dependence on his Father, enjoying comforting communion with him. It also reflects the image of two companions enjoying fellowship during a meal. According to an ancient custom, the one who reclined next to the master at a meal was the one dearest to him. (See Luke 16:22 for an example of a similar depiction, Lazarus in the bosom of Abraham, and see John 13:23 for a description of John reclining on the bosom of Jesus.) In short, the image depicts closeness, comfort, and intimate companionship. As was said before, this recalls the expression "the Word was with [face-to-face with] God" in 1:1.

has made him known. The Greek reads, "he has explained [him]." We derive the English word *exegesis* from the Greek verb *exēgeomai,* meaning "to lead through," "to narrate," or "to draw out." In context, this tells us that the Son is God's explainer, God's explicator, even God's exegete. In a sense, we could say that Christ came to take us on a tour of God, to narrate God to us, and to explain God to us. No man can know God apart from Christ, God's explainer. This mirrors 1:1, in which the Son is called the Word—i.e., the expression of God, the communicator of God.

The last verse of the prologue perfectly mirrors the first verse and artfully culminates the message of the entire prologue. In summary, John tells us that no man can see God—i.e., know God as God. But there is one who has come to explain him to us, not just in words but in his very person. This one is uniquely qualified to be God's explainer because he is (1) the one and only Son, (2) God, and (3) the one in the bosom of the Father. As the one and only Son, he alone has a unique position with God the Father; he alone can communicate the Father's message to mankind. And since he himself is also God, he is the very expression of God manifest in the flesh. Furthermore, his intimate relationship with the Father enables him to share with men the heart of God and the love of God. Throughout the rest of the Gospel of John, these three themes are reiterated and expanded upon.

ENDNOTES

[1]Schnackenburg makes much of this—with some good insights—but his exegesis of the prologue contains too much conjecture about how he supposes John to have used a particular "Logos Hymn," though such a hymn is not extant.

[2]See comments by Beasley-Murray listed in their introduction for a full discussion on the poetic structure of the prologue.

[3]Because 1:4 follows a verse pertaining to the Word's role in creation, some commentators think that 1:4 belongs to the time period prior to Christ's incarnation. This view is especially favored by those who prefer to punctuate 1:3-4 the way it appears in UBS[3] and NA[26]. They see the preincarnate Word, as God, giving life and light to men (see Ps 36:9). Although this interpretation is possible, it must be remembered that John did not maintain a strict chronology throughout this prologue. For example, 1:9-12 clearly identifies the time of Christ's incarnation, and yet it is not until 1:14 that John says that "the Word became flesh." Furthermore, it should be said again that 1:1-5 forms a kind of mini-prologue to and within the whole prologue (1:1-18). Thus, it is more likely that 1:4 pertains to the ministry of Jesus Christ begun in the flesh and now continued in the Spirit—for the light continues to shine (see comments on 1:5).

[4]In some Latin mss, this verse indicates that it was the Son of God who was born, not of blood or of the will of the flesh or of the will of man, but of God. But such a reading is not present in any of the Greek mss, all of which preserve the text in the plural (with reference to the "children of God" in 1:12), not in the singular. Obviously, some Latin scribes were attempting to provide more description of Christ's incarnation. The *Jerusalem Bible* adopted the singular reading, but this was changed to the plural in the *New Jerusalem Bible*.

[5]The manuscript evidence for the reading "God" is superior to the evidence for "Son." The papyri (𝔓66 and 𝔓75), the earliest uncials (𝕏 B C), and some early versions (Coptic and Syriac) support the first reading. Some of the earliest church fathers (Valentinus, Irenaeus, Clement, Origen, Eusebius, Serapion, Basil, Didymus, Gregory-Nyssa, and Epiphanium) knew of the first reading. Though later mss support the second reading, it was known by many early church fathers (Irenaeus, Clement, Hippolytus, Alexander, Eusebius, Eustathius, Serapion, Julian, Basil, and Gregory-Nazianzus) and translated in some early versions (Old Latin and Syriac). Thus both readings have early witness, but the first reading has earlier documentary testimony and is more likely the reading to have been changed. In a volume called *Two Dissertations* (Cambridge: Macmillan, 1976), Hort argued extensively and convincingly for the reading "only begotten God." He argued that Gnostics (such as the Valentinians) did not invent this phrase; rather, they simply quoted it. And he argued that this phrase is very suitable for the closing verse of the prologue, in which Christ has been called "God" (in 1:1), "an only One" (in 1:14), and finally "an only One, God," which combines the two titles into one.

The Beginning of Jesus' Ministry

JOHN 1:19–2:12

Jesus and His Witnesses: John the Baptist and the First Disciples
JOHN 1:19-51

EXPOSITION

The first section of John's narrative (1:19-51) provides a threefold witness to Jesus Christ's identity. The first witness comes from John the Baptist in 1:19-36. His witness has been briefly mentioned in the prologue (1:7, 15) and is here expanded. The second witness comes from the Old Testament Scriptures concerning the Messiah, referred to in this section. There is hardly any other portion in the New Testament that draws upon so many Old Testament verses and messianic appellations than the first chapter of John (see chart under "Key Words and Phrases," below). The third witness comes from Jesus' first disciples—John, Andrew, Peter, Philip, and Nathanael (1:35-51).

The disciples' witness had been alluded to in the prologue (see 1:14) and is here expanded. The scriptural witnesses to Jesus' messiahship were affirmed and realized by men who first followed Jesus because they were convinced, through the reading of Scripture and through the testimony of others, that Jesus was the awaited Messiah.

1:35-49/*Different Ways People Come to Jesus*

This passage provides an excellent portrayal of how various people come to Jesus and believe in him. All true believers are called by one Spirit to follow the one Lord and Savior, but the circumstances in conversion are not all the same. The sovereign Holy Spirit draws individuals to Christ in many different ways. John relates four separate examples of how faith is awakened. Perhaps these are foundational, to which all other experiences are connected.

The public proclamation of the gospel. The birth of faith is essentially the acceptance of testimony—the conviction that the witness given is true. It was the declaration of John the Baptist that turned two men, Andrew and John, to look at "the Lamb of God who takes away the sin of the world" (1:29, NRSV). Both of these men had been the Baptist's disciples; now they became followers of Jesus, the Messiah. Many years later, when he was an old man writing this Gospel, John was able to say, "I remember as though it were yesterday the exact day, in fact the exact time ('the tenth hour'), when life became new, different, and eternal for me." Some people may not be able to pinpoint the time of their conversion, but others who have a cataclysmic turnabout in their life remember indelibly the day and hour they were born again.

The private witness of a relative. Simon Peter became a follower of Jesus when testimony was given to him by his own brother. Perhaps this was the most significant Christian service Andrew ever did. His witness was personal, intelligent, and enthusiastic. "I've found the one we've been looking for, the one of whom the prophets wrote; my heart is changed! Come and see for yourself!" (see 1:41).

The personal call of Christ. Philip became a follower in response to a direct summons from Jesus. We might call this divine intervention. Today it could be the reading of a gospel tract, listening to a Christian radio broadcast, or some other activity in which suddenly God breaks through one's consciousness and spurs a person to respond to Jesus' gracious invitation in a positive, decisive manner.

The perceptive testimony of a friend. Nathanael turned in the direction of belief and faith by the word of a friend who spoke with deep conviction of his own experience with the Lord. Nathanael was a good and honest man, a careful reader of the Old Testament. He belonged to that very small group of pious people who were, like Simeon and Anna, awaiting the arrival of the promised Messiah. Perhaps he even knew the Scriptures better than his friend Philip, but that did not deter Philip in his testimony. He would not argue with Nathanael (over whether the Messiah could possibly come from Nazareth), but would simply say, "Come and see" (1:46).

Five men longed to know God, and though they found Christ in different ways, they all came to Christ, and thus to God. There is absolutely no other way to God than through Christ Jesus.

KEY WORDS AND PHRASES

This passage contains a number of messianic descriptions of Jesus, all of which were predicted in the Old Testament. It is well worth the time to read the following passages, first the Old Testament reference and then the verses from John's Gospel.

Title	Old Testament	John
the Lord	Isa 6:1	1:23
the Lamb of God	Isa 53	1:29, 36

the Son of God	Ps 2:7	1:34, 49
God's chosen one	Isa 42:1	1:34
the Christ ("Anointed One")	Ps 2:2; Dan 9:25	1:41
the Prophet	Deut 18:18	1:21, 45
the King of Israel	Ps 2:6; Zeph 3:15	1:49
the Son of Man	Dan 7:13	1:51

NOTES

1:19 *John's testimony.* John had been sent to give testimony to Jesus Christ (1:6-7). He was Christ's first and most important witness. John disavowed any personal status; he constantly pointed men to Christ.

the Jews. Here and in many other places in John, the phrase "the Jews" designates the Jewish leaders in Jerusalem.

1:20 *He did not fail to confess . . . "I am not the Christ."* John's response presupposes that their question ("Who are you?") in verse 19 was tantamount to asking, "Are you the Christ?" From the beginning, John the Baptist wanted to make it perfectly clear that he was not the Christ; rather, he was one who was preparing the way for the Christ. At any rate, their question indicates that the Jews were looking for the Christ, i.e., the Anointed One (in Hebrew, "the Messiah"—translated into Greek, *ho Christos,* "the Christ").

1:21 *Elijah.* The Old Testament predicted that Elijah would come to prepare the way for the Messiah (Mal 3:1; 4:5-6). John the Baptist had come to prepare the way for the Christ, but he did not claim to be Elijah. According to Luke 1:17, John came "in the spirit and power of Elijah," and according to Jesus' words in Matthew 11:14 and 17:10-12, John the Baptist was the predicted Elijah. Then why did John not acknowledge that he was this Elijah? This is difficult to answer. Perhaps John did not know he was the Elijah. Or perhaps John was just being consistent with his desire to divert attention from himself to Christ, for to claim to be Elijah would draw attention to himself and away from Christ. Whether or not John was Elijah or had come in the spirit of Elijah is not fully clarified in the New Testament, but his role and demeanor was truly Elijah-like (cf. 2 Kgs 1:8; Mark 1:6).

the Prophet. Referring to the prophet Moses spoke about in Deuteronomy 18:15-18. The Jews were looking for three predicted personages: the Messiah, Elijah (the Messiah's forerunner), and the Prophet. John 7:40ff makes it clear that the Jews thought of the Prophet and the Messiah as being two separate persons. Actually, Jesus was both the Messiah and the Prophet, according to Acts 3:20-22, and John was the Elijah.

1:22-23 *Who are you? Give us an answer to take back to those who sent us.* Befuddled by John's evasiveness and anxious to return to Jerusalem with some kind of answer, the emissaries pressed John to identify himself.

I am the voice of one calling in the desert, "Make straight the way for the Lord." John quoted from Isaiah 40, a portion that introduces the Messiah's forerunner and herald. In Isaiah 40:3-11 the herald is pictured as announcing the coming of God incarnate, the divine Shepherd. So without directly telling the Jews who he was, John indicated he was heralding the Messiah's coming. In ancient times, the function of a herald was to go before a dignitary, announcing his coming and clearing the way before him. John was doing just that, yet surprisingly, John did not see himself as being that important. He was merely a voice, calling upon people to make themselves ready for the coming one. People could get ready by repenting, confessing their sins, and being baptized. The verb "make straight" carries with it the connotation of making things morally correct. All of us are crooked and bent, morally speaking; we need an attitude of repentance in order to receive the divine rectification.

1:24-25 *Some Pharisees who had been sent questioned him.* Instead of pondering this great statement by the Baptist, they questioned him further. The Pharisees were the orthodox Jews of Jesus' day. They were zealous for the law—in fact, too zealous, for they became so engrossed in keeping every detail of the ceremonial law, to which they added their own rules, that they failed to heed the higher principles of God's law—i.e., those involving love for God and love for men. Jesus severely rebuked them for this inconsistency (see Matt 23).

Why then do you baptize? Since John did not claim to be the Christ, the Prophet, or Elijah, the Pharisees wanted to know for what purpose and by whose authority John was baptizing. In essence they were asking, "Since you don't claim an official office, what's the meaning of your baptism?" Baptism was not a new thing. Gentiles converting to Judaism were baptized as a purification and initiation rite. But John was calling upon *Jews* to be baptized. This was new and called for an explanation!

1:26 *I baptize with water.* In saying this, John may have been referring to Ezekiel 36:25ff, in which God promised to cleanse his people (with water) from their sins and then to give them a new heart filled with his Spirit. It was John's function to administer the sign of repentance; it would be Jesus' function to provide the people with a new heart and a new Spirit. John baptized with water; Jesus with the Spirit. Christian (or believer's) baptism is not the same as John's baptism. John's baptism called people to repent, which, more than an act of remorse, is a turning from unbelief in preparation for a spiritual work in one's heart and life. Christian baptism is identification with Christ in his death, burial, and resurrection and signifies a believer's walk in newness of life.

Among you stands one whom you do not know (NRSV). Perhaps Jesus had been standing among the crowds by the Jordan riverfront on several occasions prior to his own baptism and was even there at the time John uttered this. Or perhaps John's words mean that the Son of God had taken up his residence among his own people, the Jews, but they did not realize it. This latter supposition recalls John's words in the prologue (1:11-12). The Jews did not know that the Son of God had come to live among them. Some soon realized this, but most refused to believe it. This tragic note is sounded again and again in this Gospel.

1:27 *I am not worthy to untie the thong of his sandal* (NRSV). In ancient times, a slave would perform many menial tasks for his master, but unstrapping a sandal was considered the most menial task and would oftentimes not be even asked of a slave. In saying that he was not worthy to unlatch Jesus' sandals, John was saying that the Messiah was so glorious that he was not even qualified to be Jesus' lowest slave.

1:28 *Bethany.* This is the reading in the earliest manuscripts; it was changed from "Bethany" to "Bethabara" in some later manuscripts because certain scribes wanted to avoid the confusion between this Bethany and the one near Jerusalem and/or because the exact location of a "Bethany beyond the Jordan" has never been determined.[1]

1:29 *Look, the Lamb of God.* What a way to introduce the Messiah to the Jews! To every listening Jew, the title "Lamb of God" would have been pregnant with meaning. John was not citing any particular Old Testament passage when he used this term; rather, he drew upon many images concerning sacrificial lambs. No doubt, the title "Lamb of God" would be associated in the minds of the Jews with the Passover lamb (Exod 12; cf. John 19:36), the lamb led to the slaughter (Isa 53:7ff), and the lambs used in the daily sacrifices for the sin offerings (Lev 14:12ff, 21, 24; Num 6:12). In saying that Jesus was the Lamb of God, John was declaring that Jesus was the substitutionary sacrifice provided for by God. He was also telling the people the nature of the Kingdom. The announced Messiah came not to be a meditative philosopher or a teacher of morality. He came to do what we could not do for ourselves—take away sin.

It is amazing that John had the foresight to introduce the Messiah in such a way. According to the synoptic Gospels, John introduced Jesus as a lion—one who would execute the judgment of God and take his rightful rule. Perhaps if the Jews had accepted him, such would have been the case, but his time of reigning like a lion is yet to come. In his first coming, he came as the Lamb provided by God to take away the sin of the world. How we must praise our God for providing a Lamb, his only Son! Recall how God provided Abraham with a ram to take the place of his son Isaac in sacrifice (Gen 22:8, 13). God has done the same for us—only he provided his only Son as the sacrifice. For eternity we will be praising the Lamb of God. Read the book of Revelation and see how often the believers are praising the Lamb.

takes away the sin of the world. The Greek word for "takes away" (*airōn*) can also mean "take up" or "bear." Jesus took away our sin by taking it upon himself and bearing it. This is the image conveyed in Isaiah 53 (see also 1 Pet 2:24). Note that the text says sin and not sins—Jesus would take away the sin principle that had plagued the world since the fall of Adam (Rom 5:12ff). It is the Lamb's perfect, once-for-all sacrifice for sin that provides the foundation of man's renewed relationship with God.

1:30 This verse repeats 1:15, but is now placed in its proper chronological context. Just the same, John reiterates a truth that a herald is not more important than the dignitary.

1:31 *I myself did not know him.* The Greek word for "know" here is *oida.* It usually indicates absolute knowledge or perceptive knowledge. The other Greek word for "know" is *ginōskō,* meaning progressive, experiential knowledge. It was often used in describing the kind of knowledge that exists between two persons. In saying that he did not know (*oida*) Jesus as the Son of God (1:34), John made it clear to the people that he was not acquainted with Jesus the Messiah in times past. There had been no private collusion or arrangement between him and Jesus. John may have seen his cousin, Jesus, when they were little boys, but John did not know him as the Messiah previous to the baptism experience. Mary and Elizabeth were relatives; perhaps John had heard about Mary's son before he left home. The Scriptures tell us that John was in the wilderness from his early years (Luke 1:80) and thus may have never been with Jesus. Whatever the case, the language seems to indicate that John needed a special revelation from God (the one who sent him) in order to perceive Jesus as the Son of God.

the reason I came baptizing with water was that he might be revealed to Israel. Though John had not yet clearly perceived the person of the Messiah, he knew that the Messiah was coming and that his own mission was to make the Messiah's coming manifest to the nation of Israel.

1:32 *I saw the Spirit come down from heaven as a dove and remain.* The action of the Spirit descending from heaven in the form of a dove was a sign for John. According to Matthew 3:16, only John and Jesus saw this. The expression "as a dove" is adverbial—connected with "come down"; it refers to the way in which the Spirit descended, not to the physical appearance of the Spirit.

1:33 *I myself did not know him, but the one who sent me to baptize with water said to me, "He on whom you see the Spirit descend and remain is the one who baptizes with the Holy Spirit"* (NRSV). One might amplify this testimony to read, "I did not know Christ personally, though I had an impression when I first saw him coming to be baptized that he was one far greater than I—and under that impression, I hesitated to baptize him. But after his baptism, I saw clearly who he was—the Lamb of God."

He on whom you see the Spirit descend and remain (NRSV). In a well-known messianic passage, the Messiah is depicted as having the sevenfold Spirit resting upon him (Isa 11:1-2ff). Another passage, Isaiah 61:1ff, also pictures the Messiah as being anointed with the Spirit of the Lord God. This endowment with the Holy Spirit was a manifest sign of Jesus' messiahship. Hereafter, throughout his ministry Jesus would live and work in full dependence upon the Holy Spirit (Luke 4:14, 18).

the one who baptizes with the Holy Spirit (NRSV). This statement foretells Jesus' divine mission; it does not just point to the day of Pentecost, on which Jesus sent the Holy Spirit to baptize the disciples (Luke 24:49; Acts 1:8; 2:4). The statement characterizes Jesus' entire ministry. "Jesus, united with the Holy Spirit, came to immerse men in the Holy Spirit, came to bring the Holy Spirit to men—so as to make available to men the divine life and divine resources" (Morris). Throughout this Gospel, Jesus is presented as the divine life-giver; he came to give the divine life to those who believe in him and receive him. But no man could actually receive that life apart from receiving the life-giving Spirit of Jesus Christ. Thus, when Jesus offered himself as the Bread of Life for men to eat, Jesus added that the Spirit—not the flesh—is what gives life (6:63). And when Jesus offered himself as the water of life for men to drink (7:39), the apostle John explained that no one could actually drink of Jesus until he was glorified. Then they could partake of the Spirit of the glorified Jesus.

All true believers have been baptized by Jesus in the Holy Spirit. As such, we have been immersed in Jesus' Spirit. Now we can partake of the life-giving Spirit and enjoy his presence day by day. So the Baptist contrasts his work with that of the Messiah. John could baptize in water—that is, he could perform an outward rite—but to true penitents who trusted solely in Jesus, Christ alone could give an inner, actual, spiritual renewal. Water baptism was but a symbol—the power to change the heart and life came from Christ.

1:34 *this is the Son of God.* This reading is supported by several early manuscripts; however, other early manuscripts read, "this is the chosen one of God." The title Chosen One adds one more messianic title to John 1 (see introductory paragraph to 1:19-51), while "Son" is repetitive (1:14, 49).[2] Isaiah 42:1 predicts that God would put his Spirit on his "chosen one." No matter which title John used, he was declaring Jesus' special position with God, either as God's chosen one or as God's Son. God had told John the Baptist that he would reveal his sent one to him by means of the Spirit descending and remaining upon him. John saw this and declared his belief in Jesus as God's elect Son. Each believer is also given a sign at the time he or she believes in the Son of God; the sign is the Spirit given as a seal of God's ownership and a guarantee of God's fatherhood (see 2 Cor 1:21-22; Gal 4:6; Eph 1:13-14). He who receives the Spirit can also declare that Jesus is the Son of God, for it is by the Spirit that we believe and make confession (see 1 Cor 12:3).

1:35 *two of his disciples.* Andrew and John, the writer of this Gospel, had both been disciples of John the Baptist until he pointed them to the Lamb of God, Jesus Christ. This last portion of John 1 (verses 35-51) shows how the earliest believers became disciples of Jesus. Andrew and John became Jesus' followers through the testimony of their teacher, John the Baptist. Peter, Andrew's brother, became a follower through the testimony of Andrew. Philip became a disciple by Jesus' seeking him out and calling him, and Nathanael became a believer through the testimony of Philip and the revelation Jesus gave to him. Though people come to Christ by different ways, it is most unusual that one will find Christ without hearing the gospel from another. This chapter demonstrates this principle. Of all the early believers, it appears only Philip was sought out directly by Christ; the others heard from other men.

1:36 Look, the Lamb of God! The first time John said this (1:29), it was a public declaration. Here it is a private statement, a commission to these two to leave him and follow Jesus. As far as we know this is the last time the Baptist saw Jesus. He was called of God to a certain work; he was faithful to that call, and now he faded from the scene. He was called to be a forerunner, not a disciple.

1:37-38 they followed Jesus. This indicates a commitment, not an experiment.

where are you staying? An indication that John and Andrew were serious followers. They wanted to stay with Jesus and have fellowship with him in private, uninterrupted by the crowds of people.

1:39 It was about the tenth hour. John here recalls the time (about 4:00 p.m.) when he first stayed with Jesus, much like many believers recall the time they first received Jesus. It was a special time for John and Andrew—a time never to be forgotten. From this time forward, these two men followed Jesus. This, of course, does not mean that they lived with him every day—for the other Gospels indicate that there were times when they went back to their occupations of fishing. But from that time forward they were committed to following Jesus and did so until the end.

1:40-41 The first thing Andrew did [after spending a day with Jesus] **was to find his brother Simon and tell him, "We have found the Messiah"** [the Hebrew term, or "the Christ," the Greek translation of Messiah, meaning "anointed one"]. Andrew's statement implies that they had been looking for the Messiah and were attracted to the powerful preaching of John the Baptist, the Messiah's herald and forerunner. Having heard John's proclamation, "Behold, the Lamb of God," and having spent a day with Jesus himself, Andrew was convinced that Jesus was the Messiah.

1:42 he brought him [Simon] **to Jesus.** Some commentators have said that this was the best service Andrew rendered to the church.

"Simon son of John. You are to be called Cephas" (which is translated Peter) (NRSV). When Jesus beheld Peter, he saw him for what he would become—a stone in the building of Christ's church (Matt 16:16-18; 1 Pet 2:4-5). With this foresight, Jesus changed Simon's name to "Cephas," which is the Aramaic word for "stone." Throughout his days with Jesus, it appears that Simon was anything but a stone, but after Christ's resurrection and Pentecost, Simon was strengthened and fortified. He became a pillar and a foundation stone in the building

of the first-century church (Gal 2:9; Eph 2:20). Jesus not only sees what is in a person, he sees what that person can be by God's transformation.

1:43-44 Jesus' first two disciples (Andrew and John) sought out Jesus. The third disciple, Peter, was brought to Jesus by his brother, Andrew. The fourth disciple, **Philip**, was sought out by Jesus. Jesus sought him, found him, and called him to follow him. This shows yet another dimension in the whole scheme of becoming a follower of Christ—namely, that of being called out by Jesus. On one hand, the disciples of Jesus are those who are seeking him; on the other hand, the disciples of Jesus are those who never sought him but were found by him. The Christian life has two sides to it—one side shows our effort, the other Christ's.

 Philip, like Andrew and Peter, was from the town of Bethsaida. This piece of information may indicate that Philip knew Andrew and Peter before he became a follower of Jesus.

1:45 *Philip found Nathanael.* Earlier, Andrew had found Peter (his brother) and brought him to Jesus. Philip now does the same with Nathanael, who is called Bartholomew in the synoptic Gospels. (Note how Philip and Bartholomew are paired together in the list of the disciples in Matt 10:3 and Mark 3:18; here Nathanael and Philip are paired up.)

 We have found the one. Quite possibly, Philip was speaking not only for himself, but for Andrew and Peter (who may have been his friends). If this was the case, it is not unreasonable to think that the first five disciples (John, Andrew, Peter, Philip, and Nathanael) were well acquainted.

 Moses wrote about in the Law, and about whom the prophets also wrote—Jesus of Nazareth. This language indicates that Philip was also a seeker, one who read the Old Testament Scriptures and was looking for the predicted Messiah. Moses had written about him in the Law (Deut 18:15-18), and the prophets had foretold his coming. The prophets, however, never said that he would come from Nazareth, though Isaiah had predicted that a great light would arise out of Galilee (Isa 9:1-2). The Messiah was to be born in Bethlehem (Mic 5:2). And, in fact, Jesus was born in Bethlehem. But his parents' flight to Egypt and later return to Galilee, where Jesus was raised, gave Jesus the reputation of being a Galilean, specifically a Nazarene from the hill country of Nazareth. This was the cause of stumbling for many Jews because they could not accept a Messiah who had not come from Bethlehem. And since Jesus never told them this, they continued to believe that he was reared from birth as a Galilean, as a Nazarene (see comments on 7:52ff).

 the son of Joseph. Philip was speaking of Jesus' pedigree per common knowledge; in other words, this was how Jesus was known among them (Luke 3:23—it was supposed that Jesus was Joseph's son). But actually he was not Joseph's son; he was (and is) God's Son.

1:46 *Can anything good come from there?* Nathanael's statement does not necessarily mean that there was anything wrong with Nazareth; rather, the statement seems to indicate that Nathanael would not expect that anything related to God's purpose could come from Nazareth because Nazareth is not mentioned in the Old Testament. *Come and see.* Philip did the best thing. He did not argue with Nathanael about Jesus; he brought him to Jesus.

1:47 *Here is truly an Israelite in whom there is no deceit!* (NRSV). Jesus' statement about Nathanael reveals the purity of Nathanael's inner character. The Greek *dolos* was originally used to designate a trap. Taken figuratively, the word means "deceit, cunning, falsehood." Nathanael was devoid of deceit, cunning, and falsehood.

1:48 *I saw you while you were still under the fig tree before Philip called you.* Jesus here unveils his prescience to Nathanael. He had seen Nathanael under the fig tree before Philip called him. According to Jewish tradition, the expression "to sit under the fig tree" was a euphemism for meditating on the Scriptures (Morris). In telling Nathanael that before Philip spoke to him, he saw him reading the Scriptures, he was saying, "I have power to see and know all things, and I've seen into your heart and have known of your activities." The early disciples of Jesus were diligent students of Scripture, and they took their reading seriously. When the Law and the Prophets spoke about a coming Messiah, they began looking for him—and found him!

1:49 *the Son of God . . . the King of Israel.* Seeing Jesus and realizing his prescience was enough to convince Nathanael that Jesus was the Messiah. Here he proclaims his faith by ascribing to Jesus two marvelous messianic titles: Son of God (Ps 2:7) and the King of Israel (Ps 2:6; cf. Zeph 3:15). Five others in this fourth Gospel declare Jesus to be the Son of God: John the Baptist, Simon Peter, Martha, Thomas, and John the beloved disciple.

1:50-51 *You shall see greater things than that. . . . you shall see heaven open, and the angels of God ascending and descending on the Son of Man.* Jesus began by addressing Nathanael alone and then all the disciples then present (the first "you" is singular and the second is plural in the Greek). Jesus told them that they would hereafter see the angels ascending and descending upon him, the Son of Man. As students of the Old Testament, his disciples would have realized that he was alluding to Jacob's vision of the ladder connecting heaven to earth (see Gen 28:12ff). He, as the Son of Man, was the real vehicle of communication between heaven and earth, divinity and humanity. To a genuine Israelite, Jesus revealed himself as the fulfillment of the dream of Jacob (who became Israel). He had come to make this dream a reality, and now Nathanael and the other disciples would see the Son of Man living both a heavenly and an earthly existence in constant communication with the heavenly Father. Furthermore, Jesus was the true Jacob, the true Israel—the spiritual leader of God's new tribe (not the twelve sons of Jacob, but the twelve disciples).

Finally, it should be noted that this is the first place in this Gospel in which Jesus calls himself the Son of Man. This title was his favorite self-designation. He applied it to himself to identify with the messianic title contained in Daniel 7:13 and to present himself as a man among men—living in full identification with humanity, as the God who became man, the God-man. The entire first chapter of John attributes the highest titles to Jesus—he is called the Word, God, the one and only Son, the Christ, the King of Israel, etc.; but Jesus, when speaking of himself, preferred to call himself the Son of Man.

Jesus at the Wedding Feast in Cana of Galilee
JOHN 2:1-12

Jesus performed the miracle of changing water into wine as a small display of his glory—even as a preview of his coming hour of glorification. This small sign was enough to convince the disciples and gain their trust in him.

NOTES

2:1 *the third day.* I.e., two days after Jesus' encounter with Nathanael.

a wedding. In ancient times, this could last as long as a week (Gen 29:27-28).

in Cana of Galilee (NRSV). A town about ten miles north of Nazareth.

the mother of Jesus was there (NRSV). Many commentators think she may have been a hostess at this wedding because of the position she assumes throughout this passage. For example, she is the first to know about the lack of wine, and she directs the servants to follow Jesus' orders.

2:2 *Jesus and his disciples had also been invited.* Jesus' presence at this wedding indicates his approval of marriage. (See Christ's comments about marriage in Matt 5:31-32; 19:3-9.) The marriage where there is no place for our Lord and Savior cannot be blessed of God. But this young couple had made room for Jesus, and into this happy and positive occasion he brought greater joy and happiness.

2:3 *When the wine was gone.* Or running out. In ancient Israel it was very important for the parents of the bride to provide enough wine for the wedding; to fail to do so would result in social embarrassment.

Jesus' mother said to him, "They have no more wine." Mary told Jesus this fact, expecting him to do something about it. Mary had known for a long time about her son's divine commission. Her son had just been baptized by John and heralded as the Lamb of God and had attracted a small following of disciples. Perhaps she wanted Jesus to do something in the presence of her relatives and friends (who may have heard reports about Jesus) that would prove he was an extraordinary, supernatural person. For remember, it was she who carried the stigma of bearing an illegitimate child.

2:4 *Dear woman, why do you involve me?* Several commentators have pointed out that it was not disrespectful for Jesus to call his mother "woman." What sounds quite harsh in English is not so in Greek. It is like saying "lady" or "madam." On the cross, Jesus again called his mother "woman" (19:26). Although Jesus was not being harsh toward his mother, his language does show that he was distancing himself from her—not in affection, but in position. Mary now had to realize that her position with Jesus could not be that of a mother to her son. Jesus was not under her parentage but his Father's. Jesus made this clear at the age of twelve when his parents found him in the Temple, and he told them that he was there doing his Father's business (Luke 2:49).

When they become Christians, people sometimes experience a significant change in their relationships with their parents. Keenly aware that God has become their Father, they feel love and loyalty to a new, divine parent. But this does not annul their love and respect for their earthly parents; rather, their love for God strengthens their appreciation for their parents.

My time has not yet come. Jesus made it clear that he would not operate according to Mary's timetable. He lived to carry out his Father's business, according to his Father's timetable. It was as if Jesus had said, "Don't worry; leave things to me. I will take care of them at the right time in my own way." Mary thought this was an ideal time for Jesus to do something unusual and catch the attention of the hometown folks. Jesus knew that he would not be fully manifested as the Messiah until the hour of his glorification via death and resurrection. Later in this Gospel, Jesus' brothers also tried to push him into the limelight. Again he resisted, saying, "My time has not yet come" (7:3-6, NKJV).

2:5 *Do whatever he tells you.* Intuitively Mary realized that Jesus would do something about the situation. Her words show her respect for his authority— and, of course, these words extend beyond that specific situation and affect us in our life. Mary, in conceiving Jesus, the Son of God, had been submissive to God's word (Luke 1:38). We, too, need to submit to whatever the Lord would say to us.

2:6 *six stone water jars for the Jewish rites of purification* (NRSV). This statement has been subject to a great deal of allegorization—especially the number six and the water jars. But the context does not seem to call for allegorization. The most that can be said is that the empty waterpots (normally used by the Jews to purify themselves) may symbolize the emptiness of Jewish ritual. Jesus had come to give content and life to a hollow religion.

2:7 *they filled them to the brim.* This fullness showed that nothing could be added to the water. When Jesus performed the miracle, all the water was changed to wine; wine could not have been added to the water.

2:8 *draw some out.* The Greek word for "draw out" indicates that the servants were to dip deep down into the waterpots and draw out the water, which had miraculously changed to wine. There was no visible action that preceded or accompanied the drawing out. Jesus did not touch the waterpots or command the water to change into wine. He simply willed the change, and it took place. It was an act of creation—an act of God.

2:9 *tasted the water that had been turned into wine.* Lit., "tasted the water having become wine." This is the climax of the narrative. Jesus had provided as much as 180 gallons of choice wine! In our Christian life we have experienced the transformation of water into wine—that is, we have experienced how Jesus can change the ordinary into the extraordinary.

2:10 *Everyone serves the good wine first, and then the inferior wine after the guests have become drunk* (NRSV). After people have drunk two or three servings of wine, their taste buds become insensitive to the quality of further drinks. Thus it was customary to give the best wine first and the poorer wine last.

2:11 *the first of his miraculous signs.* In the Gospel of John, each miracle was performed to be a sign—pointing people to the truth that Jesus is the divine Son of God come down from heaven. According to John's Gospel, this is Jesus' first sign, and it was performed in his own region.

revealed his glory. The sign he performed was a small unveiling of his glory, or even a preview of his coming glory.

his disciples put their faith in him. This does not mean that they had not believed in him before. Evidently, they had believed, or they would not have started to follow him. In fact, Nathanael believed Jesus to be the Son of God and the King of Israel (1:49). This means that they were given cause to believe in Jesus even further. The miracle was performed and the needs of the people were met; but only the disciples seemed to be aware of the miracle, and their faith was further strengthened in him.

2:12 *he went down to Capernaum.* Capernaum, on the western shore of the Sea of Galilee, became Jesus' base of operation throughout his ministry. He, with his family, made a home there (Matt 4:13) to which he would retreat at various times throughout his three-year ministry (4:46; 6:59; Mark 2:1; 9:33). Although Jesus performed many miracles in this city (Luke 4:23), he was not believed by its citizens. Hence, Jesus proclaimed a strong anathema against Capernaum (Luke 10:15). According to his word, the city was later completely destroyed.

with his mother and brothers. Many scholars assume Joseph was no longer living at the time Jesus began his ministry (but see note on 6:41-42). If Joseph was deceased, Jesus, as the oldest brother, was responsible for the welfare of his family.

ENDNOTES

[1]"Bethany" has the best support: 𝔓66 𝔓75 ℵ B C W. This is the reading that Origen encountered in "nearly all the copies," but Origen could not locate any "Bethany" by the Jordan when he traveled

to Palestine. However, there was a town called Bethabara in the vicinity, which, according to local tradition, was the site of John's baptism. Origen, therefore, adopted the reading "Bethabara" (see Barrett).

[2]Even though the title "Son of God" has good external support ($\mathfrak{P}$66 $\mathfrak{P}$75 A B C W 083), several scholars have argued that it is more likely that the reading "the chosen One of God" (found in $\mathfrak{P}$5 $\aleph$) was changed to "the Son of God" than vice versa. For example, Gordon Fee thinks an orthodox scribe of the second century might have sensed "the possibility that the designation 'Chosen One' might be used to support adoptionism and so altered the text for orthodox reasons" (see Fee's article "The Textual Criticism of the New Testament" in *The Expositor's Bible Commentary*, vol. 1, ed. Frank E. Gaebelein [Winona Lake, Ind.: BMH Books, 1986], pp. 431–432).

Jesus Clears the Temple in Jerusalem

JOHN 2:13-25

EXPOSITION

John is fond of using a physical backdrop to display a spiritual truth. In this passage, the Temple in Jerusalem is used to reveal Jesus as God's dwelling place. The Temple that Jesus entered was the second Temple, the one rebuilt by the returned remnant of Israelites from Babylon (515 BC) and expanded by Herod the Great. It was God's house—"my Father's house," as Jesus called it. But some of the Jews had turned it into an emporium, a place for selling merchandise. Some Jews had become involved in the business of religion. They made a profit on exchanging common currency for Temple money (Temple money had no animal or human likeness engraved on it) and by selling animals to be offered in sacrifice. The people coming to participate in the Jewish holidays accepted this system because it was convenient for them not to have to bring their animals with them, contrary to what God had originally ordained (Deut 12:5-7). All this business was taking place in the outer court of the Temple, a place which had been set aside for Gentiles to come and seek God in prayer. But the Jews had turned this place of prayer into a place of haggling, cheating, and merchandising.

At another Temple cleansing, Jesus said, "Is it not written, 'My house shall be called a house of prayer for all the nations'? But you have made it a den of robbers" (Mark 11:17, NRSV, quoting Isa 56:7). With all the buying, selling, and trading taking place, how could a Gentile spend time with God in prayer? The whole enterprise was an abomination to God. And his Son, Jesus Christ, displayed his Father's wrath by cleansing the Temple. Malachi had predicted that the Lord would suddenly come to his Temple and purge it (Mal 3:1-4). Here we see at least a partial fulfillment of Malachi's prophecy.

2:13-16/Worthless Worship

Convenient worship. There are many magnificent cathedrals and church buildings today, particularly in Europe, but none filled with people and activity as was the Temple in Jerusalem. There was the inner court for only male Jewish worshipers, the next separated area for Jewish women only, and the outer court for all non-Jewish people. In this outer court were the money changers and animals to be purchased for sacrifice. The money changers were there to exchange Roman or other foreign coins for Jewish coins because no coin with the effigy of the emperor could be offered within the Temple. The sellers of animals were there because everyone offered a sacrifice for sins. To ensure that an animal was "without spot or blemish" and acceptable to the priest, one didn't risk bringing an animal from home, but purchased one at the Temple and took it to the priest for the required sacrifice.

All this was done for the convenience of the worshipers. They didn't have to come to worship *prepared.* They could take care of the necessities at the last minute, and maybe, if they were sharp enough in haggling, they could get a good deal. Surveying this scene of milling people, greedy merchants, and noisy animals, Jesus was incensed at the gross desecration of God's house.

We must beware of a religion of convenience, for it robs us of true devotion and self-sacrifice. Too many churches today do everything they can to make worship convenient for people. We call it spectator worship—no personal involvement. But worshiping God is not convenient; it demands true devotion, self-sacrifice, and personal involvement.

Worship without reverence. In the outer court there would be arguments about prices, disputes about coins, animals that were not just what the buyer wanted—in short, the chatter of the marketplace in the house of God. And how about us today? There is incongruent boisterousness, flippancy, unpreparedness, and thinking of other things rather than worshiping God. Formality without heart, impersonal giving or no giving at all, going through the motions, but not really meditating on God. Worship that is perfunctory or indifferent is not worship at all. Jesus, on another occasion, acknowledged that people are capable of honoring God with their lips while their hearts are far from him. When we attend a service of worship but keep our spirit uninvolved, we dishonor God.

Sacrifice without devotion. Isaiah called such sacrifices "meaningless offerings" (Isa 1:13). David told God, "You do not delight in sacrifice" (Ps 51:16). No animal sacrifice can ever make a person right with God. To participate in a ritual without personal involvement demonstrates a lack of devotion. Those who were uninvolved with the sacrifice, who were merely performing a requirement, did not please God. Today we often identify service to God as "doing things," but if our sacrifices are without true devotion and love toward God, they are in vain. It is a great tragedy that we can be engaged in religious activities for all sorts of evil motives. This, of course, will never injure God, but it is calamitous to us.

Activity without prayer. The outer court was the only place where Gentiles could go to worship God, and Jesus called his Father's house "a house of prayer for all the nations" (Mark 11:17, NRSV). The place of prayer had become a confusing, squabbling, stinking, shrieking mass of people, animals, and business deals. No one could pray. The purpose of worship is conversing with God, but this was hindered by making the requirements of worship convenient.

KEY WORDS AND PHRASES

The key sentence in this section is "Destroy this temple and I will raise it again in three days." The Greek for "temple" here is *naos;* it refers to the inner sanctuary (i.e., the Holy Place and the Holy of Holies). Another Greek word was also translated "temple" in 2:14-15; the word is *hieron.* It refers to the Temple proper, including the outer courts. When Jesus cleansed the Temple, he cleansed only a portion of the outer courts. When Jesus spoke of the temple that would be destroyed, he was speaking of his body as the inner sanctuary, the place of God's dwelling. Paul told the believers that each one of their bodies was a *naos,* a sanctuary for God (1 Cor 6:19). Paul also said that the church, as Christ's body, is a spiritual *naos* for God (1 Cor 3:16-17; 2 Cor 6:16; Eph 2:21). What a special privilege it is to be God's spiritual dwelling place, both individually and corporately. In the new Jerusalem there will not be a physical Temple because God and the Lamb will be the eternal *naos.* We will dwell in God forever.

NOTES

2:13 *The Passover of the Jews* (NRSV). Some commentators have said that John described the Passover as being "of the Jews" because it had become a ritualistic holiday void of spiritual reality—thus, a Passover no longer belonging to God but to custom. But it is more likely that John added "of the Jews" for the sake of his Gentile readers.

   Jesus went up to Jerusalem. According to the synoptic Gospels, Jesus visited the Temple and cleared it during his final visit to Jerusalem, just prior to his crucifixion (Matt 21:12-17; Mark 11:15-19; Luke 19:45-46). The seeming discrepancy in chronology has been debated by scholars. The simplest—and probably best— solution is to recognize that John and the Synoptics are referring to two different Temple cleansings. The language of the two incidents is quite different. John speaks of sheep and oxen; the Synoptics don't. John speaks of Jesus' comment about making his Father's house a house of merchandise; the Synoptics speak of Jesus' comment about making his Father's house a den of thieves. John records Jesus' challenge about destroying the temple and raising it up; the Synoptics do not mention this here—they do so later in connection with Jesus' trial.

2:14-15 For the convenience of the pilgrims coming to Jerusalem to worship, the priests in Jerusalem instituted a market for selling animals for sacrifice and for exchanging common currency for Temple currency (at an exorbitant exchange rate). This way the pilgrims would not have to bring their animals for sacrifice, and the priests could make money. But this ran contrary to what God had originally intended (see Deut 12:5-7). He wanted the people to bring from their own flock the best animals for sacrifice. This would make the offering more personal and self-sacrificial. With this system the Jews could bypass all this and still carry out their religious rituals.

he made a whip out of cords. Some early manuscripts read, "He made a kind of whip." Whether it was a real leather whip or one he fabricated for the occasion, this shows he was zealously bent on driving out the merchandisers. This messianic purging of the Temple was predicted in part in Malachi 3:1-4 and Zechariah 14:21. This purging or cleansing was appropriate for the season of Passover because that was the time when all the Jews were supposed to cleanse their houses of all leaven, and leaven, according to the New Testament (1 Cor 5:6-8; Gal 5:9), typifies sin. The Temple, God's house, had become infected with the sin of moneymaking; it needed to be thoroughly cleansed.

2:16 *How dare you turn my Father's house into a market!* Jesus saw the Temple as belonging to his Father, but the Jews had usurped it, turning it into a place for merchandising. The Greek word for "market" is *emporion*—a place for selling merchandise.

2:17 *Zeal for your house will consume me.* As the disciples saw Jesus' vehement action of cleansing the Temple, God's Word must have come to their remembrance, confirming the action as God-ordained. For it had been written of Christ in Psalm 69:9 that he would be consumed by zeal for God's house. The disciples, probably as much as any of the people then present, must have been shocked at Jesus' display of anger. But the disciples trusted him because they were given the divine word to affirm their faith. Not so with the others present. Outraged by Jesus' action, they demanded a sign.

2:18 *What miraculous sign can you show us . . . ?* The Jews of Jesus' day continually required Jesus to give them some spectacular sign or portent, proving beyond the shadow of a doubt that he was the Messiah. The Jews were so notorious for being sign seekers that Paul could say categorically, "For Jews request a sign" (1 Cor 1:22, NKJV). All throughout his ministry, Jesus performed miracle after miracle: He healed lepers, gave sight to the blind, and even raised the dead. Yet still the Jews did not believe. They said they would believe if they saw a sign (John 6:30)—perhaps a glorious portent radiating from heaven. Elsewhere, Jesus had told the Jews that they were evil and adulterous for seeking a sign (Matt 12:38-39). They could discern the signs that foretold weather conditions, but they could not discern the signs of their times (Matt 16:1-4). Jesus would not give them the kind of sign they wanted. He himself was the sign, for he was the Son of God come from heaven to earth as the visible manifestation of God in the flesh.

We dare not ask God to give us a sign from heaven to prove that Jesus was and is the Son of God. The unique sign has already been given: Jesus, the crucified, has risen from the dead. Believing this with our heart is the unique requisite for salvation (Rom 10:6-10).

2:19 *Destroy this temple, and I will raise it again in three days.* This was the answer to the sign the Jews were asking for: They would destroy his body, and he would raise it up in three days. In another encounter with the Jews, when they asked for a sign, Jesus told them that the only sign he would give them was that of Jonah the prophet, who spent three days and three nights in the belly of a great fish before God delivered him (Matt 12:39-40). In like manner, Jesus would be killed and after three days rise from the dead. Actually, Jesus would allow himself to be killed, for no one had any power over his life, and he of his own power would rise from the dead. John 10:17-18 says, "I lay down My life that I may take it again. No one takes it from Me, but I lay it down of Myself. I have power [or *authority*] to lay it down, and I have power [or *authority*] to take it again" (NKJV).

According to the Greek, Jesus said, "You destroy this temple." (The verb is second person, plural, aorist active imperative.) He did not say *he* would destroy the temple. But at the time of Jesus' trial, some of his accusers twisted his statement to assert that Jesus said he would destroy the Temple (Matt 26:61; Mark 14:58). This was the only accusation against Jesus that was clearly verbalized— and the accusation was false. Nevertheless, Jesus was accused of being a Temple desecrator, and this violent act of purging the Temple would help support such an accusation. Some of those standing around his cross hurled this same twisted accusation at him (Matt 27:40; Mark 15:29), and eventually the accusation became part of the Jewish lore about Jesus' crimes (Acts 6:14).

2:20-21 *"It has taken forty-six years to build this temple, and you are going to raise it in three days?" But the temple he had spoken of was his body.* The Jews thought Jesus was speaking about the physical Temple, but he was speaking about his body, the temple of God the Father, a fact the Jews never seemed to grasp. The Jews thought it was preposterous to speak of destroying a Temple that took Herod the Great and others forty-six years to construct. (Actually, Herod only added to the Temple, which had been rebuilt in the time of Ezra.) But Jesus was speaking of his body. It was quite usual for people in New Testament times to speak about death in terms of the destruction or dissolution of the body. Paul used this imagery in 2 Corinthians 5:1-4, and Peter in 2 Peter 1:13-14. The body is a temporal dwelling place for one's real inner person. Death dissolves that dwelling place and releases a person from his temporal confines. Jesus' temporal body would be destroyed through crucifixion, but he would rise again with a new, glorified body suited to his spiritual existence (see 1 Cor 15:42-45).

2:22 *After he was raised from the dead, his disciples remembered that he had said this* (NRSV). Prior to his death and resurrection, Jesus had told his disciples that he would send them the Spirit, who would remind them of all the things Jesus had taught them (see 14:26). After Christ's resurrection, they received this Spirit (20:22) and so were reminded by the Spirit of the many things Jesus had said, and in particular about his death and resurrection.

they believed the scripture and the word that Jesus had spoken (NRSV). Since there is not a particular Scripture in the Old Testament to which Jesus alluded in connection with his resurrection, we probably can understand "the Scripture" here to mean the Old Testament Scripture at large as it testifies to Christ's resurrection. For example, see Psalm 2:7 (quoted by Paul in Acts 13:33 to affirm Christ's resurrection) and Psalm 16:9-10 (quoted by Peter and Paul in Acts as a proof text for Christ's resurrection in Acts 2:24-32; 13:35-37). After Christ's resurrection, the Spirit illuminated the Scripture, substantiating this wonderful fact. And so the disciples believed the Scripture—and they believed the word that Jesus had spoken. As he predicted, his body, the temple, was destroyed, but then he raised it up in three days.

2:23 *while he was in Jerusalem at the Passover Feast.* This was during the same week he purged the Temple in Jerusalem, the festival week of Passover.

many people saw the miraculous signs he was doing and believed in his name. John did not recount any of the particular miracles Jesus performed in Jerusalem; he simply said that many people believed in Jesus when they saw the miracles he did. But as the next verse indicates, this belief was based on the wrong motives. The people believed in Jesus as a miracle worker, but not necessarily as the Christ, the Son of God. At best, they believed in Jesus as the Christ when, and only when, he performed miracles. When Jesus spoke of his divine, heavenly origin and of his destined death on a cross, the people did not believe him (see comments on 3:31-32; 6:41-42; 7:26-27, 40-43; 10:1ff). In other words, when Jesus fit their conception of the promised Messiah, they believed in him; but when he didn't, they no longer believed in him. Jesus experienced this fickle behavior throughout his ministry.

A misplaced faith is perilous. The wrong reasons for believing in Jesus may bring us to only a fickle faith. We should not believe in him because of what he can do for us or because of what miracle he may have done for us. We should believe in him for who he is—the Christ, the Son of God.

2:24 *But Jesus would not entrust himself to them.* In verses 23-24, John used the Greek verb *pisteuō* (to trust) to make a word play, as is conveyed in the following rendering: "Many *trusted* in his name . . . but he did not *entrust* himself to them." The reason for Jesus' reaction then follows—*for he knew all men.*

2:25 *He did not need man's testimony about man, for he knew what was in a man.* Jesus did not need to be told about human nature; he knew the motives of men's actions because he thoroughly knew the human makeup. He knew how fickle men are. When he miraculously fed the multitudes, they wanted to make him a king (6:15); when he spoke of his death, they called him a madman and a demon (8:40, 48; 10:17-20). Signs do not create faith; the Holy Spirit must do this. Moreover, once saving faith is present, one will believe in the word of Christ even if there is no sign.

Jesus Reveals the Need
for Regeneration

JOHN 3:1-21

EXPOSITION

The short discussion between Jesus and Nicodemus has had universal appeal. It would be difficult to find any other portion of Scripture as well-known as John 3:16, or any other statement of Scripture more popular than "you must be born again." When Jesus revealed the necessity of the new birth to Nicodemus, he unveiled mankind's paramount need. Jesus' words about the new birth and God's gift of eternal life were not just for Nicodemus or the nation of Israel. His Good News was and is for the whole world. Because God loves all humankind, he sent his only Son into the world so that whoever would believe in him would "not perish but have eternal life" (3:16).

3:1-18/*The New Birth*

In effect, Jesus said to Nicodemus, "Even though you are a faithful Jew, and a Pharisee, and a member of the Sanhedrin, and wealthy, and a great teacher in Israel, you need to be born again." In spite of how clear those words were, particularly to one who was very familiar with Old Testament Scriptures, Nicodemus did not understand. Now there are two kinds of misunderstandings. There is the failure to understand that comes from an unwillingness to understand— a deliberate refusal to accept the facts. But there is also the misunderstanding based upon a lack of knowledge or a history of misinterpreting the facts. To such a person, a good teacher will simply and carefully explain the truth until it is grasped with conviction. So Jesus cleared away Nicodemus's misunderstanding of the Father's love, people's (Nicodemus's) great need, and the incredible result of belief—everlasting life.

The Father's love. God loved the world. He loved us even while we were yet sinners—enemies of God (Rom 5:8). Some have pictured God as a wrathful judge, a tyrant, one who had to be placated. This is an erroneous view. Christ died for our sins because God loves humankind and was determined to save those who believe. God is love. His love is for our sake. He loves not just "good" people but also the unlovely and crooked and mean and lonely and cruel. He loves the person who thinks of God and the person who never thinks of God. It is difficult for us to appreciate how God could even *like* a crooked and perverse world, but the expression Jesus used is much stronger—God *loved*.

Man's great need. The new birth of which Jesus spoke is imperative because humankind is altogether devoid of spiritual life. It is not that people are ignorant and need instruction, or that they are feeble and need invigorating, or that they are sickly and need doctoring. Their case is far worse. They are dead. This is no mere figure of speech; the sinner is spiritually lifeless and needs quickening. The natural person is spiritually a corpse (no matter what good or bad things he does), and what each one desperately needs is life—divine life. As birth is the gateway to life, so we must be born again. And if we are not born again, we cannot enter the Kingdom of God. Suppose the mainspring of my watch is defective. What good would it do to polish the crystal and put on a new band? The trouble is inside the watch. So it is with the unbelieving sinner. A person is cleansed by believing the Word of God and by the work of the Holy Spirit, two things Nicodemus had not considered.

The result of belief. Believing in Jesus Christ for our salvation includes accepting with all our heart that God is what Jesus declared him to be, the God of love. The word *whosoever* is like a check or deed signed by God himself, with the place for the beneficiary's name left blank, thus inviting each of us by the act of faith to write his or her own name, accepting eternal life.

Jesus had a right to speak so confidently because he had come directly from heaven to earth. He knew the Father God intimately, and he knew most assuredly the secrets of heaven. Not sin but unbelief bars people from God's love and gift of life. But to as many as believe, God gives the right and the power to be born again.

KEY WORDS AND PHRASES

Several expressions in this passage address the new birth that gives the believer eternal life and entrance into the Kingdom of God:

- » Born again (3:3, 7)
- » Born of water and the Spirit (3:5)
- » Born of the Spirit (3:6)
- » See and enter the Kingdom of God (3:3, 5)
- » Believe and receive eternal life (3:15-16)

NOTES

3:1 *Now there was a man.* Some commentators see a connection between this statement about a man, Nicodemus, and the mention of "man" in 2:25. If John intended any kind of connection, there are two ways to interpret it: (1) John wanted the reader to know that Nicodemus was no different from any other man;

as with most men, he believed in Jesus only as a miracle worker but not as the Messiah. Jesus, knowing all men, knew this about Nicodemus from the outset. (This interpretation may be valid if the commentator understands the Greek postpositive *de* as signaling the continuation of the narrative, not as a contrastive.) (2) John wanted the reader to know that Nicodemus was different from the ordinary man; his belief was deeper and studied. (This interpretation may be valid if John intended the Greek postpositive *de* to signal a contrast.)

   of the Pharisees named Nicodemus, a member of the Jewish ruling council. Nicodemus was one of the Pharisees, the strictest, most fundamental Jewish sect of those times. He was also a ruler or leader among the Jews. Thus he was a very prominent figure in Israel; in fact, Jesus called him "a teacher of Israel" (3:10, NRSV).

3:2 **he came to Jesus** (NRSV). What motivated Nicodemus to come to Jesus? It could be that Nicodemus saw this as an opportunity to exchange theological opinions with another great teacher. More likely, Nicodemus was spiritually hungry. He was drawn to Jesus by his inner craving and by the power of God.

   by night (NRSV). Why did Nicodemus come to Jesus by night? Most likely, he did not want to be seen with Jesus in broad daylight because he feared reproach from his fellow Pharisees. The Pharisees had tremendous power over the religious affairs in Israel; to go against them was asking for trouble. Later, John said that many of the rulers of Israel believed in Jesus but would not openly confess him, fearing that the Pharisees might excommunicate them from the synagogue (12:42). As with these rulers, Nicodemus became a secret believer in Jesus. He tried to defend Jesus before the Pharisees without openly confessing his faith in him (7:50-51). But to his credit, Nicodemus joined Joseph of Arimathea in burying Jesus (19:38-39).

   Since John makes great use of the terms *light* and *darkness* in this Gospel, the expression "by night" could also suggest that Nicodemus was "in the dark" (i.e., unenlightened) about spiritual truths.

   Rabbi, we know that you are a teacher who has come from God (NRSV). Nicodemus respected Jesus as a teacher sent from God. He told Jesus this as if he, Nicodemus, were representing the Jews. He was probably not speaking on behalf of the Pharisees, for they did not believe, but on behalf of the people, of whom he was a ruler or leader.

3:3 **no one can see the kingdom of God.** Although the Bible does not explicitly state what the Kingdom of God is, it is probably safe to say that God's Kingdom is the sphere of God's rule—and from man's perspective, God's Kingdom is wherever men recognize God's control. During Jesus' earthly ministry, the Kingdom of God was present with him, for wherever he was, God's Kingdom was (Luke 17:21, RSV). To "see" the Kingdom of God, therefore, is to have a special perception or insight concerning God's absolute control.

   unless he is born again. The Greek word (*anōthen*) translated here as "again" could also be rendered "from above." The birth that Jesus spoke of was either a new birth or a heavenly birth—or both. It seems that Jesus was speaking of a heavenly birth because he later used the analogy of the wind, coming from some unknown, heavenly source, to depict the spiritual birth. But Nicodemus clearly understood Jesus to be speaking of a second birth—to be born again. Jesus explains this new or heavenly birth in 3:6-8.

To those not born again or born from above, God's Kingdom is imperceptible—an unknown domain. To those having experienced the new birth, God's Kingdom is a perceived reality. The new birth is the only way one can see the sphere of God's rule and then enter into it. Nicodemus may have thought he could participate in God's Kingdom by doing good deeds or understanding the Scriptures, but no mere human activity grants one access into God's Kingdom. Nicodemus—and all mankind—must have a spiritual rebirth to experience the reality of God's Kingdom.

3:4 How can a man be born when he is old? Surely he cannot enter a second time into his mother's womb to be born? These questions—whether spoken sincerely or sarcastically—show that Nicodemus did not perceive the spiritual intent of Jesus' words. Many people have wished that they could start life all over again by being born a second time. But such a birth would not enable them to enter the Kingdom of God, for it would be just another human progeneration. The only way one can start over in life is by being born from above—by receiving God's eternal life and the regenerating Holy Spirit.

3:5 unless he is born of water and the Spirit. This statement has perplexed commentators for many centuries. Some have believed that the water denotes physical birth (a baby is born in a sac of water) and the Spirit, spiritual birth; thus, Jesus would be saying that a man has to have two births: the first physical and the second spiritual. Others have believed that the water symbolizes baptism and the Spirit symbolizes spiritual regeneration; thus, Jesus would be saying that a person must be baptized and receive the Spirit to enter the Kingdom of God. Many Bible teachers think the water signifies "the washing of water by the word" (Eph 5:26, NRSV) or "the washing of regeneration" (Titus 3:5, NKJV). According to the Greek text, there is only one preposition before "water" and "Spirit" (ex hudatos kai pneumatos). Had there been two prepositions, we could say that Jesus was speaking of two different experiences. But the construction in Greek seems to indicate that Jesus was speaking of one experience with two aspects. Thus, the water quite likely signifies the cleansing and life-giving action of the Spirit. This is substantiated by John 7:37-39, where the Spirit is likened to flowing waters; by Titus 3:5, where the Spirit is said to both cleanse and regenerate; and by Ezekiel 36:25-27, where the cleansing and regeneration of Israel are associated.

3:6 What is born of the flesh is flesh, and what is born of the Spirit is spirit (NRSV). In other words, flesh begets flesh, and Spirit begets spirit. The one cannot beget the other. Human beings, the "flesh," can produce only more human beings; this answers Nicodemus's question in 3:4. Only God, the divine Spirit, can generate spiritual life. The divine Spirit entering into a believer generates a new spirit in the believer. This spiritual regeneration was predicted in Ezekiel 36:26-27: "A new heart I will give you, and a new spirit I will put within you; and . . . I will put my spirit within you" (NRSV). At the same time God puts his Spirit into us, we are given a new, regenerated human spirit. This makes us children born of God.

3:7 *You must be born again.* In Greek the pronoun for "you" is plural—"you all." Jesus was speaking not only to Nicodemus, but to all of Israel through Nicodemus, who was acting as their representative. All of Israel needed regeneration. After Ezekiel had been told that Israel would be given a new spiritual regeneration (see Ezek 36:25-27), he received the vision of the corporate regeneration of Israel (see Ezek 37). Nicodemus, "Israel's teacher," should have known this great truth. He who had given his life to the study of the Scripture was woefully ignorant!

3:8 *The wind blows wherever it pleases. You hear its sound, but you cannot tell where it comes from or where it is going.* Jesus used the illustration of the wind to depict the effect of the Spirit on the person born of the Spirit. In Greek the same word (*pneuma*) can mean "spirit," "wind," or "breath." In Ezekiel 37, the Old Testament passage to which Jesus may have been alluding, the word *pneuma* in the Septuagint was used by the translator to signify all three words, "spirit," "wind," and "breath." The son of man is told to prophesy to the wind, which will then come as the Spirit to breathe into the slain of Israel the life-giving breath. Very likely, Jesus had this triple image in mind. But he also used this illustration to show that the reality of the Spirit living in a person is evidenced by the effect of the Spirit on that person's life.

So it is with everyone born of the Spirit. Lit., "So is everyone that is born of the Spirit." It does not mean "So is the activity of the Spirit." The image Jesus used describes the person born of the Spirit. Westcott said, "The believer shows by deed and word that an invisible influence has moved and inspired him. He is himself a continual sign of the action of the Spirit, which is freely determined, and incomprehensible by man to source and end, though seen in its present results."

3:9-10 *You are Israel's teacher.* According to the Greek, Jesus called Nicodemus "the teacher of Israel." Having such a position, he should have known what Jesus was talking about, for the new birth is not a topic foreign to the Hebrew Scriptures. Jesus' question must have exposed Nicodemus, who perhaps had thought that he and Jesus were teachers who could entertain a dialogue as equals.

3:11 *we speak of what we know, and we testify to what we have seen.* This "we" could be (1) an editorial "we"; (2) a reference to Jesus and his Father (see comments on 9:4); (3) a reference to Jesus and his disciples; or (4) an inclusive "we," referring to all those prophets, including John the Baptist and Jesus himself, who have spoken to Israel. Of these choices, the fourth seems to be the most likely.

you people do not accept our testimony. Israel did not receive the corporate testimony from Jesus speaking on behalf of the Father or from the prophets—hence the plural "our."

3:12 *I have told you of earthly things* (NRSV). In context, this refers to the illustration of the wind, which Jesus used to depict the activity of the Spirit in a regenerated person's life.

heavenly things (NRSV). These are the things that pertain to the heavenly realm, the heavenly kingdom. Because his listeners would not understand, Jesus did not often speak of these things openly but used parables to depict heavenly mysteries.

3:13 *No one has ever gone into heaven except the one who came from heaven.* Jesus could speak the things of heaven because he came from heaven! No other man could make such a claim. None but Jesus has come to earth from heaven.[1]

3:14 *as Moses lifted up the serpent in the wilderness, so must the Son of Man be lifted up* (NRSV). According to the construction in the Greek, the primary point of comparison is between the *action* of Moses' lifting up the serpent in the wilderness and the Son of Man being lifted up on the cross. Jesus was not comparing himself directly to the serpent—although the indirect simile cannot be excluded. According to Numbers 21:6-9, Moses erected a pole on which he placed a bronze serpent as the remedy for the rebellious, snake-bitten, dying Israelites. Their salvation came when they looked upon this lifted-up bronze serpent. By way of comparison, Jesus used this incident to depict his forthcoming salvation work on the cross. To be "lifted up" in Jesus' time—according to the usage in John (8:28; 12:32-34)—was a euphemism for death on the cross, as the victim was literally lifted up above the earth.

The one who knew no sin became sin for us that we might become the righteousness of God in him (2 Cor 5:21). Christ had no sin, no serpentine nature, but he was made in the likeness of sinful flesh (Rom 8:3) in order to die on the cross for all mankind who, like the children of Israel, were infected with death-producing sin (Rom 5:12). The crucified Christ is the only cure for mankind's plight.

3:15 *everyone who believes in him may have eternal life.* In Numbers 21:6-9, the perishing Israelites looked upon the lifted-up serpent and lived: *look and live.* Here, Jesus says, *Believe and live.* The Israelites in the wilderness were not required to believe; we are required to believe—to believe that Jesus died on the cross for our sins. The Israelites were spared from death; the believer in Jesus is spared eternal destruction and given eternal life.

3:16 *For God so loved the world that he gave his one and only Son, that whoever believes in him shall not perish but have eternal life.* Some commentators have thought that Jesus' conversation with Nicodemus concluded with 3:15, to which John added the following inspired words (verses 16-21) by way of further explanation. The future orientation of these words (i.e., they address people who have lived during and after the time of Christ) seems to affirm this. Nonetheless, verses 3:15 and 3:16ff blend together so well that it is very difficult for most readers to see any separation. Whether Jesus spoke this sentence to Nicodemus, or whether John under the inspiration of the Spirit penned it, no other verse in all the Bible so encapsulates the basic message of the gospel. How often has this verse been proclaimed? In how many sermons, languages, and books does it appear? This is the Good News in a nutshell: God so dearly loved all the people in the world that he was willing to give his one and only Son, who gave his life so that no one would have to perish, but rather be given eternal life simply by believing in him, Jesus Christ, the Son of God.

3:17-18 Jesus did not come to *condemn* [judge] an already condemned world—what good would that do? All of mankind was already under God's judgment and would continue to be under his judgment because of sin, specifically the sin of unbelief. The only way to escape the condemnation is to believe in Jesus, the Son of God. He who believes in him is saved (rescued) from God's judgment.

3:19 *this is the judgment* (NRSV). Or "This is how the judgment works" (TEV), or "On these grounds is sentence pronounced" (NJB). What follows describes the grounds for condemnation.

   the light has come into the world, and people loved darkness rather than light because their deeds were evil (NRSV). The same conflict between light and darkness was presented in the prologue.

3:20 *Everyone who does evil hates the light, and will not come into the light for fear that his deeds will be exposed.* The apostle Paul helps us understand this verse when he writes, "Everything exposed by the light becomes visible, for it is light that makes everything visible" (Eph 5:13-14). The people who fear exposure from the Light are those who are practicing evil, who don't want to be known for what they really are. Man in his sin does not want to part with the evil he loves.

3:21 *But those who do what is true come to the light, so that it may be clearly seen that their deeds have been done in God* (NRSV). According to the context, to practice the truth is to come to Christ, the Light; the result of coming to the Light and living in the Light will be clearly manifest in the lives of those who believe. Paul made this clear when he said, "Walk as children of light (for the fruit of the Spirit is in all goodness, righteousness, and truth)" (Eph 5:8-9, NKJV). It is implied that the believer comes repeatedly to the light of God's Word to learn God's mind and to do that which is acceptable in his sight.

ENDNOTES

[1]The last words of this verse, "who is in heaven," appearing in the KJV, are not found in the earliest manuscripts ($\mathfrak{P}$66 $\mathfrak{P}$75 $\aleph$ B W). However, the words were known to several early church fathers

(Hippolytus, Novatian, Origen, Dionysius), were included in the *Diatessaron*, and were translated in some early versions (Old Latin, Syriac, and Coptic). There is a good possibility that the statement was written by John and then excised by several early copyists because of its enigmatic meaning; i.e., how could the Son of Man who was then and there on earth also be in heaven? Furthermore, scribes are not known for adding text that created exegetical problems. More often than not they edited the text to alleviate what they thought were problematic passages or statements. Thus, it seems unlikely that later scribes would have added this statement. Nonetheless, the reading cannot be absolutely certified as genuine because it is absent in many good, early manuscripts.

John the Baptist Extols the Superiority of Jesus

JOHN 3:22-36

EXPOSITION

This portion begins with a scene in Aenon, near Salim, in the land of Judea. Two groups were baptizing: John the Baptist with his disciples and Jesus with his disciples, though Jesus himself did not perform any baptisms (4:2). Two baptisms were going on at the same time in approximately the same place, and people were coming to one or the other. One cannot deny that the situation could create a spirit of competition. This is underscored by the foreboding words, "For John had not yet been thrown into prison" (3:24, NKJV). Both men, Jesus and John, the two prominent figures in the new movement of God, were gathering disciples, but greater crowds were coming to Jesus than to John. This bothered the disciples of John, who must have been vexed with a spirit of competition. But it did not affect John, for he knew his position in God's plan. He was the herald of the Messiah-King, or to put it in his own words, "the friend of the bridegroom" (3:29, NRSV). John was pure. Unlike his disciples, he did not have a competitive spirit. He extolled the preeminent and superior Christ; he knew that he had to decrease and Jesus increase. John rejoiced to see this happen.

3:25-36/The Unnatural Equation

The powerful person fascinates us. In our society competitive, ambitious, successful people are admired and readily emulated. To those who are anxious to develop a competitive edge, a trip to a modern library, section 658.8 will offer abundant information. Consider just a few of the many titles available in this category: *Management by Intimidation; Job Power; How to Handle Subordinates; No Nonsense Delegation; The Art of Managing People; Tough-Minded Management;* and *Power!* While these books and many more address the extraordinary requirements needed for leadership on a grand scale, their message appeals even to those who are currently on the bottom rung of the societal ladder and desire passionately to have some authority over others. The spell of leadership is so powerful an allurement that even Henry Kissenger, former secretary of state, is reported to have said that "political power is an aphrodisiac."

All this was absolutely foreign to John the Baptist. It was not that he was devoid of ambition, but that he saw the real issues most clearly. Ambition concerns our goals in life and our incentives for pursuing them. A person's ambition is what makes him tick; it uncovers the mainspring of his actions, his secret inner motivation. Egocentric ambition focuses on selfish pursuits that may be perfectly acceptable to those whose only goal is this brief life (*my* comfort, *my* wealth, *my* power, *my* status) but who are totally shortsighted in view of eternity. John saw the issue as fundamentally between Creator and creature—between the glorious personal God and man's selfish ambition. God can be served only with an entire and exclusive devotion. This is simply because he is God. To share him with other loyalties (such as egocentric ambition) is to opt for idolatry. John, knowing clearly that God is absolutely sovereign, rightfully became ambitious for his glory, his Kingdom, his righteousness. It is not natural for a man who has experienced popularity and leadership to watch it slipping away from him and not fight or become embittered by the circumstances. How was it that John was able to handle this devastation in such a magnificent manner? Three possible answers come to mind that ought to prove instructional for us.

His heritage. Our Lord's unique epithet for this unusual man was, "Among those born of women there has not risen anyone greater than John the Baptist" (Matt 11:11). From such a statement and from our selected text, you cannot help but surmise that such a good and godly man must have come from a good and godly home. Luke informs us that Zechariah and Elizabeth "were upright in the sight of God, observing all the Lord's commandments and regulations blamelessly" (Luke 1:6). For years they did not experience an affirmative answer to their prayers, yet they lived blamelessly before God. Such was their character and trust in God that though heaven apparently remained silent to their hearts' cry, they continued living for God in an exemplary manner. Then in their advanced age God gave to them a child, whom they named John, meaning "the grace of God." We assume that since these godly parents were elderly, they may have reasoned that their time with their son might be very limited. Perhaps they would have only a few precious years to instill into him a love for God and a desire "to serve him without fear in holiness and righteousness before him all our days" (Luke 1:74-75). Not expecting to have him in their home and under their tutelage for two or three decades, they made each day count. They did not rely upon the synagogue for John's instruction. They did not say to themselves, "He is too young to instruct in righteousness; wait till he is older." Like Jochebed, the mother of Moses (Exod 2:9-10), they realized that time was very limited and that each day was precious, for all too soon circumstances could alter relationships. So a blameless father and a righteous mother instructed John in the things of God, and the divine record says, "The child grew and became strong in spirit" (Luke 1:80). Parents cannot instill in their children that which they do not have. We cannot practice unrighteousness and hope to influence our children to live righteously. John's strong convictions, his spiritual insights, and his noble character came from roots going deep into his heritage.

His self-evaluation. In addition to his heritage, the Scriptures indicate that John the Baptist had an honest self-evaluation. After our Lord's interview with Nicodemus, Jesus and his disciples left Jerusalem and went to an area in Judea, near Salim, not far from where John was preaching. Those who responded to Jesus' preaching were baptized, not by Christ, but by his authority and with his supervision. Interestingly, not far from this scene, John the Baptist was still continuing his ministry of calling people to repentance. People were repenting and being baptized by both John and Jesus, not very far apart. Then some Jews who were surprised at this asked John's disciples about it. Maybe these Jews argued that Jesus' baptism was superior to John's, which the disciples of John refused to admit. An argument developed, and John's disciples went to John with their grievance and confusion. In fact, they were so defensive about this situation that in their complaint to him they didn't even mention the name of Jesus, referring to him as "that man who was with you on the other side of the Jordan" (3:26). They stated their problem to imply that Jesus was under great *obligation* to John and ought not to be competing with him. They must have felt that John had done much for Jesus by testifying of him. And now Jesus had come into John's territory and was taking the crowds away. In their view this was highly unethical. John's reply was so demonstrative of his humility that it stands as a monument to him as long as God's Word abides. He began with a statement every child of God must accept: "A man can receive only what is given him from heaven" (3:27). In effect, John said to his disciples, "I cannot take that which is not given to me. I am grateful for the privilege of being the forerunner to Christ, but now he is here, and the crowds must turn to him. He must have the preeminence."

The different tasks in life and the apparent degrees of greatness must be explained as the expression of the will of God. When men arrogate something to themselves, rob others, snatch what does not properly belong to them, or claim what is not their own, it will be taken from them, and eventually God's judgment will condemn them. What is really our portion, including our position, our work, and our success, is a gift allotted to us. Promotion, influence, leadership, and responsibility are gifts God gives; if we do not receive them from him, they are stolen. The apostle Paul chided the Corinthians concerning a misguided view of themselves when he wrote, "What do you have that God hasn't given you?" (1 Cor 4:7, TLB). This is a most important truth for us to embrace. If we do, it will make sacred our particular position in life and keep jealousy from our door.

His conviction. In addition to his heritage and self-evaluation, John the Baptist's healthy conviction of God's sovereignty protected him from the allurement of ambition. There is tremendous contrast between John's attitude and those of the religious leaders described in 11:48 who wanted to kill Jesus before he created a disturbance and the Romans took away "our place and our nation." They, like Diotrephes, desired preeminence (3 Jn 1:9). Acknowledging no authority but their own, they put themselves first, and such blatant sin is utterly obnoxious.

It is stark unbelief, for it says, "I am more important than God." John the Baptist said, "Whatever happens is really immaterial; God is most important."

In the last paragraph of chapter 3, the final words of the greatest of all God's prophets are that Jesus Christ is infinitely superior to all men. The Baptist, talking to his disciples, says, in effect, that their view of Jesus must change, since evidently they had not yet grasped the truth of who Jesus is. Actually it is a marvelous testimony, for John the Baptist uses one striking expression after another to convey the majesty of Christ. He speaks of Jesus as the bridegroom of God's people, as the one who came from above, as the one whom God had sent, as one upon whom the Spirit is given without measure, as one whom the Father loves, and as one unto whose hands all things are given. To believe him is to have everlasting life, and to reject him is to experience the eternal wrath of God.

John the Baptist was not for a moment disturbed over the loss of his popularity and his "place in the sun." He believed in the sovereignty of God, that God is in control and that all things are to bring praise to him. His contentment and ambition, which is unnatural to the natural man, was to bring glory to God. We should be eager to develop our gifts, widen our opportunities, extend our influence, and accept promotions in our work. But we should not do so to boost our own ego or build our own empire; rather, through everything we do, we should strive to bring glory to God. Lesser ambitions are safe and right, provided that they are not an end in themselves (namely *ourselves*) but always the means to a greater end—God's eternal glory, and the spread of God's Kingdom and righteousness.

KEY WORDS AND PHRASES

In this section John extols Jesus' superiority. The following comparisons reveal Jesus' preeminence over John:

John the Baptist	Jesus	Verses
"I am not the Christ but am sent ahead of him."	"Everyone is going to him."	3:26-28
"The friend of the bridegroom . . . rejoices."	"He who has the bride is the bridegroom."	3:29, NRSV
"I must decrease."	"He must increase."	3:30, NRSV
"I am from the earth."	"He who comes from heaven is above all."	3:31, NKJV

NOTES

3:22-23 *Jesus and his disciples went out into the Judean countryside . . . and baptized. Now John also was baptizing in Aenon near Salim.* These verses tell us that two baptisms were going on at the same time: one in Judea and one in

"Aenon near Salim." Although the location of the latter is disputed, Albright considers the site to be in northern Samaria. Aenon, which means "a place of many springs," provided John with enough water to perform his baptisms—thus the statement, ***there was plenty of water.*** While John was baptizing, Jesus' disciples, under his direction, were also baptizing. John's baptism prepared the way for people to come to the Messiah. Jesus himself submitted to this baptism and endorsed it. But why was Jesus baptizing? Since the synoptic Gospels do not tell us anything about Jesus initiating a baptism, and we have no other known historical mention of this, we can only postulate that Jesus' disciples carried out the same kind of baptism as John, to prepare people to receive Christ and enter into his Kingdom. At that time more and more people were following Christ, so Jesus might have thought it necessary to initiate this baptism. Whatever kind of baptism it was, the disciples of John were probably upset that the people were going to Jesus for baptism rather than to them.

3:24 *This was before John was put in prison.* This statement has two functions. First, it helps clarify the chronology of events. At the time John wrote this gospel (c. AD 85), his readers may not have known when John the Baptist's ministry ended, especially in relationship to Jesus' ministry. Second, it sets the stage for the Gospel writer to expose the spirit of competition that existed in John's disciples. Had John not been around, there would have been no cause for strife.

3:25 *An argument developed between some of John's disciples and a certain Jew over the matter of ceremonial washing.* Given the immediate context, the argument over ceremonial washing (or purification) probably involved some debate about whether or not baptism produced purification and whose baptism was superior. The Jews sought purification through various sacrifices and ablutions prescribed by God through Moses. Thus some of them must have strongly believed that baptism could not purify someone from his or her sins.

3:26 *that man who was with you on the other side of the Jordan—the one you testified about—well, he is baptizing, and everyone is going to him.* John's disciples hereby expose their competitive spirit; this is certain because of the way John responds to them in the following verses. These disciples had heard John bear witness to Jesus. In their presence he had announced Jesus as "the Lamb of God who takes away the sin of the world" (1:29). The second time John made this proclamation (1:36), two of John's disciples left him and followed Jesus. All of John's disciples could have done the same, but some stayed with John to help him with his ministry. Some of these disciples must have lost sight of their mission, which was to join John in preparing people for Christ. They should not have been surprised, much less dismayed, that all men were going to Christ—they were supposed to!

We Christians must always remember the primary focus of our ministry: to exalt Christ and point people to him. We may follow certain leaders, but we must always remember that they, too, have the same commission. We should not be affected by how well or how poorly a particular leader or movement is doing. And we must do our utmost to quench any kind of competitive spirit. All is under the sovereignty of God. Our task is to follow Christ and see that he is exalted.

3:27 *No one can receive anything except what has been given from heaven* (NRSV). John's reply to his disciples was the response of a spiritual man who knew his place in God's plan. He knew that a man is not able to do anything unless it has been given to him from heaven, that is, from God. Therefore, it would have been foolish to strive against the heavenly will. If all men were going to Christ, then all men *should* go to Christ. John's statement is one that takes a lifetime to learn and appropriate. All those who have been involved in some kind of Christian ministry should sooner or later come to the realization that no one can accomplish anything of significance for God if God has not originated the work. That which comes from self-origination needs sheer self-will to accomplish it; that which originates from the heavenly will is accompanied by God's heavenly blessing and impetus. Many Christian workers know the difference and have come to depend on God's blessing and presence (see Exod 33:15).

3:28 *I am not the Christ but am sent ahead of him.* John here tells his disciples what he already declared earlier. John had always been forthright in declaring his position so that the distinction between himself and the Christ would be unmistakably clear. Some of John's disciples had left to follow the Christ; undoubtedly any of his disciples could do the same. But John could not command them to do so, for no one can come to Jesus unless the Father has drawn him. Those who followed Jesus did so in personal response to God's calling, not an earthly reassignment.

3:29 *He who has the bride is the bridegroom. The friend of the bridegroom, who stands and hears him, rejoices greatly at the bridegroom's voice* (NRSV). John employed a beautiful metaphor to depict the way he saw his relationship with Jesus the Christ. He saw himself as being the bridegroom's friend, or as we would say in modern parlance, the best man. As the best man, John enjoyed being with his friend, the bridegroom; he did not expect to receive any attention. All the attention should go to the bridegroom and not the friend of the bridegroom. In ancient times, more attention was given to the bridegroom than the bride (see Ps 45).

John's metaphor also has theological implications. In the Old Testament, God was likened to a bridegroom and his people to a bride (Isa 62:5; Jer 3; Ezek 16; Hos 2). In saying that Jesus was the bridegroom, John was implying that Jesus was the divine husband of God's people. As such, all of God's people belonged to him—or as John said in the following verse, all of the increase belonged to him. In the other Gospels, Jesus spoke of himself as the bridegroom (Matt 9:15; Mark 2:19-20), and then later in the New Testament Christ and his church are likened to husband and wife, bridegroom and bride (2 Cor 11:2; Eph 5:22-32; Rev 19:7; 21:2).

3:30 *He must increase, but I must decrease* (NRSV). What a realization John had! He knew that his work was destined to decrease—even that he himself would have to decrease. (The Greek word for "must" is used here—*dei*, meaning "it is necessary." When this word was used previously in this chapter, it signaled a mandate—see 3:7, 14.) John *had to become less,* but his decrease was for Jesus' increase. It may be easy for Christians to repeat John's words, but it is not so easy to live them out. None of us likes to decrease, but God allows certain experiences to diminish us so that we might experientially know that our decrease brings Christ's increase.

3:31 *The one who comes from above is above all.* According to the Greek, the word for "all" could be neuter ("all things") or masculine ("all men"). In either case, John's statement reveals his attitude about Christ's preeminence over everything.

the one who is from the earth belongs to the earth, and speaks as one from the earth. John, though the greatest man born among men (see Matt 11:11), was still a man—he originated from an earthly source. As Paul puts it, "The first man was of the dust of the earth, the second man from heaven" (1 Cor 15:47). Since John had not come from heaven, he could not reveal heavenly things, as Christ could.

The one who comes from heaven is above all. Christ's heavenly origin gives him preeminence over all men.[1]

3:32 *He testifies to what he has seen and heard* (NRSV). Throughout this Gospel, John presents the truth that Jesus spoke to men what he had heard from the Father. Several of the statements intimate that this hearing from the Father began before the foundation of the world and continued throughout Jesus' lifetime and ministry. Jesus was faithful to testify to what he heard.

yet no one accepts his testimony (NRSV). Of course, not all rejected Jesus. But this describes the national sentiment about Jesus. The Jews who lived when Jesus did heard his testimony and rejected it. To refuse Christ's testimony is to treat it as a lie. By the help of the Holy Spirit and the drawing power of the Father, we who believe have been given the grace to accept Christ's testimony. We believe that he came from the Father in heaven and brought to all men the divine truth.

3:33 *The man who has accepted it has certified that God is truthful.* By way of contrast with 3:32, this verse indicates that Jesus' testimony was not rejected by everyone, for some did receive his testimony. Those who received Jesus' testimony believed that he was the Son of God come from heaven, the Messiah sent from God. Their belief in his testimony was their "stamp of approval" on the veracity of God's action of sending his Son. In other words, they tested the testimony and found it to be true, and so they could approve of it by virtue of their own experience. Of course, Jesus' testimony does not need any man's seal to certify it, for it is bona fide in and of itself. John's statement refers to the seal each believer places on his experience, not to a seal that is to be placed on Christ. "To set one's seal" to something in ancient days not only signaled certification; it also indicated identification. Therefore, to say, "I have set my seal to this" was another way of saying, "I have identified with this." In ancient days, a person would impress his personal mark on a seal and thereby label the object as belonging to him or her. The same word, *sealed,* is used in 2 Corinthians 1:22 and Ephesians 1:13 with respect to God sealing the believers with the Holy Spirit. This is God's mark of ownership on each of his children and a sign of his identification with us.

3:34 *He whom God has sent speaks the words of God* (NRSV). God's Son, Jesus Christ, does not speak his own words but the words of God.

for he gives the Spirit without measure (NRSV). This is the reading in the earliest manuscripts; other manuscripts read, "God gives him [Jesus] the Spirit without measure." The statement could mean that God gives the immeasurable Spirit—in this case, to his Son—or that Jesus gives the immeasurable Spirit when he speaks the words of God. It can be argued that Jesus Christ dispensed the Spirit via his spoken word, since John 6:63 says that his words are spirit. But most scholars favor the second option, primarily because the next verse speaks of the Father giving all things to the Son. As such, the Son was the recipient of the immeasurable Spirit for his prophetic ministry (Isa 11:1ff).

John also was a prophet, even the greatest prophet; yet he had a limited measure of the Spirit. The same is true of every believer: each child of God has a certain measure of the Spirit (1 Cor 12:7ff; cf. 12:3ff). The Son, by comparison, has an unlimited supply of the Spirit. He, in contrast to the Old Testament prophets who were anointed with the Holy Spirit only when they were speaking for God, always had the Spirit and therefore always spoke for God.

3:35 *The Father loves the Son* (NRSV). For John to say this reveals John's insight into the mystery of the divine Father-Son relationship. Although the Father loves all men, including John the Baptist, who must have been especially dear to him, he has always had a special love for his one and only Son.

and has placed all things in his hands (NRSV). The Father committed all of his divine plan to the care of his Son. What a glorious privilege and awesome responsibility. By the end of his ministry Jesus told the Father that he had accomplished everything the Father had wanted him to do (17:1-4).

3:36 *Whoever believes in the Son has eternal life.* Because the Son accomplished everything that the Father asked him to, there is nothing left for men to do but believe in God's Son. The person who believes becomes the instantaneous recipient of the divine, eternal life of God. A believer need not wonder if he has eternal life or wait for the future judgment to see if eternal life will be granted. He who has the Son has eternal life (1 Jn 5:12).

whoever rejects the Son. To reject the Son's testimony and the gospel is to disobey the Son.

will not see life. To not see life means to not experience God's eternal life.

God's wrath remains on him. God's judgment (wrath) has already come upon mankind because of the Fall and the sin that thereby entered into the human race, making all men enemies of God (Rom 5:8ff). Every person is born under God's wrath. But God provided the way of escape, the way of deliverance, by sending his Son to die on the cross to take away our sins. Whoever believes in the Son is liberated from God's wrath, but whoever refuses to believe remains under God's wrath.

ENDNOTES

[1] This clause is present in 𝔓36 𝔓66 ℵ^C A B L W, but not present in 𝔓75 ℵ * D. Good reasons could be given to explain why scribes would be tempted to add the words (as a repeat from the first part of the verse) or delete the words because they seemed redundant.

Jesus, the Life-Giver

JOHN 4:1-54

Jesus, God's Gift to the Samaritans
JOHN 4:1-42

EXPOSITION

Jesus had to pass through Samaria on his way to Galilee. Samaria was a province allotted to Ephraim and half the tribe of Manasseh in the days of Joshua. After the death of Solomon and the revolt of the ten tribes, the inhabitants of Samaria followed the idolatry introduced by Jeroboam, refusing to go to Jerusalem to worship at the Temple. Years later, after the ten tribes had been carried away into captivity, the king of Assyria put into this province a colony of various nations that soon intermingled and intermarried with the original people, causing a strange medley of religions. Second Kings 17:33 says, "They feared the LORD, yet served their own gods" (NKJV). This conglomerate of people became known as Samaritans. They adopted the books of Moses as their Scriptures and set up a place to worship on Mount Gerizim (Deut 11:26-29; 27:1-12). But they were far from having accurate knowledge about the truth, even though they knew about a coming Messiah.

When a remnant of Jews returned from the Babylonian captivity, they refused the Samaritans any participation in rebuilding the Temple or the city of Jerusalem, even though the Samaritans claimed to have the same God as the Jews. This refusal led to a bitter animosity between the two groups of people, which was succinctly summed up by John: "Jews have no dealings with Samaritans" (4:9, NKJV). They wouldn't talk to them and generally avoided going through their neighborhoods.

But Jesus went to the Samaritans and offered them the gift of life. To the Samaritans Jesus revealed himself as the expected Messiah (4:25-26). Furthermore, Jesus pointed the Samaritans to the truth about salvation, God's nature, and the worship of God: (1) Salvation comes from among the Jews (i.e., the Messiah is a Jew), (2) God is Spirit, and (3) God must be worshiped in spirit and in truth.

4:1-26/*Worship Contrasted*

Few portions of Scripture offer as many intriguing contrasts as does this fourth chapter of John's Gospel. It is quite easy to see two kinds of gifts, two kinds of water, two kinds of food, two kinds of harvest, and two kinds of worship. Not quite so apparent, but nonetheless within the text, can be found contrasted prejudice, work, priorities, and belief. What Jesus had to say about each of these subjects would be worthwhile studies providing very practical instruction in Christian living. But perhaps for the believer nothing could be more valuable from this section than to look carefully at two kinds of worship.

Misplaced worship. As the dialogue progressed between Jesus and this woman, it began to dawn upon her that she was speaking with a prophet—that is, one who revealed secrets and spoke for God. Her conscience had been stirred as she acknowledged her guilt. No doubt she at times had been bothered by her lifestyle, but now, in the presence of a prophet, she thought about worship.

Perhaps what went through her mind was something like this: *I realize that I am a sinner before God. I must offer to God an offering for my sin. I must take that offering to the house of God to put myself right with him. But where am I going to take my offering for sin? Where is the best place to make a sacrifice?* Her people had always worshiped at the nearby mountain, but it had never given her any satisfaction. Perhaps that was the mistake—maybe one ought to worship at Jerusalem, as the Jews insisted. She only knew that for her, God had never been real, personal, satisfying—and she knew she needed cleansing. But where could one obtain it? No doubt she thought of worship as a matter of form, ceremony, observance, ritual, and location. She had yet to understand that God is Spirit and not confined to things or places. To think otherwise is idolatry and an insult to the very nature of God.

Real worship. Jesus was helping this woman to see that her problem had not been with the *place* of worship, but that she had not really worshiped at all. It is not the *where* that matters, but the *how* and the *what*. She was concerned about location when she didn't even know whom she was worshiping. In order to worship God we must know him and his salvation. It is not a question of going to the mountain or going to Jerusalem. We can worship God anywhere and everywhere if we are ready to take our rightful place before him, to confess our sin and our guilt. Then we can lift our heart to him in worship.

True worship is not a question of place or ritual, but of faith, love, and spiritual reality. It is an attitude of the heart. There must be a sense of sin, a sense of need, true repentance, and a turning to the Savior. True worship operates on a clear and definite knowledge of God, derived from his Word. It is the action of a new nature seeking more of God. It is a redeemed heart occupied with God, expressing itself in adoration and thanksgiving through prayer, singing, and meditation. Real worship, spiritual worship, is decorous (proper), reverential, and doctrinally sound, occupying the worshiper with God himself. The end result is a peaceful heart and a rejoicing spirit. Since God is Spirit, gifts to God must be gifts of the Spirit: love, loyalty, obedience, and devotion. A dead spirit cannot possibly worship the living God, so unless one is born from above and has the life of God, all attempts to worship are in vain. Real worship occurs when our renewed spirit speaks to, listens to, and meets with God, who is immortal and invisible. Such worship will never be empty, boring, or mundane, because God seeks to meet with all who worship him in spirit and in truth.

KEY WORDS AND PHRASES

In this chapter, various aspects of Jesus' person are revealed. He is:

» The gift of God (4:10)
» The fountain of living water (4:10, 14)
» A prophet (4:19)
» The Messiah (4:25-26, 29)
» The Savior of the world (4:42)

NOTES

4:1 The NIV translators moved the first phrase of this verse as it appears in the Greek text to verse 3 in order to avoid the awkward statement, "When Jesus realized that the Pharisees heard that Jesus was gaining and baptizing more disciples than John." Some manuscripts read "Lord" instead of "Jesus" in the first occurrence. But the change from Jesus to Lord may also indicate scribal adjustment of an awkward expression.

The Pharisees heard that Jesus was gaining and baptizing more disciples than John. According to John 3:26 and 30, it was becoming increasingly evident that Jesus was now drawing a larger following than John the Baptist. Somehow Jesus realized, either by divine intuition or by actual report, that the Pharisees had heard about the crowds coming to hear him and to be baptized. The Pharisees were the ones who closely followed the activities of John the Baptist and sent emissaries to question him about his identity. The Baptist pointed them to a greater one, the coming Messiah. Now that the greater one had come and was, in fact, manifesting his preeminence, the Pharisees shifted their attention to Jesus of Nazareth. They were jealous of his popularity and rejected his message. They would eventually lead the nation in that awful rejection.

More men were becoming Jesus' disciples (4:1; cf. 6:60). In the wording of some translations (NKJV, NASB), Jesus was *making* more disciples than John. Undoubtedly, many of these men left John the Baptist to follow Jesus. Earlier, John the Gospel writer had done just that. He and Andrew were disciples of John the Baptist, but they left him to follow Jesus (see 1:35-37). Since he was the first to leave the Baptist and follow the Messiah, it was natural for him to have a personal interest in this matter. How did Jesus "make" disciples? Did he appoint them and give them special teachings? Or perhaps we should understand the verb "make" (*poieō* in Greek) as "create"—that is, Jesus' very presence and ministry spontaneously created disciples. Some men's hearts were drawn to Christ in such a way that they wanted to follow him completely.

4:2 *although in fact it was not Jesus who baptized, but his disciples.* The Messiah would baptize in the Holy Spirit, in contrast to those who baptized in water. Thus, Jesus never performed water baptism—that was the task of his disciples, a task they continued to perform during the days of the early church. None could boast, "I was baptized by Jesus." It is not the baptizer who gives value to the rite. Even Judas must have baptized some. It is one's belief in Christ and the testimony of what he has done in a person's life that makes baptism meaningful.

4:3 *he left Judea and started back to Galilee* (NRSV). Knowing that the Pharisees in Jerusalem had heard about his popularity and that they would begin their pursuit of him, and at the same time knowing that the time for his final conflict had not yet come, Jesus purposefully decided to leave Judea and return to Galilee. His first Judean visit had come to an end—a visit begun by his coming to Jerusalem for the Passover (2:13).

4:4 *Now he had to go through Samaria.* Lit., "And it was necessary for him to pass through Samaria." Since the Samaritans were hated by the Jews, most of the strict Jews traveling from Judea to Galilee took a route around Samaria, even though such a route would take more time. For those who were trying to make the best time, it was faster to go through Samaria to Galilee. However, the context indicates that Jesus was in no hurry to get to Galilee (4:40, 43). Thus, the necessity must be understood in a different way: Jesus was compelled by an inner urgency to go to Samaria and give them the divine life and light. He was above the Jewish prejudices.

4:5 *he came to a town in Samaria called Sychar near the plot of ground Jacob had given to his son Joseph.* Sychar was near Shechem. According to Genesis 33:19, Jacob bought a piece of land in this vicinity, where he dug a well. Joseph was buried at this site (Josh 24:32). Thus, this land was historically significant, and the well was very important to the Samaritans, who claimed Jacob as their father (4:12), just as the Jews did. This land was a "gift" from Jacob to Joseph. Jesus would play off this idea of a gift during his discussion with the Samaritan woman, inasmuch as he would present to her "the gift of God."

4:6 *Jacob's well was there.* The Greek word for "well" in this verse is *pēgē*, meaning a spring or fountain. However, in 4:11-12 the woman calls the well *threar*, meaning a man-made well or cistern. Both words are correct because Jacob's well was dug out by hand and "fed by an underground stream, which rarely gives out" (Bruce). Later in the discussion, when Jesus offered the gift of eternal life, he compared it to a *pēgē* (fountain) springing up into eternal life.

Jesus, tired as he was from the journey. Lit., "having become wearied from his journey." The Greek verb for "weary" is very often used to denote labor. He had walked from Judea to Sychar, which was probably a two-day journey. The Word made flesh was truly flesh, truly human—an important theme in John's Gospel. Jesus certainly knew what it meant to be hungry, weary, thirsty, exhausted. He experienced our humanity.

It was about the sixth hour. Noontime.

4:7 *A Samaritan woman came to draw water* (NRSV). Noon was an unusual time to go to the well because it was the peak heat of the day. Early morning and late afternoon were the favored times. Maybe she was out of water, but many commentators assume she had few female companions, and so rather than being snubbed, she chose to journey to the well when it was most likely to be free of her neighbors.

Jesus said to her, "Give me a drink" (NRSV). As the woman approached the well, she knew that the man who sat there was a Jewish teacher by the clothing he wore. She was probably highly indignant that a Jew was sitting on "our" well. So you can imagine her surprise as she approached, trying to ignore him, when he said kindly, "Give me a drink." She knew that the typical Jew would have dashed the cup to the ground had she offered a cup of water, but here was a Jew speaking kindly to her and *asking* for some water. Jesus' approach provides a good model for personal evangelism. Godet said, "He is not unaware that the way to gain a soul is often to ask a service of it."

4:8 (*His disciples had gone into the town to buy food.*) This parenthetical statement serves to inform the reader that Jesus was alone with the woman. But apart from the fact that he was alone with her, this statement implies something else. (1) The disciples of Jesus did not beg; they bought. (2) They were responsible for the money they had; i.e., while there were many people poorer than they were, they did not give away all their money. (3) Even Jesus did not live by the miraculous. He could have turned rocks to bread and changed water into wine, but he lived as we must live.

4:9 *You are a Jew and I am a Samaritan woman. How can you ask me for a drink?* The woman was triply surprised: first, that a Jew would speak to a Samaritan; second, that a Jewish male would speak to a woman of Samaria; third, that a Jew would use a Samaritan's utensil to drink from.

(For Jews do not associate with Samaritans). This parenthetical statement is found in most of the early manuscripts, but is not included in a few. Though some scholars have argued that this statement is a "gloss" that found its way into the text, it is more likely that this gloss was part of the original text, since it was customary for John to add such explanations for his Gentile readers. These are

not the words of the Samaritan woman, but of John the Gospel writer, who here provides an explanation about the relationship between Jews and Samaritans. The Greek word translated "associate" literally means "to share the use of." Some commentators, therefore, think John was saying that Jews and Samaritans would not share the same utensils or facilities. This interpretation is reflected in the TEV: "Jews will not use the same dishes that Samaritans use" (see also NIV mg). With this in mind, we can appreciate what it meant for Jesus to ask for a drink of water from a utensil belonging to a Samaritan. To do so was to go against the Jewish mores and accepted prejudices of the time.

4:10 *If you knew the gift of God and who it is that asks you for a drink, you would have asked him and he would have given you living water.* The structure of this verse is chiasmic, "the gift of God" corresponding to "living water" and "who it is" corresponding to "he." The woman was ignorant of two things: (1) God's gift, which is the gift of life, symbolized as "living water"; and (2) the giver, Jesus the Messiah. Jesus hereby turned the conversation and made a spiritual proclamation which, of course, the woman did not then understand. The Samaritan woman's reference to the well as a gift from Jacob to Joseph (see v. 12) probably encouraged Jesus to continue with the same metaphor—namely, that of a gift. But whereas Jacob gave Joseph a well, Jesus would give this woman living water.

4:11 *Sir, you have no bucket, and the well is deep. Where do you get that living water?* (NRSV). It would be very interesting if we had some way to see the changing expressions on this woman's face. She must have looked at Jesus in puzzlement and doubt. "This well is deep. Where are you going to get this spring water?" At this point the woman had no idea that Jesus was speaking metaphorically.

4:12 *Are you greater than our father Jacob, who gave us the well and drank from it himself . . . ?* She looked at this tired, dusty, thirsty traveler and said with some incredulity, "Jacob was great; he gave us this water. Just where are *you* going to get and give better water than this? Certainly you don't mean to imply you are greater than Jacob?" What caused this response? Perhaps the woman was offended that someone could claim to provide a better water supply than had their great forefather Jacob. Or perhaps the woman was beginning to have some suspicion about the greatness of Jesus (Schnackenburg). The discourse intimates the gradual enlightenment which is characteristic of John's Gospel.

The Samaritans had the highest regard for Jacob, as did the Jews, and both groups legitimately claimed him as their forefather. The Samaritans must have considered themselves very fortunate to have this well that Jacob dug and even drank from (along with his children and cattle). The Old Testament does not mention such a well, so their knowledge about its history must have come from tradition. The irony of the situation is that the original readers of this Gospel knew that Jesus, the provider of eternal life, is, in fact, greater than Jacob.

There is a lesson to be learned here: The veneration of a historical object with religious associations is an affront to the living reality of Jesus Christ. Further-more, the Samaritan woman claimed a heritage that did nothing for her spiritual life. God was not personal to her. She said, "Our fathers worshiped here." That is similar to answering the question "Are you a Christian?" by saying, "My grand-parents were Methodists." God has no grandchildren. Salvation is not transmit-ted down the bloodline. The Samaritans possessed Jacob's well, but they did not possess a relationship with God, as Jacob did.

4:13 *Everyone who drinks this water will be thirsty again.* The woman certainly agreed with that statement. How well she knew that she had come to this well again and again because of her thirst, only to be thirsty again. So also the other "thirsts" of life—they never satisfy. They create ever more thirst. The Samaritan woman had had her fill of "drinks," as she had experienced five husbands and was now with a sixth man, who was not her husband (4:18). She would have had to admit that she was not satisfied.

4:14 *those who drink of the water that I will give them will never be thirsty* (NRSV). We interpret Jesus to be saying, "Drink, or crave, the things of fleshly desires and you'll always be thirsty, but drink of the living water I give and you will thirst for nothing more. That is, drink the water I offer and you'll experience its cleansing, purifying, and soul-refreshing effects forever."

The water that I will give will become in them a spring of water gushing up to eternal life (NRSV). The recipient of living water actually receives not just a drink or even a bucket of water, but an inbuilt, indwelling fountain providing a constant supply of eternal life to enjoy. The Greek word here is *pēgē;* it denotes a fountain whose water gushes forth. How different this is from a well that requires man-ual labor to dig and to draw out the water. The gift that Jesus gives—a fountain springing up into eternal life—suggests the availability and accessibility of the divine life for the believer. The expression "to eternal life" probably means "result-ing in eternal life." The result of drinking the water Jesus gives is that the drinker receives eternal life. This drinking is not a once-and-for-all experience. Very likely this fountain is the indwelling Spirit, for Jesus later compares the Spirit to rivers of living water flowing out of the person who comes to Jesus and drinks (see 7:37-39). The same thought is apparent in 1 Corinthians 12:13.

4:15 *Sir, give me this water so that I won't get thirsty and have to keep coming here to draw water.* The woman's response reveals that she understood Jesus to be speaking of physical water, much in the same way as the crowds did when Jesus spoke about giving them the living bread: "Sir, from now on give us this bread" (6:34) (Bruce). She must have been quite excited to think that this man could give her some kind of water that really quenches thirst and does not have to be drawn from a well, because the idea had not yet dawned upon her that Jesus was using water as a symbol for spiritual life.

The Greek verb tenses in the woman's response are very revealing. The first verb is an aorist (indicating once-and-for-all action), while the other three are in the present tense (indicating continuous action). In expanded form, this statement could read: "Give me this water once and for all, so that I do not have to keep on thirsting nor continue coming here to keep on drawing out water."

4:16 *Go, call your husband, and come back* (NRSV). Jesus now turned the conversation because the woman did not perceive the spiritual intent of his words. Besides, Jesus knew that he now had to make this woman see her true condition and her real need for the true water that quenches thirst.

4:17-18 *You are right when you say you have no husband. The fact is, you have had five husbands, and the man you now have is not your husband.* The woman did not perceive the spiritual intent of Jesus' words, so he said something to awaken her conscience. Unless one is spiritually thirsty, one will not desire living water. When she saw her true condition before God, she would understand Jesus' offer. Furthermore, the unveiling of his knowledge about her life is the beginning of her revelation about his identity. He who "is the light of men" (1:4) exposes the sinful condition of each person and reveals himself as the "knower" and Savior of each person.

4:19 *I can see that you are a prophet.* In saying this, the woman acknowledged the truthfulness of Jesus' remarks about her life. Undoubtedly, she believed that a prophet had the power to see not only into the future, but also into a person's life. She reckoned that Jesus was such a prophet. This is the dawning of her realization of Jesus' identity.

4:20 The notion of Jesus' being a prophet sparked in the woman's mind a question pertaining to religion. Some have pointed out that she may have been purposefully attempting to avert any further disclosure of her personal, sinful life. However, Jesus made no attempt to return the discussion to her marital situation; rather, he entered right into a dialogue about true worship.

   Our fathers worshiped on this mountain, but you Jews claim that the place where we must worship is in Jerusalem. Her inquiry was valid. The Samaritans had set up a place for worship on Mount Gerizim in accordance with Deuteronomy 11:26-29 (cf. Deut 27:1-12), while the Jews had followed David and Solomon in making Jerusalem the center of Jewish worship.[1] Naturally, there was ongoing debate between the two groups concerning who was correct. The Scriptures absolutely affirmed Jerusalem as the true center for worship (Deut 12:5; 2 Chr 6:6; 7:12; Ps 78:67-68). Thus the Jews were correct and the Samaritans in error, even though the Samaritan "fathers" had perpetuated what they thought to be the true tradition. The Samaritan woman wanted to hear directly from a Jew and a prophet what he thought about this issue.

4:21 *the hour is coming when you will worship the Father neither on this mountain nor in Jerusalem* (NRSV). Instead of arguing for the right of Jerusalem over

Mount Gerizim, Jesus foretold the advent of a new age in which worship would not be confined to a physical place. Since both the Jews and the Samaritans relied on a particular physical setting for "proper" worship, Jesus pointed them to a new realm—that of the Spirit. It is not the *where* that matters, but the *how* and the *what.* True worship is not a question of place or ritual, but of spiritual reality. True worship is of the heart and in the spirit.

There are many Christians who need to heed this new direction, for they have become dependent on a physical building or setting as providing the proper place and environment for worship. God, who is Spirit, is not so confined. He can be worshiped anywhere at any time, as long as it is done in spirit and in truth (see 4:23-24).

4:22 You Samaritans worship what you do not know; we worship what we do know, for salvation is from the Jews. In addressing the Samaritan woman, Jesus was speaking to all the Samaritans; the "you" here is plural. The Samaritans worshiped, but their worship was done in ignorance of that which they were worshiping. The Greek text says "that which" instead of what might be expected: "he whom." Probably this points to the entire system of worship and does not confine itself specifically to the knowledge of God (Morris). Since the Samaritans used only the Pentateuch, they were ignorant of the rest of the Old Testament Scriptures and the truths they expressed about the full scope of worship. The Jews, with whom Jesus explicitly identifies himself here, did know what they worshiped, for they had the full canon of Old Testament Scriptures. These Scriptures revealed, especially in the Psalms and Prophets, that salvation would come from the Jews because the Messiah would come *from* the Jewish race and *for* the Jewish race. The Greek text speaks of "the salvation"; most likely this refers to the messianic salvation that had long been the hope of the chosen people (Luke 1:69, 71, 77; Acts 13:26, 47).

4:23 Yet a time is coming and has now come. Jesus here announced that a new age had come, an age in which **the true** [real, genuine] **worshipers will worship the Father in spirit and truth.** Worship would take on two new aspects: it would be in spirit, and it would be in truth. The phrase "in spirit" speaks of a locality (the phrase is locative in Greek), in contrast to Jerusalem or Mount Gerizim, the two localities previously discussed. Both the Jews and the Samaritans were oriented to a physical location for worship; this had to change. The true place to worship is in spirit—i.e., man's human spirit, which is the ethereal inner being in each person, that God-breathed entity that corresponds to the nature of God himself, who is Spirit. In the New Testament age, the church is called "a dwelling place of God in the Spirit" (Eph 2:22, NKJV), for God indwells the spirits of the believers, and it is there where true worship takes place.

The phrase "in truth" speaks to the fact that the Samaritans' system of worship was invalid because it was based on inaccurate knowledge of the Scriptures. The Samaritans had relied only on the Pentateuch for their knowledge about worshiping God, and that knowledge was incomplete. The phrase "in truth" also means "in a true way" or "with genuineness."

True worship operates on a clear and definite knowledge of God derived from his Word. It is the action of a new nature, born from above, seeking more of God. True worship proceeds from a redeemed heart occupied with God, expressing itself in adoration and thanksgiving, through prayer, singing (praise), and meditation (teaching of the Word). True worship is spiritual, reverential, and orderly, occupying the worshiper with God. The end result of true worship is a peaceful heart and rejoicing spirit. God is not a stone deity or a wood deity; therefore idol worship is an insult to the very nature of God. God is Spirit and not confined to space, objects, or location.

4:24 *God is spirit.* "Spirit" comes first, for emphasis: "Spirit is what God is." Here is a simple yet profound definition of God as to his nature. God, by nature, is spirit. In the immediate context, the statement "God is spirit" speaks of God's omnipresence—God is not limited to any locality (such as Jerusalem or Mount Gerizim); he can be worshiped anywhere. But **his worshipers must worship in spirit.** This is a must; there is no other way to truly worship God. Since God is spirit, a man can only rightfully worship in a way that corresponds to God's nature. Of course, a person cannot commune with God if his spirit has not been regenerated by God's Spirit. Unless one is born from above, it doesn't matter where one worships, for no worship is ever done. But if you are born again, you can worship God anywhere!

4:25 *I know that Messiah is coming* (NRSV). The best manuscript evidence supports the reading "I know that a Messiah is coming." But a few manuscripts read, "We know that a Messiah is coming." The second reading, very likely a scribal emendation, has the Samaritan woman speaking on behalf of the Samaritans from start to finish.

When he comes, he will proclaim all things to us (NRSV). Jesus' mention of a "coming hour" with a new kind of worship must have triggered a thought in the Samaritan woman's mind about the coming of the Messiah. Perhaps she thought it would be the role of the Messiah to declare what would be in the coming age; if so, she may have been testing him to see if he would affirm his identity as the Messiah. Following their tradition, the Samaritans believed in the coming of the *Taheb* (meaning "the restorer"), or Prophet, foretold by Moses (Deut 18:15-18). Very likely, they had also heard of the coming Messiah from John the Baptist, who had been baptizing in northern Samaria. They, along with the Jews, probably did not consider the Prophet and the Messiah to be one and the same person. The woman had perceived that Jesus was "a prophet" (4:19), and perhaps now she was beginning to think he was *the* Prophet, or even the Messiah.

4:26 *I who speak to you am he.* Lit., "I am [he], the one speaking to you." Whereas Jesus avoided telling the Jews plainly that he was the Christ (see

10:24ff)—because of their misconstrued notions about what and who the Messiah should be—he told this Samaritan woman directly that he was the Messiah. The one who sat there with her on the well was the coming Christ, now come.

4:27 Just then his disciples came. They were astonished that he was speaking with a woman (NRSV). The disciples of Jesus were startled to see their rabbi speaking with a Samaritan woman. Rabbis did not carry on conversations with women because it was considered frivolous, even evil. For example, Rabbi Jose ben Johanan (c. 150 BC) said, "He that talks much with womankind brings evil upon himself and neglects the study of the Law and at the last will inherit Gehenna" (*Pirqe 'Aboth* 1.5). But the disciples did not question Jesus concerning his motives, for they must have come to realize that Jesus did all things with good purpose. If he had been anyone else, he would have been called to account.

4:28 The woman then left her waterpot, went her way into the city, and said to the men (NKJV). This action has symbolic meaning; it speaks of the woman leaving behind that which could not give her true life or satisfaction. The waterpot could give her water from the well but not the water of life. Now she had been given the real source of life—living water from the Messiah. It is interesting that she spoke to the men of the city, not the women; perhaps this underscores her situation as an "outcast among women."

4:29 Come, see a man who told me everything I ever did. Although this statement is an exaggeration, it still contains the truth. In essence, the Samaritan woman was saying that Jesus could have told her everything about her life—for in telling her about her previous and present relationships with various men, he revealed his knowledge about her history.

Could this be the Christ? According to the Greek, this is a tentative question: "Perhaps this may be the Christ?" "It is as though a negative answer might be expected, but a positive one is hoped for" (Morris).

4:30 They left the city (NRSV). The verb tense is a historic aorist here.

and were on their way to him (NRSV). The verb tense here is imperfect. It indicates ongoing past action—"they kept on coming to him"—that is, the crowds increased as more and more people kept coming.

4:31-34 I have food to eat that you know nothing about. After the woman left for the city, the disciples urged their teacher to eat. His response mystified them. Just as the woman did not immediately grasp the meaning of living water, so the disciples were perplexed about what Jesus meant by "food that you know nothing about." They thought he was speaking of physical food (cf. Matt 16:5-12; Mark 8:14-21). Jesus was spiritually satisfied by having witnessed to the Samaritan woman, for in so doing he accomplished his Father's will: **My food**, Jesus said, **is to do the will of him who sent me and to finish his work.** This statement provides a window into the spiritual life of Jesus, as one who lived to please his Father and in so doing found spiritual satisfaction (see 17:4). To finish God's work speaks of completing the God-ordained task—all the way from sowing the seed to reaping the harvest (see following verses).

The disciples had earlier left Jesus tired, thirsty, and hungry. Now upon their return he seemed refreshed and no longer hungry, and they wondered, *What happened?* Jesus had had a great emotional experience and was anticipating more to come. The woman had believed in him, and now the whole village was on the way to hear him. As is the case with high or low emotional experiences, the natural body appetites seem suspended. During great sadness or great excitement one is not hungry. Jesus was tremendously happy in doing the Father's will. That pleasure was, as it were, food for his soul.

As those who live a life to please the Lord, we find true spiritual satisfaction and fulfillment in carrying out his will. Some so-called spiritual activities do not give us true spiritual fulfillment because they were not engendered by the Lord or motivated by him. In the end, he is not pleased, nor are we.

4:35 *Do you not say, "Four months more, then comes the harvest"?* (NRSV). Perhaps, as Jesus was talking to his disciples, it was seed-planting time, and perhaps they could see off in the distance farmers planting. Very likely Jesus was not quoting the words of the disciples, for they had not made any comment about how the harvest in that region would be coming in four months. Rather, Jesus was probably citing a rural adage or popular saying; this is suggested by the rhythm of this statement in the Greek.[2] Approximately four months elapsed between the time of the end of sowing and the beginning of reaping. So Jesus says, "You think of harvesttime as being four months from now . . . but I tell you it is harvesttime right now."

look around you, and see how the fields are ripe for harvesting (NRSV). From Jesus' perspective, the time for harvesting had already come. The Samaritans, who were now coming out to him en masse, were ready to be harvested.[3] In telling the disciples to lift up their eyes and look on the fields, Jesus was probably directing them to look at the approaching Samaritans. The image of the harvest is often found in the Bible to depict the gathering together of God's people to participate in some joyful event (see Ruth 3:2, 7; Isa 9:3). There was about to be a joyful harvest in Samaria—one begun by Jesus and later continued by his disciples (Acts 1:8; 8:1; 9:31; 15:3). In fact, John himself (with Peter) was responsible for going to the first Samaritan believers after Pentecost and providing the way for them to receive the baptism of the Holy Spirit (Acts 8:14-17). It could be for this reason that John devoted a chapter of his book to the Samaritans' reception of Jesus and the gospel.

4:36-37 *the reaper draws his wages . . . he harvests the crop* [or *gathers fruit*] *for eternal life.* The reaper of this spiritual harvest enjoys the benefits of the harvest as his wages. His wages are not monetary but spiritual, derived from his satisfaction of bringing others into the experience of receiving eternal life. This parallels Jesus' experience with the Samaritan woman; he was satisfied by giving her the gift of life. The expression "gathers fruit into eternal life" draws upon the image of grain being brought into the barn at harvesttime (Matt 13:30; Luke 3:17). The "fruit" are those who believe in Jesus as the Christ and, as a result of their faith, are given eternal life.

the sower and the reaper may be glad together. Jesus now mentions the sower in addition to the reaper. The sower and the reaper are identical—just as the sowing and the reaping in 4:35 became one event (Barrett). Jesus, as both sower and reaper, sowed the seed of the gospel into the Samaritan woman and reaped a harvest of an entire Samaritan city. This sowing and reaping transpired so quickly that the sower and reaper could rejoice together. Normally, the sower does not rejoice; the reaper does. The two do not have the same experience, which is the point of the next verse.

Thus the saying "One sows and another reaps" is true. This saying may have come from verses like Deuteronomy 20:6; 28:30; Job 15:28 (LXX); 31:8; Micah 6:15; but it is not a direct quotation of any known biblical passage. The saying could have also come from some Greek literary sources, or it might have been a rural adage commonly quoted in the Galilean hill country.

It is easy to understand the wages a reaper receives. The joy and satisfaction of seeing one "born from above" is the divine payment. It is not as easy to see how the sower receives divine wages if he is not the reaper as well. But Jesus says that the harvest—that is, the divine compensation—belongs to both sower and reaper.

4:38 *I sent you to reap that for which you did not labor. Others have labored, and you have entered into their labor* (NRSV). This must have been spoken with respect to the coming harvest of Samaritan believers—both at that time and in the days of the early church (Acts 1:8; 8:1; 9:31; 15:3). The others who labored may have been some of the Old Testament prophets and then John the Baptist, the last of the prophets preceding Christ. According to 3:23, John the Baptist had been laboring in Samaria; thus, his ministry prepared the way for Jesus' coming. Every reaper must keep this in mind. Our work is not solitary. Others have made a contribution, so the harvest truly belongs to both sower and reaper.

4:39 *Many Samaritans from that city believed in him because of the woman's testimony* (NRSV). The Samaritans, as Jesus had just declared, were ripe and ready to receive the gospel. Many of the Samaritans believed in Jesus through the testimony of the woman; others believed when they heard Jesus for themselves.

4:40-42 After Jesus had spent *two days* with the Samaritans, many more believed in him because of his message. Jesus' message, heard over a period of two days, enlightened and quickened his Samaritan listeners. As a result, many more believed, and those who had initially believed because of the testimony of the woman became sure in their faith.

They said to the woman, "We no longer believe just because of what you said; now we have heard for ourselves, and we know that this man really is the

Savior of the world." To hear about Jesus from a witness can produce faith, but to hear Jesus himself produces faith and personal conviction based on a surer knowledge. The Greek expression for "know" (*oidamen*) suggests the attainment of absolute knowledge and complete perception. The Samaritans had come to know absolutely and positively that Jesus was "the Savior of the world." This last expression is the climax of this passage concerning Jesus with the Samaritans, for it speaks of how Jesus had come, not just to be the Jews' Messiah, but to be the world's Savior—the deliverer of all those who put their trust in him.

It is interesting to note the contrast here with what happened in Jerusalem. There he performed miracles and few believed. Here he performed no miracles and many believed. Sometimes that is true today. Those we feel ought to be interested in the gospel are not, while some who seem so hopeless and indifferent are the most receptive.

Jesus in Galilee: The Healing of the Royal Official's Son
JOHN 4:43-54

The first few verses of this section give the reason for Jesus' going into Galilee, and they relate the reception he received there. The interpretation of verse 44 is critical to understanding his motive for returning to Galilee: Did he go there because he knew he would not be received there or because he knew they should welcome him there? There are many interpretations (see comments on 4:44). Whatever Jesus' motives, he went to Cana in Galilee and healed a royal official's son. But along with the healing came Jesus' reproval of people's belief being based on seeing signs and wonders, not on trusting in Jesus himself.

NOTES

4:43 *After the two days he left for Galilee.* In the midst of much popularity in Samaria, Jesus departed for Galilee (northern Israel).

4:44 *(for Jesus himself had testified that a prophet has no honor in the prophet's own country)* (NRSV). This verse must connect with 4:3 and provide an explanation for Jesus' departure from Judea to Galilee. But which "country" (lit., "father country" or "native place"—Greek, *patridi*) was the country in which he would not be honored? Some commentators argue that the native country was Judea; thus, Jesus departed there because he was not really received in Judea and went to Galilee, where he knew he would be received. The strength of this interpretation comes from 4:45, which says that the Galileans welcomed Jesus. But there are problems with this interpretation. First, John 4:1ff indicates that Jesus left Judea not because he was rejected but because his popularity was growing there. Second, in the synoptic Gospels, Jesus' statement about not being received in his own country is spoken with respect to being rejected in his own hometown, Nazareth of Galilee. In all three occurrences (Matt 13:57; Mark 6:4; Luke 4:24), the word *patridi* is used to describe Nazareth. Therefore, it is unlikely that Jesus thought of Judea as his *patridi* (native country). Finally, the entire tenor of the passage that follows (4:46-54) speaks of apparent reception but actual rejection. In other words, the Galileans welcomed him as a miracle worker but not as a prophet, much less the Messiah. Jesus, knowing that he would not really be honored in Galilee, went there anyway, to confirm his prediction.

4:45 When he arrived in Galilee, the Galileans welcomed him. They had seen all that he had done in Jerusalem at the Passover Feast, for they also had been there. This statement refers to 2:23, which says that the people assembling in Jerusalem (among whom were these Galileans) during the Passover believed in Jesus because of the signs they saw him perform. But Jesus did not trust this kind of belief (see 2:24-25 and compare 4:48).

4:46 Then he came again to Cana in Galilee where he had changed the water into wine. Now there was a royal official . . . in Capernaum (NRSV). He was very likely an official in Herod's court, serving in some capacity in Capernaum, which was about fifteen miles from Cana.

whose son lay ill (NRSV). This is a different incident from that recorded in Matthew 8:5-13 and Luke 7:2-10, which both relate the story of Jesus' healing a centurion's slave in Capernaum. Nevertheless, it is instructive to compare all three narratives and to note the similarities.

4:47-48 When the royal official requested that Jesus *come and heal his son, who was close to death*, Jesus responded, *"Unless you people see miraculous signs and wonders . . . you will never believe."* In speaking to the man, Jesus spoke to all the Galileans and rebuked them for being sign-seekers whose faith was based on seeing miracles, not on seeing Jesus for who he really was.

4:49-50 Oblivious to what Jesus said, the man desperately begged Jesus to heal his child or he would die. Jesus responded, not by going to Capernaum and laying his hands upon the dying child, but by speaking the healing into being: *"You may go. Your son will live."* Then the text says, **The man took Jesus at his word and departed.** The man believed Jesus' word, and the healing was performed.

4:51-53 The details given in these verses tell the reader that the healing occurred at exactly the time Jesus spoke the words "Your son will live." This affirmed the reality of the miracle and produced faith in every member of the household (whether slaves or kinsfolk): **So he and all his household believed.** The man believed that if Jesus would come to his house, his boy would be healed. Then he believed the word of Jesus. Now he believed in Jesus, and his entire household followed him in that life-changing belief (see Acts 10:2; 16:15, 33 for other examples of household faith).

4:54 *This was the second miraculous sign that Jesus performed, having come from Judea to Galilee.* The first sign was that of changing the water into wine at a festive wedding party in Cana (2:1-11). The second sign performed in Galilee was in a darkened home, under the shadow of death, when a dying child was healed. The point is this: True belief in God means belief in his Word. Jesus' miracles, according to the Gospel of John, were signs pointing the people who witnessed them to the one who performed the signs—Jesus, the Messiah, the Son of God. If the miracle produced faith only in a miracle worker and not in the Son of God, then the purpose of the sign was missed.

ENDNOTES

[1]In the text of the Samaritan Pentateuch, in Exodus 20:17, the tenth commandment imports the statement from Deuteronomy 11:29 regarding the importance of Mount Gerizim as the center of worship. This was an obvious alteration by Samaritan scribes intended to validate the Samaritans' place of worship.

[2]Dodd, in *Tradition*, said the clause in Greek forms an "iambic trimeter, with the initial foot resolved into a tribrach."

[3]The final Greek word of 4:35 (*e͏̄de͏̄*), translated "already," could be joined with the end of 4:35 (giving the rendering "Look on the fields, that they are already white for harvest") or with the beginning of 4:36 (giving the rendering "Look on the fields, that they are white for harvest. He who reaps is already receiving wages"). Some of the earliest mss (𝔓66 ℵ * A B) have no punctuation here at all. 𝔓75 C³ and 083 have a punctuation mark after *e͏̄de͏̄* (thereby including it with 4:35); ℵᶜ C* D L W have a punctuation mark before it (thereby including it with 4:36). There is no consensus among the modern English translations. For example, the RSV, NEB, and TEV include "already" with 4:35, whereas the NASB and NIV join it with 4:36. Good arguments, from an exegetical viewpoint, can be advanced for either position. Jesus could have been saying that the harvest was already white, or he could have been saying that the reapers were already reaping the harvest. Both were true.

Jesus, the Divine Healer

JOHN 5:1-47

After the Jews discovered that Jesus had healed the paralyzed man on a Sabbath day, they confronted Jesus concerning what authority he possessed for violating the Sabbath. Jesus told them he was working in cooperation with his Father. This infuriated the Jews even more. They realized that in calling God "my Father" (5:17), Jesus was saying, "I am God's Son." And for Jesus to indicate that he was God's Son was to make himself equal with God (5:18-19). This was unthinkable to the Jews; it was blasphemy! One of the reasons this was unthinkable was that the Jews had never considered the Messiah to be divine. To their way of thinking, the Messiah would come from the loins of David. He would be a man—a wonderful man, but still a mortal human. They had no thought that the Messiah would or could be God, even though this was prophesied of the Messiah in such verses as Isaiah 7:14; 9:6-7; and Micah 5:2. The Jews could not imagine that David's son could be God's Son (see Jesus' statement concerning this in Matt 22:41-45). So for Jesus to claim divine sonship was blasphemy, and therefore, from that point forward the Jews sought to kill him.

5:1-47/Who Are You?

Most people have a seemingly insatiable desire to learn something new about the rich and the famous. We wonder how they really live, what they believe, and how they act in their private lives. This is epitomized in the popular play *Camelot* when the monarch's loyal subjects ask, "I wonder what the king is thinking tonight?" Almost anyone who achieves a high degree of public recognition is certain to be questioned and interviewed by media anxious to supply fresh information to the waiting public. Of course, there were no mass media in Jesus' day, but he was nevertheless repeatedly interrogated and questioned by the religious authorities. It wasn't just what he did that amazed or infuriated them; it was what he said about himself that was to them so unbelievable. His words of personal revelation seem plain enough, but they were largely disbelieved in his day and argued over in this day. Two books of yesteryear, *Who Is This Man Jesus?* and *The Man Nobody Knows*, give a clue to the ongoing search for the authentic Jesus.

In this chapter Jesus very clearly enunciates who he is and by whose authority he was working. Nowhere else in the Gospels do we read of our Lord giving such a formal, systematic, orderly statement of his unity with the Father, his commission, and his authority. It is the considered opinion of many Bible students that this solemn discourse was delivered to a number of the nation's religious leaders, if not to the entire Sanhedrin. It is the most complete formal defense of his deity and messiahship. In four unequivocal, crystal-clear statements Jesus tells the religious leaders who he is.

My Father and I do the same work. Jesus told the leaders that if they charged him with Sabbath breaking, they would have to charge his Father, with whom he was working in the closest possible cooperation. "You charge me with Sabbath breaking, you charge God with breaking his own law!" The Jews perfectly understood what Jesus meant, for they were outraged that he made himself equal with God. Those today who allege that Jesus never called himself God—equal with the Father—must reject this portion of the Bible or, in some other convoluted way, circumvent this declaration.

I am the Son of Man. The prophet Daniel indicated that the Son of Man, the Messiah, would bring with him a new age. His kingdom would overcome the terrible powers that have abused, conquered, and enslaved mankind. Godly Jews longed for the appearance of the Son of Man to establish God's Kingdom on earth. To many, such a kingdom had overtones of laudatory nationalism; nonetheless, it was of divine implementation. So when Jesus called himself the Son of Man, they understood him to say, "I am the long-awaited sent one of God."

My actions back up my words. Publicly healing the paralytic man by the pool of Bethesda was a sign that Jesus was the Messiah. Isaiah's picture of the new age when the Messiah arrived is partially described in chapter 35, where he says, "Then will the lame leap like a deer" (v. 6). Jeremiah and other prophets foretold that when the Messiah came, the lame and the blind would be healed. In the fulfilling of these and many other prophecies, Jesus demonstrated by his actions that he was the anointed one sent from God.

I am the raiser of the dead and their judge when they are raised. The Jews knew their Scriptures, and they were well aware of 1 Samuel 2:6, "The LORD kills and makes alive" (NKJV), and Deuteronomy 1:17, "Judgment belongs to God." Jesus very clearly claimed functions, privileges, and powers that belonged to God and no one else. Since God the Father and God the Son are equal in essence and in works, they must be equally honored as well. He who does not hear and obey the Son is not really honoring the Son. Someday all those who dishonor him will be judged by him. Against such a terrible prospect is the wonderful promise, "I tell you the truth, whoever hears my word and believes him who sent me has eternal life and will not be condemned; he has crossed over from death to life" (5:24). Knowing who Jesus is makes life abundant now and glorious eternally .

KEY WORDS AND PHRASES

In this chapter Jesus does not directly declare his deity by saying, "The Father and I are one" (this comes later—especially in ch 10). Rather, he affirms his deity by pointing to the divine power manifest in his works, and he calls upon a five-fold testimony as a witness to his divine being:

1. John the Baptist (5:33-35)
2. Jesus' works (5:36)
3. The Father himself (5:37)
4. The Scriptures (5:39-40)
5. Moses (5:45-47)

All these witnesses were accessible to the Jews, and each pointed them to Jesus as their Messiah—if only they would receive the testimony and believe in him.

NOTES

5:1 *Jesus went up to Jerusalem for a feast of the Jews.* While the particular feast is not named,[1] we know that the Jews observed their religious functions with great exactitude, as if that were all God required. The expression "of the Jews" was added by John as a help to his Gentile readers.

5:2 *Now there is in Jerusalem near the Sheep Gate a pool.* This statement represents the way most translators handle the expression in Greek. John did not specify the noun after the expression in Greek, literally meaning "pertaining to sheep." Very likely those readers familiar with Jerusalem would have known he was speaking about the Sheep Gate (mentioned in Neh 3:1, 32; 12:39). But a few other translators understand the entire expression to be in the dative case and thus translate, "Now at the Sheep-Pool in Jerusalem there is a place . . ." (NEB; see also NJB). Those who defend this interpretation assert that all of the ancient exegetes coupled together *probatikē* and *kolumbēthra*, thus Sheep Pool.

in Aramaic. The name of this pool appears with different spellings in various manuscripts: Bethzatha, Bethsaida (meaning "house of fish"), Bedsaidan, Belzetha, Bethesda (meaning "house of mercy").[2] Many scholars prefer the reading "Bethesda" because it is indirectly attested by the Copper Scroll discovered in Qumran, which calls this place Beth'eshdathain (3Q15, column 11, line 12), meaning "the place of the twin outpouring" (Bruce). Recent excavations show this site (near the Church of St. Anne) to have had two pools, with five **colonnades**. The name "house of mercy" accords well with the passage, for it is here that men and women sought mercy from God for their healing.

5:3a *In these lay many invalids. blind, lame, and paralyzed* (NRSV). The multitude of sick people lay underneath the five colonnades. Such a scene reminds modern readers of similar gatherings in Fatima and Lourdes.

5:3b-4 This portion, noted in the NIV mg, was not written by John because it is not found in the earliest manuscripts, and where it does occur in later manuscripts, it is often marked with obeli or asterisks to signal probable spuriousness. Undoubtedly, the passage was a later addition—inserted to provide an explanation about the troubling of the water mentioned in John 5:7.

5:5 *an invalid for thirty-eight years.* A few commentators have pointed out that the thirty-eight years might be symbolic of the period of time Israel was in the wilderness (see Deut 2:14), experiencing the harsh effects of sin. Though this man had suffered because of his sin (see 5:14), it is not likely that John intended the reader to see him as an antitype of Israel. The duration of his sickness simply shows the seriousness of his ailment and the extent of his desire to be cured.

5:6 **When Jesus saw him lying there and learned** [or *knew*] **that he had been in this condition for a long time.** This gives us a glimpse into the extent of Jesus' knowledge. He knew this man's condition and how long he had suffered.

Do you want to get well? Jesus' query shows us that he will not force himself upon anyone; he seeks a person's permission before doing anything in that person's life.

5:7 *I have no one to put me into the pool when the water is stirred up* (NRSV). The man indirectly answers Jesus by telling how he has not been able to get healed because another person always gets into the water before he does. But in saying this, he acknowledges that he needs the help of another.

5:8-9 *At once the man was cured; he picked up his mat and walked.* This miracle should have revealed to the Jews in Jerusalem that the Messiah was in their midst (see Isa 35:5-6).

The day on which this took place was a Sabbath. Jesus purposely healed on the Sabbath (see Mark 2:1–3:6) in an attempt to show the Jews that they had become enslaved to their traditions about how to observe the Sabbath and had forgotten that God seeks mercy above duty. Thus Jesus performed acts of mercy on Sabbath days.

5:10 *It is the Sabbath; the law forbids you to carry your mat.* There is nothing in the law given by God concerning a person not carrying a mat on the Sabbath. This regulation was the last of thirty-nine rules in the "tradition of the elders," which stipulated what kind of work could not be done on the Sabbath (Bruce). In the synoptic Gospels, Jesus told the Jews that they had annulled the commandments of God by their traditions (see Matt 15:3).

5:11-13 In this exchange between the man who was healed and the Jewish leaders in Jerusalem, the man claims not to have known who healed him. (This claim was probably true, for Jesus had not identified himself and had immediately left the scene.) At the same time, he put the blame on this healer for having him walk around with his mat. Even though the people lived in fear of breaking the tradition of the elders and being caught by them, this man should have countered their interrogation with an exclamation of joy concerning his healing.

5:14 Jesus sought out this man and *found him in the temple.* Perhaps the man had gone there to give thanks to God for his healing.

Stop sinning or something worse may happen to you. Jesus' instruction implies that the man's sin was responsible for his sickness. At first glance, this seems to contradict Jesus' remark concerning the blind man in 9:1ff. In that instance, Jesus told his disciples that the man was born blind not because of his sins (or the sins of his parents), but so that God might be glorified. But in neither case was Jesus making universal statements about the cause of suffering and sickness. In the case of the invalid man, he had been sick because of his sin; and if he continued in his sin, Jesus warned him, he might suffer something worse than what he experienced before, such as the eternal consequences of living in sin.

5:15-16 *it was Jesus who had made him well.* After this encounter, the man told the Jews what he could not tell them before. How do we interpret this action? Was this a betrayal? If so, would this not be a heinous sin against the one who had healed him, sought him, and warned him not to continue in sin? Or was this just a simple report to fulfill orders from the Jewish leaders? John does not tell us this man's motives, so we do not know. What we do know is that this action triggered the Jews' persecution of Jesus, which continued from that day until the time Jesus was arrested and crucified. And why did they persecute him so vehemently? The reason is stated in verse 16: *because Jesus was doing these things on the Sabbath, the Jews persecuted him.*

5:17 *Jesus answered them* (NRSV). This is not an answer to a question, but a response to the Jews' intent to persecute him for breaking the Sabbath (cf. comments on 8:12).

My Father is still working, and I also am working (NRSV). With this statement Jesus challenges the notion that God has been at rest since the seventh day of creation. God has been at work and continues to work in sustaining his creation; so does his Son, Jesus (Col 1:17; Heb 1:3). In making this statement, Jesus identified himself as God's Son and coworker. (In Mark 2:28, he identifies himself as "Lord of the Sabbath"—i.e., he who has the sovereign right to determine what should and should not be done on the Sabbath.)

5:18 *For this reason the Jews tried all the harder to kill him; not only was he breaking the Sabbath, but he was even calling God his own Father, making himself equal with God.* The Jews realized that Jesus' words "my Father" intimated that he possessed a very personal relationship with God, specifically that of a son with his father. No mortal, they believed, could make such a claim (see Isa 40:25). They did consider God to be their Father, but not in any kind of personal sense. Thus Jesus' claim about working in unity with God as his very own Father meant that Jesus was claiming equality with God (see comments on 10:30-33). His Sabbath breaking, they may have reasoned, was not just an isolated event but "proceeded from Jesus' view of his own person and was consistent with it" (Morris). In the four Gospels, Jesus is shown to break the Sabbath seven times by performing various healings (see Mark 1:21-28; 1:29-31; 3:1-6; Luke 13:10-17; 14:1-6; John 5:1-18; 9:1-16). To them, Jesus was a lawbreaking rebel and blasphemer, worthy of death.

5:19 *the Son can do nothing by himself; he can only do what he sees his Father doing, because whatever the Father does the Son also does.* In this and the following verses (vv. 19-30), Jesus affirms his oneness and equality with the Father on the basis of their cooperative work—especially in two areas: giving life and executing judgment. Jesus begins this argument by declaring his dependence upon the Father. Jesus does not say that he *will not* do anything independent of the Father but that he *cannot* do anything independent of the Father. His unity of nature with the Father, which is manifest in continual communion (as intimated in the words "what he sees the Father doing"), does not allow independent action. In short, the Father and Son cannot act independently from one another because they are one. The Son performs the tasks the Father wants done, not by way of mechanical imitation, but by natural manifestation—or as Westcott said, "not in imitation, but in virtue of his sameness of nature."

5:20 *The Father loves the Son and shows him all that he himself is doing* (NRSV). John may have chosen the Greek word *philei* ("is fond of") rather than the more usual word *agapa* ("loves") to emphasize the personal quality of the Father's love for the Son. Because there is no opaqueness in the relationship between the Father and the Son, they are fully unveiled to one another. This is not so for us, who see our Lord as in a poor reflection in a mirror (1 Cor 13:12) and as a result are not always clear about what he wants us to do. Because of their transparent relationship, the Son always saw what the Father was doing and worked in harmony with him to see it accomplished.

he will show him greater works than these (NRSV). According to the following verses, the greater works are manifest in the Son's ability to give life to the dead and to execute judgment. What greater works are there than these?

5:21 *For just as the Father raises the dead and gives them life.* This statement would have been acceptable to most of the Jews hearing Jesus speak, for it is clearly stated in the Old Testament that it is only God who can raise the dead (see Ezek 37:13) and give life (see Deut 32:39; 1 Sam 2:6; 2 Kings 5:7).

even so the Son gives life to whom he is pleased to give it. This statement would have shocked Jesus' audience because it ascribes to the Son what was exclusively the activity of God the Father. The Son has the divine prerogative to give life to whom he chooses; as a case in point, he had just selected the invalid man and given him life. According to what follows, Jesus gives spiritual, eternal life to those who are spiritually dead, and he will give resurrection life to those who are physically dead.

5:22-23 Moreover, the Father judges no one, but has entrusted all judgment to the Son. The topic of raising the dead leads quite naturally to that of judgment because after the resurrection comes the judgment. The Jews knew that it was God's task to execute a final judgment. But now Jesus informs them that this task has been given to him so **that all may honor the Son just as they honor the Father.**

He who does not honor the Son does not honor the Father, who sent him. This statement was directed specifically to those Jews who were persecuting him because they, while claiming to honor God, were dishonoring his Son. Jesus exposed their hypocrisy.

5:24 whoever hears my word and believes him who sent me. According to the Greek, this describes one response in two phases: "the one hearing and believing." True hearing results in believing, for as Paul says, "Faith comes by hearing, and hearing by the word of God" (Rom 10:17, NKJV). An unusual aspect of this statement, however, is that it speaks about believing in the one who sent Jesus, while the Gospel usually speaks about believing in Jesus himself. But in this context the statement affirms the unity of the Father and the Son. To believe in the Father is to believe in the one he sent.

has eternal life. The believer becomes the recipient of eternal life with God. A believer need not be uncertain about whether he has eternal life, for as John says in his first epistle, "He who has the Son has life" (1 Jn 5:12, NKJV).

will not be condemned. For the believer, the judgment has passed. He has already **crossed over from death to life** (see 1 Jn 3:14, where John uses the same expression). According to 3:18, this world is presently under God's judgment. The full effect of that judgment will be realized on the last day. The only escape from this judgment is to believe in Jesus. For those who do, God transfers them out of the domain of death into the realm of life (cf. Col 1:13).

5:25 Very truly, I tell you, the hour is coming, and is now here, when the dead will hear the voice of the Son of God, and those who hear will live (NRSV). When Jesus speaks of the coming hour that "is now here," he sees the eschatological moment as happening in the present. That is, for one to receive eternal life now is a present experience assuring eternal life in the future, and for one to believe in Jesus now is to presently escape the future judgment. In the future, the physically dead will hear the voice of the Son of God and will be raised from the grave (see 5:28). This verse, however, refers to those who are spiritually dead. But how can the dead hear? That is the miracle of vivification—activated by the life-giving Spirit inherent in the words of God's Son (see 6:63 and comments). One should also note that this is the first time Jesus uses the term "the Son of God" when speaking about himself; the next two occurrences are 10:36 and 11:4 (cf. 19:7; 20:31).

5:26 For just as the Father has life in himself, so he has granted the Son also to have life in himself (NRSV). Human beings do not have life in themselves; they receive their life from God. But God does not receive his life from any exterior source. He has life in himself and is life; he is the source of his very own life. In eternity past, the Father gave his Son the same capacity—to have life in himself (cf. 1:4, which says "in him was life"). This is a uniquely divine characteristic, unshared by any created being. Bruce says, "The Father's bestowal of life-in-himself on the Son [is not] something which began with his ministry on earth, or with the Incarnation; it is an eternal act, part and parcel of the unique Father-Son relationship which existed already 'in the beginning.' In the eternal order the Father, as Father, imparts to the Son, as Son, that life-in-himself which it is the Father's to possess and impart; on the temporal plane the Son reveals that life to men and women."

5:27 And he has given him authority to judge because he is the Son of Man. In the Greek, the last phrase reads, "he is Son of Man" (without an article). This emphasizes his humanity: Jesus, as man, will judge men. In this way, the Father has given all the honor to the Son, for everyone must answer to him (see Phil 2:5-11). Behind Jesus' statement must be Daniel 7:13-14, for in this prophetic passage about the final judgment the Son of Man is described as exercising dominion over all the earth.

5:28-29 the hour is coming (NRSV). Compare this with 5:25, which has the added expression "and is now here." This shows that 5:28 is speaking only about a future event—that of the coming resurrection.
all who are in their graves will hear his voice and will come out—those who have done good, to the resurrection of life, and those who have done evil, to the resurrection of condemnation (NRSV). Every person will be resurrected when the Lord returns, but there are two results of the resurrection; one ends in life, the other in judgment. Eternal life is granted to those who have done good things (cf. Rom 2:7); these are those who have come to the light and believed in Jesus Christ. But judgment is executed upon those who practiced evil throughout their lives; these are those who refused to come to the light. God's pronouncement of judgment is already upon them. It will be executed by the Son of Man after the resurrection (see 3:18-21 and comments).

5:30 By myself I can do nothing; I judge only as I hear, and my judgment is just, for I seek not to please myself but him who sent me. Even though the Father committed to the Son the task of executing judgment, the Son cannot and will not perform as his own authority and by his own initiative (see NASB). He hears the Father perfectly, without distortions; therefore his judgment is free of bias and self-consequence. Those who seek their own will can never judge without personal bias.

5:31-32 If I testify about myself, my testimony is not valid. There is another who testifies in my favor, and I know that his testimony about me is valid.

During a later visit to Jerusalem, Jesus was accused by the Jews on this same issue: "Here you are, appearing as your own witness; your testimony is not valid" (8:13). As Bruce puts it, "A testimonial to oneself is no testimonial at all." According to the Jewish law, the testimony of one man is not a valid witness. Truth or validity has to be established by two or three witnesses (Deut 17:6; 19:15). Therefore, Jesus' self-witness would not validate his claims; he needed the witness of another. That other witness was not John the Baptist, but his Father (see 5:33-37 and comments). In the following verses, Jesus will draw upon several witnesses to affirm his claims, but actually he needs only one witness, his Father's (see 8:12-18 and comments).

5:33-34 *You sent messengers to John, and he testified to the truth. Not that I accept such human testimony, but I say these things so that you may be saved* (NRSV). John the Baptist was Jesus' first human witness (see comments on 1:6-8). His testimony concerning Jesus' being the Son of God, Lamb of God, bridegroom, etc. (see 1:34; 3:27-36), was necessary for the Jews, not for Jesus. The Jews needed his testimony to prepare them for salvation.

5:35 *John was a lamp that burned and gave light.* John 1:8 explicitly states that John the Baptist was not "the light." This is underscored here where it says he was "a lamp." In other words, he was a vessel for the light, not the light itself. In saying this about John the Baptist, Jesus was showing that John's witness fulfilled messianic prophecy: "There I will make the horn of David grow; I will prepare a lamp for My Anointed" (Ps 132:17, NKJV). John was this lamp prepared by God for his anointed one. The verb "was" probably indicates that at this point in time John the Baptist was deceased (Schnackenburg).

you chose for a time to enjoy his light. The ministry of John the Baptist produced great excitement about a coming Messiah, but the Jewish leaders did not really understand his message or receive the illuminating revelation concerning the one to whom John gave witness—Jesus, the Son of God. In two other Gospels Jesus said of himself and John, "We played the flute for you, and you did not dance; we sang a dirge, and you did not mourn" (Matt 11:17; Luke 7:32). In other words, they may have enjoyed hearing the tune—whether joyful or sad—but they did not really respond to it.

5:36 *But I have a testimony greater than John's. The works that the Father has given me to complete, the very works that I am doing, testify on my behalf that the Father has sent me* (NRSV). All the works Jesus did were part of the one great work the Father had sent him to accomplish (see 17:4; Westcott). These works were signs providing witness to Jesus' being the one sent from the Father.

5:37-38 *And the Father who sent me has himself testified concerning me.* "The Father gave direct witness to his Son at his baptism (Matt 3:16-17), on the mount of transfiguration (Matt 17:5), and before his crucifixion (John 12:28); but Jesus' present hearers had never received such audible or visible communication of the

Father's testimony to the Son" (Bruce). But they did have God's living oracle among them, the Word. As Hebrews 1:2 says, God "has spoken to us by his Son."

You have never heard his voice nor seen his form, nor does his word dwell in you, for you do not believe the one he sent. They had three strikes against them: (1) They had never heard God's voice. Moses had heard God's voice (Exod 33:11), and so had the children of Israel (Deut 4:12). They could not claim the same. (2) They had never seen God's form (or visage). The Greek word for "visage" is *eidos;* it is used in the Septuagint to describe the "face" of God, which Jacob (Israel) saw (Gen 32:30). (3) They did not have God's Word residing in their hearts. The psalmist treasured God's Word in his heart (Ps 119:11), but they lacked this devotion. Even though the Jews to whom Jesus was speaking had not received the kind of revelations some of their forefathers had, they still possessed the Word of God—God's written revelation to his people. If that Word had been abiding in their hearts (see 8:31; 15:7), they would have recognized the one to whom the Scriptures give testimony (see 5:39). Even more so, they had the greatest of all God's manifestations standing right before their eyes—Jesus, the Word, the visible expression of God to men.

5:39-40 You diligently study the Scriptures. Or this could be translated, "You research the Scriptures"—or as an imperative, "Search the Scriptures." The Greek word for "search" or "research" implies intense scrutiny and tracking down. The Jewish scribes devoted their lives to studying the letter of the Law. But the letter on the page cannot give life; the spirit of the Scriptures gives life (see 2 Cor 3:6).

because you think that by them you possess eternal life. The Jews were mistaken to think that they could obtain eternal life by diligently studying the Scriptures. In fact, there is no verse in the Old Testament that indicates eternal life is gained through researching the Scriptures, but several rabbis made such claims. For example, Hillel said, "The more study of the law the more life, . . . if one has gained for himself words of the law, he has gained for himself life in the age to come" (*Pirqe 'Aboth* 2.7). Paul counters this notion when he says, "For if a law had been given that could impart life, then righteousness would certainly have come by the law" (Gal 3:21). Life is not found in studying the Scriptures, but by studying the Scriptures one can ascertain the source of life: Jesus Christ, the Son of God.

These are the Scriptures that testify about me. Failing to see this testimony means missing the very purpose for which the Scriptures exist. If there were no such person as Jesus Christ, the Scriptures would have no value. The Bible's value lies in its testimony to and about him.

you refuse to come to me to have life. Christ is the unique source of life (1:4; 5:25; 14:6). Men cannot obtain this life in any other way but by coming to him and receiving it from him.[3]

5:41-42 I do not accept glory from human beings (NRSV). Just as Jesus did not receive (or need) the testimony from men (5:34), so he does not need to receive glory (praise and honor) from men. If he were seeking to be accepted and praised by the Jews, he would not criticize them.

But I know that you do not have the love of God in you (NRSV). Jesus knew their condition: they did not really love God; they loved their religion. Therefore, they could not accept the beloved Son of God.

5:43 I have come in my Father's name. This means Jesus came as the Father's personal representative (see 14:7-11).

and you do not accept me. Jesus' claims of being the one sent by the Father were unacceptable to the Jews.

if someone else comes in his own name, you will accept him. Very likely Jesus was speaking about other persons claiming to be the Messiah. There were many such men who made the claim. For example, in AD 132 one called Simeon ben Kosebah claimed to be the Messiah. Akibah, the most eminent rabbi of the day, upheld this claim by saying that Simeon was the "star out of Jacob" predicted by Balaam in Numbers 24:17. Simeon's messianic pretensions brought ruin upon himself, his followers, and the people of Judea (Bruce). Israel had seen several such pretenders before the coming of Jesus (see Josephus *Antiquities* 20:97-99, 170-172 for a list).

5:44 How can you believe if you accept praise from one another, yet make no effort to obtain the praise that comes from the only God?[4] This condemning word exposes one of the main reasons the Jewish religious leaders could not believe: They were so engrossed in mutual admiration and mutual acceptance that the individual could hardly make a stand that differed from the group. Their solidarity of unbelief and opposition to Jesus was hard to overcome (see 9:22; 12:42-43). For example, Nicodemus found it extremely difficult to speak out on behalf of Jesus in the face of this hard-core, corporate opposition (see 7:45-52). Instead of seeking what would honor God and bring glory to him, which in this case would be to believe in his Son, they continued to seek honor and glory from one another.

5:45 Do not think that I will accuse you before the Father; your accuser is Moses, on whom you have set your hope (NRSV). Note the verb tenses: "I will accuse" and "one accusing" (according to the Greek); there is no need for Jesus to go to the Father at some point in the future and accuse them, because they were already being accused by Moses. This could mean that Moses was then and there in the presence of God accusing them (cf. Matt 17:3), but it is more likely that "Moses" here stands for what Moses wrote, as is indicated in the next two verses. To say that Moses was accusing them was a brilliant display of litigation on Jesus' part. They thought Moses was on their side, but Jesus calls upon Moses as his last witness against them! This ironic twist must have left them dumbfounded.

5:46-47 If you believed Moses, you would believe me, for he wrote about me. But since you do not believe what he wrote, how are you going to believe what

I say? Moses had written about Christ (see Deut 18:15-18; cf. Luke 24:44); but since they had not believed in the Christ when he came, they had not really believed in the writings of Moses. "Disbelief in Moses involved disbelief in Christ" (Westcott). Neither the written word nor the spoken word penetrated these Jews; even when they read the writings of Moses, a veil was over their hearts (see 2 Cor 3:12-15). How they needed to turn their hearts and be infused with the quickening word of Christ!

ENDNOTES

[1]According to the majority of early manuscripts (𝔓66 𝔓75 A B D W), there is no article before "feast." Thus the feast is unspecified. Some other manuscripts (ℵ C L 33) read "the feast," which would indicate the Passover Feast. This reading shows the work of interpolation—the scribes added the article to specify the feast.

[2]The name of this pool appears with different spellings in various manuscripts: Bethzatha (ℵ L 33); Bethsaida, meaning "house of fish" (𝔓66* 𝔓75 B W 0125—note: 𝔓66* reads "Bedsaidan," 𝔓66ᶜ reads "Bedsaida"); Belzetha (D); Bethesda, meaning "house of mercy" (A C 078 Maj.).

[3]An ancient manuscript called Papyrus Egerton 2 (dated 140–160) and a few Old Latin and Old Syriac mss read, "You search the Scriptures; these writings, in which you think to have life, are those that bear testimony of me."

[4]Some of the earliest manuscripts (𝔓66 𝔓75 B W) read, "the only One" (*tou monou*); other ancient manuscripts (ℵ A D) read, "the only God" (*tou monou theou*). It has been argued that the Greek word for "God" dropped out accidentally due to homoeoteleuton (words with like endings). Although this is a possibility, it seems much more likely that "God" was added by scribes to fill in what would otherwise seem incomplete. According to Edwin E. Abbott in his book *Johannine Grammar,* the expression *tou monou* is a title, which could be translated as "the only One" or "the unique One." This reading suits the passage well. Since the Jews were seeking to receive glory from one another, they had neglected to seek the glory that comes from the unique one, the only one who gives glory.

Jesus, the Bread of Life

JOHN 6:1-71

EXPOSITION

As is often the case in this Gospel, a physical setting is first put forth as a platform for presenting some spiritual truth about Christ. The Temple in Jerusalem served as a good backdrop for Christ to be presented as the real sanctuary of God, and the well in Samaria was an excellent figure of Christ as the fountain of living water. Here in John 6, the multiplication of the loaves provides the way for Christ to present himself as the Bread of Life.

After the multiplication of the five barley loaves and two fish and the subsequent feeding of the five thousand, the people wanted to make Jesus their king. And they would have forced this upon him had Jesus not fled away. Meanwhile, Jesus' disciples boarded a boat and started to cross the Sea of Galilee westward. A storm arose, putting the disciples in grave danger; but Jesus, walking on the water, came to them and rescued them. After this, the multitude who had eaten of the loaves found Jesus on the other side of the sea. They were seeking him because he had satisfied their appetites, not because they had seen a sign (6:26). Jesus told them, "Do not work for the food that perishes, but for the food that endures for eternal life" (6:27, NRSV). This was Jesus' introduction to his great and profound discourse on the Bread of Life.

6:15-21/Miracle at Midnight

Many significant events stand out in this, the longest chapter of John's Gospel. We could consider the importance of the feeding of the multitude, since it is the only miracle recorded by all four Gospel writers. Or we could very profitably turn our attention to our Lord's marvelous contrast of manna and living bread. Certainly any time spent in studying what Jesus meant by "feeding" on him would be profitable, since many followers found those words difficult to accept and consequently left him. But because much of what Jesus enunciated at the Capernaum synagogue is repeated later on, we will give attention to the famous incident of Jesus walking on water.

After Jesus miraculously fed the five thousand, there was an almost spontaneous clamoring among the people to take him by force and make him their king. They thought of free meals and no more work—a utopian kingdom—but Jesus knew their hearts wanted only physical sustenance, not him. So amidst the clamor of the people, he told the disciples to get in a boat and head for Capernaum. All by himself he subdued the crowd, dismissing them and telling them to go home, and then he slipped away in the gathering darkness to pray up in the hills. As darkness fell, the crowd was milling about and reluctantly dispersing. The disciples were in the boat rowing across the lake, and Jesus was up on the mountain in prayer. Suddenly, a tremendous windstorm swept across the lake, churning up the water and creating great waves that nearly swamped the boat. All they could do was desperately row. One of the other Gospels tells us that they rowed most of the night and were completely fatigued. No doubt the disciples fully anticipated a watery grave that night.

Jesus watches. The disciples didn't realize that Jesus could see them (Mark 6:48); that they were the object of his prayers never crossed their minds. In their difficulty, the tempest fully occupying their energies, they forgot about him. They thought they were all alone in a very hostile environment, but they were never abandoned from the care and keeping of the Savior. We, too, are frequently nearly engulfed by the stormy seas of temptation, trouble, tragedy, and grief, but all the while we must be assured that Jesus is aware of our situation. He intercedes for his own (Heb 7:25). We appreciate it when other believers pray for us, but it is comforting beyond measure to contemplate Christ praying for us. Whatever your circumstances today, in spite of your feelings of loneliness and helplessness, be assured Jesus sees you and is aware of your need.

Jesus comes. When the disciples had rowed three or four miles and fought that awful storm until they were about ready to give out, they saw Jesus coming toward the boat, walking on the water, and they were afraid. Howling winds, crashing waves, and now they imagined they saw a phantom or ghost coming toward them! Circumstances so overwhelmed them that they failed to recognize Jesus. Today also faith is required to see him, for we experience Jesus by faith, not by sight. But it is easy to be so preoccupied with the problems at hand that we do not recognize when he comes to help us. We can become so distraught in our afflictions, troubles, and adversities that we do not see him coming to give us deliverance. It is our great privilege by the eye of faith to believe—even in the worst storms of life—that he meant it when he said, "Never will I leave you; never will I forsake you" (Heb 13:5). We are not left to go it alone.

Jesus helps. As the Savior drew near, he said, "Don't be afraid." When they willingly received him into the boat, immediately everything was changed. The storm subsided, the gale ceased, and the waters calmed, for the Creator of bread is also the Controller of waters. It was as though he had said to those amazed disciples, "I have refused to be crowned King on the basis of free food, but make no mistake about it, I am King—King in every realm, King of nature, King everywhere." Many of the things that now frighten Christians and fill us with anxiety would cease to overwhelm us if we would only realize that in all things the Lord Jesus is in control.

Jesus brings us to the haven. It seemed to John, as he remembered this episode, that as soon as Jesus arrived, the keel of the boat grated on the shore and they were safe. In the presence of Jesus, the longest journey is short, and the hardest battle is easier. The psalmist reflected on this principle and wrote, "They were glad when it grew calm, and he guided them to their desired haven" (Ps 107:30). Someday, perhaps sooner than any of us anticipate, Christ shall bear our boat safely through that last storm and harbor us in that great port where we shall nevermore experience storms.

KEY WORDS AND PHRASES

In this chapter, physical bread and spiritual bread are continually contrasted. The multitudes, having been fed by Jesus' miraculous multiplication of the loaves, want more physical bread. But Jesus tells them that this bread never satisfies. Jesus came from heaven to feed the world with the true spiritual bread—himself.

The physical bread:
cannot satisfy
and cannot give eternal life   6:26-27
even those who ate manna still died   6:31, 49

The spiritual bread:
satisfies man's real hunger and gives eternal life   6:27, 33
because this bread came from heaven   6:41
and is the Bread of Life   6:35, 48, 58

NOTES

6:1 *Some time after this, Jesus crossed to the far shore of the Sea of Galilee.* Some time (which John leaves unspecified—cf. 5:1 and 7:1) after the events recorded in John 5, Jesus went across the Sea of Galilee.

Tiberias. The Sea of Galilee was given the name "Sea of Tiberias" by Herod Antipas in honor of Emperor Tiberias in AD 20.

6:2 *and a great crowd of people followed him because they saw the miraculous signs he had performed on the sick.* Even though John does not specify these many acts of healing, he informs the reader that Jesus did perform many signs (see 20:30-31). John chose to call the healings "signs" rather than "miracles" because they should have pointed the viewers to the divine activity present in the act. Most of those who followed Jesus saw the signs but did not come to really believe in the divinity of the one who performed them (cf. 2:23-25).

6:3-4 Just as John begins to describe the scenario for the feeding of the five thousand, he inserts the words, **the Jewish Passover Feast was near.** His mention of the Passover provides a time frame for his narrative. Three Passovers are mentioned in this Gospel: the first in 2:13 (during which Jesus was in Jerusalem), the second here (during which Jesus remained in Galilee), and the third in 11:55ff (during which Jesus went to Jerusalem and was crucified). Later in the chapter it will become apparent that the mention of the Passover provides a foreshadowing of certain key elements in Jesus' discourse—especially the discussion on Israel's journey in the wilderness and the words about Jesus shedding his blood.

6:5-13 There are some interesting details in this eyewitness account, giving us a glimpse of the genuine, honest relationship between Jesus and Philip (cf. 14:8-12). When Jesus tested Philip concerning the provision of food for the multitude, Philip exclaimed that eight months' wages (which is the equivalent of two hundred denarii, according to the NIV) would not be enough to feed them. Andrew (who is usually presented in the Gospels as Simon Peter's brother and takes a subordinate position to him) points out that the only food available is that of a poor boy's lunch (five barley rolls and a couple of cooked fish). But that was enough for Jesus. He took the bread and fish, gave thanks for them, and distributed the multiplied miracle meal to the multitude numbering five thousand males (the Greek word used in 6:10 is *andres*), plus women and children. After all had eaten and were thoroughly satiated, there was more food left over than what Jesus had started with. Thus the text says, **So they gathered them and filled twelve baskets with the pieces of the five barley loaves left over by those who had eaten.**

This is the only miracle (besides Christ's resurrection) recorded in all four Gospels. All four writers must have been impressed with the undeniable miraculousness of the event. And Christian expositors (both with the pen and from the pulpit) have used this event to teach several lessons, the most obvious of which is this: Give what little you have to Jesus; he can bless it and multiply it to meet the tremendous needs around you.

6:14 **After the people saw the miraculous sign that Jesus did.** Again, John indicates that the people saw the sign that Jesus did—who could have failed to see it!

Surely this is the Prophet who is to come into the world. Their seeing the sign led them to believe that Jesus was the prophet whom Moses had predicted would come (Deut 18:15-18). And as Moses was a prophet who (they thought) fed the children of Israel in the wilderness (see comments on 6:31-32), so Jesus must have been the prophet predicted by Moses, who was now feeding them in the wilderness. John does not say they were wrong to think of Jesus as the prophet, but the next verse shows that they conceived this prophet to be a military leader. In this they were wrong.

6:15 **When Jesus realized that they were about to come and take him by force and make him king, he withdrew again to the mountain by himself** (NRSV).

Nationalistic fervor was high; the people wanted a king, a leader who would lead the Jews in rebellion against Rome in order to gain freedom for Israel. The people expected this from the coming Messiah and from the coming Prophet (it was not clear to the Jews that one person would be both). When Jesus realized their intentions, he departed. He, the true King of Israel, would not be made the kind of king they wanted. According to Mark 6:45-46, Jesus made the disciples board a boat and head out into the Sea of Galilee, then he went up to the mountain to pray. Perhaps Jesus "saw that they were being infected with the crowd's excitement" (Bruce).

6:16-21 Prior to evening, the disciples had boarded a boat headed westward toward Capernaum on the Sea of Galilee. When they were near the middle of this lake (which is about seven miles across), they encountered a sudden storm (blowing from west to east), for which that lake is notorious. They had gone without Jesus, who was on a mountain praying until evening. Curiously, the text says, *Jesus had not yet joined them* (6:17). This could not mean that they were expecting him to come to them in the middle of the lake, for they were terrified when he did so. It could be that John said this for the sake of his readers who already knew the story and for the sake of pinpointing the time during the evening when the disciples encountered the storm—it was before Jesus had come to them (see Morris). When Jesus did come to them, he did it by way of a miracle— he walked on the sea. This miracle greatly strengthened the disciples' faith (see 6:67ff). After they received Jesus into the boat, immediately the boat reached the shore where they were heading. Either this statement reflects that John felt the voyage to shore flew by in Jesus' presence, or it suggests that a second miracle occurred that evening.

6:22-25 These verses can be confusing because of the statement about the boats coming from Tiberias. Apparently this is what happened: Jesus had performed the miracle of feeding the five thousand somewhere on the eastern shore of the Galilean sea. That evening his disciples had boarded a boat headed west toward Capernaum; Jesus came to them during the storm and together they arrived at Capernaum (presumably before dawn). The crowd had noticed that the disciples—without Jesus— boarded the one boat that was there. The next morning they saw that the boat was gone and that Jesus was gone—but they knew he had not gone in that one boat. During the evening the storm had blown in some boats from Tiberias (on the western shore). The people in the crowd used these boats to cross the sea to Capernaum, searching for Jesus. When they found him in Capernaum in the synagogue (6:59), they asked him not *how* he got there (which seems to be the right question), but *when* he got there, for they would not have thought that he came any other way than by boat. But Jesus did not answer their question—rather, he had something to say about their motive in seeking him (see following comments).

6:26 *Very truly, I tell you, you are looking for me, not because you saw signs, but because you ate your fill of the loaves* (NRSV). Jesus recognized that the crowd had the basest motive for seeking him: He had satisfied their hunger. They had seen the miracle and been fed by it, but they had failed to see it as a sign of divine activity (see 6:14 and comments).

6:27 Do not work for the food that perishes (NRSV). Jesus pointed out that the bread that fills the stomach, whether produced by a miracle or produced at the mill, is perishable—not spiritual or eternal. And the eater will perish with the food. There is another kind of food, **the food that endures for eternal life, which the Son of Man will give you** (NRSV). In fact, he himself is this food (as he later revealed).

For it is on him that God the Father has set his seal (NRSV). In those days, a seal was used to show ownership and authenticity. The Son belonged to his Father. Furthermore, Jesus was the authentic Son of God, the giver of eternal life. The Father's seal of approval was on no one else.

6:28 What must we do to do the works God requires? The crowd, missing Jesus' words about how he would *give* the food that lasts to eternal life and latching on to his words about working, wanted to know what they could do to carry out the works of God (or taken as an objective genitive, to "do God's work") and thereby please him. This was a natural response for those who were taught to earn God's favor by performing the tasks required by the Law.

6:29 The work of God is this: to believe in the one he has sent. Jesus' answer to their question was straightforward. They spoke of works; he spoke of one work (or activity), and that one activity was to believe in him as the one sent by God. The only work God requires from us is to believe in his Son.

6:30-31 What miraculous sign then will you give that we may see it and believe you? What will you do? Amazingly, the crowd still asked for a sign. Had they not just seen the miracle of the multiplication of the loaves? But they wanted more—not just one day's supply of bread but a lifetime's supply! Their argument was that their **forefathers ate the manna in the desert**—which, of course, was available every day for nearly forty years. And furthermore, they argued that **he gave them bread from heaven to eat** (Exod 16:4; Neh 9:15; Ps 78:24-25). They reasoned that Jesus' one act of feeding five thousand men in one day with a few loaves and fish was nothing by comparison to the hundreds of thousands of Israelites fed with manna from heaven for nearly forty years. In those days there was an expectation that the coming of the Messiah would be accompanied by a renewed heavenly dispensation of manna. A midrash on Exodus 16:4 also says that as the former redeemer (Moses) caused manna to descend from heaven, so the latter Redeemer would cause manna to descend.

6:32-33 In these verses and those that follow, Jesus will explicate the verse they quoted ("He gave them bread out of heaven to eat") according to a new, Christocentric interpretation. First, Jesus makes it clear that it was **not Moses** who gave the heavenly bread. In this, the midrash noted above was wrong, and the populace was also mistaken—just as they were mistaken about comparing Jesus to Moses. According to the Greek, Jesus could have said, "[It was] not Moses [who] has given" or "Moses has not given." The first negates Moses as the giver; the second negates the action of giving. In either case, the tense is perfect, thereby emphasizing the fact that Moses—then or now—had not given them any kind of lasting bread. Then Jesus shifts to the present tense: *It is my Father who gives you the true bread from heaven.* The Father who continually gave the manna to the Israelites is the one who gives (and keeps on giving) the true bread out of heaven. Just as the Israelites ate manna every day, so the true bread was also provided for daily sustenance. The Jews wanted a daily supply of physical bread; God had given them his Son as the true heavenly bread to meet their daily spiritual needs. Again, the idea of the continual supply is emphasized by the present tense: *For the bread of God is he who comes down from heaven and gives life to the world.* Just as manna came down every day, so the Son, as it were, comes down continually (not in the sense of repeated incarnations, but in the sense of an abiding presence) and keeps on giving life to the *world* (not just to the *Jews*).

6:34 *From now on give us this bread.* The crowd was unaware that Jesus was speaking about himself as the Bread of Life.

6:35 *I am the bread of life.* Jesus answered them directly: If they wanted this bread, they must come to him and believe in him. Note again how Jesus put this in the present tense (signifying ongoing action): *He who comes* [or *keeps on coming*] *to me will never go hungry, and he who believes* [or *keeps on believing*] *in me will never be thirsty.* There are two ways to understand Jesus' statement: (1) The believer will never again thirst after carnal things, or (2) the believer need never go thirsty and hungry because he will have a continual supply (see comments on 4:14).

6:36 *you have seen me and yet do not believe*[1] (NRSV). The crowds had seen Jesus, the very Bread of Life, standing before them, and yet they did not believe in him. Until they did, they would go on hungering and thirsting.

6:37 *All that the Father gives me will come to me.* In the Greek, the words "all that" (*pan ho*) are neuter singular; they indicate the total collective entity of all believers, which is given as a gift to the Son from the Father (see comments on 17:2, 24). This statement undoubtedly speaks of God's selection. Only those selected by God can come to the Son and believe in him.

whoever comes to me I will never drive away. While the first part of this verse speaks of the collective whole of believers, this phrase speaks about the individual believer. He can be assured that once he comes to Jesus he will not be cast out (cf. 10:28-29).

6:38-40 *For I have come down from heaven not to do my will but to do the will of him who sent me.* This gives the basis of Jesus' acceptance of those who come to him. It is not based on his own biases of selection. He will accept whomever the Father has chosen—for Jesus had come, not to do his own will, but the Father's. And the Father's will is that of *all that he has given* the Son, none would be lost. As in 6:37, the Greek words for "all that" (*pan ho*) are neuter singular; they indicate the total collective entity of all believers. This is affirmed by the following statements in Greek: "I shall not lose of it [neuter singular]" and "I will raise it [neuter singular] up on the last day." Thus in 6:39 Jesus speaks of the total group of believers as an entity that was given to him, that would not be lost, and that would be raised up on the last day. In 6:40 he speaks of the individual: *Everyone who looks to the Son and believes in him shall have eternal life, and I will raise him up at the last day.* The same pattern appears in 6:37, which goes from the collective entity of believers to the individual believer. The individual believer's eternal selection and eventual resurrection are realities dependent upon his or her inclusion in the corporate selection and resurrection. Nonetheless, each individual is important to God. And each person who beholds (or gazes upon) Jesus and really sees that he is the Son of God and believes in him is one who has eternal life—as a present possession and a guarantee of everlasting life.

6:41 *I am the bread that came down from heaven"* (NRSV). The Jews in Jesus' audience hardly heard a word he said about selection, resurrection, etc., for they were stunned by his claim to be the bread that came down from heaven. Had we been there, we too would have been stunned. There was a buzzing in the crowd as they spoke to one another about his statement.

6:42 *Is this not Jesus, the son of Joseph, whose father and mother we know? How can he now say, "I have come down from heaven"?* (NRSV). In the Gospel of John there is a running theme concerning the controversy over Jesus' identity and origin. The Jews expected an earthly Messiah, not a heavenly deity; a son of man, not a Son of God; a descendant of David, not one descended from heaven. They had no thought that God's Son would come from heaven to be their Messiah. They expected a great man to come from the line of David to be their Messiah. Jesus had moved from Nazareth to Capernaum at the beginning of his ministry (see Matt 4:13; Mark 1:21; John 2:12). It is certain that his mother and siblings went with him. Possibly Joseph was alive and also present in Capernaum, given the testimony of the crowd, "whose father and mother we know." In any case, the Jews in Capernaum knew Jesus' parents, and they thought they knew who Jesus was—the son of Joseph.

6:43-45 Jesus tells them to stop talking among themselves. Not one of them could know his true identity if the Father had not revealed it to him. Jesus relied on this revelation. He did not attempt to explain that—as to his humanity—he was the son of David born in Bethlehem, and that—as to his divinity—he was the Son of God from all eternity. In short, he did not attempt to explain the incarnation of eternal deity. This requires revelation. And that is the point of his next two statements: (1) *No one can come to me unless drawn by the Father who sent me; and I will raise that person up on the last day*; and (2) *It is written in the prophets, "And they shall all be taught by God." Everyone who has heard and learned from the Father comes to me* (NRSV). Note the four verbs in these statements: *drawn, taught, heard,* and *learned.* A person cannot come to Jesus if he has not been drawn by the Father, been taught by the Father, heard the Father, and learned from the Father. The Father is the initiator, attractor, and teacher of every person who comes to Christ. No one can claim to have come to Christ by his own initiative, volition, and power. If the Father draws, the person comes. This is Jesus' clear teaching backed up by the Prophets (see Isa 54:13; Jer 31:34; Mic 4:2).

6:46 *No one has seen the Father except the one who is from God; only he has seen the Father.* Jesus' previous statement about people being taught by God (and hearing and learning from the Father) does not mean that anyone other than himself could have direct access to the Father. He is "the one being [existing] from God" (Greek)—or to put it another way, he is "the one whose existence is from God." Only he "has come forth from the presence of God" (Barrett), and only he has seen the Father. This last statement in itself implies divine privileges, for no man has ever seen God (see 1.18 and comments; cf. 1 Tim 6:15-16).

6:47 *whoever believes has eternal life* (NRSV). Jesus had already said that the believer would be raised up on the last day (6:39-40, 44). Here he makes it plain that the believer "has eternal life here and now, without waiting for the last day" (Bruce).

6:48 *I am the bread of life.* This is another of Jesus' "I am" declarations. It is affirmative and exclusive. No one else but he is the bread that gives eternal life.

6:49-50 *Your ancestors ate the manna in the wilderness, and they died. This is the bread that comes down from heaven, so that one may eat of it and not die* (NRSV). The Jews had boasted in the fact that their forefathers had eaten manna, and they were looking forward to a messianic reenactment of this (see comments on 6:30-31). But manna doesn't give eternal life. The Israelites who ate it died in the wilderness. If the Jews in Jesus' day also were given manna, they too would die. God had something better to give than manna from heaven; he gave his Son from heaven as the Bread of Life. Whoever would eat of that bread would not die—that is, would not experience ultimate death but instead participate in the resurrection (see comments on 6:51).

6:51 *I am the living bread that came down from heaven. Whoever eats of this bread will live forever; and the bread that I will give for the life of the world is my flesh* (NRSV). This is the seventh and penultimate time this chapter speaks of Jesus coming down out of heaven (see 6:32-33, 38, 41-42, 50-51, 58). He came as the living bread that possesses eternal life and gives eternal life to those who eat it. To eat this bread means to assimilate it and make it part of one's life now. The partaker of this living bread will live forever. But before Jesus, the Bread of Life, could be eaten by anyone, he had to die. This is conveyed in the words "the bread I will give for the life of the world is my flesh." The Greek word underlying "for" is *huper* (meaning "on behalf of," also translated as a benefactive "for" in English). It is used by John and other New Testament writers with respect to Jesus' death to signify his substitutionary, benefactive death on the cross (see 10:11, 15; 11:50, 52). To give of his flesh meant Jesus gave over his body to death on the cross, so that by his death the world (i.e., humanity) could have life. This theme is expanded in the following verses.

6:52 How can this man give us his flesh to eat? Some of the Jews must have understood Jesus' words at the literal level; they did not perceive the spiritual intent behind his utterance (see comments on 6:63). Others must have known that he was speaking figuratively but could not discern the intent of his words. As a result, they argued with one another about Jesus' statement concerning the eating of his flesh.

6:53 unless you eat the flesh of the Son of Man and drink his blood, you have no life in you (NRSV). Instead of directly telling them how he could give them his flesh to eat, Jesus emphasized the necessity of eating his flesh and—he now added—drinking his blood. If the Jews were offended when Jesus spoke about eating his flesh, they must have been repulsed to hear him speak about drinking his blood because they were commanded by the Law not to drink blood (Lev 3:17; 7:26-27; 17:10-14). But he who resists this eating and drinking is void of life, for "life" must be ingested in order to be received. But no one could receive this life until the giver of it died by shedding his own life's blood. When Jesus speaks of his blood, he refers to it as separated from his body—a sure indication of death. Thus what Jesus is saying is that a person must accept, receive, and even assimilate the significance of his death on the cross in order to receive eternal life.

6:54-55 Whoever eats my flesh and drinks my blood has eternal life, and I will raise him up at the last day. In this verse, there is a different Greek word for eating than occurs previously in this discourse. John shifts from *esthiō* (the most common word used for eating) to *trōgō* (a word generally used in the Greek language to describe animals munching and crunching their food). If this shift was intentional (and not merely a stylistic change), Jesus' language would have been all the more offensive. The word *trōgō* appears again in 6:56-58 and is best translated "feeds on" (as in NLT and the first edition of the NIV). The person who feeds on Jesus' flesh (which is said to be **real food**) and drinks his blood (which is said to be **real drink**) is one who appropriates by faith Jesus' sacrificial death and thereby receives eternal life. And, as is repeatedly stated in this discourse, this reception of eternal life is a sure sign that the receiver will be raised up by Jesus on the last day.

6:56-57 *Those who eat my flesh and drink my blood abide in me, and I in them* (NRSV). This is the first mention in this Gospel of "mutual indwelling" (i.e., a simultaneous indwelling of two persons in each other). This spiritual, even mystical, union is developed in Jesus' last discourse (chs 14–17)—especially in the section on the vine and the branches (15:1-11). The recipient of Jesus is indwelt by Jesus and also indwells him. This mutual indwelling speaks of intimacy and dependency, which is made explicit in the next statement.

Just as the living Father sent me, and I live because of the Father, so whoever eats me will live because of me (NRSV). Jesus now points to himself in his relationship with the Father as a model of the vital union and mutual dependency that he would share with each believer. As the Son is dependent upon the living Father for his (the Son's) life (see comments on 5:26) and lives "because of" the Father (i.e., the Son lives because the Father lives, and the Son is a recipient of that life), so the believer who "feeds on" Jesus will derive his life supply and live "because of" Jesus (i.e., the believer lives because Jesus lives, and the believer is a recipient of Jesus' life). Note how the language shifts from "eat my flesh and drink my blood" to "eat me." "This way of putting it makes it clearer than ever that it is the taking of Christ within oneself that is meant by the metaphor of eating and drinking" (Morris).

6:58 *This is the bread that came down from heaven. Your forefathers ate manna and died, but he who feeds on this bread will live forever.* This verse, providing a summary for the discourse, repeats the major points of Jesus' message. He again contrasts himself, as the bread that gives life, to the manna that could not give eternal life to those Israelites who ate it. Jesus, the true manna from heaven, gives eternal life to those who feed on him. (Note that the two words for "eat" appear in this verse; first *esthiō*, then *trōgō*. See comments on 6:54.)

6:59 *He said these things while he was teaching in the synagogue at Capernaum* (NRSV). The Greek expression underlying "in the synagogue" is literally "in synagogue." Morris says, "The absence of the article in the Greek seems to indicate an assembly for worship, and not simply the building." Apparently, Jesus had spoken these words (6:26-58) during an assembly.

6:60-62 *On hearing it, many of his disciples said, "This is a hard teaching. Who can accept it?"* At this time in Jesus' ministry there were several who were following him who could loosely be called "his disciples" (see 4:1 and comments). These "disciples" were different from the twelve disciples, and many of them were offended by Jesus' teaching—for it was *sklēros* (meaning "harsh" and "rough"). It is not that his words were hard to understand, but that the import of his message was difficult to accept. Jesus, knowing that they were struggling, asked, *"Does this offend you?"* (or more literally, "Does this cause you to stumble?"). (The Greek word *skandalizō* means "to ensnare, to trap, to cause to stumble"; it is often used in the New Testament to indicate a falling away into unbelief.) The next verse seems to indicate that they were especially offended to have heard a mortal declare that he had descended from heaven. Thus, Jesus asked them, **"What if you see the Son of Man ascend to where he was before!"** If they saw Jesus return to heaven, would they then believe? According to 6:64, they would not, for they were not true believers. From this exchange, we could surmise that Jesus had been purposely harsh so as to separate the true believers (i.e., those with revelation—see 6:65) from those who were accompanying Jesus for various other reasons. To those without revelation, Jesus' words probably sounded like those of a madman and a raving lunatic. Imagine hearing someone tell you that he had come from heaven and that you must eat him in order to live forever! You would perceive such a person to be insane or divine. Your perception depends upon your revelation or lack thereof.

6:63 The Spirit gives life; the flesh counts for nothing. The words I have spoken to you are spirit and they are life. This statement gives us the key to interpreting Jesus' discourse. His hearers had not understood the spiritual intent of his message. Some of them may have taken Jesus' words about eating his flesh literally; thus Jesus' clarification, "the flesh counts for nothing." This statement also applies to the correct mode of interpretation. A fleshly interpretation of his words would yield nothing; one must apply a spiritual interpretation to Spirit-inspired words. Morris says, "A woodenly literal, flesh-dominated manner of looking at Jesus' words will not yield the correct interpretation. That is granted only to the spiritual man, the Spirit-dominated man." The key to interpreting Jesus' words is in recognizing that his very words are spirit and life. Therefore, the interpreter must depend upon the life-giving Spirit to appropriate Jesus' words. What Jesus spoke was in itself *pneuma* (spirit) and *zōē* (life) and, activated by the life-giving Spirit, was capable of giving life to those who really heard him and believed him. Thus, to receive Jesus' word was (and is) equivalent to receiving his life and was (and is) the same as eating and drinking him. The key, therefore, to eating and drinking Jesus is to receive his word as spirit and life. Those who believed there and then were those who received his word in this way and, as a result, were recipients of eternal life. Peter was one such believer who had come to realize that Jesus had the words of eternal life (see 6:68). Those who believe now are also those who receive Jesus' word as spirit and life and are thereby regenerated.

6:64 "Yet there are some of you who do not believe." For Jesus had known from the beginning which of them did not believe. Jesus knew that some of those following him did not believe in his true identity as the Son of God come from heaven. He had this knowledge "from the beginning"—which means either from the beginning of his ministry or from the very beginning mentioned in 1:1. If John intended the latter, this is the only instance in the New Testament where there is a mention of divine foreknowledge concerning unbelievers. Elsewhere, the Scriptures speak about God's foreknowledge of the elect.

and who would betray him. This was Judas, the son of Simon Iscariot (see 6:70-71).

6:65 And he said, "For this reason I have told you that no one can come to me unless it is granted by the Father" (NRSV). This repeats (hence the imperfect tense, "was saying" in Greek) what Jesus declared before (see 6:44-45 and comments).

6:66 From this time many of his disciples turned back and no longer followed him. The Greek expression for "turned back" means "went away to the things behind" (cf. Phil 3:13). These disciples, lacking revelation and faith, no longer accompanied Jesus.

6:67 "You do not want to leave too, do you?" Jesus asked the Twelve. In the Greek, this question expects a negative answer. Jesus knew they could not say yes, for they had been chosen by God to believe in him.

6:68-69 Lord, to whom can we go? You have the words of eternal life (NRSV). Peter gave the perfect (and candid) response. There was nowhere else for them to go. They had found the only one who spoke the words that give eternal life (see comments on 6:63).

  We have come to believe and know that you are the Holy One of God (NRSV). Peter, speaking for the rest, declared that their faith in him still remained—it was an abiding faith (indicated in Greek by the perfect tense). And through personal, experiential knowledge (indicated by the verb *egnōkamen* in Greek—also in the perfect tense), they had come to realize that Jesus is "the Holy One of God." This declaration parallels the one Peter made at Caesarea Philippi. In each of the synoptic accounts, Peter's declaration is slightly different: "You are the Christ, the Son of the living God" (Matt 16:16); "You are the Christ" (Mark 8:29); "[You are] the Christ of God" (Luke 9:20). The textual evidence for John 6:69 supports the reading, "the Holy One of God." Other manuscripts betray the work of scribes attempting to conform the wording in John to one of the synoptic Gospels.[2] Though the title "Holy One of God" is rare in the New Testament (the only other occurrences are in Mark 1:24 and its parallel verse in Luke 4:34), Peter spoke of Jesus as being "the Holy One" on two other occasions (see Acts 2:27; 3:14).

6:70-71 Then Jesus replied, "Have I not chosen you, the Twelve? Yet one of you is a devil!" (He meant Judas, the son of Simon Iscariot, who, though one of the Twelve, was later to betray him.) Peter thought he was speaking for the Twelve, but Jesus wanted to make it clear that Peter was not speaking for all of them. One among them, even one chosen by Jesus, was a devil. He was the traitor who would betray Jesus. According to 13:2, 27, the devil put the idea into Judas's heart to betray Jesus and then entered Judas to instigate the actual betrayal; thus Judas was specifically a devil in the act of betrayal. Jesus foreknew this, and yet he still chose Judas (see comments on 13:1ff).

ENDNOTES

[1]This is the reading in many early manuscripts (B 𝔓66 𝔓75vid D T W); a few manuscripts (ℵ A) omit "me."

[2]The reading "the Holy One of God" is decidedly superior to all the other readings because of its excellent documentary support ($\mathfrak{P}$75 ℵ B C* D L W) and because most of the other variant readings are obvious assimilations to Matthew 16:16 ("the Christ, the Son of the living God") or some derivation thereof. Quite interestingly, $\mathfrak{P}$66 and a few Coptic manuscripts display a conflated reading: "the Christ, the Holy One of God." This tells us that some manuscript prior to $\mathfrak{P}$66 (perhaps its exemplar) had the reading "the Holy One of God."

Jesus, the Smitten Rock

JOHN 7:1-52

EXPOSITION

At this juncture in the narrative, John begins to focus on the inability of the Jews to recognize Jesus' true divine identity. Their imperceptiveness revealed their blindness, and that blindness led to hatred. From this chapter forward, Jesus is shown as the suffering Messiah—suffering the unbelief of his own brothers, the fickle opinions of the crowd, and the persecution of the Jewish religious leaders in Jerusalem. It is in the midst of this persecution that one figure emerges: the smitten Rock flowing forth with life-giving water. As part of the Feast of Tabernacles, it was a tradition to pour water over a rock in commemoration of the rock smitten during the wilderness wanderings (Exod 17:6). At the appropriate time, Jesus presents himself as the archetype and reality of that desert experience. Smitten with suffering and with death on the cross, he would give forth the living water.

7:37-38/The Overflowing Life

It was on the last great day of the Feast of Tabernacles that Jesus made his supreme claim to crowded Jerusalem, that in his person he fulfilled all the great realities symbolized by the Feast. This happy celebration was a time to remember the wilderness journeys—specifically the time when the Jews' forefathers were so thirsty and Moses gave them water from the riven rock. Each day of the feast, except the last day, a golden bowl of water was carried from the pool of Siloam to the Temple and poured out at the altar. During the pouring out of the water, the watching multitudes chanted the words from Isaiah, "Come, all you who are thirsty, come to the waters. . . . With joy you will draw water from the wells of salvation" (Isa 55:1; 12:3).

On the last day of the feast, the "greatest day" (John 7:37), this particular ceremony was not done, perhaps to suggest the blessedness of entering the land of Canaan or even to indicate the thirst for greater spiritual blessings that the prophets had written about, which had not yet been realized. Think of the packed and crowded Temple that day: The water-pouring ritual had been omitted, and the people were thinking about it when Jesus stood up in a place where all could see him and cried with a loud voice, "If anyone is thirsty, let him come to me and drink" (7:37).

Approach Christ. Jesus was claiming that he was for the weary, unsatisfied, thirsty world what the riven rock had been for Israel of old—utterly satisfying. Their fathers had eaten manna in the wilderness and had died. They drank from the smitten rock and had died. But that day, to the countless souls and weary multitudes who were thirsty and distressed, Jesus said, "Come to me and drink."

There are some passages in Scripture that deserve to be printed in letters of gold—not that it would add any value to the particular verse, but that attention might be more carefully drawn to the priceless truth. Certainly this great declaration of Jesus is one of those that might well be printed in gold leaf. This is one of those wonderful, all-inclusive invitations that makes the gospel the Good News. The words seem to leap off the page—*Thirst. Come. Drink.*

If any thirst, come. Those who are grimed with sin, those who are up and coming and those who are down and out, those who are persecutors and procrastinators—all are included in this grand invitation. Richard Baxter is quoted as saying that if his name had been on this page, he would have feared the invitation belonged to some other who had the same name, but since the Lord had said "any," he knew even he was welcome.

Here is a universal, yet personal, offer that has been substantiated by many witnesses since the day Jesus made his offer. Think of the appetites Christ can satisfy. For pleasure: "You will fill me with joy in your presence, with eternal pleasures at your right hand" (Ps 16:11). For things: "He who did not spare his own Son, but gave him up for us all—how will he not also, along with him, graciously give us all things?" (Rom 8:32). We could continue with a list of humanity's thirsts, and in all of these Christ alone is the satisfying portion. Jesus Christ boldly offers to you this great invitation, as though your name and social security number were included in verse 37. And you may boldly respond to his invitation.

Appropriate Christ. Those who drink from the fountain (Jesus Christ) receive lasting satisfaction for themselves, but in addition, they become a channel of abundant blessings to others. Believers should prove to be a blessing to those about them. If rivers of living water flow out of believers, our lives should be to those around us as refreshing as streams of water in a dry and thirsty land. The Holy Spirit, the presence and power of the risen Christ always within us, makes the rivers of living water flow. The Holy Spirit's purpose, to glorify Christ, is fulfilled in and through the believer, who, seeking to refrain from grieving the Lord, presents himself to God as a living sacrifice. Before the ascension of Christ, the Spirit of God had rested upon men, fitting them for particular service, but Jesus promises henceforth the Holy Spirit is to be *in* men. In regeneration the Holy Spirit does, in fact, indwell each believer.

Why then are so many of us content with a trickle of blessing when Jesus here promises "rivers"? Is the Holy Spirit unequal to the pressures and problems of our advanced timetable? Is he still able to make an overflow in the lives of believers? The answer, of course, is that he is able! The tragedy is that his life in us may be stunted, dwarfed, or repressed, as plants in a sickly atmosphere or as streams choked with debris. We need to remove the silt and the rubbish, the flotsam and jetsam of life's activities that clog the full blessing and sense of his presence. Let us put away the sins that grieve him. Let us be done with those things and desires that have crowded him from the preeminence in our lives. Let us keep our hearts in an eager, believing attitude toward Jesus, not asking for a new blessing but appropriating more of what we already have when we receive Christ as Savior. This is the overflowing life Jesus promised to all who believe.

KEY WORDS AND PHRASES

Opinions about Jesus abound in this chapter. Consider what the crowds thought of him:

- » Some questioned his teaching credentials (7:15)
- » Some accused him of having a demon (7:20)
- » Some wondered if the rulers knew whether or not Jesus was the Christ (7:26)
- » Others claimed that no one could know where the Christ came from (7:27)
- » Some thought he was a miracle worker (7:31)
- » Others considered him the Prophet (7:40)
- » Some thought he was the Christ (7:41)
- » But still others wondered how the Christ could come from Galilee (7:41)
- » And others were convinced that he, a Galilean, could not even be a prophet (7:52)

We need revelation to see Jesus as he really is—the Messiah, the Son of God (see 20:30-31).

NOTES

7:1 *After this Jesus went about in Galilee. He did not wish to go about in Judea because the Jews were looking for an opportunity to kill him* (NRSV). Since the Jewish religious leaders in Jerusalem were seeking to kill him, Jesus left Judea and stayed in Galilee for the next twelve months. He did not leave because he was motivated by fear. Rather, he left because it was not yet his time to die on the cross. According to chapters 7–9 of Mark's Gospel, Jesus, using Capernaum as his home base, continued his ministry throughout Galilee. John records one long dialogue in the synagogue in Capernaum and is silent about Jesus' other activities during this year.

7:2 *the Jewish Feast of Tabernacles was near.* The Feast of Tabernacles was enjoyed by the Jews every year in celebration of the autumn harvest, occurring in the month of Tishri, which is about mid-September to mid-October in our calendar (see Exod 23:16). It was a time of great rejoicing when many Jews went to Jerusalem and built temporary booths (or tabernacles) in which they lived for a full week while enjoying the festivities (see Lev 23:40-43). Great crowds would gather in Jerusalem for this festival because it was one of the three festivals (the other two being Passover and Pentecost) required by Mosaic law.

7:3-5 *Jesus' brothers said to him, "You ought to leave here and go to Judea, so that your disciples may see the miracles you do. No one who wants to become a public figure acts in secret. Since you are doing these things, show yourself to the world." For even his own brothers did not believe in him.* Jesus' brothers— James, Joseph, Judas, and Simon (Mark 6:3), the sons of Joseph and Mary—did not believe that their brother was the Messiah (cf. Mark 3:21, 31). Apparently, they remained unbelievers until after Jesus' resurrection. Jesus made a post-resurrection appearance to his brother James (1 Cor 15:7), and we are told in Acts 1:14 that shortly thereafter his brothers were gathered with the believers. But prior to their conversion, his brothers viewed the activities and claims of Jesus with disbelief. They could not understand why he would remain in relative obscurity (in Galilee, at home with them) if he was trying to show the world he was the Messiah. They urged him to prove his identity by performing miracles (the kind he had done in Galilee for the last year) in Jerusalem, so that all the world (i.e., all the Jews assembling in Jerusalem for the Feast of Tabernacles) could see that he was who he claimed to be. It is possible they were daring him to prove himself. This was no new experience for Jesus. Satan had tempted him to prove himself, and Mary urged him to demonstrate his uniqueness before the wedding guests. In our present-day vernacular, we might say, "Why are you hanging around here? If you are who you claim to be, why aren't you down at the state fair, where all the crowds are, doing your thing? Besides, if you're such a good Jew, you should be at the feast."

7:6 *My time has not yet come* (NRSV). Elsewhere in John, Jesus speaks about his "hour" (Greek, *hōra*) having not yet come (2:4; 7:30; 8:20), but here he refers to his "time" or "opportune time" (Greek, *kairos*) having not yet come. The "hour" refers to the crucifixion-resurrection event; the "opportune time" refers to the same event, but in this context it addresses the notion of seizing the opportunity. It was as if Jesus said, "If I go up to the feast just now, I will not get the opportunity I am looking for."

but your time is always here (NRSV). His brothers could do whatever they wanted whenever they wanted, but he could not, because he lived according to a different timing—his Father's predetermined schedule and course.

7:7 *The world cannot hate you, but it hates me because I testify against it that its works are evil* (NRSV). Jesus' brothers, in their unbelief, were so much in harmony with the spirit and practice of the world that they had nothing to fear from the world. They were in tune with the unbelieving world, and the world had no quarrel with them. But Jesus knew that his early appearance at Jerusalem would only incite his opposition to violent hatred because he exposed the religionists for their hypocrisy.

7:8 *I am not yet going up to this Feast.*[1] This is the reading in the earliest manuscripts; however, other manuscripts read, "I am not going up to the feast." Despite the early testimony for the inclusion of "yet," most scholars consider the inclusion to be a scribal addition, since it would be natural for scribes to want to rid the text of any appearance of contradiction (i.e., Jesus says he will not go to the feast, but then he goes—7:10). The wording "I am not going up to the feast" very likely means (1) "I am not going up to the feast the way you, my brothers, want me to go—that is, in open manifestation, proclaiming myself to be the Christ." (2) Included is the idea that "I am not going up to the feast until the Father tells me to do so," which is implied by the next statement.

because for me the right time has not yet come. This was not the time to bring to a climax the Jews' hatred and Jesus' death.

7:9-10 *he stayed in Galilee.* True to his word, Jesus did not go up to Jerusalem when his brothers wanted him to. He stayed in Galilee until after they went up, and then *he went also, not publicly, but in secret.* He went up to Jerusalem unobserved, without any entourage.

7:11-13 The Jewish leaders fully expected to confront Jesus at this national festival, and the word was going around, *"Where is he?"* (NRSV). He was the subject of conversation and nearly everyone had an opinion about him. Some thought he was *a good man*; others thought he was one who *deceives the people*—that is, by his miracles, he deceived the people into thinking he was the Messiah. The people's opinions about Jesus abound in this chapter (see introduction to this chapter). No one spoke too favorably of Jesus in public because as yet the Sanhedrin had not pronounced its official verdict, and no one wanted to find himself on the wrong side of the religious authorities.

7:14-15 *About the middle of the festival Jesus went up into the temple and began to teach. The Jews were astonished at it, saying, "How does this man have such learning, when he has never been taught?"* (NRSV). Halfway through the feast (the fourth day of an eight-day event), Jesus came out from secrecy to teach in public view. He did his teaching in the outer court of the Temple (indicated by the Greek word *heiron*) over a four-day period. The Jewish leaders' criticism was that Jesus was quite "unlettered" because he had never studied with the rabbis. They were not wondering about his ability to read or write, and they were not questioning his knowledge of the Scriptures (all Jewish males should have had some knowledge of the Scriptures). They were marveling that he could interpret the Scriptures the way the rabbis did without having the same education they received. It is exactly the same accusation that was made against Peter and John when they stood before the Sanhedrin in Acts 4:13. No rabbi ever made a theological pronouncement on his own authority. He would likely say, "There is a teaching that . . . ," or "It is generally believed. . . ." Jesus did not teach that way. He spoke with authority. So the Jews were saying, "A man must be taught in our schools, or he spouts his own ideas. You have not been taught in our schools; therefore your words are unreliable."

7:16-18 *My teaching is not my own. It comes from him who sent me.* In essence Jesus was saying, "I need no teacher. I don't need to quote your rabbis for authenticity. My authority comes from God. I am not self-educated. I am not giving you my words, but my teaching is directly from my Father." Clear knowledge depends upon honest obedience. Only one who does God's will can understand God's truth. In seeking to do the will of God (repent, believe), one will recognize the veracity of Jesus' teachings. Freed from seeking glory for himself, Jesus was able to transmit the message from the one who sent him to humanity, thereby bringing glory to God. Therefore, Jesus could rightfully claim about himself: *he . . . is a man of truth; there is nothing false about him* or, as in NJB, "He is sincere and by no means an impostor."

7:19-20 Once every seven years at the Feast of Tabernacles, the Law was read publicly so that all would hear it. Perhaps it had just been read and Jesus made the point that some of those proud defenders of the Law were actually breaking the Law by plotting murder. The Jewish leaders were planning to kill Jesus because on his previous visit to Jerusalem (nearly a year earlier) he had healed a man on the Sabbath day (5:8-9). In an ensuing debate after this healing, Jesus implied equality with God, his Father. The Jewish religious leaders wanted to kill Jesus for Sabbath breaking and blasphemy. Therefore, Jesus said to them: *"Did not Moses give you the law? Yet none of you keeps the law. Why are you looking for an opportunity to kill me?"* (NRSV). The irony of the situation is obvious. In seeking to enforce Mosaic laws concerning Sabbath breaking and blasphemy, they were about to break another law: "You shall not murder." The people denied that anyone wanted to kill Jesus, even though it was common knowledge in Jerusalem that the leaders wanted to do away with him (7:25). Even worse than lying, they blasphemed Jesus by charging him with demon-possession. Those who accused Jesus of Sabbath breaking and blasphemy were not only liars, but the real blasphemers.

7:21-24 In these verses Jesus argues that circumcision is a work done on the Sabbath to fulfill the law of Moses; therefore, the Jews should not protest that he performed an act of mercy on the Sabbath when he healed the invalid man. The Jews were so engrossed with their regulations about Sabbath keeping that they failed to see the true intent of Jesus' actions. They judged his actions *by mere appearances* and failed to *make a right judgment.* They needed to look deeper than surface events, which may seem to be wrong.

7:25-27 *Some of the people of Jerusalem* had heard that the religious rulers were *trying to kill* Jesus. But since he was speaking openly and none of the rulers attempted to stop him, they questioned if the rulers had reconsidered and now recognized (Greek, *ginōskō*) that Jesus was *the Christ*. Yet their question, according to the Greek, expects a negative answer, as in the NASB: "The rulers do not really know that this is the Christ, do they?" for they themselves could not believe this. They thought they could trace Jesus' origins back to Nazareth, and they were convinced that no one was supposed to recognize *where* the Christ *is from*. The Jewish leaders in Jerusalem knew that the Messiah was to be born in Bethlehem (Matt 2:1-6; cf. Mic 5:2), but the populace entertained some other idea about the origin and appearance of the Messiah.

7:28-29 Jesus, knowing that the people did not believe in him due to their preconceived notions of who the Messiah was and where he was supposed to come from, *cried out* in the Temple while he was teaching, *"Yes, you know me, and you know where I am from."* Some versions render this sentence as a question rather than as a statement because it seems more poignant as a query than a declaration, e.g., "You *think* you know *me* since you know my home and family?" The fact that Jesus grew up in the home of Mary and Joseph reveals nothing about his true origin or mission.

I am not here on my own, but he who sent me is true. You do not know him, but I know him because I am from him and he sent me. In this deeply emotive declaration, Jesus reveals his divine origin and divine commission. From Jesus' proclamation, we can gather that it is not important *where* Jesus came from, but from *whom* he came. Jesus never once defended himself by pointing to his Bethlehemic birthplace; he always pointed to his divine origin. To recognize his divinity requires revelation. The people did not know him because they did not know the one who sent him; however, he knew the one who sent him. In 7:27-30 the Greek word for "know" (*oida*) is used four times; it signifies absolute knowledge and complete perception. Here is the heartbreaking irony: The people thought they absolutely knew where Jesus came from, but they absolutely did not know because (1) they misjudged appearances, and (2) they did not know God the Father.

7:30-32 Their anger was so great that they made a spontaneous attempt to arrest Jesus, followed by an official attempt (by the chief priests and Pharisees who sent the Temple police). Their efforts failed because he was supernaturally protected, for *his time had not yet come*. In the midst of these attempted arrests, John tells us that *many in the crowd put their faith in him.* Their faith was based on the miracles he had performed, and they concluded that if the Messiah came, he would not perform more signs than Jesus had; therefore Jesus must be the Messiah.

7:33-36 Aware that the Jewish religious leaders were seeking to kill him, Jesus alluded to his coming death: *"I am with you for only a short time, and then I go* *to the one who sent me."* This statement indicates that no one would take Jesus' life from him; rather, he would depart this life according to his preordained time to return to his Father. Jesus said to them, *"You will look for me, but you will not find me; and where I am, you cannot come."* The Greek word for "look" or "seek" (*zēteō*) speaks of that which "one desires somehow to bring into relation with oneself or to obtain without knowing where it is to be found" (Bauer, Arndt, and Gingrich, pp. 338–339). In this context, it has a double meaning: (1) "You will seek me and not find me because I will not be here on earth"; and (2) "You will seek me and not find me because of your unbelief" (see 8:21; 13:33). Or perhaps we could combine the two: "You will seek me and not find me because your unbelief has caused me to leave." Even after Jesus (the true Messiah) left, the Jews would continue to seek for the coming of the Messiah but would not find him because he had already come.

The Jews, not understanding that Jesus' statement referred to his departure via death, wondered if he was speaking about going to where the Jews were *scattered among the Greeks* (the Dispersion), where he would also *teach the Greeks.* "The Dispersion" is a technical term referring to "the large number of Jews who at this time were dispersed throughout the Roman Empire and beyond" (Morris). Some of the Jews were dispersed among the Greeks. The Jews listening to Jesus wondered if he was about to depart Judea and go to these Jews to teach them and the Greeks among whom they lived. Some commentators have wondered if perhaps the tone of Jesus' voice was filled with so much disgust that they picked up on it and said, "Oh, so now you are going to leave us and go to the Greeks!" Jesus, of course, never went to the Greeks himself (see comments on 12:20-24), but his Spirit through the church brought the gospel to them. At the time John wrote this Gospel, many Greek churches existed—most notably the one John served in his later years, Ephesus. Thus there is irony in the question the Jews ask, for little would they have imagined that the gospel of Christ would go to the Greeks.

7:37-38 On the last and greatest day of the Feast. This would be the eighth day, the climax of the festival. During the Feast of Tabernacles, the Jews celebrated the memory of how God tabernacled with their forefathers in their sojourning, guiding them on their way and providing them with manna and water from the smitten rock. Every day during this feast except the last one, a priest, standing in front of the Temple, would take a golden pitcher of water and pour it on a rock in commemoration of the water flowing out of the smitten rock (see Exod 17:6). While the water flowed out, the people standing by would chant, "With joy you will draw water from the wells of salvation" (Isa 12:3). Bengel remarks that a priest would also read Zechariah 14:8 on the first day of this feast: "On that day living water will flow out from Jerusalem." These promises of living water were wonderful, yet they were in reality unfulfilled promises; consequently the people were still thirsty. Thus on the last day of the feast *Jesus stood and said in a loud voice, "If anyone is thirsty, let him come to me and drink. Whoever believes* *in me, as the Scripture has said, streams of living water will flow from within him."* Jesus' invitation can be rendered in two ways: one way (as above) has the believer being the one from whom the living water flows, and the other has Jesus being the source from which the living water flows (as in the following): "Jesus stood and cried out, 'If any man thirsts, let him come to me. And let him drink who believes in me. As the Scripture said, out of his innermost being will flow rivers of living water'" (see NEB, NJB, RSV mg, NIV mg). In the first rendering, "within him" refers to the believer; in the second, "his" refers to Jesus. The second rendering seems more suitable, for it is Jesus who is the antitype of the smitten rock, not the believer.[2] But the first rendering seems to follow the Greek more closely and naturally (although Bruce argues that the second more closely corresponds to the original Aramaic utterance).

The Scripture cited by Jesus does not help us determine if he was speaking about himself or the believer as the source because there is no one verse in the Old Testament that exactly says, "Out of his innermost being [lit., "belly"] will flow rivers of living water." Jesus was either paraphrasing a verse like Psalm 78:16 ("He made streams come out of the rock, and caused waters to flow down like rivers," NRSV), Isaiah 58:11 ("You will be like a well-watered garden, like a spring whose waters never fail"), or a number of other verses (Isa 12:3; 44:3; Ezek 47:1-12; Joel 3:18; Zech 14:8). The psalm passage is the closest to what Jesus said and affirms that Jesus was speaking about himself as the antitype of the smitten rock. But the other verses generally speak of the believers' experience of receiving spiritual, living water.

Jesus would become the true smitten Rock by being crucified on the cross and giving forth the life-giving water. Even prior to his crucifixion he suffered the blows of persecution, insult, and unbelief. He did not retreat or withdraw in the face of suffering. Rather, he took the smiting as a chance to let the living waters flow and give life to others. The Christian should take God's appointed suffering as an opportunity to let life flow forth for others to drink. Paul had learned this secret, for he said, "Death is at work in us, but life is at work in you" (2 Cor 4:12). After Jesus' declaration in 7:37-38, John provides an explanatory note in the next verse.

7:39 *By this he meant the Spirit, whom those who believed in him were later to receive. Up to that time the Spirit had not been given, since Jesus had not yet been glorified.* There are several textual variants in this verse, but the most significant one pertains to the expression "the Spirit had not been given."[3] Most translators, except those of the NJB and NRSV, have felt compelled to add "given," but this addition slightly modifies the meaning of the original wording. In context, this statement was part of an explanation provided by John to help the reader understand Jesus' declaration in verses 7:37-38. Jesus had just promised that anyone who believes in him could come drink of him and experience an inner flow of living water. John's parenthetical remark makes it clear that Jesus was promising the believer an experience of the Spirit that could not happen until after he was glorified and the Spirit was made available. John's words do not mean that the Spirit did not exist at the time Jesus spoke or that believers had not received the spirit and life of Jesus' words. John's note pointed to a time when the Spirit of the glorified Jesus would become available through a special dispensation to all who believed in him. Thus, the availability of the Spirit is linked with the glorification of Jesus, for it was after Jesus' glorification via death and resurrection that the Spirit became available to the believers. In other words, once Christ became the life-giving Spirit through resurrection (see 1 Cor 15:45; cf. 2 Cor 3:17-18), he could be received as the living water.

7:40-42 Jesus' exclamatory invitation in 7:37 caused a mixed reaction among the people. Some were saying, **"Surely this man is the Prophet,"** i.e., the Prophet predicted by Moses in Deuteronomy 18:15-18. Others were saying, **"He is the Christ."** But many would not believe. They were convinced that **the Christ** would not **come from Galilee** because, **"Does not the Scripture say that the Christ will come from David's family and from Bethlehem, the town where David lived?"** These unbelievers were correct in saying that the Christ, as David's offspring, should come from Bethlehem (Mic 5:2). And in fact, Jesus was David's son (Matt 1:1-16; Rom 1:3-4) born in Bethlehem (Matt 2:1-6; Luke 2:1-11). Soon after his birth Jesus was taken to Egypt to avoid the sword of Herod, then later was reared in Nazareth of Galilee, the hometown of Joseph and Mary. Once Jesus began his ministry, he suffered the disgrace of being known as a Galilean and a Nazarene, not a Judean or a Bethlehemite. One of his greatest sufferings was to have his true identity misunderstood. However, Jesus never once discussed his Bethlehemic birth; rather, he always pointed to his divine, heavenly origin. If a person knew the one he came from, he would know that Jesus was the Christ. In any case, the Jews were inaccurate when they said that the Christ would not come from Galilee, for Isaiah 9:1-2 indicates that a "great light" would appear in the region of Galilee.

7:43-49 some wanted to seize him, but no one laid a hand on him. Because, as it says in 7:30, "his hour had not yet come" (NRSV). There was an aura about him they feared. The **temple guards** (very likely Temple police under the jurisdiction of the Jewish religious rulers, not the Romans) who had been sent by **the chief priests and Pharisees** to arrest Jesus also returned empty-handed. When asked why they did not bring him, they said, **"No one ever spoke the way this man does"**—or as F. F. Bruce renders it, "No human being ever spoke as he does." When the officers heard Jesus, they recognized that they were listening to a man like no other, for in fact they were listening to the God-man. "Their testimony was expressed in few and simple words, but it has stood the test of nineteen centuries" (Bruce). The Pharisees, rejecting this simple testimony, asked these officers (whose job was simply to carry out orders), if they **also**, like the ignorant populace, had been **deceived** into believing that Jesus was the Messiah. If he really were the Messiah, they argued, at least some of the religious rulers would have believed in him. But they were assured that none *of the rulers or of the Pharisees believed in him.* They were convinced that the populace believed in him because they knew *nothing of the law.* Therefore, there was *a curse on them* for their ignorance. In other words, the common people, not knowing the Scriptures, were confused. Of course, in saying this the Jewish leaders were claiming to have known the Scriptures and, by that knowledge, to have determined that Jesus, having come from Galilee, could not be the Christ.

7:50-52 *Nicodemus, who had gone to Jesus before, and who was one of them, asked, "Our law does not judge people without first giving them a hearing to find out what they are doing, does it?"* (NRSV). The Pharisees were convinced that not one of them had believed in Jesus. This tells us that if Nicodemus had become a believer after his visit with Jesus (3:1-21), he had not made it known. Perhaps Nicodemus was a secret believer but, as with other rulers, would not confess his belief for fear of being put out of the synagogue (12:42). Nevertheless, Nicodemus attempted to make his fellow Pharisees adhere to the law they claimed to know. An accused person, according to Deuteronomy 1:16, must first be heard before being judged. But these Pharisees would not listen even to "the teacher of Israel" (NKJV). They retorted sarcastically, *"Surely you are not also from Galilee, are you? Search and you will see that no prophet is to arise from Galilee"* (NRSV). This is as much to say, "If not even a prophet is said, in the Scriptures, to come from Galilee, how much less the Christ?"[4] So the Pharisees and religious rulers were confident that they could reject Jesus as having any claim to messiahship because of his Galilean origin. But they were wrong on two counts: (1) Jesus had been born in Bethlehem, the city of David (Luke 2:4-11), and therefore had legal claim to messiahship (Mic 5:2); and (2) the Scriptures do speak of the Messiah as a "great light" arising in Galilee (see Isa 9:1-7; Matt 4:13-16). Jesus alludes to this prophecy in his response to their affirmation (see 8:12 and comments).

7:53–8:11 This passage is discussed in Appendix A; it is not discussed as part of the text of John for the following reasons: The passage about the adulterous woman is not included in any of the earliest manuscripts. Its first appearance in a Greek manuscript is in the fifth century, but it is not contained in any other Greek manuscript until the ninth century. No Greek church father comments on the passage prior to the twelfth century—and then Euthymius Zigabenus declares that the accurate copies do not contain it. When this story is inserted in later manuscripts, it appears in different places: after John 7:52, at the end of John's Gospel, or after Luke 21:38. And when it does appear, it is often marked off by asterisks or obeli to signal its probable spuriousness. The story is part of an oral tradition that was included in the Syriac Peshitta, circulated in the Western church, eventually finding its way into the Latin Vulgate, and from there into later Greek manuscripts, the likes of which were used in formulating the Textus Receptus (Metzger).

Beyond this impressive external evidence is the clear observation that the insertion of this story at this point in John greatly disrupts the narrative flow. We have noted that the setting of John 7 and 8 is at Jerusalem during the Feast of Tabernacles. During this feast, the Jews would customarily pour water over a rock, commemorating the smitten rock in the wilderness, and light lamps, commemorating the pillar of light that accompanied the Israelites in their wilderness journey. With reference to these two ritualistic enactments, Jesus presented himself as the true source of living water and as the true light to be followed (8:12). To add this pericope in this place in the text disrupts the continuity between these great declarations of Jesus.

Further, John 8:12 contains a response—even though indirect—to John 7:52. In John 8:12ff Jesus was speaking to the Pharisees who had boldly told Nicodemus that the Scriptures make no mention of even a prophet (much less the Christ) being raised up in Galilee. With respect to this assertion, Jesus made a declaration in which he implied that the Scriptures did speak of the Christ coming from Galilee. He said, "I am the light of the world. Whoever follows me will never walk in darkness but will have the light of life" (NRSV). This statement was probably drawn from Isaiah 9:1-2, which contains images parallel to those in John 8:12. Both speak about the light, walking in darkness, and the shadow of death versus the light of life.[5]

ENDNOTES

[1]The reading in the NIV, "I am not yet going," is the reading in many ancient manuscripts (𝔓66 𝔓75 B T W); however, other manuscripts (𝔑 D and some ancient versions) read, "I am not going." The editors of UBS[3] and NA[26] selected the second reading on the basis of intrinsic probability versus documentary evidence that strongly favors the inclusion of "yet."

[2]It is interesting to note that the two earliest manuscripts (𝔓66 and 𝔓75) both indicate a full stop after "drink." If John intended his readers to understand this statement according to the first reading, it implies that the believer who drinks of Christ as the Rock will experience the living water flowing out from him. Westcott put it this way: "He who drinks of the Spiritual Rock becomes in turn himself a rock from within which the waters flow to slake the thirst of others."

[3]There are several textual variants in this explanation, but the most significant one pertains to the expression "the Spirit was not yet," attested to by 𝔓66ᶜ 𝔓75 𝔑 T. According to other manuscripts (𝔓66* L W), this reads, "the Holy Spirit was not yet"; and still other manuscripts (B and some early versions) read, "the Holy Spirit was not yet given." The best-attested reading is the shortest one: "the Spirit was not yet." Various scribes could not resist the temptation to add "Holy" to "Spirit," an addition that frequently happened throughout the course of the transmission of the New Testament text.

[4]One Greek manuscript, 𝔓66*, definitely reads *ho prophētēs* (the prophet), which was then corrected to *prophētēs* (a prophet). 𝔓75 is questionable; it could read either way because there is a lacuna in the manuscript that could be filled with *ho prophētēs* or *prophētēs*. Thus as is stated in the TEV mg, there is only one manuscript that reads, "the Prophet."

[5]For more on this, see Comfort's article "The Pericope of the Adulteress (John 7:53–8:11)," in *The Bible Translator,* January 1989.

Jesus, the I Am

JOHN 8:12-59

EXPOSITION

A very large portion of John's narrative is devoted to detailing the controversy over Jesus' true identity. No other portion of this Gospel, or even of the Bible, is so focused on this controversy as chapters 7–8. The religious rulers were convinced that Jesus could not be the Christ because he did not fit their preconceived notions of who the Messiah should be and how he should behave. Jesus never directly told them, "I am the Christ," as he had done with the Samaritan woman (4:25-26). Rather, he declared something even greater about himself—that he is the eternal God!

8:12-59/*The Light of the World*

John 8:12 is a grand text because the words are so simple that even a child can grasp their meaning, yet they express realities so profound, the most educated may ponder them. Jesus is the Light of the World—not just what he taught, but what he is. All other religions or religious leaders look for, search for, and seek the light, but Jesus Christ alone can say, "I am the Light." He didn't say he came to bring light. He didn't put himself on the level with other teachers who simply enlighten the minds of men, but he said that he himself was the Light. The fullest simplification of that statement is, "I and I alone, and no other, am the Light."

The announcement. When Jesus boldly said that he is the Light of the World, he was acknowledging the truth that mankind is in moral and spiritual darkness. Every believer certainly recognizes the fact that the world is in a dark condition. The vast majority of men neither see nor understand the true nature of God, nor their natural spiritual condition, nor the reality of the world to come. In spite of all the discoveries of science and education, Isaiah's words are still true: "Darkness covers the earth and thick darkness is over the peoples" (60:2). Philosophy, science, education, humanism, and man-made religions have all promised mankind light in his darkness, but mankind, apart from Christ, still gropes in the darkness. Unregenerate people can weigh moral issues because they have a conscience (Rom 2:15), but they do not have spiritual light. When Jesus said, "Whoever follows me . . . will have the light of life," he meant spiritual light for life's journey. The unbeliever walks in darkness, with no one to guide him when important decisions are to be made and no one to comfort him when sorrows come. When death comes, the unbeliever has no one to be with him. When judgment comes, he has no one to defend him.

The analogy. During the Feast of Tabernacles two huge golden candelabra were lit in the Temple. The lighting of these two huge lamps was meant to be symbolic of the pillar of fire that led the children of Israel in their wilderness wanderings. The camp of Israel might be pitched in a desolate place, away from any delightful oasis or palm trees, or surrounded by foes of various kinds. No matter! As long as the pillar was motionless, no one broke camp. It might be two days or two months; if the pillar stayed, the children of Israel journeyed not. When it did move, no matter how short had been the halt, how weary the people, or how pleasant the camping place, the tent pegs were pulled up, and immediately they were on their way. The true commander was not Moses but the pillar, God's light.

On this day it was as if Jesus had said to those about him, "You have all seen the blaze of the Temple illumination, the golden candelabra piercing the darkness. Well, I am the Light of the *World,* and for the person who follows me there will be light, not just during the dark hours, but for the entire pathway of life. That light in the Temple is merely symbolic, and it ceases, but I am the Light that lasts forever and ever."

The candelabra were an external light, but the light of which Christ speaks is an inner illumination. The believer has him. The natural darkness of the soul is banished when he comes into the heart to dwell. Christ taught that he was the Bread of Life for the hungry, the Water of Life for the thirsty, and the Light of Life for his followers.

The answer. It is not enough that we gaze upon or study or discuss the Light. Our response, our answer, is to irrevocably follow that Light. He who follows Christ shall no longer live in ignorance and darkness, but shall have spiritual light on his pathway, now and in the world to come. To follow Christ is to be delivered from darkness and have a guide through all the perplexities of life. We need not stumble, because we do not walk in darkness when we walk with him. How gentle and loving is that guidance! How wise and sure that light. Spurgeon says, "Jesus is too good to do me wrong. He is too wise to make a mistake. So even though my eye cannot immediately see his way, my heart will trust his guidance."

The word *follows,* as used by Christ in 8:12, has a rich and full meaning. The word in Greek could be used in at least five different ways, all interrelated.

1. A soldier following his captain—on long marches or campaigns in strange lands, or merely completing boring details in camp. The Christian is like a faithful, loyal soldier following Christ in the battles of life.

2. A slave accompanying his master—faithful by accompanying and serving in excellence. The Christian follows Christ best when his greatest joy is in selflessly serving the Lord Jesus.
3. A person following a wise counselor's guidance—be it legal advice or financial counsel or some other needed guidance. The Christian is the person for whom Christ is counselor and expert in the insurmountables of life.
4. A citizen following the laws of the state—the Christian is a citizen of heaven, and he endeavors to follow the laws set down in the Word of God.
5. A person following the gist of a line of reasoning—the believer is the person who has understood the meaning of the teachings of Jesus. He not only understands, but accepts the truth and follows in happy obedience the ways of Christ. To do so is to walk in the light.

KEY WORDS AND PHRASES

In this chapter Jesus asserts his divine identity through a series of seven "I am" statements:

» "I am the light of the world." (8:12)
» "I am not alone." (8:16)
» "I am one who testifies for myself; my other witness is the Father." (8:18)
» "I am from above." (8:23)
» "I am not of this world." (8:23)
» "I am he [i.e., the Christ]." (8:24, 28, NRSV)
» "I am!" (8:58)

NOTES

8:12 *I am the light of the world. Whoever follows me will never walk in darkness, but will have the light of life.* In John's original writing, this verse immediately follows 7:52. The intervening passage, 7:53–8:11, known as the pericope of the adulteress (see comments on this passage in the previous section), interrupts the true narrative continuity from the end of chapter 7 to the beginning of chapter 8. Both these chapters record the dialogues Jesus had with the Jewish leaders in Jerusalem during the Feast of Tabernacles. During this feast, the Jews would customarily pour water over a rock (in commemoration of the water supply coming from the smitten rock in the wilderness) and light lamps in the Temple (in commemoration of the pillar of light that accompanied the Israelites in their wilderness journey). With reference to these two ritualistic enactments, Jesus presented himself as the true source of living water (7:37-39) and as the true Light to be followed (8:12). John 8:12 contains a response—even though indirect—to John

7:52. In John 8:12ff Jesus was speaking to the Pharisees, who had boldly told Nicodemus that the Scriptures make no mention of even a prophet (much less the Christ) being raised up in Galilee. With respect to this assertion, Jesus made a declaration in which he implied that the Scriptures *did* speak of the Christ coming from Galilee. The statement in 8:12 was probably drawn from Isaiah 9:1-2, which contains parallel images. Both speak about the light, walking in darkness, and the shadow of death versus the Light of Life. Thus 8:12 parallels Isaiah 9:1-2 and thereby provides a reproof to the Pharisees' declaration in 7:52.

In declaring himself "the light of the world," Jesus was making a claim for his unique position as the one true luminary source for all mankind. The expression "the light of life" can mean "the light which gives life" or "the light which is life" or "the light which springs from life" or "the light which illuminates life" (Morris). The Greek construction emphasizes this reading: "I and I alone and no other am the light."

8:13-19 These verses contain a continuing discussion concerning the validity of Jesus' testimony, "I am the light of the world." After he said this, **the Pharisees challenged him, "Here you are appearing as your own witness; your testimony is not valid."** The Jews insisted that a statement such as the one Jesus made could not be regarded as accurate because it was not supported by sufficient witnesses. In other words, they were saying, "When you call yourself the Light of the World, you are boasting. No one confirms your testimony, so it cannot be true." Jewish law required two witnesses to establish the validity of a statement (Deut 17:6; 19:15). Jesus did not disagree with the Jewish requirement for two witnesses. He simply replied that his testimony was true even if no one else bore witness, because there was another one bearing witness—his Father. The Father who sent Jesus was with Jesus, so that the Son was **not alone**. Because they did not know Jesus' divine origin and considered him to be no more than a pretender to the messiahship from Galilee (that is, they judged him according to **human standards**), they were unenlightened. They did not understand that the Father and Son lived in each other (in what theologians call co-inherence) and were with one another. Therefore, even though the Son **came from** the Father and was **sent** to earth by the Father, he was not separate from the Father: The Father who sent the Son came with him and provided testimony for him. The Pharisees, mystified about Jesus' reference to his Father, asked him, **"Where is your father?"** In other words, "Show us this 'witness.'" This was probably said scornfully. Their question clearly revealed that they had totally rejected the claims of Christ. Since it is only through the Son that the Father reveals himself, and only through the Son that one knows the Father, these religionists demonstrated their ignorance of God the Father.

8:20 He spoke these words while he was teaching in the treasury of the temple (NRSV). This area was part of the Temple grounds where women were permitted to go. In this Court of Women there were thirteen trumpet-shaped collection containers for the reception of various offerings. This treasury was very close to the hall where the Sanhedrin met. Its proximity to the Sanhedrin is significant inasmuch as Jesus' words in 8:12-19 were addressed to those Pharisees who had just met in the Sanhedrin and had denounced Jesus for his Galilean origins (see comments on 8:12).

but no one arrested him, because his hour had not yet come (NRSV). Men may plot and scheme, but God is in control, and his timetable will be followed exactly.

8:21-23 Speaking again (probably on another occasion, later the same day or another day) to the Jewish religious leaders, Jesus boldly said, *"You will die in your sin. Where I go, you cannot come."* If the Jewish religious leaders would not believe in Jesus while he was there with them as God-incarnate, they would not have any further opportunity to receive eternal life. Remember, he was addressing men who had seen his works of power and had heard his teaching, who had been urged to receive him as the living bread and come out of the darkness to the Light of the World, and then refused to believe. The ultimate experience of such blindness is to die in one's sins. Elsewhere the Bible speaks of dying in one's own sin (Ezek 3:18) but never completely explains what exactly that means. "It points to a horror which is all the more terrible for being unexplained. To die with one's sin unrepented and unatoned is the supreme disaster" (Morris). In contrast, consider the words of Revelation 14:13: "Blessed are the dead who die in the Lord." All die, either in unbelief or in faith. The Jews could not comprehend Jesus' words. They surmised that he might have been speaking about death, maybe even suicide, when he spoke about going away, but they could not understand how he would die: **Will he kill himself?** In the Greek, the question expects a negative answer. Instead of answering their query, Jesus explains why they were unable to comprehend his statements. They did not understand because they were *from below*—that is, they were *of this world*, as compared to Jesus, who is *not of this world.* Those of this world are earthly, born of the flesh; they cannot understand the heavenly and spiritual things, as the apostle Paul declared in 1 Corinthians 2:14.

8:24 you will die in your sins unless you believe that I am he (NRSV). In this context a predicate nominative should be supplied after the statement in Greek, *egō eimi* (I am); most scholars select "he" or "the one," referring to the Christ. In 8:58 it is more appropriate not to supply a predicate nominative and let it stand as "I am." It is a statement of fact. Those who do not believe will die in their sins because faith in Jesus is the only means of escaping eternal judgment. Unbelief keeps one separated from God. To die in such a condition is to remain forever estranged and at enmity with God.

8:25-26 Who are you? Possibly said in derision, "You, who are *you?*" In other words, "You are a nobody."

Just what I have been claiming all along. The Greek answer can be translated in a number of ways: "I am what I have said to you from the beginning," or "I am what I say I am," or—taken as a question—"Why do I speak to you at all?" Interpreted this way, Jesus did not need to give them any further explanations; he had already, through his previous speeches, unveiled his identity to them. In short, the Word revealed himself through his words. The Pharisees remained unable to understand his speech because they were deaf to his words (8:43).

I have much to say in judgment of you. But he who sent me is reliable, and what I have heard from him I tell the world. In essence Jesus was saying, "I have many things to say concerning you, which would actually judge you. In spite of your vehemently uttered rejections and your unbelief, what I say is true because the one who sent me is true, and I only speak his words to the world." The Father's word was reliable—i.e., it was true and real; it was not just for the Jews, but for the entire world.

8:27-29 The Pharisees had not realized that Jesus had been speaking **to them about his Father.** They did not understand that Jesus had come from God the Father and was still accompanied by God the Father. Jesus was not alone; the Father who sent him came with him. Jesus asserted this twice: **"The one who sent me is with me"** (8:16, 29). Jesus had not come on his own, and he did not do anything of his own initiative (8:28, 42). He was completely dependent upon the Father. He spoke only what he heard from his Father and was taught by his Father. In short, he lived to please his Father. The Pharisees would not recognize that Jesus was the Messiah and that he had come from God the Father until after his crucifixion, resurrection, and ascension. This is implicit in Jesus' statement: **"When you have lifted up the Son of Man, then you will realize that I am he, and that I do nothing on my own"** (NRSV). The expression "lifted up" signifies being lifted up on the cross; it also connotes exaltation. The Jews in Jesus' day clearly understood "lifted up" to signify crucifixion. To be willing to be "lifted up" certainly indicates he was doing another's will, for death on the cross exhibited his absolute submission to the Father's desires.

8:30-32 Frequently, in the midst of hostile rejection, John will inform us that "some believed." Even as Jesus spoke, several of the Jews in the audience were enlightened concerning Jesus' divine identity and began to believe, for the text says, **Even as he spoke, many put their faith in him. To the Jews who had believed in him, Jesus said, "If you hold to my teaching, you are really my disciples. Then you will know the truth, and the truth will set you free."** Jesus urged the new believers to remain in his word, to adhere to his teachings in order to become true followers of Jesus. The Greek word for "hold to" also means to "abide," a word that has great spiritual significance in the Gospel of John. To abide in Christ is to put oneself in subjection to him and remain there, drawing life from his words. This abiding produces ongoing discipleship. Jesus made it clear that discipleship is to follow initial belief. A disciple will come to know the truth by knowing Jesus through a lifelong process of abiding, continuing, and obeying. If we recognize this truth, we will be free from the bondage of sin.

8:33-34 The Jews were offended to hear anything about needing liberation, for they were convinced that they, **Abraham's descendants**, had **never been slaves to anyone** (NRSV). This was an incredible response from these unbelieving Jews. They denied the bondage the Jewish nation had under the Egyptians, the Assyrians, the Babylonians, and even then under the yoke of Roman rule as Jesus spoke. But whatever they had in mind, Jesus makes it clear that what he is talking about is a different form of liberation—that of the soul set free from sin. Jesus said, **"Everyone who commits sin is a slave to sin"** (NRSV). Paul develops the same idea in Romans 6:12-23.

8:35-36 **The slave does not have a permanent place in the household** (NRSV). Lit., "does not remain in the house forever."

the son has a place there forever (NRSV). This aphorism amplifies the difference between a slave and a son. Not a member of the family, a slave has no permanent standing in his master's house; he can easily be sold to another. But a son always has a place in his father's house; once a son, always a son (Bruce). The Jews had a false sense of security because they claimed to be sons of Abraham, when actually they were slaves of sin. As such, they had no permanent standing in the Father's house. This same idea is expressed in the synoptic Gospels, where John the Baptist said, "Do not begin to say to yourselves, 'We have Abraham as our ancestor'; for I tell you, God is able from these stones to raise up children to Abraham" (Luke 3:8, NRSV). Thus, they couldn't claim spiritual reality based on their heritage. Spiritual reality comes from true faith in Jesus, and with this reality comes the privilege of becoming a permanent member of God's family.

The reference to "the son" in this verse has double significance: (1) It refers to a son, as opposed to a slave, who has a permanent place in his father's house, and (2) it refers to the Son of God, who has an eternal place in his Father's house. The next verse affirms the second meaning. **So if the Son makes you free, you will be free indeed** (NRSV). The Son of God alone has the power and authority to liberate men from their bondage to sin. This is the purpose of our Lord's incarnation, as suggested by Luke 1:74-75, "that we, being rescued from the hands of our enemies, might serve him without fear, in holiness and righteousness before him all our days" (NRSV).

8:37-44 In these verses, Jesus exposes as false the Jews' twofold claim of having Abraham as their father and God as their Father. The Jews could rightfully claim to be **Abraham's descendants**, but they were his sons only by physical lineage, not moral likeness; they were not children of faith. In seeking to kill Jesus, they exposed their relationship with another "father," namely, the devil. They did not behave like Abraham, who believed God's words. Jesus specifically pointed to their sin of wanting to kill him because this would convict them and convince them that they really were enslaved to sin. It was impossible to have God as their Father when they rejected the Son, whom they were seeking to kill. In response to Jesus' charge that God was not their Father, the Jews said, *"We are not illegitimate children* [lit., "We were not born of fornication"]. *The only Father we have is God himself."* It is unlikely that the Jews were here charging Jesus with having an illegitimate birth. How could they have known about his unusual beginnings? It was always assumed by the unenlightened that he was the son of Joseph. Rather, their retort shows that they took offense at being told that God was not their Father, since it implies that they had committed spiritual fornication and gone after false gods. Actually, at this time in Israel's history, they were devout monotheists, but it was in form only. They did not truly know the God whom they claimed as their Father. Jesus said, *"I declare what I have seen in the Father's presence"* (NRSV). And again he said, *"[I have] told you the truth that I heard from God"* (NRSV). Derived from his relationship with his Father before the world began, the Son's words to men on earth were those that originated from God, not from man.

Jesus declared that he *came from God*; he had *not come* on his own. He came as the one sent by the Father to bring God's word to his people. If Jesus had come on his own, the Jews' hatred of him would have been focused on him alone, but their rejection of him showed that they did not love God or the one sent by God. The Jewish religious leaders had not received the word. Jesus told them, "My word finds no room in you" (lit.), and, *"You are unable to hear what I say."* They were hardened and deaf; the life-giving, enlightening word could not penetrate. Instead of being open to the words of God, they were receptive to the lies of the devil. Jesus told them, *"You are from your father, the devil, and you choose to do your father's desires"* (NRSV). This statement, developed in 1 John 3:7-15, indicates that a person's actions are a manifestation of his true source of being. The intent to murder comes from the father of murder, the devil. The devil was the instigator of Jesus' murder and the perpetrator of the lies the Jews believed about Jesus. Jesus said, The devil *"was a murderer from the beginning, not holding to the truth, for there is no truth in him. When he lies, he speaks his native language, for he is a liar and the father of lies."* The devil, through his lies to Eve (Gen 3:4-5), gave death a way to enter into the world, causing Adam and Eve and all their posterity to be alienated from God (Rom 5:12). In this sense, the devil was a murderer from the beginning. Furthermore, the devil is an incurable liar, for falsehood constitutes the nature of his being. "The devil utters falsehood as naturally and spontaneously as God utters truth" (Bruce).

8:45-47 In contrast to the devil, who habitually speaks lies, Jesus speaks *the truth*, and for that reason he was disbelieved, because people who speak lies cannot entertain truth. The Jewish leaders charged Jesus with being a Sabbath-breaker and blasphemer (5:18), to which Jesus answered, *"Can any of you prove me guilty of sin?"*—i.e., "Of what sin do you convict me?" His words to them were very penetrating and exposing. Only *he who belongs to God hears what*

God says. Nothing could be clearer; either we hear (receive, obey) his words, or we don't.

8:48-50 *The Jews answered him, "Are we not right in saying that you are a Samaritan and have a demon?"* (NRSV). This is the only instance in the Gospels where Jesus is charged with being a Samaritan. For a Jew to call another Jew a Samaritan was equivalent to calling him a heretic, a schismatic, and a foreigner; it's like saying, "You're not one of us; you're one of them." They leveled this charge at Jesus because he, a fellow Jew, had charged them with not being true descendants of Abraham. They also accused Jesus of being demon possessed (see 7:20; 8:52; 10:20). In the synoptic Gospels, this blasphemous accusation was counted as the most heinous sin, a sin that would never be forgiven (see Matt 12:24ff; Mark 3:22ff). Jesus did not respond to the charge of being a Samaritan, but he did refute the blasphemous charge of being demon possessed, saying it dishonored him who always sought to honor and glorify his Father. The Father would seek glory for his Son (which is the meaning of the words **there is one who seeks**) and consequently would judge those who dishonored the Son.

8:51-53 *Whoever keeps my word will never see death* (NRSV). According to the Greek, the latter clause means "he will not experience the eternal death." Jesus had sobering words for those who rejected him and great promises for those who believed him. Of all the promises, this is the greatest one. Jesus' words, when received and kept, give eternal life. But his words to these Jews seemed like the speech of a madman.

Now we know that you have a demon. Abraham died, and so did the prophets; yet you say, "Whoever keeps my word will never taste death." Are you greater than our father Abraham, who died? The prophets also died. Who do you claim to be? (NRSV). The Jews realized that no one—not even great people like Abraham or the prophets—had escaped death. (Had they forgotten about Elijah?) Thus for Jesus to claim that he could prevent death was for him to claim to be greater than any man who ever lived—indeed, it meant he was claiming to be God. These Jews were convinced that only a madman (one who was demon possessed) would make such a claim.

8:54-55 Again Jesus defers the matter of his divine identity to his relationship with his Father. He could never make the kind of claims he made apart from his intrinsic union with the Father. If he had come of his own accord, his **glory** would be **nothing**. The Father had sent him, and the Father would glorify him, even if the Jews would dishonor him. The crux of the matter was that the Jews did not know the Father from whom Jesus came, even though they claimed he was their God. The one who really knew the Father and kept his word knew that these Jews were lying.

8:56-59 In these final verses of chapter 8, Jesus makes one of his greatest claims to eternal deity. He begins by telling his listeners, *"Your ancestor Abraham* *rejoiced that he would see my day; he saw it and was glad"* (NRSV). According to rabbinic tradition, Abraham was supposed to have been given foresight into future events pertaining to the descendants who would come from his loins. Jesus, perhaps knowing this tradition, pinpointed the one event that would have made Abraham the happiest—the day when the Messiah, his seed, would come to deliver the Jews. Note that Jesus did not say "his day" but "my day"—a clear reference to his personal claim to the messiahship. The expression "my day" refers to the time of Christ's presence on earth.

Thinking on the literal level, the Jews said to him, *"You are not yet fifty years old* [this is a roundabout way of saying that he was not yet an old man], *and you have seen Abraham!"*[1] Jesus had not claimed to be a contemporary with Abraham or that he had seen Abraham; he had said that Abraham had seen his day. Jesus astounded them with his answer: *"before Abraham was born, I am!"* In one breath, Jesus asserted his eternal preexistence and his absolute deity. Abraham, as with all mortals, came into existence at one point in time. The Son of God, unlike all mortals, never had a beginning. He was eternal, and he was God. This is evident in the words "I am" (*egō eimi*), for this statement refers to the Septuagint translation of Exodus 3:14, in which God unveiled his identity as the I AM THAT I AM. Thus, Jesus was claiming to be the ever-existing, self-existent God. No other religious figure in all of history has made such claims to deity. Either Jesus was God or he was a madman.

The Jews, offended by this claim to deity, *picked up stones* in order to execute him for blasphemy. Perhaps Jesus had purposely incited them to this extreme so that they could see themselves for who they really were—murderers. He had told them this before and had used it to show that they belonged to the devil, a murderer from the beginning. When he said it, they could have internally denied it, but not now. They were exposed.

but Jesus hid himself. Lit., "was hidden" (perhaps referring to the divine passive—"was hidden by God"). He went out *from the temple grounds.* The time had not yet come for him to die, and so he escaped their stoning.

ENDNOTES

[1]This is the reading in 𝔓66 ℵ C A Bᶜ C D L. A few other early manuscripts (𝔓75 ℵ *) read, "and Abraham has seen you." This reading may be an assimilation to the preceding verse, in which Jesus indicated that Abraham rejoiced to see his day, or it may be the true reading because it focuses on the longevity of Jesus' life, not Abraham's foresight. The length of Jesus' existence is affirmed in the next verse.

Jesus, the Sent One, the Light of the World

EXPOSITION

When the Bible is taught as literature, this chapter is often included because it is considered a classic example of an ancient short story that makes full use of irony, contrasting the blindness of the Jewish leaders with the enlightenment of the healed blind man. The key statements in this chapter are found in verses 4 and 5: "We must work the works of him who sent me" (NRSV) and "I am the light of the world." As in other places in this Gospel, John uses a physical object (or person) to depict or symbolize a certain spiritual aspect of Christ. Earlier the writer used Jacob's well as the setting where Christ presented himself as the fountain of living water, the manna from heaven to illustrate Christ as the Bread of Life, and the rock at the Feast of Tabernacles to show Christ as the source of living water. Later, Lazarus serves as a physical illustration for the spiritual reality of resurrection. Here in chapter 9, John uses the pool of Siloam to symbolize Christ as "the sent one" (*Siloam* means "sent"), and he focuses on the healing of one blind man to illustrate the spiritual truth that Christ is the Light of the World. Furthermore, the events of this chapter offer continuing evidence of Jesus' messianic identity, for the prophet Isaiah said that the Messiah would heal the blind (Isa 29:18; 35:5; 42:7).

9:1-38/*The Blindness of Sight*

This story possesses an irresistible and unfailing charm. Just a casual reading evokes various emotions, and the more one studies this action-packed drama, the more one sees much hidden truth. There is a subtle humor that pervades the dialogue between the Pharisees and the man who had been born blind. The former blind man's irony is almost amusing as he exasperates the Pharisees and ruffles their dignity. But most important to see in this story is that this miracle is an acted-out parable of the life that issues from faith in Christ. We have as the central figure a poor, blind beggar, helpless and beyond the aid of men, sought out by Christ, and forever changed by that meeting. The story is easily divided into three parts.

The miracle. The Scripture tells us that "as [Jesus] went along, he saw a man." The man was blind and desperately needed help, and the Lord was not indifferent to his needs. In fact, Jesus was interested in this man long before the man was interested in Jesus. Others may observe need and go their indifferent way, but not so with Jesus. He is moved by our need.

Now this man bore a heavy load. Blind from birth, he had never seen his loved ones, the light of day, or the world around him. The disciples brought up a theological question: "Who sinned, this man or his parents, that he was born blind?" They recognized that sin has consequences and wanted to know who should be blamed for this poor fellow's plight. Sometimes in human tragedy no one is specifically at fault, but the experiences of disease, sorrow, suffering, limitation, and handicap are the effects of man's separation from God. We must be careful not to get wrapped up in theorizing and philosophizing while remaining indifferent to human needs. Rather than argue, debate, and question who has sinned, we ought to look at each situation as an opportunity for God to manifest his grace.

Jesus placed some mud on the sightless eyes and told the blind man to go wash in the pool of Siloam. He gave no other command, no promise, no added encouragement, no assistance. Jesus could have spoken the word or merely touched the sightless one and healed him, but for his own purposes he ordered him to a specific pool of water to wash away the mud. God cannot be forced into a certain mold—he deals with each of us differently and reveals himself in unique ways.

The Scripture says that *Siloam* means "sent." During the reign of King Hezekiah, the water source for Jerusalem was outside the wall, which meant they were very vulnerable in any time of siege. So the king ordered a conduit to be dug underground from the spring to the center of the city. The workmen began at either point and started digging toward each other through solid rock on almost a zigzag course. The distance was 583 yards (nearly the length of six football fields), and they met in the center perfectly in line with each other. In 1880, a tablet was found adhered to the tunnel wall, telling of the digging, which is described in 2 Chronicles 32:2-8, Isaiah 22:9-11, and 2 Kings 20:20. Now the reason the pool was called Siloam, or "Sent," was that the water had been sent through the conduit to the city. Jesus said, "Go to the pool 'Sent' and wash," imaging the command, "Go to the 'sent one' and be washed of sin." For spiritual cleansing one must go to the true Siloam, Jesus Christ. In other words, when you realize that Jesus is the "sent one" from the Father, you will *see*.

The blind man obeyed—he found the pool, he washed, and he could see! And today we rejoice that Jesus can open the eyes of the most sinful and ignorant and make them see things they have never seen before. He can send light into the darkest heart and cause blindness and prejudice to disappear. "We who have sat in darkness have seen a great light" is the testimony of every believer.

The meddlers. After this man washed and his eyes were opened, he went home, and the neighbors got in an argument over whether this was the same man who was formerly blind.

"Are you the man who was blind?"

"Yes!"

"Who healed you?"

"A man called Jesus."

"Who is he?"

"I don't know."

So they took him to the Pharisees because they thought there ought to be an investigation. Rather than rejoicing that the man had received his sight, the Pharisees were greatly agitated that the man had been healed on the Sabbath! They argued that God would not break their laws of the Sabbath; therefore, Jesus was not from God, and this whole thing was from the devil! But the healed man said, "He is a prophet." The Pharisees were so blinded by their own sin and rejection of Jesus that in their unbelief they refused to acknowledge God at work. And today unbelievers are just as blind to what Jesus can do for those who trust him.

The Pharisees then turned to the man's parents. They said, "We know he is our son. He used to be blind; now he can see. That's all we know." They spoke in fear, for the Pharisees had said that those who confessed Christ as the Messiah would be put out of the synagogue. They would be persecuted, have no fellowship with friends, and be treated as outcasts, separated from the household of Israel.

The Pharisees then said to the man, "Give God the praise." This was a phrase used in cross-examination that literally meant, "Speak the truth in the presence and in the name of God." The man replied, "I don't know whether Jesus is a sinner or not, but one thing I do know, I was blind, but now I see." There was no denying *that* truth. Neither can men deny the reality of our salvation if they can see evidence of it in our lives. We who are saved—we who "see"—are not resting on someone's say-so, but on the authority of God's eternal Word and the ever-deepening knowledge of the abiding presence of Jesus Christ. The children of God are people who *know* they have moved from spiritual blindness to sight.

The Pharisees lost all reason and began to revile, belittle, and ridicule the healed man, ultimately excommunicating him from the synagogue. They bragged that they were disciples of Moses, but their actions demonstrated they were utterly blind to spiritual truth. Those who were tragically blinded by unbelief condemned those who could see the truth.

The master. Hearing that the man had been excommunicated, Jesus set out to find him and asked, "Do you believe in the Son of Man?"

He replied, "I would like to believe, but who is he?"

Jesus said, "You have *seen* him. I am he."

With all the earnestness of his soul the young man cried out, "Lord, I believe!" This great confession of faith indicates that the man's mind had been prepared by the Holy Spirit. The more he contemplated the wonderful thing that had happened to him, the more convinced he was that it was the Messiah who had healed him. He began by calling Jesus a man (v. 11). He then called Jesus a prophet (v. 17), and finally he worshiped him as the Son of God (v. 38). In worshiping Jesus, he gave ample evidence that he was truly converted.

This story started with a beggar groping in his blindness. He had no hope that he would ever see the light of day. Then Jesus came, and that made all the difference in the world. His night was changed to day. His hopelessness was changed to hope. His destiny was changed from hell to heaven. From blindness to sight. From darkness to enlightenment. From sin to worship of the Savior. What a wonderful change occurs when Jesus touches us!

KEY WORDS AND PHRASES

In this chapter the blind man has progressive revelation about Jesus' identity. His physical eyes were opened immediately; his spiritual eyes opened gradually. The enlightening was in four stages:

1. At first the man recognized our Lord as "the man they call Jesus" (9:11),
2. then as "a prophet" (9:17),
3. then as one who was "from God" who had performed a miracle never done before (9:32-33),
4. and then finally, as "the Son of Man," the Messiah (9:35-39).

NOTES

9:1-3 *he saw a man blind from birth* (NRSV). Jesus' notice of the blind man was not accidental or incidental. Not only did he care for the blind man, he used the man's predicament to correct some erroneous ideas. Seeing the blind man, the disciples asked a theological question, *"Rabbi, who sinned, this man or his parents, that he was born blind?"* (NRSV). One of the beliefs of Jesus' time was that the sins of the fathers are visited upon the children (see Exod 20:5; 34:7; Num 14:18; Deut 5:9). But God had explained to Ezekiel that that was no longer the case, "'The fathers eat sour grapes, and the children's teeth are set on edge.' . . . As surely as I live, declares the Sovereign LORD, you will no longer quote this proverb in Israel. . . . The soul who sins is the one who will die" (Ezek 18:2-4).

Neither this man nor his parents sinned. The disciples believed that blindness was a punishment for sin. But whose sin, the disciples wondered—the man's or his parents'? Jesus taught them that it had nothing to do with his sin or his parents' sin.

he was born blind so that God's works might be revealed in him (NRSV). These words do not imply that God heartlessly inflicted blindness on a newborn baby; rather, he allowed nature to run its course in this case so that the victim would ultimately bring glory to God through the reception of both physical and spiritual sight.

9:4-5 As long as it is day. While Christ was in the world, direct light was in the world; it was "day." It was Israel's day of visitation.

we must do the work of him who sent me. Evidently Jesus was speaking of himself and his disciples as coworkers. They were to learn from him because they would continue his work as his sent ones (see 20:21). He included the disciples in this work, although they did nothing for this blind man, because they would continue to shine the light of Jesus after his departure (see Phil 2:15).

Night is coming, when no one can work. "The coming night was the period of his withdrawal from the world" (Bruce). This is intimated in 13:30.

I am the light of the world. Christ used the beggar's blindness as an illustration of the spiritual darkness that gripped the world and could only be alleviated by his work of giving the light of life.

9:6 he spit on the ground, made some mud with the saliva, and put it on [lit., "anointed"] **the man's eyes.** Why would Jesus do it this way? Why not just touch his eyes or merely speak the word of healing? Because Jesus is not limited to any one means or method. In Mark there are two incidents of miraculous healing in which Jesus used his saliva: to cure a deaf and mute man in the Decapolis and to heal a blind man in Bethsaida (Mark 7:33; 8:23). John's account, however, is the only record of Jesus spitting on the ground and forming clay from it. Some ancient commentators, such as Irenaeus, saw this act as resembling God's creation of man (Gen 2:7). In any case, the action could speak of creation or creative power. From antiquity, spit or saliva was thought to have medicinal power. The Jews were suspicious of anyone who used saliva in healing because it was sometimes associated with magical arts. But there is no magic here. It is a gracious Savior giving a blind man the golden opportunity to obey his command and be healed.

9:7 wash in the pool of Siloam (NRSV). "Siloam" is a Greek translation of the Hebrew name *Shiloah,* which means "sent." The water in Siloam got there by being sent into the pool through a channel from the Spring of Gihon in the Kidron Valley. This tunnel channeled the water into the pool of Siloam inside the city walls. Located in the southeast corner of the city, the tunnel and pool were originally built to help Jerusalem's inhabitants survive in times of siege. If the city were ever surrounded by enemy armies, the people inside could always get fresh water without having to leave the city (2 Kgs 20:20; 2 Chr 32:30). It was a tremendous engineering feat to bring water nearly six hundred yards through solid rock and into the city.

However not all appreciated the water, for we are told in Isaiah 8:6 that the Jews refused the waters of Siloam, just as in this chapter the Jews refused Jesus (Barrett). But the blind man obeyed the word of the sent one, and his obedience demonstrated his faith. He washed in the water of Siloam and **came home seeing**. These waters symbolized the work that Jesus had come to do. The man's positive response to Jesus' words physically displayed the truth that spiritual healing and cleansing come as the result of following Jesus' word. Many Christians in the early church saw this "washing" as portraying baptism. In fact, several second-century depictions about baptism in Roman catacombs include the blind man's washing at the pool of Siloam.

9:8-12 In these verses John records the various reactions of the blind man's neighbors after his healing. Some thought he looked like the **same man who used to sit and beg.** (In ancient cultures, as in many modern cultures, those who were blind had no choice but to be beggars.) Others positively identified him: **"It is he"** (NRSV). Still others objected, **"No, he only looks like him."** In response, the blind man kept saying, **"I am the man."** Realizing that he who once was blind now had his sight, they asked, **"How then were your eyes opened?"** The newly sighted man lost no time in testifying to the healing power of Jesus by very accurately recounting what had happened to him.

9:13-14 They brought to the Pharisees the man who had formerly been blind (NRSV). Why did they bring him to the Pharisees? The people were confused. They knew that Jesus was not accepted by the religious leaders, and they wanted to know, "What's going on? Here is someone we've known for years who has been suddenly, dramatically healed. We have never seen or even heard of such a miracle before; yet this miracle worker is not accepted by the religious leaders. Why?" Adding to their confusion was the fact that this took place on the Sabbath. There was that same problem again: Can a person do good deeds even if it means breaking Sabbath laws? It was prohibited to heal on the Sabbath and to anoint on the Sabbath with any kind of substance other than what was used normally during the week (Barrett). Healing, along with many other actions defined as work, was strictly controlled on the Sabbath and was only to occur in cases of life or death. The blind man's healing was not a matter of life or death.

9:15-23 First the Pharisees asked all about the healing (9:15), and then some of the Pharisees condemned the healer as being **not from God** because he had done this work on the Sabbath (9:14, 16). To charge Jesus with being not from God was tantamount to saying he was a deceiver performing miracles that would lead people astray (see Deut 13:1-5). But some other Pharisees questioned this condemnation: **"How can a sinner do such miraculous signs?"** (9:16).

So they were divided. This is the first time the Gospel of John indicates a division among the Pharisees concerning Jesus' identity (see 10:19-21). The staunchest Pharisees, refusing to believe the healed man, attacked him with a renewed attempt to break down his testimony. The newly sighted beggar responded with even more illumined praise for his benefactor than he had offered previously—he called him *a prophet* (9:17). The Pharisees called in the man's parents in the hope that they would refute their own son's testimony. The parents refused to disavow their son's story, but they were afraid to say anything about Jesus for fear of being put out of the synagogue: *for already the Jews had decided that anyone who acknowledged that Jesus was the Christ would be put out of the synagogue.* The Greek expression for "be put out of the synagogue" states an action similar to excommunication. The expression is uniquely Johannine (used here and in 12:42; 16:2). According to Jewish regulations, there were two kinds of excommunication: one that would last for thirty days until the offender was reconciled, and one that was a permanent ban accompanied by a curse. In a tight-knit community, it was a terrible judgment to be removed from the synagogue, the very center of Jewish life. Many Jews in John's day had been "de-synagogued" because they confessed Jesus to be the Christ. An ancient document found in the Cairo Genizah (c. AD 80–90) contains a curse against the Nazarenes, banning them from participating in the synagogue. Perhaps John included this story for particular encouragement to those Christians who were experiencing such treatment.

9:24-25 *A second time they summoned the man who had been blind.* Not content with their first examination of the healed man, the Pharisees called him in a second time with a command, *"Give glory to God."* This was a phrase used in cross-examination that literally meant, "Speak the truth in the presence and in the name of God." It was used by Joshua when he interrogated Achan (Josh 7:19). It does not mean give glory to God instead of giving glory to Jesus. The Pharisees were trying to make him admit his wrong in thinking that Jesus was a prophet and to confess that Jesus was a sinner. But the healed man would not give in; he would not say whether or not Jesus was a sinner. What he would say was what he had experienced: *"One thing I do know. I was blind but now I see!"* There was no denying that truth! Future generations of Christians, having once been blind and then having received spiritual sight, have testified the same!

9:26-33 The relentless questions and even curses of the Pharisees were unable to throttle the healed beggar's willingness to testify for Jesus. In fact, the more the Pharisees questioned the man, the clearer he became about Jesus. Their blind obstinacy augmented his clarity. At first, the man recognized our Lord as "the man they call Jesus" (9:11), then as "a prophet" (9:17), then as one who was "from God" and had performed a miracle never done before (9:32-33). Then finally, when confronted by Jesus, he saw him as the Son of Man, the Messiah (9:38-39). While the Pharisees questioned him, they persistently defended their adherence to Moses because they were confident God had spoken to him (cf. 6:45-47). They were not sure where Jesus came from and therefore questioned his relationship to God. This reasoning astonished the healed man, so he tried to explain to them that Jesus' act of giving him sight proved that Jesus was a man whom God listened to: *"We know that God does not listen to sinners, but he does listen to one who worships him and obeys his will. Never since the world began has it been heard that anyone opened the eyes of a person born blind. If this man were not from God, he could do nothing"* (NRSV). There are many Scriptures that support the first part of the man's statement: Job 27:9; 35:13;

Psalms 66:18; 109:7; Proverbs 15:29; Isaiah 1:15; and 1 John 3:21. God does not listen to the requests of sinners but to the requests of those devoted to him. The Greek word *theosebēs,* which appears only here in the New Testament, literally means "God-fearing" and can be translated as "pious," "devout," "godly," and "a worshiper of God." Another expression in Greek, "since the beginning," appears only here in the New Testament; it can mean "since time began." The man was right; since the beginning of human history there was no record of a man *born blind* being healed. Jesus had done the unprecedented. But the Pharisees were blind to the Old Testament predictions that specifically speak of the Messiah giving sight to the blind (see Isa 29:18; 35:5; 42:7). Indeed, the healing of the blind was thought of as the most distinguishing and significant messianic miracle because there was not any record of such a healing in the Old Testament.

9:34 The healed man's condemnation of the Pharisees' irrational rejection of Jesus proved too much for them to take, so *they threw him out.* "They expelled him from the synagogue" with a curse about his presumed guilt from birth: *"You were steeped in sin at birth; how dare you lecture us!"*

9:35-38 Later Jesus found him and asked him, *"Do you believe in the Son of Man?"* This is the reading in all the earliest manuscripts; later manuscripts read, "the Son of God."[1] Since "Son of Man" is a title of the Christ, Jesus was asking the man if he believed him to be the Christ. In this context, it was important for the man to acknowledge his faith specifically in Jesus as the Messiah. (Later in history it was important for people to confess their faith in Jesus as the Son of God, so later scribes changed "the Son of Man" to "the Son of God.")

There are three other good reasons why "Son of Man" completely suits the text. First, this passage ends with Jesus affirming his role as the Judge (9:39-41), and the title "Son of Man" is used for Jesus as the Judge of all men (5:27). Second, since "Son of Man" was a surrogate title for "Messiah," Jesus was asking the man if he believed in the Messiah—knowing full well that this confession would affirm his expulsion from the synagogue. Third, for the blind man to realize that Jesus was the Son of Man was to realize that Jesus was the revelation of God to man. This is important to chapter 9, wherein we are presented with the gradual spiritual enlightenment of the blind man, culminating in this realization.

When the man asked who the Son of Man was, Jesus responded, *"You have now seen him; in fact, he is the one speaking with you."* These climactic and potent words, "you have now seen him," have double impact, referring to the enlivening of the man's physical sight and spiritual sight. The man could now see in both respects; he had been enlightened by the "light of life." He believed in Jesus as the Son of Man, and he showed it by worshiping Christ as one would worship God.[2]

9:39-41 *Jesus said, "I came into this world for judgment so that those who do not see may see, and those who do see may become blind"* (NRSV). Christ spoke these words to the healed man in the presence of the Pharisees. The Pharisees quickly understood that Jesus had directed this statement at them, but they were not fully sure of the meaning of his words (9:40), so Jesus expanded his statement with the rather cryptic condemnation in 9:41—*"If you were blind, you would not have sin. But now that you say, 'We see,' your sin remains"* (NRSV). In contrast to the man who had received his double sight, the Pharisees had sight but no light. They were spiritually blind, though they thought they were enlightened. They presumed they knew all about the Messiah, but their knowledge blinded them from seeing the very Christ of God who stood in their midst. Those who admitted blindness could receive the light and see, but those who thought they saw would remain in their darkness. These verses provide a good conclusion to a chapter that began with a question about the relationship between sin and blindness. According to Jesus, the real sin is to be blind as to who Jesus really is.

ENDNOTES

[1]All the earliest manuscripts ($\mathfrak{P}$66 $\mathfrak{P}$75 $\aleph$ B D W) read, "the Son of Man"; later manuscripts read, "the Son of God."

[2]All of 9:38 and the first part of 9:39 ("He said, 'Lord, I believe.' And he worshiped him. Jesus said") are not included in $\mathfrak{P}$75, $\aleph$ *, W, Coptic mss, and the *Diatessaron*. It could be argued that the omission may be the result of a transcriptional error, but not in so many diverse manuscripts. Brown suggests that the words may be "an addition stemming from the association of John ix with the baptismal liturgy and catechesis." Calvin Porter makes a strong argument for this portion being a liturgical addition. See his article, "John IX. 38, 39a: A Liturgical Addition to the Text" in *New Testament Studies* 13 (1967), 387–394.

Jesus, the Shepherd

JOHN 10:1-42

EXPOSITION

The first twenty-one verses of this chapter are most likely a continuation of Christ's remarks to the Pharisees (cf. 9:39-41 with 10:19-21). The thematic connection between the two chapters centers on the blind man having become a believer in Jesus as the Christ and subsequently having been expelled from Judaism. And so this one believer becomes typical of all those believers who would come out of Judaism to follow Jesus, as sheep following their shepherd.

This chapter begins with a "figure of speech" (10:6), which is something like a parable, but not exactly. In a parable all the items lead to one total meaning; each item in a parable may not have an equal significance. But it is relatively easy, and very instructive, to give symbolic meaning to the figures used by Jesus in this story. The Good Shepherd is Christ; the sheep are the Jewish believers; the sheepfold is Judaism; the "other" sheep are the Gentile believers; the gatekeeper is the Father God; the stranger is a false messiah; and the wolf is some kind of destructive pretender. But what is the gate into the sheepfold? It would seem that the gate is the messiahship—that is, the office of the Messiah. Only one person could qualify: Jesus. Since he was the true Messiah, God the Father opened the gate to him, giving him legitimate access into the sheepfold of Judaism. Anyone who tried to enter that fold had to do so by some other means, for no one else was qualified to be the Christ.

Jesus' similitude seems to have one parable inside the other. The larger parable pertains to the sheep and the shepherd; the parable within this pertains to the gate. Christ is both the gate and the shepherd. The gate comes first (10:1-3a) and then the shepherd (10:3b-5), each with its own interpretations—the gate is explained in 10:7-9, and the shepherd in 10:11-18. Finally, it should be noted that the entire passage is set against the backdrop of Ezekiel 34, wherein the false shepherds are castigated and the true shepherd is predicted to come and provide God's people with genuine care and leadership.

10:1-16/The Shepherd and His Sheep

The picture of the shepherd is deeply woven into the language and the imagery of the Bible. This is due in part to the fact that Judea was a pastoral rather than an agricultural country. The most familiar figure of the Judean uplands was the shepherd tending his sheep. For many Christians today, there is no better-loved depiction of Jesus Christ than the portrayal of him as the Good Shepherd. The very idea conjures up in our mind warm thoughts. It is therefore somewhat of a shock to note in this tenth chapter that with the conclusion of Christ's self-revelation as the Good Shepherd, there were those who tried to kill him. Their actions simply reinforced the words of Jesus that they were not part of his flock.

To correctly interpret chapter 10, it is important to remember that it follows chapter 9 concerning the healing of the blind man. In other words, Jesus is explaining to the crowd what *really* happened to the formerly blind man. Failure to make this connection has led to some incorrect interpretations of Jesus' words. Perhaps you have heard someone say, "If anyone tries to get into heaven in some other way than through Jesus Christ, he is a thief and a robber." It is perfectly true that if you try to enter heaven by some way other than by trusting the Lord Jesus Christ, you will be like a thief trying to break into a place where you don't belong. But that is the wrong application here. Jesus is not talking about getting into heaven. Heaven is not a sheepfold. *Judaism* was the sheepfold!

Further explanation may be needed before we look carefully at this parable. Those who have carefully studied the "land and the Book" tell us that in Israel there were two kinds of sheepfolds. One near a large village or town was a communal fold, where various flocks were kept at night. The owners of the sheep hired a porter—a doorkeeper or guardian—and he let in only those shepherds whom he knew personally as rightfully belonging to the sheep. The other kind of fold was out in the hills and away from any village. It frequently was a walled enclosure, without roof, and had a small hole in the wall through which the sheep entered at night and across which the shepherd lay to sleep—so that the shepherd was, indeed, a door. Nothing could enter or leave unless the shepherd allowed it.

The true shepherd. In this parable, Judaism was the sheepfold tended by God's prophets, the last of whom was John the Baptist. In effect, Jesus is saying that many have tried to get in and control the sheep, but they tried to get in as thieves, never via the door—in this case the Scriptures—but always in some way other than God's appointed means. The Pharisees and leaders of official Judaism were bad shepherds. They had not entered by the door into the sheepfold; like thieves and robbers, they had climbed in some other way. Their power over the flock had been secured illegitimately. They were like thieves in their deceit and hypocrisy and like robbers in their violence.

Jesus, on the contrary, had come on a divine mission and in the office of the Messiah. John the Baptist, a prophet, had given him access to the flocks. And as sheep recognize the voice of their shepherd, so, like the blind man whom Christ had healed, those who truly love God would gladly accept Christ as the Messiah. Jesus came and called to the Jews, but only his flock responded—the disciples, the woman at the well, Zacchaeus, and many others. They came out to follow the true Shepherd, Jesus Christ. The called ones (*ekklēsia* in Greek) form the true church today, God's flock, Christ's bride. The true Shepherd does not view his sheep as a group; he knows each one by name. We are promised in Revelation 3:5, "He who overcomes will, like them, be dressed in white. I will never blot out his name from the book of life, but will acknowledge his name before my Father and his angels."

The only Door. Demonstrating tragic unbelief, the Jews responded to Jesus by saying that they did not understand him. Incredulously they asked, "Are you saying that *we* are blind? We do not see what you are talking about" (9:40). So with great emphasis, Jesus says again, "I am the door for the sheep, I and no other— the only door through which sheep enter." There is simply no other entrance! There are no limitations either of sex or nationality—anyone may come, but only through Jesus Christ.

If such a person comes to Jesus, he will be saved and can "go in and out" and find pasture. This is an old Hebrew way of describing *life without fear.* It represents security, liberty, free activity. The country is at peace; law and order are in control. No secret police. No Gestapo. No bands of thieves ready to pounce on an unsuspecting person. It is a beautiful picture of a person perfectly at peace and secure in all things because he is a part of God's flock. This threefold promise, for security, liberty, and free activity, is given to those who enter the Door.

There is freedom in loving God; not bondage, but grace controls the situation. There is nourishment—through the Door we find the bounty of his provision. One cannot enter the fold through baptism, church membership, good works, or human relationships. There is just one way to enter the fold: through repenting and receiving Jesus Christ as Savior.

The Good Shepherd. Unfortunately the English language cannot do justice to the simple words *the Good Shepherd.* What is implied is that he is altogether lovely, in a class all by himself, par excellence, none beside him. Maybe you have heard someone at some time say of a certain physician, "He is a good doctor." They are not only thinking of the doctor's efficiency and skill as a physician; they are thinking of his manner, his kindness, his friendliness, his sympathy, and his graciousness. That is a quality inherent in the title the Good Shepherd—the altogether lovely one.

The reason that he is the Good Shepherd is that he lays down his life for the sheep. Four times in just a few sentences he says, "I lay down my life for the sheep." In order to understand this, one must enter the realm of divine love, best viewed at a place called Calvary. There we see one dying not for his own sins but for the sins of others. "Greater love has no one than this, that he lay down his life for his friends" (15:13). But we were not his friends. We were ungodly sinners, without strength, enemies of God—there was nothing in us to commend us to God. He lays down his life for the sheep. When he died for us, he did not merely die on our behalf; he died in our place. He went through something so terrible we cannot fully understand it in order that we who believe might never go through it. We who believe shall never die as he died, for he has promised that we shall not taste death. Our bodies shall wear away and cease functioning, but we will not taste death because the Good Shepherd loves us and gave himself for us.

KEY WORDS AND PHRASES

The symbolic figures in this story represent the following:

- » The Good Shepherd is Jesus Christ.
- » The sheep are the Jewish believers.
- » The other sheep are the Gentile believers.
- » The sheepfold is Judaism.
- » The gate is the office of the Messiah.
- » The gatekeeper is God.
- » The pasture is the abundant life.
- » The wolf is the intruding destroyer of God's people.
- » The hired hand is a selfish religious leader.

NOTES

10:1-2 *he who does not enter the sheepfold by the door, but climbs up some other way, the same is a thief and a robber* (NKJV). It would seem that the door is the messiahship. Christ, the sent one, was the only person who could qualify for the office of Messiah.

The man who enters by the gate is the shepherd of his sheep. Because he was the true Messiah, God the Father opened the door to him, and once he entered, Christ became that door. He alone had legitimate access into the sheepfold of Judaism. Anyone else who tried to enter that fold had to do so by some other means, for no one else was qualified to be the Good Shepherd. Furthermore, as the gate, Jesus provided the way into eternal life (see 14:6).

Judaism was the sheepfold tended by God's prophets, the last of whom was John the Baptist. Now, Jesus says, many have tried to get in and control the sheep, but they came in as thieves, and their control of the flock was illegitimate. The intent of the robber was to destroy what belongs to God.

10:3-5 *The gatekeeper opens the gate for him, and the sheep hear his voice* (NRSV). Within the fold of Judaism were some of God's people who had awaited the coming of their Shepherd-Messiah (see Isa 40:1-11). Jesus came and called to the Jews, but only his true sheep responded. When the shepherd came, he would lead his people out to good pasture (see Ezek 34). He *calls his own sheep by name and leads them out* of the fold. This was exactly what happened to the blind man in the previous chapter. It is said that shepherds in the East would name each sheep and that each sheep would respond to the shepherd calling its name. This helps to explain the next verse: ***They will not follow a stranger, but they will run from him because they do not know the voice of strangers*** (NRSV). Because sheep in Palestine were primarily raised for wool, they were with their shepherd for years and easily recognized his voice. Likewise true believers recognize their Shepherd's voice and would never follow one pretending to be their shepherd.

10:6 *this figure of speech.* The Greek word *paroimia* can mean "proverb" (as in 2 Pet 2:22) or "enigmatic saying" (as in 16:25, 29), or "similitude." John did not use "parable," which is common in the synoptic Gospels, and the Synoptics do not have the word *paroimia*. Most scholars consider the two words to be nearly synonymous. The only difference is that in John's Gospel the word *paroimia* may connote the idea of a similitude. Whatever the exact definition, Jesus' "similitude" was not understood by his listeners. Clearly they were not his sheep! Earlier they had said, "Are we blind too?" (9:40). Here they frankly admit they cannot understand his teaching.

10:7 *I am the door of the sheep* (NKJV). Some readers may have expected Jesus to say here, "I am the shepherd of the sheep."[1] But Jesus thought it first necessary to explain the symbolic meaning of "the door," which was the way out of Judaism into the true flock of God.

10:8 *All who ever came before me.* meaning "all who ever came pretending to be the Christ." The words "before me" are not present in some of the earliest manuscripts.[2] On one hand, it can be argued that these words were added—in some manuscripts before the verb and in others after it—in an attempt to clarify an otherwise mysterious statement: "All who came are thieves and robbers." On the other hand, it can be argued that the words "before me" were dropped "in order to lessen the possibility of taking the passage as a blanket condemnation of all Old Testament worthies" (Metzger). The statement was not directed at Old Testament saints and prophets, but at those who came on the scene pretending to be the promised Messiah. The emphasis is on the verb "came"—i.e., came pretending to be the Messiah. All such pretenders were actually ***thieves and robbers***. These terms are further descriptions of the one Jesus previously called "a stranger." Such terms could depict evil Jewish religious leaders (see Matt 23:13) or false messiahs (see Matt 24:5).

but the sheep did not listen to them. Those who are truly born again recognize the truth when it is taught and sense something wrong when false teachers speak (see 1 Jn 2:20-27; 4:1).

10:9 *I am the door. If anyone enters by Me, he will be saved* (NKJV). Since Jesus was the genuine Messiah, the sheep could enter through him to find salvation, liberty, and provision. He is the Door, not to the fold but to eternal life (cf. 14:6). The expression "will be saved" or "will be kept safe" (NIV, first edition) points to spiritual salvation and spiritual security.

will go in and out (NKJV). This comes from an Old Testament expression describing the normal activity of daily life. It is a life without fear (see Deut 28:6; Ps 121:8; Jer 37:4). In short, the Shepherd would provide his sheep with deliverance, freedom, and nourishment.

10:10-11 As opposed to the *thief* (who may represent the false Christ, the antichrist, the one in league with the devil, or just someone whose intention is to harm the sheep) and the hired hand (who symbolizes the religious leader who abuses his leadership over God's people for self-gain—see Ezek 34), Christ is the devoted and dedicated Shepherd—*the good shepherd*. In contrast to those whose intentions were to **steal and kill and destroy** the sheep, he came **that they may have life, and have it to the full**. Jesus gives abundant life to his sheep. This is divine, eternal life, a gift that becomes the possession of every believer for now and continuing throughout all eternity. Jesus would provide his sheep this eternal life even if it would cost him his own life. Four times in this passage Jesus says that he **lays down his life for the sheep** (10:11, 15, 17, and 18). When Jesus talks of laying down his "life," he uses the word *psuchē*, which means "soul." This is the word Peter used when he told Jesus he would lay down his life for him. In response, Jesus said to him, "No, you won't. You can't! You, Peter, can't give your soul for another. But I will give my soul, that you—and all my flock—might have life" (see John 13:37-38). Isaiah 53:10 says the Messiah would "make His soul an offering for sin" (NKJV).

10:12-15 In these verses Jesus seems to be contrasting the Good Shepherd with the **hired hand,** who is not really a shepherd at all. The hired hand has no inner relationship to either the shepherd or the sheep. He has no concern for the sheep. Jesus probably had the Pharisees in mind when he used the term "hired hand" (see Matt 23:1-36; Luke 11:39-52), but it need not be limited to only those fake shepherds. Basically, the hired hand is only interested in money. The **wolf** refers to false prophets or others who take advantage of God's people, the sheep (see Matt 7:15; 2 Pet 2:12). True spiritual leaders should be on the watch for such people and guard the sheep from their destruction (Acts 20:28-29).

10:16 *I have other sheep that do not belong to this fold* (NRSV). Prior to this statement, Jesus had spoken of leading his sheep from out of the fold of Judaism. All of his disciples came out of this fold, as did all those Jews who had come to believe in him as their Messiah. Jesus knew, however, that he had other sheep that would not come from Judaism. These "other sheep" are non-Jews, the Gentile believers.

So there will be one flock, one shepherd (NRSV). The Good Shepherd, as the true David, came to gather God's people into one flock (cf. Ezek 34:11-14, 23). The Jewish believers who left Judaism, along with the future Gentile believers, would form one flock that was altogether outside of Judaism. This imagery pictures the same togetherness that Paul depicted as the one body, the church, composed of Jewish and Gentile believers (Eph 2:14–3:6). After his death and resurrection, Jesus would gather together into one flock all the children of God who had been scattered over the face of the earth (John 11:52).

10:17-18 *The reason my Father loves me is that I lay down my life—only to take it up again.* The Father loved the Son for his willingness to die in order to secure the salvation of the believers. His was a voluntary offering for sin, and yet it was in obedience to the Father. The Father loves the Son because of the sacrifice by which he wins the sheep.

No one takes it from me, but I lay it down of my own accord. I have authority to lay it down and authority to take it up again. Jesus' death was not the demise of a captured martyr, not an accident, not the result of mob violence, not that of a helpless victim, but the voluntary sacrifice of the omnipotent Son of God. Jesus Christ was utterly invincible. No one could take his life from him against his will. Jesus himself had the authority to lay down his life and to take it up again in resurrection. Since a dead man needs a living God to raise him from the dead, Jesus' statement means that he is God. To say, "I will raise myself from the dead" is to say, "I am God." This act of Jesus is absolutely without any analogy.

Death was the first step in his glorification process. The grain of wheat had to fall to the ground and die before it could bring forth fruit (12:23-24); Jesus had to experience resurrection himself before he could impart resurrection life to others—before he could give his sheep the "abundant life" he promised them. As risen Lord he can fully care for his sheep, now and forever.

This command I received from my Father. The Son's authority to lay down his life and take it up again did not originate with himself; it came from the Father.

10:19-21 *Again the Jews were divided* (NRSV). When Jesus speaks there is a division! Some of the Jews who heard him, darkened in their minds and unable to comprehend Jesus' similitude, pronounced a twofold judgment against him: *"He has a demon and is out of his mind"* (NRSV). Jesus had already been accused of being demon possessed (7:20; 8:48), but this is the first and only time in John's Gospel that Jesus is accused of being insane (lit., "he raves"). In those days the Jews believed that insanity was the result of demon possession.

Others were saying, "These are not the words of one who has a demon. Can a demon open the eyes of the blind?" (NRSV). Some other Jews in Jesus' audience were impressed with both Jesus' words and his miraculous deeds. Loving and caring for the sheep does not sound like a lunatic, nor does giving sight to a blind man seem demonic. Thus, they disagreed with those who said, "He isn't worth listening to." But they merely disagreed with the ridiculous charges hurled at Jesus; they did not affirm his divinity.

10:22 *the Feast of Dedication.* Between verses 21 and 22 there is a break of some two and a half months (from the time of the Feast of Tabernacles in October to the time of the Feast of Dedication in late December). Jesus had made his tender and wonderful offer to be the Jews' Shepherd and was rejected. He left

Jerusalem, only to return after several weeks for the Feast of Dedication. He left at the end of this discourse (10:39), not to return until the next spring, during the Feast of the Passover, where he met his death.

The Feast of Dedication was not one of the official festivals prescribed by the Pentateuch. It was instituted by Judas Maccabaeus in 165 BC to commemorate the purification of the Temple from its profanation by Antiochus Epiphanes. The festival, called Hanukkah, is held in December and lasts eight days. Similar to the Feast of Tabernacles, it was a time of great rejoicing. (For the history of this event, see 1 Macc 4:36-59; 2 Macc 1:9; 10:1-8.) Bruce writes, "To this day it is celebrated as the Feast of Lights, so called from the lighting of the lamps or candles in Jewish homes to honor the occasion."

It was winter. This added detail helps explain why Jesus was in a covered part of the Temple precincts.

10:23 *Jesus was in the temple area walking in Solomon's Colonnade.* Solomon's Colonnade (or portico) was located on the east side of the Temple; it provided a walled shield against the winter winds. The earliest Christians met in the same location (Acts 3:11; 5:12), probably because they had become accustomed to meeting there with Jesus. The expression "Jesus was walking" could mean that he was teaching as he walked, for the Greek expression *periepatei* in this context could signify peripatetic teaching—a style of teaching exemplified by Plato, wherein the teacher paced back and forth as he engaged his students in dialogue. While Jesus often taught while he walked, we also know that on occasion he sat and taught (see Matt 5:1-2), which was the usual habit of a rabbi when he instructed his students.

10:24 *So the Jews gathered around him and said to him, "How long will you keep us in suspense? If you are the Messiah, tell us plainly"* (NRSV). Jesus had never plainly told the Jews in Jerusalem that he was the Christ. He had told the Samaritan woman (4:25-26) but not the Jews, because the term "Messiah" in some minds connoted a military leader. Therefore Jesus wisely avoided using that term with the Jews. But the Jewish leaders wanted to hear an open declaration from Jesus' lips. Was he the Christ or not? It is doubtful, however, that a plain declaration would have convinced them, for they had already made up their minds on the issue. Their request was not a search for truth but a trap to catch Jesus in the act of blasphemy, as is shown by their actions a few moments later. Furthermore, Jesus purposely spoke in parables to outsiders so that an understanding of his words would depend on the reception of divine revelation, not human intelligence.

10:25 *I did tell you, but you do not believe. The miracles I do in my Father's name speak for me.* Jesus had never told them, "I am the Christ," but through parable and allegory he had clearly indicated his unity and equality with God the Father, his heavenly origin, and even his eternality. Besides, Jesus had just identified himself as "the Son of Man," a messianic term, to the healed blind man. The healed blind man had tried to convince the religious leaders not to oppose Jesus but they were hardened. Even the miraculous signs Jesus performed in their midst did not convince them that he was the Messiah. His works did not convince them, and neither would his words.

10:26-28 Jesus told the Jewish leaders surrounding him, *"You do not believe because you are not my sheep."* This could be interpreted as an explanation or a condemnation. It was a fact stated by Jesus; they could interpret as they wanted. Only those who were given to Jesus by the Father (10:29) were his sheep. Of these Jesus said, *"My sheep listen to my voice; I know them, and they follow me. I give them eternal life, and they shall never perish; no one can snatch them out of my hand."* In this grand statement, Jesus summarized the blessings of the gospel as presented in John. The believer in Jesus knows him personally, has eternal life, will not perish, and is secure in his care. In Greek, the expression "shall never perish" (*apolōntai*) means "will not experience eternal destruction." Eternal life is not futuristic. Heaven is futuristic, but eternal life is now. It is a quality of life, God's life.

10:29 *My Father, who has given them to me, is greater than all.* This statement appears in the ancient manuscripts in three ways.[3] The first, as just cited; the second, "That which the Father has given me is greater than all"; the third, "My Father, as to that which he has given me, is greater than all." Of all the readings, the first one makes the most sense and seems to be characteristically Johannine, for the Son often spoke of the Father as the one who had given various things to him (see 5:26-27; 6:37, 39; 17:2). However, the simplicity of this reading, as compared to the others, has caused it to be suspect, for what scribes would change a simple, direct reading to a very difficult one? Thus it is quite possible that John wrote the second reading. Elsewhere in his Gospel, John used the neuter singular ("that which") to designate the corporate entity of believers (which encompasses all Christians as one unit) that was given to him as a gift from the Father (see 6:37, 39; 17:2, 24). Given the context of this chapter, Jesus would be saying that this one corporate entity, which could be called the church, was given to the Son by the Father, was under the protective care of the Father's hand and the Son's hand, and would be invincible to the attack of the enemy. Therefore it would be greater than all the enemies mentioned in John 10. The third reading noted above seems to be impossible Greek, but some exegetes, such as Barrett and the NJB translators, have made sense of it and render it as noted.

  no one can snatch them out of my Father's hand. The impossibility of true believers being lost in the midst of all the temptations they may encounter does not consist in their fidelity and decision, but is founded upon the power of God.

10:30 *The Father and I are one* (NRSV). Since the word for "one" in Greek is neuter, it could be rendered "are one in purpose" (i.e., that of securing the sheep).

The oneness of purpose comes from their oneness of *essence,* also intimated by the use of the Greek neuter case. This verse is widely regarded by conservative scholars as a succinct intimation of the essential unity and personal distinctiveness of the three members of the Godhead, even though only two members are specified in the verse. Augustine was right in saying that the plural verb *esmen* (we are) condemns the Sabellians (who denied the distinction of persons in the Godhead), while the word *hen* (one) condemns the Arians (who denied the unity of their essence). No matter how we understand this bold statement, it is obvious that the Jews who heard it recognized it as a claim to deity, which to them was blasphemy. They asked for plain words, and when Jesus spoke plainly, they were enraged.

10:31-32 *Again the Jews picked up stones to stone him.* When Jesus previously made claims to unity with the Father and to eternal preexistence, the Jews' response was the same (see 5:17-18; 8:58-59): They wanted to execute this blasphemer. But Jesus restrained their violent act by asking them, *"I have shown you many great miracles from the Father. For which of these do you stone me?"* Jesus knew he would not be stoned to death, which was the form of capital punishment under Jewish law. Jesus knew that his death would be on the cross, the form of capital punishment under Roman law.

10:33 The Jews answered that they were not stoning him for any good deeds he had done, **but for blasphemy, because**, they said to him, *"you, a mere man, claim to be God,"* which could also be translated, "you, being human, make yourself deity." If the Jews in Jesus' audience clearly understood his words to constitute a claim to deity, how can modern critics say that Jesus never claimed to be God? Jesus' greatest critics have mistakenly thought that he was nothing more than a man, while his greatest enemies recognized that he was claiming to be God.

10:34-36 *Is it not written in your Law, "I have said you are gods"?* Jesus used Psalm 82:6 to counter the Jews' charge of blasphemy. (The term "law" was often used in the New Testament to encompass the entire Old Testament.) In Psalm 82 the supreme God is said to rise in judgment against those he calls "gods" (Heb., *'elohim*), even "sons of the Most High," because they had failed to extend just equity to the helpless and oppressed. These "gods" were those who were the official representatives and commissioned agents of God; they were the judges executing judgment for God. But God would execute judgment against them.

If he called them "gods," to whom the word of God came—and the Scripture cannot be broken—what about the one whom the Father set apart as his very own and sent into the world? Why then do you accuse me of blasphemy because I said, "I am God's Son"? Jesus argued that it was not blasphemous to call himself the Son of God when, in fact, he was the one the Father sanctified and sent into the world. The judges of Israel, to whom the word of God came, represented God and therefore were called "gods." The Jews could not argue against this because it stands written in the irrefragable Scriptures (i.e., the Scriptures are an entire entity from which no one can excise any individual portion). Jesus was greater than those men who received messages from God, for he himself was the very message from God to men. Whereas they were earthly men selected by God to represent him, the Son of God came from heaven as the sanctified one (i.e., set apart from all earthly things) to fully represent the heavenly God. The Word of God, who was God himself sent into the world to become man, was therefore justified in calling himself the Son of God.

10:37-39 *even though you do not believe me, believe the miracles.* There was in Christ's person, independent of any miracles, a self-evidencing truth, which, to those who had any spiritual perceptibility, should have produced faith. But for those who lacked this faith, the works were a mighty help.

that you may know and understand. According to excellent documentary support,[4] the verse contains the Greek words for "know" twice, in two tenses: aorist and present, suggesting inceptive knowledge and continuous knowledge. This knowledge depends on revelation.

that the Father is in me, and I in the Father. This reiterates Jesus' claim to essential oneness with the Father. The oneness of the Son and the Father is described by John in terms of mutual indwelling. Jesus' explanations did not change the Jews' minds; they were intent on stoning him for blasphemy. But when they attempted to arrest him, *he escaped their grasp.*

10:40-42 *He went away again across the Jordan to the place where John had been baptizing earlier* (NRSV). Jesus went to the east side of the Jordan, in Perea (see 1:28). He would not return to Jerusalem again until the day he made his triumphant entry.

Many came to him, and they were saying, "John performed no sign, but everything that John said about this man was true" (NRSV). Many of the people in this region had heard John the Baptist preaching a few years earlier, proclaiming the coming of the Messiah. His words had left a permanent impression on them and had properly prepared them for the coming of the Messiah. As a result, when Jesus came, *many believed in him* (NRSV). John the Baptist never performed a miracle, lest people think he was the Messiah. (In this regard, John was different from Elijah.) When Jesus came, performing miracles and speaking the words of God, the people were ready to accept him as the Messiah.

ENDNOTES

[1] Only one Greek manuscript (𝔓75) reads, "I am the shepherd," while all other Greek manuscripts read, "I am the door."

[2] The words "before me" are found in 𝔓66 ℵ^C A B D L W, but not in 𝔓45^vid 𝔓75 ℵ * and several other witnesses.

[3] 𝔓66^C and 𝔓75^vid support the first reading; B*, the second; and ℵ D L W, the third.

[4] The documentary support is found in 𝔓45 𝔓66 𝔓75 B L W.

Jesus, the Resurrection and the Life

JOHN 11:1-57

EXPOSITION

John 11, the midpoint of this Gospel, presents the apex of the Lord's ministry of life. Prior to this chapter, Jesus had presented himself as life (or the giver of life) to various people. For Nicodemus, the gift was eternal life; for the Samaritan woman, the water of life; for the invalid man, the quickening life; for the hungry multitude, the Bread of Life; for the believers in Jerusalem, the rivers of living water; for the blind man, the light of life; and for his sheep, the abundant life. Now in this chapter Jesus is life (Gr., *zōē*) in its ultimate expression—resurrection life—to a man (Lazarus) in his ultimate state, death. Here Jesus' life is shown to be the true life that conquers death. Jesus himself would experience death but then come forth in resurrection because death could not subdue the eternal life of God embodied in Jesus. The living one who raised Lazarus from the dead said, "I am the resurrection and the life. Those who believe in me, even though they die, will live" (11:25, NRSV). Lazarus died, and Jesus raised him. This resurrection became a sign of Jesus' ultimate life-giving power and a prefiguring of Jesus' resurrection to come.

The resurrection of Lazarus is the greatest miraculous sign in the Gospel of John. It is the fitting climax of all the previous signs. Jesus turned water into wine, healed a sick young man, cured an invalid, miraculously fed five thousand, healed a man born blind, and then raised a man from the dead. It is this miracle, done in the presence of so many people from nearby Jerusalem, that aroused the multitude's excitement about Jesus and caused them to give him such an enthusiastic welcome when he made his Triumphal Entry.

The synoptic Gospels, in not including an account of the raising of Lazarus, fail to provide any background information for the surprising Triumphal Entry. Out of nowhere, it seems, Jesus enters Jerusalem and is suddenly welcomed by the masses. Why didn't the synoptic writers include an account of Lazarus's resurrection? It could be conjectured that they purposely omitted any mention of Lazarus, because the Jewish leaders discussed killing Lazarus (see 12:10). And so to protect Lazarus (who must have been still living from AD 50 to 70 if our theory is correct), they did not include his story. But by the time John wrote his Gospel (c. AD 85), Lazarus must have died. So John had the freedom to record this event that is so significant to Jesus' ministry and so critical to providing a complete narrative.

11:1-45/*The Raising of Lazarus*

We are approaching the last days of our Lord's earthly life. As the scene opens in this chapter, we look in on a godly home located in Bethany, which was two miles from Jerusalem. Bethany could be known for a great many things, but in God's record this village was known as the town of Mary and Martha. There were many who lived there, but to Jesus—to God himself—it was the town of Mary and Martha. In this particular home three devoted hearts believed Jesus, and that meant more to God than all the other notable things for which Bethany might be known.

When God thinks of your city, does he pass by the famous, the influential, the powerful, and looking at your residence, say to the angels, "There is one of my choice servants, one who really loves me and in whose home I am honored"? Jesus especially liked to visit that home in Bethany. It wasn't the great meals prepared by Martha or the comforts provided by Lazarus that attracted Jesus to that home. It wasn't creature comforts; it was relationships. He enjoyed their hospitality because they loved him and had a great desire to learn from him. We do well to ask ourselves, If Jesus came to my town, would he want to come to my house? Would he feel comfortable? Would I?

When common events turn bad. One day while Jesus was on a preaching tour, Lazarus became ill. Maybe it was a cold that turned into severe influenza, or some other minor malady that turned into something very serious. Sickness is a common experience. Some believe that all sickness is an error of the mind, but we know that is not true. Some believe that all sickness is the direct result of personal sin, but we know that is not true. Some of the choicest Christians in the world have been invalids and suffered much pain, while some of the most wicked men have enjoyed robust health. For those believers who struggle with illness in this life, we have God's own promise that in heaven there will be no sickness and no pain.

Sickness often comes as a blessing in disguise. It may give us a truer perspective of things transitory and things eternal. For this and many other reasons, devoted saints have believed that sickness is often sent for our own good. It may have nothing to do with divine discipline, but rather is lovingly purposeful and allowed by God. Such was the case with Lazarus. His illness was for the glory of God.

Whatever Lazarus's symptoms, it became apparent to his sisters that the situation was deteriorating rapidly and his condition was very serious. All of a sudden events were beyond human control. Mary and Martha desperately sent a message to Jesus, a message that was very brief, very urgent, very personal: "Lord, the one you love is sick." Amazingly they didn't tell Jesus what to do! They didn't ask him to hurry to the bedside of their brother or beg him to offer a prayer on Lazarus's behalf. They knew Jesus loved Lazarus and that he would do what was best. When our situation is confusing and desperate and events have turned bad, when we don't know what to ask for in our prayers, we should simply, earnestly, believingly say, "Lord, you know the situation; do what is best for me and what will bring glory to you."

When it seems God doesn't care. It took the messenger at least one day to reach Jesus, and when he arrived, Jesus said, "This sickness will not end in death. No, it is for God's glory." This statement did not mean that Lazarus would not die. As a matter of fact, Lazarus was already dead when the messenger arrived. The words of Jesus meant that death was not the final word. Its victory was only temporary, for out of the death of Lazarus would come glory to God and a greater happiness for that little family in Bethany because many would come to believe in Christ.

Incredible as it may seem, Jesus did not rush to Bethany to be with those he loved. He stayed where he was for yet another two days. By this time the messenger had returned. Mary and Martha must have been greatly disappointed. The days that Lazarus was dead must have been the longest, most excruciating days these two sisters ever experienced. They probably were overcome with the terrible perception that apparently Jesus didn't care! They were no doubt experiencing what we feel when it seems there is no answer to our prayers. Events around us seem disastrous, and we pray earnestly for God to help us, but it seems that he remains aloof. May the Lord give to each of us godly patience and peace as we wait for his timing and good pleasure.

In accordance with his own timetable, Jesus arrived at Bethany. Martha ran out to meet him, saying, "Lord, if only you had been here." The same thought is expressed by many believers today—*Lord, if you had been here, this tragedy, this accident, this disaster would not have happened!* But we must forever keep in mind that he *is* here with us. His angels do keep watch. He knows our situation better than we know it. He has not left us nor abandoned us as orphans. He cares; he loves; he keeps.

"Martha," said Jesus, "it's not all over when death comes. This isn't the end of the story. There is going to be a resurrection. Your brother will rise again!"

"I know, I know," replied Martha, "in that last day, we shall rise again, but that still doesn't take away the pain, the sorrow I feel right now."

Then Jesus made one of the most marvelous pronouncements ever spoken. "I am the resurrection and the life. He who believes in me, even though he dies, will live." That is a simple sentence, but we always want to mentally add a word to it . . . *again.* Jesus was telling Martha that those who believe in him, though they die—by all appearances as interpreted in this earthly level—they are not dead; they are alive. That is the great gospel declaration. That is the believer's hope. It is not life *again* after some interminable period, but life now, in Christ Jesus. Life without interval. Life forever.

Evangelist Dwight L. Moody has been quoted many times, but it bears repeating: "Someday you will read in the papers that D. L. Moody of East Northfield is dead. Don't you believe a word of it. At that moment I shall be more alive than now. I shall have gone up higher, that is all—out of this clay tenement into a house that is immortal; a body that death cannot touch, that sin cannot taint, a body fashioned like unto his glorious body. That which is born of the Spirit will live forever."

When Christ doesn't respond as expected. Having been told by Martha that Jesus had arrived, Mary went out to the pathway to meet him. She was weeping, and the many Jews with her were weeping. When Jesus observed all this emotion, he groaned as if he was in deep pain; he stood in the presence of death. Death is the ultimate result of sin. Contemplating this indignation, anger surged through him at the human misery and pain resulting from mankind's sin, causing death, broken hearts, and unrelenting sorrow. It is a remarkable revelation of the emotions of Jesus as he voluntarily identifies with the sorrow that comes from sin. He wept! Tears ran down his face. But his tears and those of the Jews were different. Theirs were a wailing, a moaning, an expression of grief. His were the tears of sympathy for Martha and Mary and resentment at all the sorrow caused by sin and death.

As they arrived at the grave site, Jesus was weeping, Mary and Martha were weeping, the Jews were wailing, and Jesus said, "Take away the stone!" Immediately all grew quiet. Mary and Martha had no idea what Jesus might do next, but they certainly didn't expect him to do this! His response to the situation completely baffled them. In fact, they may even have momentarily thought that Jesus was disoriented. "Lord, do you know what you are doing? You surely do not mean to open up that tomb. We had expected you to come and heal Lazarus, not to open a grave!" Sometimes we fail immediately to see the answer to our prayers because we fully expect Jesus to respond in a certain manner. We have it all planned just how God must respond to our situation. We limit God, who desires to do more than we can ask or think.

All was quiet. When the weeping and wailing ceased, the crowd heard Jesus praying to the Father. He was praying for their benefit, wanting them to realize that he and the Father are one, and the miracle he was about to perform he was doing because he is the source of life.

Then, when the stone was removed, Jesus cried with a loud voice, "Lazarus, come out!" He spoke to someone who could hear him. Lazarus was not dead. Dwight L. Moody said that if Jesus hadn't used the name of Lazarus, he would have emptied the graveyard that day. Someday, he shall cry with a loud voice across the face of this earth, "Come out," and the sea and the land shall give up their dead.

Jesus gave the startled bystanders something to do. He said, "Take off the graveclothes and let him go." Was this a resurrection? Yes, but not like Jesus' resurrection. In this instance Jesus called the spirit back to the body. Lazarus was held by grave wrappings. When Jesus was resurrected, grave bindings could not hold him. And on that day when the dead in Christ shall rise, graveclothes, caskets, vaults, cement, marble, or earth shall not hold us.

This certainly wasn't what Mary and Martha expected, but they greatly rejoiced. And the Word of God says that because of this miracle, many believed in Jesus.

KEY WORDS AND PHRASES

This chapter is filled with language about death and resurrection. Here are Jesus' words:

» "Lazarus has fallen asleep; but I am going there to wake him up." (11:11)
» "Your brother will rise again." (11:23)
» "I am the resurrection and the life." (11:25)
» "He who believes in me will live, even though he dies." (11:25)
» "Lazarus, come out!"—The dead man came out (11:43-44).

NOTES

11:1-2 *Now a certain man was ill, Lazarus of Bethany, the village of Mary and her sister Martha* (NRSV). Of all Jesus' acquaintances, none were so dear to him as Lazarus, Mary, and Martha. They were his intimate friends who provided him with hospitality on his visits to Jerusalem, since Bethany was a village just outside of Jerusalem (see comments on 12:1).

Mary was the one who anointed the Lord with perfume and wiped his feet with her hair (NRSV). In keeping with Jesus' prediction (Matt 26:13), this Mary was well known in the Christian community because of her display of love and devotion to Jesus (Matt 26:6-13; Mark 14:3-9). Therefore, John identified her with this event even before he described it (12:1-7).

11:3 *So the sisters sent word to Jesus, "Lord, the one you love is sick."* John used the Greek word *phileis* for "love" to signify that Jesus was very fond of Lazarus. Though Lazarus is mentioned only in John 11–12, this verse and 11:5 show that Lazarus had been a friend of Jesus. This verse also shows that Mary, Martha, and Lazarus must have stayed in constant touch with Jesus and tracked his whereabouts, for they knew where to send the message.

11:4 *When he heard this, Jesus said, "This sickness will not end in death. No, it is for God's glory."* The Greek preposition *pros* (translated "for") is significant here, for it suggests direction. Lazarus's sickness did not point to death as its ultimate end; Lazarus was not headed for death. Rather, his sickness was for another purpose: the glory of God. In other words, when Jesus heard of Lazarus's sickness, he knew it would lead to death, but not to absolute death, because his friend's death would be the means through which the glory of God would be manifested. Yet we all would ask, "How could the compassionate Messiah ignore the needs of one of his friends?" As in many of our own trying experiences of life, the answer lay in what follows: *that God's Son may be glorified through it.* As in the case of the blind beggar who was healed (9:1-5, 24-38), alleviating human suffering often gives God greater glory than the everyday blessings we enjoy (Matt 5:45).

11:5-6 *Jesus loved Martha and her sister and Lazarus* (NRSV). This parenthetical statement serves two purposes: (1) it affirms Jesus' love for each member of the family, and (2) it serves to explain that it was not lack of love that kept Jesus from going to them. Humanly speaking, Jesus would have wanted to go to them immediately, but he was constrained by the Father's timing (see following comments).

after having heard that Lazarus was ill, he stayed two days longer in the place where he was (NRSV). Lazarus had been dead for four days by the time Jesus arrived in Bethany. Reconstructing the events, it seems clear that the messenger(s) must have taken at least one day to reach Jesus; Jesus remained where he was for two days; and he must have taken a day to reach Bethany. Therefore, Lazarus must have died even before they found Jesus and shortly after they left Bethany. Even had he left immediately, Jesus could not have arrived in Bethany soon enough to prevent Lazarus's death.

11:7-8 *Then he said to his disciples, "Let us go back to Judea."* The disciples could not believe what they heard. Why would their teacher want to go into Judea again when the Jews there had just recently attempted *to stone* him?

11:9-10 *Are there not twelve hours of daylight?* Our Lord's "day" (i.e., his time on earth) was now reaching its final hour. In this twilight hour of his ministry on earth, some would still be given the chance to be enlightened and believe.

A man who walks by day will not stumble, for he sees by this world's light. On one level this refers to the actual sunlight of the physical world. Jesus' time to walk in the sunlight was now growing short, less than thirty days. He still had work to do before his death. On another level "this world's light" refers to Christ's presence among people. While he was among men, he was their light. "Men should make the most of the presence of Christ, the light of the world. For when he is withdrawn from them there is no possibility of their 'walking' without stumbling" (Morris). For the Christian, following Christ is to be walking in the day (light), and there should be no fear of stumbling or losing one's way.

11:11-14 *Our friend Lazarus has fallen asleep, but I am going there to awaken him* (NRSV). Just as the beaming rays of the sun awaken a man from slumber, the Light of Life was going to awaken Lazarus from his "sleep." The disciples missed the meaning of this euphemism for death. *"Lord, if he has fallen asleep, he will be all right"* (NRSV). It is amazing that these disciples never seem to mature.

Even after three years with Jesus, they are ready to argue with him! But then *Jesus told them plainly, "Lazarus is dead"* (NRSV).

11:15 *and for your sake I am glad I was not there.* This suggests that Jesus would not have allowed Lazarus to die if he had been present. Had Lazarus not died, the disciples and others would have missed a most important lesson, that is, the truth about the resurrection. Jesus allowed Lazarus to die to demonstrate his power over death.

that you may believe. They already "believed" (2:11), and here Jesus knows they will believe even more. We have noted already that in John's Gospel the point is made respectfully that belief is a growing experience.

11:16 Thomas missed the meaning of Jesus' words and volunteered all the disciples for what he thought was sure suicide: *"Let us also go, that we may die with him"* (NRSV). This is a remarkable statement by Thomas. He is remembered as the doubter, but here he is saying, in effect, if we go to Bethany, it means death. The irony is that the disciples deserted Jesus when he was arrested, tried, and crucified.

11:17-19 *When Jesus arrived, he found that Lazarus had already been in the tomb four days* (NRSV). Jesus was never pushed by events. He was always in charge. He kept a divine schedule. When he arrived in Bethany, there were already many people from Jerusalem there for the purpose of consoling Lazarus's family. Since Bethany is about two miles from Jerusalem, it was convenient for many to come from the city to grieve with Mary and Martha. Thus the stage was set for Jesus to perform the miracle of resurrection, not just before a few close friends, but also in the presence of many Jews from Jerusalem.

11:20-24 *Martha . . . went out to meet him, but Mary stayed at home.* Martha, as the older sister, was the head of the household; it was quite natural for her to be the first to go out to meet Jesus. She also may have been watching, waiting for his arrival. Mary remained in the house, mourning. This description of the differences in the two sisters accords with the record in Luke 10:38-42. Upon seeing Jesus, Martha said to him, *"Lord, . . . if you had been here, my brother would not have died."* This is not a rebuke as much as it is a plea, very likely spoken by Martha and Mary many times after Lazarus's death. It is often on the lips of modern believers, "If only Jesus were here in the flesh. . . ." Martha was confident that Jesus' presence would have prevented her brother's death. Mary makes the same comment later (11:32). Yet Martha seemed to believe that Jesus could even now bring their brother back to life: *"But I know that even now God will give you whatever you ask."* Martha did not take her own suggestion very seriously, for when Jesus replied with a simple affirmative answer (*"Your brother will rise again"*), she attributed it to the future resurrection—*the resurrection at the last day.* She believed in a future resurrection event, but her response in 11:39-40 also shows that she did not believe Jesus could raise Lazarus from the dead.

11:25 I am the resurrection and the life. Martha was thinking of an event; Jesus revealed that he, a person, is the resurrection and the life. You must believe in Jesus, not an event. Belief in Jesus separates the believer from those who vaguely believe in "an afterlife." All will be resurrected, but only those who believe in Jesus will be resurrected to life eternal. Life that is really life (1 Tim 6:19) is by its very nature resurrection life because it can stand the trial of death. Only one kind of life—the life of God (Eph 4:18), the indissoluble life (Heb 7:16), designated *zōē* in the New Testament—is truly life. All else that is called life eventually dies. Jesus is this *zōē* life; therefore he is also the resurrection (cf. Rev 1:18).

11:26 whoever lives and believes in me will never die. Lit., "will not die into the age"; i.e., will not experience death that lasts forever. Eternal life is not a gift given beyond the grave. Those who believe in Christ have eternal life now. Lazarus had been a believer in Jesus; therefore even though he died, he would live. He, and every believer, is spared from eternal death. Christ did not promise the prevention of physical death; he promised the life that guarantees resurrection and eternal life. Christ did not prevent the death of Lazarus, but he would guarantee his eternal life.

11:27 I believe. In the Greek, it's in the perfect tense, "I have believed." The perfect tense indicates that her past belief was still very much present. Even though she found it difficult to believe that Jesus could raise Lazarus from the dead at that moment, she still believed that Jesus was **the Christ, the Son of God, who was to come into the world.** "Like Andrew, she confessed him as the Messiah (1:41); like Nathanael, she confessed him as the Son of God (1:49). He was the one whose coming Moses and the prophets foretold (1:45); now he had come" (Bruce). Martha's confession, a high point in John's Gospel, shows us a believer recognizing that Jesus is the Christ, the Son of God. John wrote this Gospel to promote exactly this kind of faith (see 20:30-31).

11:28-31 she went back and called her sister Mary aside. "The Teacher is here," she said, "and is asking for you." The Gospel writers sometimes leave gaps, and here is one—we don't have the request of Jesus to speak to Mary. It would have been great if Martha had said, "The resurrection and the life has come and called you!" *That* was the truth Jesus was trying to convey. Martha spoke to Mary secretly so that the visiting Jews would not follow her to where Jesus was— somewhere outside the village, perhaps at the cemetery. However, when Mary **got up quickly and went to him**, she was followed by the entourage of mourners, since in Jewish society prolonged mourning for the dead was considered an essential part of every funeral.

11:32 Lord, if you had been here, my brother would not have died. Mary repeated Martha's statement. Perhaps it was said as only a close personal friend might speak. No one else approached Jesus on such intimate terms.

11:33-34 *When Jesus saw her weeping, and the Jews who came with her also weeping, he was greatly disturbed in spirit and deeply moved* (NRSV). The Greek word for "deeply moved" can also be rendered "agitated" or "indignantly angered." This Greek verb is consistently used in the Septuagint and New Testament to express anger or agitation (see Lam 2:6; Dan 11:30 LXX; Matt 9:30; Mark 1:43; 14:5). Jesus may have been angry and agitated by the mourners with their excessive sorrow, Martha's lack of understanding, Mary's faithlessness, and the general unbelief, or he may have been angry at what death does to families, friends, and life itself.

11:35 *Jesus wept.* Lit., "Jesus shed tears," or taken as an ingressive aorist, "Jesus began to cry." What made Jesus cry? Was it his love for Lazarus? Was it the presence of sadness and death? Or was it the faithless grief that surrounded him? Whatever the reason, the situation caused Jesus to shed some tears.

11:36-37 The Jews interpreted Jesus' tears as a sign of Jesus' great love for Lazarus: *"See how much he loved him!"* Their interpretation was only partially correct. Then some of them, following Martha and Mary, also asked the question, *"Could not he who opened the eyes of the blind man have kept this man from dying?"* Now the crowd adds to the intensity and pressure of the moment. Their question is the same as that of Mary and Martha, but not in the same spirit.

11:38-39 *Jesus, once more deeply moved* [the same word used in 11:33— "angered"] *came to the tomb.* Lazarus was buried in *a cave with a stone laid across the entrance.* This burial spot was similar to the one in which Jesus was buried. (This type of burial indicated wealth, which was not true of Jesus. His was a borrowed tomb.) When Jesus asked that the stone be removed, Martha protested, saying, *"But, Lord, . . . by this time there is a bad odor, for he has been there four days."* Martha wondered why Jesus would want to view the body.

11:40 *Did I not tell you that if you believed, you would see the glory of God?* The whole event was for Jesus to exhibit the glorious power of God, which is what Jesus promised from the moment he heard about Lazarus's sickness.

11:41-42 *Father, I thank you for having heard me. I knew that you always hear me, but I have said this for the sake of the crowd standing here, so that they may believe that you sent me* (NRSV). While the crowd waited beside the tomb—now with the stone rolled away from its entrance—Jesus glorified his Father publicly so that, upon seeing the miracle of resurrection, the people might recognize that Jesus had been sent by God and then believe in him. It was not a public prayer as such, but more an intimate word with the Father spoken out loud.

11:43-46 *Jesus called in a loud voice, "Lazarus, come out!"* Lazarus's resurrection provides proof of Jesus' earlier words: "The dead will hear the voice of the Son of God and those who hear will live" (5:25). Then *the dead man came out,* completely wrapped in his graveclothes. There was no question that a dead man had risen from the grave. Because of this stunning miracle, *many of the Jews who had come to visit Mary, and had seen what Jesus did, put their faith in* Jesus as the Messiah, which was the purpose of the miracle. Yet in the presence of such an outstanding miracle, other Jewish onlookers did not believe. Their reaction was to go back to Jerusalem and report what they saw to the Pharisees, who did not believe in Jesus and who were seeking to destroy him (see following comments).

11:47-48 *Then the chief priests and the Pharisees called a meeting of the Sanhedrin.* The Sanhedrin was composed of seventy-one members: the high priest presiding over seventy religious leaders, the majority being Sadducees and the minority, Pharisees. This was a powerful religious council governing the religious and political affairs of the Jews. The council feared that if they permitted Jesus to *go on like this, everyone will believe in him, and then the Romans will come and take away both* their *place and . . . nation.* If all the Jewish populace would hail Jesus as their Messiah-King, the leaders feared that the Romans would take away their limited privileges of self-rule, as well as take away what the leader called "our place"—an expression that could refer to their political position(s) or to the Temple (cf. Acts 6:13; 21:28), the center of their religious life. They feared that their limited autonomy would be taken away because it would appear to the Romans that Jesus had created an uprising in Israel. Talk about false shepherds! They were not going to let a Messiah mess up their power structure. The common people gave loyalty, respect, and allegiance to these religious leaders, but if the people followed a Messiah, the leaders could lose their control. Forty years later in AD 70, a Jewish insurgence against Rome culminated in the destruction of Jerusalem and the Temple and the expulsion of the Jews from their homeland. By the time John wrote his Gospel, this had already occurred.

11:49-53 *Caiaphas, who was high priest that year* (NRSV). The expression "that year" refers to that one momentous year in which Jesus was crucified; it does not mean that Caiaphas served as a high priest for only one year. In fact, he served for eighteen years, from AD 18 to 36.

"You know nothing at all! You do not understand that it is better for you to have one man die for the people than to have the whole nation destroyed" (NRSV). Caiaphas's words clearly indicate that he was convinced that nothing short of murdering Jesus would save the nation of Israel from Roman destruction. But the next statements, inserted by John, show that God used Caiaphas as high priest to utter a prediction about the worldwide efficacy of Christ's death.

He did not say this on his own, but being high priest that year he prophesied that Jesus was about to die for the nation, and not for the nation only, but to gather into one the dispersed children of God (NRSV). For Caiaphas, this was an unconscious prophecy. He was saying to the Sanhedrin, "Our problem is one man. If we let him continue, we'll lose everything. Therefore he must die, and our nation will be safe." The irony is, Caiaphas was talking about the nation of

Israel being saved from the wrath of Rome, while the prophecy—as John turns it—is that Jesus will die for people all over the world so they could be saved from God's wrath! Whereas Caiaphas thought this death would save Israel from destruction and dispersion at the hands of the Romans, Jesus' death actually would be for the spiritual salvation of Israel and of all the world. The further irony is that Israel would experience the great Diaspora (scattering) in AD 70 as a result of the destruction of Jerusalem, whereas Jesus' death (and subsequent resurrection, which is here implied) would bring about the gathering together (as opposed to scattering) of all God's children, both Jews and Gentiles, who had come to believe in Jesus as the Messiah. The readers of this Gospel would have known about the destruction of Jerusalem and the Diaspora, so they would have understood the irony here. The Jewish leaders at the time, however, missed the prophetic import of Caiaphas's statement and immediately began plotting **to put him to death** (NRSV).

11:54 Aware of the plot against his life, Jesus (with his disciples) **withdrew to a region near the desert, to a village called Ephraim.** Most commentators identify this place as Ophrah, near Bethel, in the hill country east of the Jordan (see 2 Chr 13:19). Jesus remained there until the time of the Passover celebration.

11:55-57 When it was almost time for the Jewish Passover, many went up from the country to Jerusalem for their ceremonial cleansing before the Passover. Most commentators think this is the Passover that occurred in AD 30, the year of Jesus' death. The Jewish people were lawfully preparing themselves for the Passover (cf. Exod 12:14-20; 13:1-9). However, the people's thoughts were not on the Passover but on Jesus—and what would happen if he came to Jerusalem for the Passover. Everyone knew that **the chief priests** ("chief priests" were of the Aaronic priesthood line) **and Pharisees** wanted to **arrest him**, and everyone knew that they were to report his whereabouts if he was discovered. The scene was set for Jesus' entry into Jerusalem. But before he would go there for his final visit, he would stop by Bethany to visit his friends Lazarus, Martha, and Mary.

Jesus, Received yet Rejected

JOHN 12:1-50

EXPOSITION

John 12 is the epitome of paradox concerning the people's reaction to Jesus. In this chapter he is seemingly received but actually rejected, seemingly believed but actually disbelieved, seemingly honored but actually hunted. Of course, this paradox pertains to the greater picture of all the Jews in Judea, not to each and every Jew, because there were those who really loved him.

Among those who loved him most were his friends at Bethany. In a world that would not welcome him, among his own people who would not receive him and, moreover, who were plotting to kill him, how comforting it must have been for him to have a place of privacy, rest, and love. In Bethany, in the home of Martha, Mary, and Lazarus, Jesus' friends were there to receive him and serve him (see Luke 10:38).

12:1-8/*Love's Extravagance*

The twelfth chapter of John serves to close the story of our Lord's public ministry and to introduce the narrative of his death. The three main incidents recorded all have a bearing one way or another upon the subject of his impending demise. Whether we look at the devotion of his friends, the spiritually hungry foreigners, or the murderous envy of the chief priests, each episode illuminates the ultimate purpose of Christ's advent. Knowing what lay before him, the awful horror and darkness of soul as he bore our sins, Jesus longed for human fellowship with those who loved him. This may be one reason why he returned to Bethany and his closest friends in the final week of his life.

The gratitude of sinners. The friends of Jesus planned a wonderful supper for him. In Matthew's account (Matt 26:6) we read that this dinner was held in the home of Simon the Leper, who was no longer a leper, an outcast, a derelict of society having to cry out, "Unclean, unclean!" whenever anyone approached. One day Simon the Leper had met Jesus and was changed forever. We have all been affected with the leprosy of sin—utterly unclean and lost. It is a wonderful day when by faith we meet Jesus and he says, "Be clean," and all our sins are removed from us. What a wonderful moment that is. So in great appreciation, Simon the

Leper prepared a dinner party for Jesus and his disciples, Mary, Martha, and Lazarus. At least seventeen people were at the party, and before the evening was finished, some interesting attitudes and actions were displayed. Simon hosted, Martha served, Mary worshiped, Lazarus fellowshiped, the disciples grumbled, and Judas found fault.

Martha served, and it was not grudging service this time. In Luke's record (Luke 10:40), she once prepared a meal for a few people and was decidedly upset. Here she is cooking and serving a small crowd, yet not a word about being distracted. Perhaps she had learned something from Jesus that had settled her spirit. Now she served gladly. We do well to inspect our attitudes behind our service for Jesus Christ. May it always be in gladness and joy.

Lazarus sat with Jesus. It is amazing that we do not have one recorded word from Lazarus. Did the disciples ask him, "What was it like being absent from the body?" Surely someone would want to know more about his experience, but nothing is recorded for our satisfaction. Lazarus was fellowshiping with Jesus, a tiny prefigurement of that great marriage supper of the Lamb when we, his bride, shall be gathered with him forever.

The gift of Mary. Sometime during the meal, Mary came and bowed at the feet of Jesus in adoration and worship. The life of Mary is painted for us in three memorable scenes, in each of which she is found at the feet of Jesus. She is seated at his feet listening to his word (Luke 10:39). She had fallen at his feet, seeking sympathy and help (John 11:32). Here she is anointing his feet to express her devotion and love. On another occasion Mary was contrasted with Martha, who was disgruntled (Luke 10:40). But here she is contrasted with Judas, whose motive was deceit and thievery.

Because of her love and devotion to Jesus, Mary took some very costly perfume and, breaking the seal, poured the entire contents on Jesus in an unparalleled act of worship, love, and sacrifice. The perfume, "genuine, expensive spikenard," represented a year's wages, or the savings of a lifetime! No synthetic or substitution could ever match the fragrance or the expense of spikenard. After pouring the costly myrrh on his feet, Mary began to wipe off the excess with her hair. Certainly she was totally unconscious of those present, in her adoration and her preoccupation with his impending death. The unsaved cannot understand such reverence. Judas couldn't!

The grumbling of Judas. Judas quickly reckoned the value of the ointment and concluded that such a gift was too expensive to waste on Jesus. He, of all the disciples, seemed to know the value of such a gift. The others might have recognized the perfume as expensive; he knew exactly what it cost. He had so accustomed himself to gauge things in terms of money that spiritual values were unreal to him. His horizons were so narrowed and bounded by money that he had no place left for love's expressions of devotion and sacrifice. Christ's estimates of gifts are not according to market value. He once declared to the disciples that the poor widow's offering of half a cent in the Temple was more than the gifts of the wealthy that day, because her gift bore the hallmark of sacrifice (Luke 21:1-4).

Judas said, "Why was this fragrant oil not sold for three hundred denarii and given to the poor?" (12:5, NKJV). The *first* words of Judas recorded in the Gospels reveal his true character—a heart filled with criticism and a spirit dominated by money. In fact, Judas was so consumed with money that he became first a thief and then a traitor for the sake of money. Mary's veneration focused attention on the Lord, while Judas attempted to turn people's thoughts from Christ to condemnation of Mary's actions. Judas had no love for the poor—his hypocrisy is made clear by the divine record. He wanted the money put in a common purse so he could steal it. The Word of God says that Judas was a thief, and we might well rejoice that Christ allows his money to be taken from him, but never his sheep!

Mary's worship clashed with Judas's critical censorship. Her heart had been touched by heaven's love, and in a reciprocal action, she had to demonstrate her dedication to Jesus. Love begets love.

There are some things we can do almost any time, and there are some things we never do unless we grasp the opportunity when it arises. Only once did Mary have this opportunity to offer her alabaster jar, and she did not count the cost. We all have, as it were, an alabaster jar—something precious—that we can unreservedly give to Christ. Streams of mercy flow with the breaking of our alabaster cruse and pouring out of what we have for Jesus. The most precious gift is ourselves, poured out in living sacrifice for the Lord Jesus, who loved us and gave himself for us.

KEY WORDS AND PHRASES

In this chapter, the last record in John of Jesus' public ministry, there are many intimations of Jesus' imminent death:

» Speaking of Mary's anointing, Jesus said she did it "for the day of my burial" (12:7).

» At the height of glory during the Triumphal Entry into Jerusalem, Jesus predicted his death—"Unless a kernel of wheat falls to the ground and dies, it remains only a single seed. But if it dies, it produces many seeds" (12:24).

» Shortly thereafter, Jesus' "heart is troubled," and he spoke of his coming "hour"—the hour of his trial and crucifixion (12:27).

» Jesus spoke of the impending judgment on this world that is concurrent with his being "lifted up" on the cross (12:31-33).

» Knowing his time was short, Jesus said, "You are going to have the light just a little while longer. Walk while you have the light." (12:35).

» Jesus gave his final public appeal, urging the people to believe while they still had time (12:44-50).

NOTES

12:1 *Six days before the Passover, Jesus arrived at Bethany.* As far as we know, whenever Jesus came to Jerusalem, he did not lodge there. Rather, he would go to Bethany (about two miles away) to stay with his friends Martha, Mary, and Lazarus (see Matt 21:17; Luke 10:38). This would be his last visit with them because he would be crucified as the true Passover Lamb during the Passover celebration.

where Lazarus lived, whom Jesus had raised from the dead. Only a few weeks had gone by since Jesus had raised Lazarus from the dead. This miracle, while causing many Jews to believe in Jesus, stirred up the flames of murderous intentions in the hearts of the Jewish religious leaders. Thus Jesus had to leave the one he had raised from the dead and the ones he so dearly loved. Now he would be reunited with them in a wonderful time of fellowship before his death.

12:2 *There they gave a dinner for him. Martha served, and Lazarus was one of those at the table with him* (NRSV). John's description of Martha and Mary is consistent with that of Luke: Martha is depicted as one who serves Jesus and Mary as one who loves and worships Jesus (cf. Luke 10:38-42). Lazarus is present, but surprisingly he says nothing. In all of the Bible Lazarus does not say a word, but he is a testimony to God's power. This dinner was given in honor of Jesus. According to parallel accounts of this story (see Matt 26:6-13; Mark 14:3-6), this very significant dinner party was held in the house of Simon the Leper. He also lived in Bethany and very likely had been healed of his leprosy by Jesus.

12:3 *Mary took a pound of costly perfume made of pure nard, anointed Jesus' feet, and wiped them with her hair. The house was filled with the fragrance of the perfume* (NRSV). Mary had been keeping a very expensive, precious ointment for just such an occasion. This ointment or perfume made of nard (cf. Song of Songs 1:12; 4:14) was genuine and pure (i.e., unadulterated, unmixed); it was of the highest quality and, therefore, very expensive. Very likely this nard had been imported from the mountains of India. Since this kind of pure nard was often used to anoint kings, Mary may have been anointing Jesus as her king.

When supper was finished, she took this perfume and anointed the feet of Jesus! This action certainly surprised everyone at the meal. Even more surprising, she wiped the perfume on Jesus' feet with her hair (cf. Luke 7:38). Imagine how the whole house must have been saturated with the overpowering scent.

12:4-5 *Why wasn't this perfume sold and the money given to the poor?* It was one of the disciples, Judas Iscariot, who verbalized the offense. But according to Matthew and Mark, all the disciples were offended by Mary's extravagant waste of this expensive ointment (Matt 26:8; Mark 14:4). Maybe this judgmental attitude was based upon the fact that their lack of love was shown up by Mary's exuberant love.

It was worth a year's wages. The perfume was worth three hundred denarii. Think of the grossly poor taste of this man Judas—a guest in a home, served a gracious meal, and he carped about this "waste." What's more, he knew the price of this very costly perfume!

12:6 He did not say this because he cared about the poor but because he was a thief; as keeper of the money bag, he used to help himself to what was put into it. John provides this parenthetical explanation as to the motive behind Judas's statement. The last part of this verse can be translated "he carried the money bag" or "he took [lit., "lifted"] what was in the money bag" (i.e., he pilfered the money bag). The context favors the second rendering. John's statement gives significant insight into the character of Judas. He was a thief and really had no compassion for the poor; yet Jesus entrusted to him the common purse (see 13:29). The love of money was very likely Judas's tragic flaw, a flaw that made him susceptible to "selling out" Jesus for thirty pieces of silver. But even here Jesus did not rebuke Judas for his terrible gaucherie.

12:7-8 "Leave her alone," Jesus replied. "It was intended that she should save this perfume for the day of my burial. You will always have the poor among you, but you will not always have me." Jesus defended Mary's action. This ointment was not wasted! Yes, the money could have been given to the poor, but although they would always have the poor, they would not always have Jesus. Mary had perceived the preciousness of having him with them. Besides, her anointing would serve as a burial ointment (cf. Matt 26:12; Mark 14:8).

We doubt if anyone was truly aware that Jesus was about to die. According to the synoptic Gospels and John's record, Jesus had given his disciples plenty of warning. But his word about his death did not sink into their hearts. Who among his loved ones realized that Jesus was about to die? Did his disciples, absorbed as they were with the coming glory? Did Lazarus, recently raised from the dead? Did Martha, totally involved with her serving? Possibly Mary alone perceived the imminent death of Jesus, or perhaps she just sensed that this evening would be her last with him. Seizing the moment to express her love to him, she poured upon his feet this extremely costly perfume. Jesus was so touched with this out-pouring of affection that he declared that the report of Mary's act should always accompany the testimony of the gospel (Mark 14:9).

May we all realize how precious Jesus is—to have him with us is the best we could ask for in life. Let us seize the opportunities to show our love to him, keeping in mind that whatever our station in life, what we give to the Lord in love must be our best.

12:9-11 When the great crowd of the Jews learned that he was there [in Bethany], **they came not only because of Jesus but also to see Lazarus, whom he had raised from the dead** (NRSV). Having heard of the miracle of Lazarus's resurrection and now discovering that Jesus had returned to be with Lazarus, a large multitude of Jews from the area just had to come and see both of them. Jesus and Lazarus had become quite an attraction! Lazarus was a living testimony to Jesus' power—something every believer ought to be, for we were dead in our sins and have been raised to new life in him.

So the chief priests planned to put Lazarus to death as well, since it was on account of him that many Jews were deserting and were believing in Jesus (NRSV). The chief priests had already formulated a plan to kill Jesus (11:50-53). All they could think of was murder, and now they included Lazarus in their death warrant. Matthew 27:18 tells us that "it was out of envy" that they wanted Jesus killed. They were envious that many Jews were "deserting" or "going over" or "going away" (i.e., leaving their allegiance to Judaism and to the Jewish religious leaders) and "were believing in Jesus" (or "were beginning to put their faith in him"). The raising of Lazarus from the dead really was a pivotal point—many believed, and the opposition turned violent.

12:12-13 The day after Jesus was in Bethany, he made his Triumphal Entry into Jerusalem. The *great crowd that had come for the Feast* had *heard that Jesus was on his way to Jerusalem. They took palm branches and went out to meet him*. The stage was set for something to happen! It is almost as though revolution was in the air. The whole city was in a big stir, with thousands ready to meet Jesus on the day of the feast. The momentum was gaining before Lazarus was raised from the dead, and now it seemed the whole city was moving in Jesus' favor. No wonder the chief priests could think only of murder in their attempt to stop this man. This is as close as the Jewish people came to accepting Jesus. The national leaders did not, but a lot of defectors did. (See Ps 118:20-27 for an amazing prophecy related to this event.)

As Jesus entered, they began to shout, *"Hosanna!" "Blessed is he who comes in the name of the Lord!" "Blessed is the King of Israel!"* As they shouted "Hosanna" (Hebrew meaning "save now"), they were probably expecting that the conquering Messiah had come to save them from Roman domination. Believing that the one "who comes in the name of the Lord" was "the King of Israel" (see Ps 118:25-26; Zeph 3:15; John 1:49), the Jews were hailing the arrival of their King! Indeed, their King was coming to them—but not to inaugurate the kind of kingdom they expected.

12:14-15 *Look, your king is coming, sitting on a donkey's colt!* (NRSV). Jesus came to them in the way prophesied by Zechariah: "Behold your king is coming to you; he is just and endowed with salvation, humble and mounted on a donkey, even on a colt, the foal of a donkey" (Zech 9:9, NASB). The King, in this coming, would not be a conqueror riding on a horse or in a chariot, but a humble servant riding on a donkey. He would not be exalted to the Davidic throne, but lifted up to die on a cross. Of course, the people would never have imagined that his entrance into Jerusalem was an entrance into the throes of death. As they shouted Scriptures from Psalm 118:25-26, they probably never thought that the very same psalm (v. 22) ironically foretold that the cornerstone would be rejected by the builders.

12:16 *At first his disciples did not understand all this. Only after Jesus was glorified did they realize that these things had been written about him and that they had done these things to him.* This lack of understanding refers only to the Old Testament prediction about Jesus entering into Jerusalem on a donkey, not to the crowd's enthusiastic acceptance of King Jesus. The disciples probably accepted at the time that Jesus was being hailed as the messianic King, but they would not have understood that the Scripture foretold his entrance as such— riding into Jerusalem on a donkey as the king of Israel. After Christ's resurrection and subsequent glorification, the disciples began to reread and reflect on Old Testament Scriptures, and the Holy Spirit opened their understanding and enlightened them about what this event and others actually signified (see note on 2:22).

12:17-18 As Jesus entered, he received special accolades from *the crowd that had been with him when he called Lazarus out of the tomb. . . . It was also because they heard he had performed this sign that the crowd went to meet him* (NRSV). This statement emphasizes the superficial enthrallment that possessed most of the cheering throng. They were welcoming a miracle worker, perhaps a deliverer from Rome's bondage, but certainly not a savior from sin.

12:19 *The Pharisees* were exasperated by the scene of such exultation. Their efforts to stop Jesus had failed. He was more popular than ever. Their statement *"the whole world has gone after him"* was probably said out of frustration, but by the time John wrote this Gospel, many people all over the Greco-Roman world had become followers of Jesus. Many of these believers were Greeks—to whom he wrote this Gospel and who are mentioned in the following verses.

12:20-22 *Now there were some Greeks among those who went up to worship at the Feast. They came to Philip.* They requested an interview with Jesus. These men were either visitors from Greece, Greek-speaking Gentiles, proselytes to the Jewish religion, or God-fearing Gentiles. Whoever they were, they had very likely been among the Passover celebrants who greeted Jesus as he rode into Jerusalem on a donkey. These Greeks selected Philip, himself a visitor to Jerusalem from northern Galilee, as their emissary to Jesus, perhaps because of his Greek name (although he himself was a Jew), or perhaps just because he was standing alone and was most accessible. It seems Philip hesitated to approach Jesus with the Greeks' request, but after discussing it with **Andrew** (with whom Philip is often associated—1:41-46; 6:7-8; Mark 3:18), both of them approached Jesus together.

12:23-24 There is great irony in Jesus' response to the Greeks' request. The whole world had gone after him (12:19); even the Greeks wanted to see him (12:20).

That should have been the time for Jesus to seize the hour! But *the hour* had *come for the Son of Man to be glorified* through death and resurrection. The hour had come for him to be buried in the earth like a *kernel of wheat*. The picture of a grain of wheat dying was a very popular idiom throughout the Near East. The destiny of the seed grain was to be buried—the outer shell to die and the inner germ of life coming forth to multiply. Just as seed grain is destined to be buried in the earth, Jesus was destined to die in order to give abundant life to the world. He would forego the momentary exaltation for the eternal glory. The buried grain would eventually bring forth *many seeds*—more fruit than could have been gained had he then and there become the king of Israel on an earthly throne. Indeed, Jesus, through being lifted up on the cross, would draw all men to himself. How many have been drawn to Christ in the last two millennia! How many grains have come from that one seed! If Jesus had not died, the seed would have remained *only a single seed,* a picture of nonfulfillment. If he had not gone to the cross, he would have remained single and alone, like an unplanted grain. But his death, like a planting, brought germination and multiplication. Thus, the one grain multiplied and, in so doing, became the bread that gives life to the entire world.

12:25-26 Following Jesus' metaphor, he gives an extended response to the Greeks or anyone who would "see" him. If one would truly "see" Jesus, then one must follow him in a lived-out death to self-sufficiency. *"The man who loves his life will lose it, while the man who hates his life in this world will keep it for eternal life. Whoever serves me must follow me; and where I am, my servant also will be. My Father will honor the one who serves me."* The believer "dies" in accepting the substitutionary death of Jesus, and in that acceptance one really lives, now and eternally. This is the first place in John's Gospel where serving Jesus is mentioned. This servanthood is the lived-out expression of death to self. Servanthood is not doing things, but is an *attitude*. What a promise—those who die this way will be honored by God!

12:27 Now my soul is troubled (NRSV). Here at this emotionally great hour of his ministry—when the multitudes are acclaiming him—Jesus was not for a moment basking in earthly glory. He came not for this but to die, and this greatly troubled him. The other Gospels wait until the Garden scene to reveal his tremendous agony, but here we see the awful agony of his experience. Here and at 13:21 are the only indications in John's record that Jesus was troubled by the approaching hour.

And what should I say—"Father, save me from this hour"? No, it is for this reason that I have come to this hour (NRSV). This verse is like a window into the soul of Jesus, where we see him arguing with himself. In his humanity he would naturally shrink from the terrible ordeal ahead, yet Jesus resolutely set his face toward those final, awful events.

12:28-30 Father, glorify your name! Turning from his own agony, Jesus directed his thoughts back to the Father and to the purpose for which he had come to earth: to glorify his Father. He had glorified his Father in life; he would glorify him in death. Thus, the Father responded, *"I have glorified it, and will glorify it again."* The Father's voice was audible but not understood or correctly perceived by those standing around. This is the third instance of God affirming his Son from heaven. The first was at Jesus' baptism (Matt 3:13-17; Mark 1:9-11; Luke 3:21-22). The second was at Jesus' transfiguration (Matt 17:1-13; Mark 9:2-13; Luke 9:28-36). John records only this one.

Some thought *it had thundered;* others thought that *an angel had spoken to him.* Whatever their interpretation of the sound, it could not be denied that the phenomenon was supernatural. Jesus made it clear that he did not need this "voice" (he knew that the Father would glorify him). The voice had come for the sake of the people. Something out of the ordinary was taking place, which should have caused the people to pay attention to what Jesus was saying.

12:31 Anticipating his glorification via death and resurrection, Jesus made a proleptic proclamation: *"Now is the judgment of this world; now the ruler of this world will be driven out"* (NRSV). These are two hugely significant statements. Jesus saw the judgment of this unbelieving world and the casting out of Satan as being accomplished by his death on the cross. Not limited by time as we are, he saw this judgment as completed. The Son of God had not been sent into the world to judge the world; the world is self-condemned by its own unbelief. The Son had come to destroy the works of Satan, who, as the prince of the world, controlled the minds of men, producing unbelief. The world would be judged in the sense that Satan, the ruler of the world (see 14:30; 16:11; 2 Cor 4:4; Eph 2:2; 6:12), would be ejected from his sphere of power.

12:32-33 *"And I, when I am lifted up from the earth, will draw all people to myself." He said this to indicate the kind of death he was to die* (NRSV). As earlier (see 3:14; 8:28), Jesus again spoke of his death in terms of "being lifted up." This, a common idiom of the day, meant being hoisted up on a cross. Everyone in the crowd must have understood he was predicting how he would die (i.e., on the cross—see 12:34). But there is a double significance to the expression "lifted up": it means lifted up on the cross and lifted up in exaltation. Actually, Jesus' death on the cross was the first stage of his exaltation, and it would become a spiritual magnet, attracting all who would come to Jesus.

12:34 *We have heard from the Law that the Christ will remain forever, so how can you say, "The Son of Man must be lifted up"? Who is this "Son of Man"?* The people had heard from the Law (i.e., the Old Testament Scriptures—see 10:34) that the Messiah would live and reign forever (see Pss 72:17; 89:4, 36; 110:4; Isa 9:6-7; Ezek 37:25; Dan 7:13-14). They had believed that Jesus had been making a claim to be the Messiah by calling himself the Son of Man. But now it was difficult for them to believe he was the Messiah when he spoke of his imminent death on a cross! Because this did not at all coincide with their preconceived notions about the Messiah, they wondered if Jesus was talking about someone else when he spoke of the Son of Man. Actually, there is just as much prophecy in the Old Testament about the suffering of the Messiah as about the eternal kingdom of the Messiah. But no reader of the Old Testament would have imagined that passages such as Psalm 22 and Isaiah 53 pertained to the Messiah. The illumination on these passages came after Jesus' crucifixion. Even today people need divine enlightenment to perceive the truth about Jesus.

12:35-36 *The light is with you for a little longer. Walk while you have the light, so that the darkness may not overtake you* (NRSV). Rather than attempting to correct the people's misconceptions about the Messiah, Jesus replied with an easily understood admonition to live in "the light" while he was still with them. The enlightened ones would have realized that Jesus was the Messiah. Those walking in darkness were headed toward utter destruction, and they didn't realize it. But the ones enlightened by God would know who was among them. They had **put their trust in the light** and had **become the sons of light.** The same opportunity was available to all, but not for much longer, since Jesus was about to depart this world. The following statement affirms this both actually and symbolically: Jesus spoke these things, and he departed and **hid himself from them.** Thus Jesus concluded his public ministry. After this chapter in the Gospel of John, Jesus is depicted as being in seclusion with his disciples until the time of his arrest and crucifixion.

12:37-41 *Although he had performed so many signs in their presence, they did not believe in him* (NRSV). Jesus had performed enough signs to evoke faith in him. The greatest of all signs, raising Lazarus from the dead, should have been enough to elicit faith from all those who saw it and even heard about it, and yet the Jewish people would not believe that Jesus was the Messiah. Their unbelief was predicted by the prophet Isaiah. In the beginning of his description of the suffering Savior, Isaiah asked, *"Lord, who has believed our message, and to whom has the arm of the Lord been revealed?"* (NRSV). Isaiah 53:1 is quoted by John in 12:38, as well as by the apostle Paul (see Rom 10:16). It took revelation from God to see that the suffering Jesus was "the arm of the Lord" (i.e., the one through whom God demonstrated his power via many signs). But the Jews lacked this revelation. Why? Because it was prophesied, claimed John, who again quotes Isaiah (6:10): *"He has blinded their eyes and hardened their heart, so that they might not look with their eyes, and understand with their heart and turn—and I would heal them"* (NRSV). This quotation appears quite often in the New Testament because it provides a prophetic explanation for why the Jews did not perceive Jesus' message nor receive him as their Messiah (see Matt 13:14-15; Mark 4:12; Luke 8:10; Acts 28:26-27). The Isaiah passage does not necessarily mean that the Jews were fated to be incapable of belief, but simply that their unbelief was predicted (Bruce). As a consequence, the Jews remained unenlightened, hardened, imperceptive, unturned, and not healed. They had not seen what Isaiah saw. ***Isaiah said this because he saw his*** [Jesus'] ***glory and spoke about him*** (NRSV). Isaiah had seen the Lord of glory, who is none other than Jesus, and because of his vision, Isaiah predicted the blindness to come. This blindness of Israel was only in part, as some did respond to the light.

12:42-43 ***Yet at the same time many even among the leaders believed in him. But because of the Pharisees they would not confess their faith for fear they would be put out of the synagogue; for they loved praise*** [lit., "glory"] ***from men more than praise*** [lit., "glory"] ***from God.*** John did not specifically identify these leaders, but since the same word (i.e., "leader") is used of Nicodemus in 3:1, we can infer that these men were societal leaders—the rich, the powerful, and the influential. Several of these men had come to have some kind of faith in Jesus but were afraid to make an open confession of this faith lest the Pharisees expel them from the synagogue. We could call such believers "secret believers," such as were Nicodemus and Joseph of Arimathea (19:38-39), or we could say that these believers had not yet entered into any kind of discipleship. The Gospel of John does, in fact, speak of faith at different levels of enlightenment and commitment (see 2:23-25; 8:31ff; 10:38). Those rulers who believed in Jesus were not willing to experience any kind of personal sacrifice for Jesus' sake. They still wanted to be accepted and approved of by their peers (see 5:44).

12:44-46 Jesus had left the crowds temporarily, but here in one final public appearance he appealed to his hearers to believe in him and thereby walk in his light. In this appeal, he affirmed his union with the Father: ***"Whoever believes in me believes not in me but in him who sent me. And whoever sees me sees him who sent me"*** (NRSV). To believe in Jesus was to believe the one who sent him. To see Jesus was to see the one who sent him, because the Son sent by the Father is the visible expression of the Father to mankind. Those who believe this have come out of the darkness and have received the light.

12:47-50 Verse 47 reiterates the important truth that Christ came not to judge the world but to save it (see comments on 3:17; 8:15-16); even so, his rejected words will condemn all unbelievers in the judgment at the last day (3:16-17, 35-36; 5:24-29, 39-40). Sometimes we use the expression "Mark my words, you'll regret this"—meaning "I won't have to be present to tell you what you did wrong. My words of warning will be recalled, and they will judge you." Jesus closed his message with one final appeal to accept the words he had spoken as coming from the Father and thereby receive eternal life. These verses (12:44-50) provide the essence of what Jesus had preached in his public ministry.

Jesus, Master and Servant

EXPOSITION

From John 13 to 17, Jesus is seen alone with his disciples. With his public ministry over, he now turned all of his attention and affection to those he loved the most. This would be his last evening with them before his crucifixion. They enjoyed a dinner together, which very likely was the Passover meal. Jesus washed the disciples' feet as a sign of servanthood and an example of humility for the disciples to emulate. This pleasant evening, however, was later marred by the inception of Jesus' betrayal. The devil, the prince of this world, would manipulate those involved in the betrayal, but he had no control over Jesus' destiny. The Son of God was in control. He had even chosen the man, Judas Iscariot, who would be used by the devil to betray him (see 6:70-71). The betrayal was a necessary act in the foreordained drama of redemption. The Father had given all things into his Son's hands, even his death. Of his own initiative and power, Jesus would lay down his life and take it up again; it would not be taken from him by some external power (see 10:18).

13:1-17/A Dinnertime Demonstration

One unique way of teaching is to act out the intended message. Under certain conditions, this method of teaching instills a visual image more powerfully than using other communication skills. A friend of mine recently hired some laborers for miscellaneous construction work. One day he was particularly bothered by the fact that three or four of these hourly employees had been standing around talking and not working. After about half an hour he walked over to them, and without a word, took a fifty dollar bill from his pocket, struck a match, and watched the flame consume the money. When it was gone, he said to the startled men, "That's what your standing around has cost me today," and he walked back to his office. Judging from my reaction to *just hearing* the story, I believe those men never forgot that illustration on cheating an employer.

The Old Testament gives us an interesting record where acting was part of a crucial event. King Ahab and King Jehoshaphat were one day deciding whether or not to fight Syria, and King Ahab's four hundred false prophets said, "Go, for the Lord will give it into the king's hand" (1 Kgs 22:6). So brazenly sure were they of their counsel that the false prophet Zedekiah made some horns of iron and pretended to gore and push the Syrians until they were destroyed (1 Kgs 22:11). It must have been a dramatic moment in that temporary courtyard when God's prophet, Micaiah, was summoned to confirm or deny Zedekiah's symbolic actions.

Likewise, it must have been a dramatic moment for all who watched Jesus give a silent lesson on the night he was betrayed, as he shared an important meal with his disciples and began to instruct them regarding the closing events of his life. It was a very sobering time as the disciples sensed the serious demeanor of our Lord. These were to be his last hours with them, and what he wanted to share with them was incredibly important. He began his teaching with a demonstration.

Jesus demonstrated his self-abasement. Midway through the meal our Lord rose from the table, laid aside his garments, and tied a long linen towel about his waist. In the Eastern culture of the day, a towel girded about the midsection was the sign of a servant or slave. According to Luke's account (22:24), we know that at this supper the disciples were arguing among themselves about who was the greatest! While this contentious spirit manifested itself, Jesus put on the badge of a servant. In such a setting, our Lord stooped to the menial act of washing the feet of the disciples. Incredible as it may seem, the disciples were actively arguing among themselves as to who was the greatest, while the Lord of Glory, God in the flesh, knelt to carefully, lovingly, humbly wash their feet in an actual parable of his divine mission to this world—of his laying aside his glory to become obedient even unto death. Amazingly, the Creator of worlds, by whose power all things are held together, he whom numberless angelic hosts serve, knelt and did the work of a servant while others bickered. The importance of this incident lies not only in the literal act, but in the symbolic significance of the redemptive cleansing of sinners. To picture it another way, from the feasts of heavenly communion he rose up to become the Servant of Jehovah and assume the task on earth that involved so much abasement. The robes of majesty were laid aside in exchange for the humble garb of human flesh. Instead of a basin of water, he brought to this deeper cleansing a divine fountain that washes away the debilitating stain of sin.

Jesus described the basis of fellowship. Perhaps Simon Peter had been watching Jesus as he proceeded around the table washing the disciples' feet, and when our Lord knelt before him, the fisherman said with embarrassment, "Lord, are *you* going to wash *my* feet?" (emphasis added). In other words, "I'm not sure I understand what's going on here, but I'm sure of one thing: you are not going to perform a slave's duty on me. You are not going to wash the dirt from my feet!" Peter saw the incongruity of the Master washing the disciples' feet, but he was unaware of the incongruity of a disciple telling his Lord what to do and what not to do!

Patiently Jesus responded to Simon by saying that someday he would understand. An amplified paraphrase would be, "After my death, burial, resurrection, and ascension—after the outpouring of the Holy Spirit—the full measure of the foot washing and my entire work of humiliation will become clear to you, Peter. Trust me. You don't understand now, but someday you will." Many times the children of God, incapable of clearly seeing the purposes of God being worked out in their lives, have been comforted by this thought: "You do not realize what I am doing, but later you will understand."

> God knows the way, he holds the key,
> He guides us with unerring hand.
> Sometime with tearless eyes we'll see
> Up there, yes up there, we'll understand.

Still Simon Peter refused the Lord's attempts to wash his feet, failing to understand what Jesus was portraying. So Jesus said that in order for him to have daily fellowship or communion with the Master, he needed to learn about daily cleansing. There is a difference between the washing of regeneration and the washing for continued fellowship, sanctification, and communion. Our daily contact with the evil all around causes the dust of defilement to settle upon us so that the mirror of our conscience is dimmed and the spiritual affections of our heart dulled. The believer's initial cleansing cannot be repeated—and does not need to be, for it cannot be canceled. But our daily walk must be brought under review and everything removed that would hinder the full experience and enjoyment of our privileges as children of God. We are human and, therefore, easily defiled by the world. We don't need to be saved again, but we do need to have the grime of the journey of life washed from us. Ephesians 5:26 speaks of our sanctification and cleansing with the washing of water by the Word. The Word of God is likened to water, and its daily application to our lives keeps us in fellowship with our Lord.

Jesus directs us toward servanthood. Completing the washing of the disciples' feet, Jesus said, "You should do as I have done for you." While a very small minority of Christians have taken these words literally, we do not read elsewhere in the New Testament of the church observing this as an ordinance like baptism and the Lord's Table. We interpret these words to mean that his action as a servant in humility ought to be the symbolic attitude of Christians toward one another. He gave us an example of the need to serve one another in humility. To do this is to prayerfully and humbly apply the Word of God to a fellow believer whose walk with the Lord is compromised. "Brothers, if someone is caught in a sin, you who are spiritual should restore him gently" (Gal 6:1). When we seek to apply the Word of God to a brother's situation, we must act in humility as a true servant would.

Many years after this incident, Simon Peter wrote to the exiled Christians, "When the Chief Shepherd appears, you will receive the crown of glory that will never fade away. Young men, in the same way be submissive to those who are older. All of you, clothe yourselves with humility toward one another, because, 'God opposes the proud but gives grace to the humble' " (1 Pet 5:4-5). Where did Peter learn that? If we were to ask him, he might answer: "On the Passover night in the upper room, I saw him do that. I saw him gird himself with humility." In verse 17, Jesus said, "Now that you know these things, you will be blessed if you do them." We have the promise of Jesus that the practice of humility imparts blessedness.

KEY WORDS AND PHRASES

The opening scene of this chapter (13:1-17) is symbolic of Jesus' coming from God to serve humanity and his subsequent return to God. This symbolism is verbalized in Philippians 2:5-11. Note the following parallels between John and Philippians:

John	*Philippians*
Jesus got up from the table and took off his outer robe.	"Being in very nature God, [Jesus] did not consider equality with God something to be grasped" (2:6).
Jesus tied a towel around his waist.	"[Jesus] made himself nothing, taking the very nature of a servant" (2:7).
He began to wash the disciples' feet with the towel.	"He humbled himself and became obedient to death—even death on a cross" (2:8).
He put his robe on again and returned to his place at the table.	"God exalted him to the highest place" (2:9).
Jesus told his disciples that they should call him Teacher and Lord.	"[God] gave him the name that is above every name, that . . . every tongue confess that Jesus Christ is Lord" (2:9-11).

NOTES

13:1 *before the festival of the Passover* (NRSV). In AD 30 (the year of Jesus' crucifixion), the Passover was celebrated on Thursday evening (which was the fourteenth of Nisan in the Jewish calendar), immediately followed by the Feast of Unleavened Bread, which lasted from the fifteenth of Nisan (Friday) to the twenty-first of Nisan. If this meal was the Passover meal, then any subsequent verses in John that mention a feast yet to come must refer to the Feast of Unleavened Bread, not to the Passover meal (13:29; 18:28; 19:14). According to 13:30, Judas went out after the Passover meal was finished to betray Jesus, but the disciples thought he was sent by Jesus to buy provisions for the upcoming feast. According to 18:28, the Pharisees did not want to defile themselves by entering Pilate's palace (the home of a Gentile), thereby prohibiting their participation in the feast, which must be the Feast of Unleavened Bread. The real conflict in the chronology comes in 19:14, which speaks of "the preparation for the Passover." If Jesus and his disciples celebrated this the evening before, this must not mean the Passover meal but the whole week of festivities that followed, which in New Testament times was called both the Passover and the Feast of Unleavened Bread.

Jesus knew that his hour had come to depart from this world and go to the Father (NRSV). Six times earlier Jesus had said, "My hour is not yet come," but now he knew the time had come. He would soon fulfill his mission and return to his Father.

Having loved his own who were in the world, he loved them to the end (NRSV). The last part of this verse could also be rendered, "He loved them to the utmost." The statement means that Jesus continued his devotion to his disciples until the very end of his life, and "he showed them the full extent of his love." Jesus could have been absorbed with his own imminent death; instead, he was absorbed with love for his disciples. They, who had been his companions for over three years, were very dear to him. Before he left them, he wanted to express his love to them, one by one—and this he did by washing each one's feet.

13:2 *The evening meal was being served.* This is a translation of a variant reading found in various manuscripts. Another reading could be translated "supper having happened."[1] The meal being served was probably the Passover meal, which Jesus and his disciples partook of before Jesus instituted the Lord's Supper (cf. Matt 26:17-30; Mark 14:12-26; Luke 22:7-30).

the devil had already prompted. Lit., "the devil having now put into the heart"—the text does not specify whose heart was involved: Judas's or the devil's. According to the best manuscripts, it very likely means the devil's heart (i.e., the devil decided to instigate the betrayal). According to inferior documentary evidence, in which Judas Iscariot appears in the genitive ("of Judas Iscariot"), it is the heart of Judas Iscariot.

to betray Jesus—See comments on 13:21ff.

13:3-5 *Jesus, knowing . . . that he had come from God and was going to God* (NRSV). Jesus had an absolute knowledge (Gr., *oida*) of his origin and destiny. He knew that he had come as God's servant to accomplish redemption and that he would rise again and return to the Father. His actions that evening illustrated what it meant for him to have come from God and return to God. That Jesus *got up from the meal* and *took off his outer clothing* portrayed how he, who existed in God's form, equal with God (Phil 2:6), was willing to divest himself of that privileged position. The action of tying *a towel around his waist* depicted how he humbled himself to take the form of a servant. After washing *the disciples' feet* (a sign of his cleansing ministry), he put his garments on again and returned to his former position (13:12), exhibiting his return to glory and to God. The entire scene is very close to what Paul verbalized in Philippians 2:5-11. John 13:3-12 provides the portrait, Philippians 2:5-11 the caption.

13:6-11 In between the act of rising from his place at the meal and then returning, Jesus washed the disciples' feet. If Peter and John were the nearest to Jesus at the meal, it would mean that Jesus began with John and ended with Peter. All the disciples accepted the washing, perhaps reluctantly but without voicing any protest, until Jesus came to Peter, who questioned Jesus: **"Lord, are you going to wash my feet?"** Jesus did not provide Peter with an explanation, other than that he would understand the significance of the washing sometime in the future— that is, after Jesus' crucifixion and resurrection. But Peter refused to let Jesus wash his feet: **"No,"** he said, **"you shall never wash my feet."**

Jesus responded, **"Unless I wash you, you have no part with me."** Then Peter wanted to be bathed completely: **"Lord, not just my feet but my hands and my head as well."** But a bath is not necessary for one who has been bathed and who is completely clean and will remain that way—except for his feet, which are soiled by the dust of the ground.[2] What a bathed person needs is a foot washing. In speaking to Peter, Jesus used two different Greek words (*niptō* and *louō*) to convey two different kinds of washing. The Greek word *niptō*, appearing in 13:5-6, 8 and in the last part of 13:10, is used throughout the Septuagint and New Testament to indicate the washing of the extremities (i.e., the hands and the feet). The Greek word *louō* (from which is formed the perfect participle *lelouomenos* in 13:10) specifically means bathing. According to the social customs of those times, once a person had bathed his body, he needed only to wash his feet before partaking of a meal. In his response to Peter, Jesus used both words in order to advance a precious truth: As he who has been bathed needs only to wash his feet daily, so he who has been bathed by the Lord, through his Word (John 15:3; Eph 5:26; Titus 3:5;), needs only to wash himself daily from the filth and defilement he accumulates by his contact with the world.

13:12-15 Do you know what I have done to you? (NRSV). There was probably a great silence among the disciples as they tried to comprehend all the meaning of Jesus' actions. Since no one answered Jesus, he explained the spiritual significance of the foot washing. The act of Jesus washing the disciples' feet demonstrated the service of love. Jesus, the **Teacher and Lord**, had stooped to a position of humility and service because he loved those he served.

For I have set you an example, that you also should do as I have done to you (NRSV). Jesus commanded his disciples to serve one another in love according to the example he set. Since his action of foot washing ultimately pointed to the forgiveness and cleansing of sins, Jesus' admonishment to act as he did was an encouragement for the disciples to forgive one another.

13:16-17 servants are not greater than their master, nor are messengers greater than the one who sent them (NRSV). This maxim would help the disciples understand that it was their position to be subservient to one another, even as Jesus had been subservient to his Father and was the perfect embodiment of servitude. *If you know these things, you are blessed if you do them* (NRSV). Knowledge should lead to practice, for it is in the performance of what we have learned that we are blessed. The generality of this verse (note the plurals: "these things" and "them") seems to indicate that Jesus was helping the disciples understand the truths of servitude and humility more than prescribing foot washing as a practice to be performed among them. Indeed, in the entire book of Acts there is no record of foot washing. This is not to say, however, that it was not practiced among the early Christians. From 1 Timothy 5:10 we know that some of the Christians washed the feet of other believers as an act of Christian service. The attitude is what matters: foot washing, or any other act, must be a demonstration of love and servitude, and if this is the heart attitude, one will be *blessed* (that is, spiritually contented and fulfilled).

13:18 *I am not referring to all of you; I know those I have chosen.* Jesus' previous statements about serving one another and loving one another did not apply to all of his disciples because, in fact, Judas was about to betray him. Nor did his words of cleansing apply to Judas—he had his feet washed, but he was not inwardly clean. However, this betrayal was not an unexpected event. Jesus had known from the beginning that one of the men he chose would betray him (see 6:70-71).

this is to fulfill the scripture. Jesus' betrayal was necessary to fulfill Scripture, specifically Psalm 41:9: "He who shared my bread, has lifted up his heel against me." The expression "to lift up the heel" in Hebrew means "he has made his heel great against me"—i.e., "has given me a great fall" or "has taken cruel advantage of me" (Bruce). The expression is a "metaphor derived from the lifting up of a horse's hoof preparatory to kicking" (Morris). Psalm 41 is a very fitting portion of Scripture for Jesus to quote because it describes one of David's companions, perhaps Ahithophel, who had turned against David and then hanged himself (see 2 Sam 16:20–17:3, 23). In Psalm 41:9 David laments the actions of one he calls "my close friend, whom I trusted," but this part of the verse was not cited by Jesus because Jesus had not trusted Judas, knowing all along that Judas would betray him. (Judas also hanged himself—see Matt 27:5.) When David wrote Psalm 41, he was deeply hurt. Jesus, too, was hurt by Judas's treachery.

13:19 *I tell you this now, before it occurs, so that when it does occur, you may believe that I am he* (NRSV). This would strengthen their faith. Belief can be of such different levels. They believed he was the Messiah, but as yet they did not believe he was from God and was going back to God. Like ours today, theirs was a progressive faith, from Messiah to Lord to Savior to God. Jesus predicted the betrayal in the presence of his disciples so that they could realize, when the betrayal actually occurred, that it was prophesied in Scripture (cf. Acts 1:16).

13:20 *whoever receives one whom I send receives me; and whoever receives me receives him who sent me* (NRSV). Jesus here emphasized a truth he had already mentioned and would state again—that is, one who receives the Son receives the Father, and one who receives the apostles receives the Son. This was significant in the early church (cf. 1 Jn 1:3), but this "chain of connection"—Father-Son-apostles—has been greatly abused over the centuries. Today, many people in the evangelical tradition glide right past these words, but we should note that Jesus said whosoever received the apostles was receiving him. This ended the discourse on servanthood.

13:21 *Jesus was troubled in spirit.* The Gospels record some of the deep emotions Jesus felt in his human spirit. Luke says Jesus was full of joy (Luke 10:21); Mark says he "sighed deeply in His spirit" (Mark 8:12, NKJV); and John earlier tells his readers how Jesus (before Lazarus's tomb) was agitated in his spirit (11:33). Such descriptions show the true humanity of Jesus Christ. In this instance, Jesus is seen to be deeply affected by the devastating experience of betrayal. He expressed inner pain even though he knew that the betrayal was foreordained (as was his coming crucifixion) and that he was in control of the situation.

"I tell you the truth, one of you is going to betray me." Now Jesus' talk about the betrayal becomes explicit and pointed: One of the twelve disciples would betray him. No informer told him of Judas's plan. No disciple whispered in Jesus' ear that Judas was up to something. Imagine the awkward stillness around the table, each looking at the other with incredulity, thinking, *Are you the one?*

13:22-26 *His disciples stared at one another, at a loss to know which of them he meant.* Wanting to know who the betrayer was, Peter gestured to **the disciple whom Jesus loved**. This is the first time in this Gospel that the writer uses the term "the disciple whom Jesus loved." The person so identified is John the apostle, the writer of this Gospel (see Introduction). The expression "the disciple whom Jesus loved" (which appears again in 20:2; 21:7, 20) is used to point out the intimate relationship this one had with Jesus (even among the Twelve) and thereby bolster the authenticity of the writing. The Gospel narrative can be trusted because it was written by John, who provided reliable, intricate details about the events in Jesus' history. John was the right one for Peter to ask because he was the one reclining next to Jesus during the meal. **Leaning back against Jesus**, John asks, **"Lord, who is it?"** In those days it was the custom for people to recline around a meal. The host would be at the head of the group, with the rest spreading out to his left and to his right in a U shape, and a special guest to the right of the host would have his head near the host's chest. Thus, John occupied this special place. Jesus identified the betrayer as **"the one to whom I will give this piece of bread when I have dipped it in the dish."** Very likely Jesus dipped the piece of bread in sauce made of dates, raisins, or sour wine (cf. Matt 26:22-25; Mark 14:19-20; Luke 22:23). Usually, this act singled out the guest of honor. But since Judas was the dishonorable one, the act was ironic. Nonetheless,

Judas was not thereby publicly exposed to disgrace. Jesus sent Judas on his horrid task discreetly after he dipped the morsel and gave it to him.

13:27-29 Jesus' identification of Judas was done so tactfully that all the disciples except John missed the significance of the act. Invisible to all, Satan entered Judas. This is the completion of the satanic influence. Thus the betrayal was set in motion; so Jesus told Judas, *"What you are about to do, do quickly."* The disciples thought Jesus was sending Judas out to *buy what was needed for the Feast, or to give something to the poor* because Judas *had charge of the money* (see comments on 12:6). They had no inkling that Jesus urged Judas to work speedily in his traitorous deed so that he would die on the day the sacrificial lamb was being prepared. After these events they would realize that Jesus was in complete control. He alone knew what lay before him, and he eagerly faced his humiliation. Verse 28 explains to the reader that the disciples had no idea Judas was going out to betray their Master.

John (and perhaps Peter) knew that the betrayer was Judas, but they could not imagine the enormity of that act, nor could they have realized that Judas was going then to betray Jesus. If so, Peter would have tried to stop Judas! But none of the disciples thought Jesus' talk about betrayal indicated an imminent event—just as they did not realize that Jesus would die on the cross the next day.

13:30 *As soon as Judas had taken the bread, he went out. And it was night.* The stage was quickly being set. This last statement is poetically ominous. It speaks of Judas's participation in a dark deed motivated by the prince of darkness, Satan. It also speaks of the end of Jesus' ministry—no longer would the daylight shine, for the end of Jesus' life had come. Finally, it tells the actual time.

ENDNOTES

[1] The significant textual variant involves a single letter in the Greek: *ginomenou* (happening), found in ℵ * B L W, versus *genomenou* ("having happened"—or, taken as an ingressive aorist, "having been served"), found in 𝔓66 ℵᶜ A D.

[2] Arguments have been advanced for both the inclusion of "except for his feet" and its omission in 13:10 (see Beasley-Murray's summary). 𝔓66 B C, attesting to the inclusion of this phrase, probably preserve the original text. The mention of only feet needing the exterior cleansing is important to Jesus' complete illustration.

Jesus: The Way,
the Truth, and the Life

JOHN 13:31–14:31

EXPOSITION

Jesus' final discourse begins in 13:31 (not in 14:1) and ends at 17:26 with the conclusion of Jesus' prayer. Beginning with the theme of glorification (13:31), Jesus focuses on the spiritual realities his glorification would provide the believers. This glorification is the key to interpreting the following discourse. All that follows is built upon the fact that Jesus viewed his glorification, through death and resurrection, as already accomplished. As a result of this glorification, Jesus in resurrection would be able to live in his disciples and they in him. It is essential to keep in mind when reading John 14–17 that most of the discourse is framed in terms of Jesus' anticipation of his resurrection and what that resurrection would create in respect to his spiritual union with the disciples. Indeed, in John 15 the Lord envisions himself and the disciples already organically united as vine and branches, for he says, in the proleptic present tense, "I am the vine; you are the branches" (15:5). This, of course, could not be realized until Jesus, in resurrection, imparted his life to his believers.

The last discourse and final prayer could have taken place together in one setting during the evening meal, or it could have been delivered in stages: (1) 13:31–14:31 after the meal in the room, (2) 15:1–16:33 en route to Gethsemane, and (3) 17:1-26 on the west side of the Kidron Valley before entering the Garden of Gethsemane.

The first portion of John 14 traditionally has been interpreted with the understanding that 14:2 refers to God's house in heaven. Accordingly, many commentators think that Jesus was speaking about his Father's house in heaven, to which he had to go in order to prepare some rooms and from which he would return one day to take back his believers to be with him in heaven. The day of that return usually has been designated as the Second Advent or perhaps the Lord's personal visitation to each believer when they depart this world.

The traditional exegesis has several problems. First, "heaven" is not mentioned in John 14. Second, the going away and coming again, according to the context of John 14–16, would be but for "a little while" (see 14:19-20; 16:16-23), not two or more millennia! Indeed 14:20 and 16:20-22 make it evident that "that day" would be the day of Christ's resurrection, the day in which the disciples would realize that they had become united to the risen Christ. Third, John 14:4, 6 indicate that Jesus was talking about the believers coming to the Father through him, the unique way. This access to the Father is not reserved for the Second Advent or for the time of each Christian's departure from this world.

Nevertheless, the Lord did indicate that he was going to the Father (14:12; 16:28), and we know this ascent did take him to heaven. As such, it could be inferred that he was going to heaven, and that was where he wanted to take his disciples. But his immediate purpose was to bring them into a living relationship with the Father through himself (the Son) and the Holy Spirit.

14:1-6/Heaven

We do not need a Gallup poll to tell us which are the all-time favorite Scriptures. The most frequently read and beloved Scriptures are Psalm 23 and John 14:1-6. In the soul's darkest night, there is great solace in hearing the promise of God that we are not left alone. The believers' unyielding hope is in the fact that God loves us, that he will care for us along life's pathway, and that he will take us to heaven at the end of the way. Such hope-filled conviction brings peace to the troubled heart.

It is difficult to overlook the eleven disciples' gloom and despair at this upper room meal. Just consider what was happening. Judas had left the dinner party to bargain for the betrayal of the Savior. Jesus had told the eleven he would very shortly be leaving them and that they could not follow. Peter had been told that he would deny, before daylight, that he even knew Jesus. There was an undercurrent of contention among the disciples as to who was the greatest. It was not a very pleasant atmosphere! Gloom must have completely overwhelmed the disciples. It was then that Jesus said, "Do not let your hearts be troubled. Trust in God; trust also in me." They, of course, believed in God. They believed his Word. Even though they had never seen the God who is invisible, they were conscious of his love and care. In the very same manner, Jesus tells them, "You must have full confidence in my existence—in my love and care for you—even though I am removed from your sight." The cure for troubled hearts, when the future seems dark and present circumstances are very troubling, is faith directed to Jesus, faith such as we have toward God, for Jesus is God. In the face of betrayal, in the face of denial, in the face of mock trials, even in the face of hate-filled crucifixion, utterly trust Christ and you will not suffer heart trouble.

Our Lord further comforts his disciples—and all future believers—by saying that he is going to prepare a place for them. In this way he describes his death as a journey, a departure, but not a permanent withdrawal. Without his death there would be no *place* for believers, and without his resurrection there would be no place *prepared* for those who follow him. The matchless comfort for grieving hearts is simply this: If there were no heaven, Jesus would have told us! Now there are many ways of describing heaven, but it seems in this passage that heaven can be described as a place and a Person.

Heaven, a place. Heaven is the everlasting abode of those who love God. In Luke 19:12 heaven is called a country, suggesting its expanse, its magnitude, its far-reaching greatness. In 2 Peter 1:11 heaven is called a kingdom, suggesting a monarchy, orderliness, and authoritative rule. In Hebrews 11:10, 16 heaven is termed a city, suggesting citizenship (our names are recorded in heaven), population, valuables (our treasure is stored in heaven), and activity. In John 14:2 heaven is called home, suggesting family, comfort, security, companionship, and good times. Little wonder we are profoundly captivated by heaven!

Jesus says that in his Father's house there are many dwelling places. Of all descriptions he might have used, he chose "home" as the most appropriate. What really constitutes a home? Not the building—but the loved ones who dwell there. Someday in heaven we shall resume the relationships death severed and enjoy perfect fellowship with those of kindred spirit. No earthly family reunion can even begin to compare to that great family gathering of the redeemed.

"Many dwelling places" (NRSV) suggests spaciousness. There is no lack of accommodations. Heaven will contain immense throngs without being crowded. "Many mansions" (NKJV) further suggests great variety, not just one great hall or dormitory building. He knows us, each one. He has planned our dwelling place accordingly. He will keep our place for our arrival. It will not suit another and will not be given to another. If it were not so, he would have told us!

Heaven, a Person. While we may be intrigued thinking of heaven as a place and all that it involves, the essence of heaven is a person. Jesus spoke of going to the Father. For him, heaven as a place and as a person were synonymous. Here, Thomas was thinking of heaven as a place and in honest puzzlement blurted out, "Lord, we don't know your destination, and if we don't know where you are going, how can we possibly know how to follow you?" In patient response, Jesus, who was still thinking of heaven as a Person, said, "I am going to the Father, and the only access to him is through me." Philip was totally frustrated, and he said, "If my final destination is the Father, *please* show us the Father. Call him down to us. Have him appear in this room right now. If I could just see the Father, I wouldn't be puzzled anymore."

Consider the irony of it all. Philip was pleading for a manifestation of the Father, and all the while God was before his very eyes, talking to him. "Don't you see it, Philip—don't you get it? I am God. I'm right in front of you." The only way the Father can be seen is in Jesus. The Father and Son are one. Philip was asking for an impossibility—according to his faulty conception—but the impossible has become possible. The Father could be seen. He was there, in their midst in the person of Jesus Christ. Whether the upper room or heaven, the only manifestation of God we will ever see is the Lord Jesus Christ.

Heaven, a promise. How can we be absolutely sure of getting to heaven, i.e., the Father? Jesus says, "I am the way and the truth and the life." He himself is the Way—the only way to the Father. Across the infinite gulf that separates humanity from God—the creature from the Creator, the sinner from the Holy One—is Jesus, bridging that gulf with his sinless obedience, his fulfillment of all righteousness, and his atonement for our alienation, our rebellion, our enmity. His death and resurrection prove him to be the only way to the Father.

Not only is he the Way, but he is the Truth. Truth is the opposite of falsehood and all that is shadowy and unsubstantial. Jesus Christ, who is absolute Truth, is stable, as opposed to the unrealities that hold mankind in bondage. He is also true Life. Apart from him, every person is spiritually dead, that is, little more than a walking corpse. No one has experienced life until they have received, by faith, Jesus Christ, who is life eternal. As we live our life in Christ Jesus, we know the truth and advance in the way. Or turning it around, as we follow the way, we learn the truth and are filled with the life. He who is Life and Truth is the only way to heaven, the Father. In other words, all who have reached the Father's house have come through Jesus Christ, and all who have come through him arrive at last in the place he has gone to prepare.

How may people come to the Father? Not by a ritual, not by a creed, not by an institution, not by an ethic, but only by a Person. He is the Way; there is absolutely no other access, no other door, no other entrance to heaven. He is the Truth; there is no knowledge of God apart from Jesus Christ. He is the Life; there is no family relationship possible with God, except in Jesus Christ.

The true value of the Way is never realized until we are following it. If you are not walking God's way today, you cannot begin to appreciate the confidence it brings to be traveling this way of life eternal. There is only one way to heaven, to the Father God. It avails nothing that a person is clever, learned, highly gifted, amiable, charitable, kindhearted, generous, or even zealous toward some sort of religion. For without Christ, people are wanderers; they are not in the Way. Without Christ Jesus, people are under the dominance of Satan. Not knowing the Truth, they are held by lies. Without Jesus Christ, people are dead in their sins; they do not have life. The Way brings men to God. The Truth makes men free. The Life produces fellowship.

KEY WORDS AND PHRASES

Of all the profound statements in this passage, the most outstanding is "I am the way and the truth and the life. No one comes to the Father except through me" (John 14:6). The goal of Jesus' mission, according to the Gospel of John, was to express the Father to mankind and to bring the believers to the Father. Jesus repeatedly indicated that he was in the Father (10:38; 14:10-11), and he prayed in John 17 that the disciples would also be with him in the Father (17:21-24). Jesus came to provide believers with a way to approach and live in the Father here and now (see Eph 2:18).

But there is another outstanding statement: "I will ask the Father and he will give you another Comforter, and he will never leave you. He is the Holy Spirit, the Spirit who leads into all truth. The world at large cannot receive him, for it isn't looking for him and doesn't recognize him. But you do, for he lives with you now and some day shall be in you. No, I will not abandon you or leave you as orphans in the storm—I will come to you" (14:16-18, TLB). In this statement Jesus tells the disciples that he will be present with them and live in them through the Spirit. The Spirit is the Son's way of living in the believers and carrying on a relationship with them. Thus, Jesus provides believers with the way to come to God, and the Spirit gives God a way to come to the believers.

NOTES

13:31 When he [Judas Iscariot] **was gone, Jesus said, "Now is the Son of Man glorified and God is glorified in him."** With the hasty departure of Judas, a different tone or atmosphere is appropriate. These are his final words to the remaining eleven. The Greek puts this clause in the past tense, which reads strangely to us: "Now *was* the Son of Man glorified," meaning that to Jesus, his death and resurrection were so absolutely certain that he considered them already accomplished. God was already glorified through the glorification of his Son. All that follows through 17:26 should be understood as the result of the glorification of Jesus.

13:32 If God is glorified in him, God will glorify the Son in himself, and will glorify him at once. The first clause is not present in several ancient manuscripts. The rest of the verse is unquestionably genuine. Speaking of the Son's glorification, Westcott says, "Even as God was glorified in the Son of Man, as man, when he took to himself willingly the death which the traitor was preparing, so also it followed that God would glorify the Son of Man in his own divine Being, by taking up his glorified humanity to fellowship with himself."

13:33 Little children, I am with you only a little longer. You will look for me; and as I said to the Jews so now I say to you, "Where I am going, you cannot come" (NRSV). This is the only place in John's Gospel where the diminutive form for "children" appears (Gr., *teknia*); it connotes intimacy and fondness. (John used the word frequently in his first epistle when he addressed his readers.) Jesus, as a comforting father, now tells his "little children" that the time of his departure is nearing. In fact, John used the Greek word *mikron*, from which we get "micro," to indicate that very little time will elapse before this event takes place. As Jesus had told the Jewish leaders earlier (see 7:33-34), he now tells his disciples that though they seek him, they will not find him. Jesus, as the God-man, would be going to the Father (14:6, 28) to rejoin him in that sphere of fellowship and glory that the Father and Son enjoyed from all eternity (see 17:5, 24 and comments). The disciples would not be able to join him in that fellowship just yet. But Jesus prayed that they (later on) could be with him and the Father and see Jesus' glory as the Son of God (see 17:24).

13:34-35 *I give you a new commandment, that you love one another. Just as I have loved you, you also should love one another* (NRSV). A command to love one another is not a new commandment; such had been mandated in the Old Testament (Lev 19:18, 33-34). The newness of Jesus' command rests upon the reality that because our hearts have been changed by experiencing the love of Jesus, we should reach out in reciprocal fashion to all those touched by that same love. At times it may not be easy to do, but grace helps us. Jesus commanded them to love one another "as I have loved you." This love would be the mark of distinction: *By this everyone will know that you are my disciples, if you have love for one another* (NRSV). Tertullian said that the Gentiles saw this love and commented, "How they love one another" (*Apology* 39.3.46). One of the major themes in John's first epistle is that of brotherly love (see 1 Jn 3–4). It is a distinguishing mark of a Christian to serve others rather than oneself.

13:36-38 *Simon Peter*, whose thoughts are on what Jesus said about going away (13:33), asks Jesus, *"Where are you going?"* Again, Jesus says, *"You cannot follow now,"* and to this he adds, *"but you will follow later."* Jesus' statement has two meanings: (1) Peter would later follow Jesus in the way of death (see 21:15-19), and (2) Peter would later follow Jesus into glory. "'Following' is the basic requirement of one who would be a disciple of Jesus, and to follow Jesus must mean in the end to follow him both to death and glory" (Barrett). Simon Peter must have somewhat understood that Jesus' words about his departure indicated death. Peter could not imagine living without Jesus, the one for whom he had forsaken all others to follow for three years. Thus Peter exclaims, *"Lord, why can't I follow you now? I will lay down my life for you."* The last statement repeats what Jesus said in 10:11, 15, 17 about laying down his life for his sheep. Jesus would really do this; Peter would not. Maybe Peter expected a fight, and he was ready to fight even to the point of death. Peter made his boast in front of the other disciples. But Jesus said, in effect, "In spite of all your boasting, you will actually deny me three times before daylight." When the time of trial came, Peter would **disown** Jesus **three times** (cf. Matt 26:69-75; Mark 14:66-72; Luke 22:54-62). This prediction silenced Peter. He must have been utterly devastated! In the rest of the discourse, Peter says nothing. In fact, the next time Peter speaks again is when he denies knowing Jesus (see 18:17ff).

14:1 *Do not let your hearts be troubled.* Because this statement immediately follows Jesus' prediction of Peter's denial, most readers would assume that Jesus addressed this statement to Peter alone. But in the Greek, the possessive pronoun "your" is plural; therefore Jesus was speaking to Peter (to whom Jesus had just said, "You will disown me three times" in 13:38) *and* to all the other disciples. In the parallel passage in Luke 22:31, the pronoun is also plural: "Satan has demanded to sift all of you like wheat" (NRSV). This verse has also been incorrectly interpreted as applying only to Peter. All of the disciples, not just Peter, must have been troubled about Jesus' predictions of betrayal, denial, and departure.

you believe in God, believe also in Me (NKJV). This could also be translated, "You trust in God; trust also in me." Jesus urged his disciples to maintain their faith in the Father and in the Son.

14:2-3 The customary interpretation of 14:2-3 has serious flaws (see the introduction above). Normally commentators say that this passage is speaking of the Lord's second advent and the believers' ascent to heaven, or the believers' ascent to heaven at the time of death. Of these two interpretations, the first is not very Johannine, although possible; but the second is highly unlikely (the Scriptures nowhere speak of the Lord's coming again and again for each deceased believer). It is far more likely that the passage is speaking of the believers' immediate access to God the Father through the Son. Nevertheless, most commentators think Jesus was talking about going to a place (heaven) and not to a Person (the Father). But let us look at the critical words in this passage to determine if the traditional exegesis is valid or not:

In my Father's house. The same expression, "Father's house," appears in 2:16, in which it is clear that the Temple in Jerusalem was the Father's house. Yet in the next few verses (2:17-21) Jesus likened himself to a temple, a temple that would be destroyed and raised again in three days. The Son, through the process of crucifixion and resurrection, would become the temple, the Father's house, prepared to receive the believers. He, as the temple, the Father's house, would be the means through which the believers could come to dwell in the Father and the Father in them (see MacGregor). Other commentators prefer to see the "Father's house" as being the church, the dwelling place of God (see 1 Cor 3:16, 17; Eph 2:20-22; Heb 3:2). As such, the promise in 14:2-3 is then thought to relate to the corporate fellowship that would be possible through Christ's departure and return in the Spirit (see Gundry). In this view, the "many rooms" would be the many members of God's household. Christ went to prepare a place for each member in God's household (cf. 1 Chr 17:9); the preparation was accomplished by his death and resurrection.

are. Jesus did not say, "In my Father's house, there *will be* [future tense] many rooms." This was spoken proleptically (as also was 15:2). The believers are viewed as having already inhabited the Son, or as having already been joined to him, though this could not be actualized until after the Lord's death and resurrection because it required preparation. Therefore though the believers are viewed as already being rooms in the Father's house, a place needed to be prepared for them.

many rooms. The Greek word *monai* shares the same root as the word for "abide" (Gr., *menō*); it simply means a dwelling place, a room. "Mansions" in the KJV, according to current usage, is misleading because it connotes a spacious, luxurious house. The Greek word translated here as "rooms" is used only twice in the entire New Testament, both places in John 14 (vv. 2 and 23). Could the "rooms" be different rooms? According to John 14:23, each believer becomes a room of the Father and the Son; since there are many believers, these must be the many rooms in the Father's house. In 14:2, the rooms are spoken of as already existing, but in 14:23, we see how these rooms will actually come into existence.

I am going there to prepare a place for you. When Jesus said he was going to prepare a place for the disciples in the Father's house, could he not have been suggesting that he himself was that house? Did not the Father live in him and he in the Father? The way for the disciples to dwell in the Father would be for them to come and abide in the Son. In other words, by coming into the one who was indwelt by the Father, the believers would come simultaneously into the indweller, the Father. Clearly, this was the Lord's desire and design (see 14:20; 17:21-24). Therefore when he said he was going to prepare a place for them, does it not mean that he, through the process of death and resurrection, was going to make it possible for the believers to live in him? Gundry observed that the many rooms are not "mansions in the sky but spiritual positions in Christ, much as in Pauline theology." This view is confirmed by the analogy of the vine and branches presented in the next chapter, in which Jesus makes it clear that the believers abide in him and he in them in an organic union.

I will come again and will take you to myself (NRSV). Notice that Jesus did not say, "I am coming again and will receive you to *heaven*"; he said, "I am coming again and will receive you to *myself.*" A Person, not a place, is the destination. The Greek here is in the present tense and should properly be translated "I am coming," showing the immediacy of the Lord's return. His coming to them again would be realized in a short while. (This is confirmed by 16:16—note the similar use of "again.") When Jesus said, "I am coming again," that "coming again" occurred on the day of his resurrection (see Dodd). However, many commentators say he is speaking of the Parousia, the Second Coming. Still other commentators see this "coming again" as referring to both the Resurrection and the Parousia—the former foreshadowing the latter. Those who hold this view, therefore, extract a double meaning from Jesus' words in 14:2-3; they say the passage speaks both of the believers being brought into the risen Christ as the many rooms in the Father's house and of the believers being brought by the returned Christ into the Father's house in heaven. Gundry's summary is worth repeating:

> The two meanings illustrate the proleptic theology of John, the tension and correspondence between the already and the not yet. According to the first meaning Jesus speaks of his going to the cross, his preparing by his death spiritual abodes in the Father's household or family, his return to the disciples immediately after his resurrection, and the sending of the Spirit to minister his continuing presence until he comes to receive those who are already in him so that they may be with him eternally. And all of that anticipates the second meaning according to which Jesus speaks of his going to the house of heaven, his preparing there abodes for believers, his return, and his taking believers to be with him in heaven forever since they

have already come to be in him by faith. In the last point the two meanings merge. ("In My Father's House Are Many Monai," Zeitschriftfür die Neutestamentliche Wissenschaft, 58 [1967]: 68–72.)

14:4 *And you know the way where I am going* (NASB). This reading has the best manuscript support; other manuscripts have an expanded reading, "And where I go you know and the way you know."[1] Furthermore, several modern translations have other expansions based upon the traditional exegesis explained previously (see comments on 14:2-3). For example, the NIV, the NRSV, and TEV have supplied words that indicate Jesus was going *to a place*: "the way to the place" (NIV and NRSV) and "how to get to the place" (TEV). But in context and in accordance with Johannine thought, Jesus was preparing the way through himself to the Father. The destination is not a place but a Person. Commentator Thomas Merton says, "Where is this place? It is not a place, it is God."

14:5-6 **Thomas** expresses his bewilderment by asking Jesus, *"Lord, we don't know where you are going, so how can we know the way?"* To which Jesus replied: *"I am the way and the truth and the life. No one comes to the Father except through me."* Jesus' response reveals that the destination was not a place but a Person (the Father), and the way to that destination is another Person (the Son). Jesus is the way to the Father. Jesus is the Truth (or reality) of all we find in the Father when we get to him. And Jesus is the Life that is given to us by virtue of our access to God.

14:7 *If you had known Me, you would have known My Father also* (NKJV). In 14:2-6 Jesus unveils the truth that he is the unique way to the Father. In 14:7 and following, he reveals that he is the visible manifestation of the Father. If the disciples were to realize that coming to dwell in the Son was equivalent to coming to dwell in the Father, they would have to realize that the Son was the Father revealed, the manifestation of the Father (see John 1:18; Col 1:15; Heb 1:3). If they had come to know the Son, they should have perceived the Father also. This reading is supported by several ancient manuscripts; other ancient manuscripts read, "If you have come to know me, you will know my Father also."[2] This reading may represent what John intended. However, it seems more likely that Jesus was reproving the disciples. Jesus was not promising the disciples that they would come to know the Father as they had known the Son, but that they should have already known the Father as manifest in the Son. If he was making a promise, how could the Lord say in the very next sentence: *"And from now on you know Him and have seen Him"* (NKJV)?

14:8-9 *Philip said to him, "Lord, show us the Father, and we will be satisfied." Jesus said to him, "Have I been with you all this time, Philip, and you still do not know me? Whoever has seen me has seen the Father"* (NRSV). Philip's question exposes his ignorance of Jesus. To see Jesus is to see the Father, for

Jesus is the visible expression of God (see 1:18 and comments). It would be impossible to show the Father outside of the Son because the Son has always been his unique expression. Philip and the disciples should have come to know and recognize that the one in their midst was the very expression of God the Father.

14:10-11 *I am in the Father and the Father is in me* (NRSV). To know the Son is to know the Father and vice versa because the two exist in one another. This coinherence (mutual indwelling) is the basis of the oneness between the Father and the Son (see 10:30, 38; 17:21-24). The reason the Son could boldly assert that seeing him was equivalent to seeing the Father is that he and the Father are one by virtue of their coinherence.

14:12-14 *He will do even greater things than these.* The difficulty with interpreting this passage is that it is a promise made to an individual, not to a collective group (such as the church). Since no one in history has done greater miracles than Jesus did, this could not refer to miracles. Perhaps Jesus' statement refers to the preaching of the gospel (proclaiming to others what Jesus did). Some individuals have proclaimed the gospel to more people than Jesus did: Peter, Paul, John Wesley, George Whitefield, and Billy Graham. Thus, this promise may refer to the work of evangelism, or what we could call "fruit bearing" (cf. 15:7-8). Jesus had fed thousands at a single sitting (6:1-14) but had never seen multitudes converted within a few minutes, so far as we know from the Gospel records. Yet Peter and the other apostles initiated unprecedented mass evangelism (Acts 2:37-43, 47; 4:1-4; 6:7).

I will do whatever you ask in my name, so that the Son may bring glory to the Father. The promise of answered prayer described in these verses is true if properly understood within the context of Jesus' last discourse. Jesus was promising the disciples that their requests concerning fruit bearing would be answered because this would bring glory to God, as clarified in the next chapters (15:7-8, 16; 16:23-24). Jesus was not promising that every request made in his name would be fulfilled. Prayer must be made according to God's will (see 1 Jn 5:14-15).

14:15 *If you love me, you will keep my commandments* (NRSV). Prior to this, Jesus urged the disciples to love one another. Now he speaks of them loving him. An important part of loving him is to do what he commands. This is emphasized in John's first epistle (see 1 Jn 5:2-3). The disciples (and all believers) would be able to have a love relationship with Jesus because he would continue to be with them in and through the Spirit (see comments on 14:16).

14:16 *and I will ask the Father and he will give you another Comforter, and he will never leave you* (TLB). In the first part of the chapter, Jesus focused on his relationship with the Father because the disciples needed to see that their union with the Son meant union with the Father, for the two are one. In this part of the chapter, Jesus reveals his relationship with the Spirit because his union with the Spirit is the Son's way of living in believers and carrying on a relationship with them. Thus Jesus provides believers with the way to come to God, and the Spirit gives God a way to come to believers.

In 14:16 Jesus said that the Father would give the disciples "another Comforter." This expression in Greek (*allon paraklēton*) means "another comforter of the same kind as the first," implying that Jesus was the first Comforter (see 1 Jn 2:1) and that the Spirit would be the same kind of Comforter. The Greek word *paraklētos* denotes the office of one who comes to the aid of a person in need (lit., "one who comes to [our] side when called upon"). Properly speaking, this is the office of an advocate; but this title hardly suits the context of John 14 (cf. 1 Jn 2:1, where the title Advocate is very fitting). Titles like Comforter, Helper, Counselor, or Consoler fit the context of John 14, but none of the titles fully expresses the Paraclete because he does more than comfort, help, counsel, and console—he also advocates, exhorts, and teaches.

14:17 In this verse Jesus identifies the Comforter. He is **the Spirit of truth**—or the Spirit of reality—inasmuch as he is the Spirit who reveals the reality about God (cf. TEV). The world cannot receive (or appropriate) this Spirit of reality because the world does not see him or know him. But the disciples should know him. Jesus said, **"You know him, because he abides with you, and he will be in you"** (NRSV). This statement indicates that (1) the Spirit embodied in Jesus was then and there abiding with the disciples, and (2) the same Spirit of Jesus would, in the future, be in the disciples. In other words, the one who was *with* them would be *in* them.[3] Notice the shift of pronouns from verse 17 to 18—"he [the Spirit] will be in you . . . I [Jesus] am coming to you" (NRSV). This implies that Jesus through the Spirit would be coming to the disciples and indwelling them. Note that in 14:20 Jesus says, "I in you" (NRSV). Compare this with 14:17, where Jesus says that the Spirit "will be in you." When we put all these statements together, it should be clear that the coming of the Comforter is none other than the coming of the Lord in the Spirit.

Several commentators remark on this wonderful truth. For example, Morris says, "He [Jesus] comes in the coming of the Spirit"; and R. E. Brown indicates that Jesus' presence after his return to the Father was fulfilled in and through the Paraclete. One finds the same kind of statements in devotional writings. For example, A. B. Simpson says, "The coming of the Comforter is just the coming of Jesus himself to the heart" (*When the Comforter Came*). And Watchman Nee affirms the same: "This Comforter, who is the Holy Spirit, is just the Christ that will dwell in you" (*The Normal Christian Faith*, 134). Thus the Spirit did not come as the Son's replacement or representative, but as the Son himself in his spiritual form. "It is not for an instant that the disciples are to have the presence of the Spirit instead of having the presence of the Son. But to have the Spirit is to have the Son" (R. C. Moberly, *Atonement and Personality*, 168).

The unity between Jesus and the Spirit is essential to the proper interpretation of the Lord's last discourse, and specifically to the verses (16-18) we have been discussing.

14:18-19 *I will not leave you as orphans.* This statement shows Jesus' fatherly care for his own, those he loved (see 13:1). It also underscores the exegesis of 14:17 by affirming Jesus' presence with the disciples through the Spirit of truth. *I will come to you.* Lit., "I am coming to you." Jesus' assurance to his disciples that he would come to them when the Spirit was given to them (see comments on 14:17) was fulfilled on the evening of the Resurrection, when Jesus breathed into his disciples the Holy Spirit (20:22). This coming would be only in *a little while* (NRSV), during which time Jesus would experience crucifixion, burial, and resurrection (see 16:16-23 and comments).

The world would *not see* him *anymore*, but they would see him in his resurrection appearances (see 20:20, 26; 21:1, 14). In resurrection, the living Jesus would become the disciples' life because they would become united to him like branches to the vine. This is the intent behind the words, *Because I live, you also will live.* As the Son's life was (and is) dependent upon the Father's life (5:26; 6:57), so the believer's life is dependent on the Son's life.

14:20 *On that day.* I.e., the day of resurrection. After Jesus' resurrection, the disciples would come to *realize* that the Son is in the Father, and they are in the Son, and the Son is in them: *I am in my Father, and you in me, and I am in you.* This is the climax of John 14 because the mutual indwelling is made complete; God and the believers are depicted as living in one another.

14:21-24 *He who has My commandments and keeps them, it is he who loves Me. And he who loves Me will be loved by My Father, and I will love him and manifest Myself to him* (NKJV). In these verses, the mutual indwelling is made personal. The one who loves Jesus demonstrates his love by keeping Jesus' commands. In return, this lover is loved by the Father and Jesus himself. Furthermore, Jesus manifests himself to those who love him. The Greek word underlying *manifest* means "to be brought into light, to appear, to be made visible." The word is used in 21:1 in connection with the Lord's final resurrection appearance. Jesus manifested himself to his disciples visibly and physically; thereafter to all his other followers he is manifested in his invisible, spiritual presence (see 20:29; 2 Cor 4:6). In 14:22, *Judas* (not Judas Iscariot, but Judas the son of James—see Luke 6:16) asked Jesus how he was going to *manifest* himself to the disciples *and not to the world.* The disciples had been expecting Jesus to make a public manifestation in which he would present himself to the world as the long-expected Messiah. Judas wanted to know why Jesus spoke only of manifesting himself to the disciples. It is a very good question. Why didn't Jesus show himself to the world after his resurrection? Wouldn't this appearance convince the Jews that he was the Messiah? Why would he appear only to his select few?

If anyone loves Me, he will keep My word; and My Father will love him, and We will come to him and make Our home with him (NKJV). Jesus' response doesn't seem to be a direct answer to Judas's question, but its intent is to reassure Judas and the disciples that neither Jesus nor the Father would be abandoning them. To the follower of Jesus, the Son and the Father would come and make a permanent abode with him (14:23). Note: it does not say, as might be expected by the context of John 14, that the Father and Son make an abode *in* the one who loves God, but *with* him. The Greek preposition used here (*para*) denotes a side-by-side, mutual activity, as between two lovers who make a home with each other. The RSV and NIV convey this thought with the rendering, "we will come to him and make our home with him." Earlier in this chapter, Jesus revealed how he and the Father were a habitation for the believers. Now each believer becomes a dwelling for the Father and the Son, as well as the Spirit (see 14:17-18).

14:25-26 *the Counselor* [Comforter]*, the Holy Spirit, whom the Father will send.* In 15:26 Jesus says that he will send the Spirit from the Father. The word variation does not imply a contradiction, but shows that the Spirit would be sent by both the Father and the Son.

in my name. The Spirit comes in the Son's name, the name of Jesus Christ, because the Spirit brings the Son's presence to the disciples and continues the work of the Son. Perhaps this is why "the Spirit" in certain verses in the New Testament has taken on the names Lord ("the Spirit of the Lord," 2 Cor 3:17-18), Jesus ("the Spirit of Jesus," Acts 16:7), Christ ("the Spirit of Christ," Rom 8:9; 1 Pet 1:11), and Jesus Christ ("the Spirit of Jesus Christ," Phil 1:19).

will teach you all things and will remind you of everything I have said to you. The Spirit would continue Jesus' teaching ministry. The Spirit would also remind the disciples of those things that Jesus had taught. This gives us some insight into how the Gospel writers, such as John, who wrote his account nearly sixty years after the events occurred, could recall all those things that Jesus had said. They did so through the help of the Spirit. (For more on the ministry of the Spirit, see comments on 15:26; 16:13-15.)

14:27 *Peace I leave with you; my peace I give you.* The Greeks' notion of "peace" was absence of war. The Jews' notion of "peace" was blessing and unity. Jesus' bestowal of peace accords with the Jewish view: He was giving his disciples true spiritual peace (his very own peace)—a peace that would keep them through the time of trial ahead. After three days the risen Jesus would come to them and again bestow his peace upon them (20:19).

14:28 *You heard me say to you, "I am going away, and I am coming to you"* (NRSV). See 14:3 and comments.

If you loved me, you would rejoice that I am going to the Father, because the Father is greater than I (NRSV). Jesus, about to leave his beloved disciples, was ready and looking forward to returning to his beloved Father. In a sense, therefore, Jesus was asking his disciples to forget their own sorrow about his departure and instead rejoice with him because he was returning to the one who sent him. If they truly loved Jesus, they would understand this. In saying that "the Father is greater than I," Jesus was not contradicting his previous statement, "I and the Father are one" (10:30). This verse pertains to his voluntary position as servant under God (as one sent by the Father), while 10:30 pertains to his essential coequality with God (as one sharing the Godhead with the Father).

14:29 I have told you now before it happens, so that when it does happen you will believe. The disciples were told about Jesus' imminent departure and return so that they would recognize this as a "fulfillment of Jesus' words and believe that he is the person he claims to be" (Bruce).

14:30-31 I will not speak with you much longer, for the prince of this world is coming. He has no hold on me, but the world must learn that I love the Father and that I do exactly what my Father has commanded me. In view of his imminent death, Jesus would not be able to be with his disciples much longer. He had to face death and, in so doing, face the prince of this world (12:31), who has the power of death (Heb 2:14). Yet the devil would not be able to exert this power over Jesus, for Jesus would conquer death. Death would take Jesus but not hold him. When Jesus went to the cross, it would look like the prince of this world was in control, but actually the Father was in control—and Jesus was fulfilling his plan by going to the cross to accomplish redemption. Jesus faced death as one who did so out of love for his Father, because his Father had sent him to die for the sins of the world. The Father's love for humanity ("the world") sent his Son to the cross. The Son's love for his Father motivated him to go to the cross.

Come now; let us leave. Many attempts have been made to reconcile this statement with the fact that Jesus doesn't seem to go anywhere, but rather keeps speaking in chapters 15–17. However, it is not unlikely that Jesus continued to speak to the disciples as he walked, in peripatetic fashion. Perhaps the final prayer was uttered just outside the Garden of Gethsemane before they entered it (see 18:1). Another explanation is that there could have been a time interval between chapter 14 and chapters 15–17 of a day (Wednesday evening to Thursday evening), which would help harmonize John with the Synoptics on the time of the Last Supper. Or there could have been an interval of hours, which would help explain why Jesus said no one asked him where he was going (16:5), when in fact, they had just asked him in chapter 14.

ENDNOTES

[1]The shorter reading is in 𝔓66ᶜ ℵ B C* L W; the expanded reading ("And where I go you know and the way you know") is found in 𝔓66* A C³ D.

[2]The reading "if you had known me, you would have known my Father also" is in A B C L; the reading "if you have known me, you will have known my Father also" is in $\mathfrak{P}$66 ℵ D W.

[3]It should be noted that several manuscripts ($\mathfrak{P}$66[c] $\mathfrak{P}$75 ℵ A D L Q W) read, "because he abides with you and will be in you"; a few other ancient manuscripts ($\mathfrak{P}$66* B D* W) read, "because he abides with you and is in you." The external evidence for both readings is strong, and so is the internal evidence. If the text originally had two present verbs, Jesus' statement about the Spirit could be understood to describe, proleptically, the twofold location of the Spirit in relationship to the believer. In other words, the Spirit is viewed in his future state as present *with* and *in* the believer. If the text originally had a present-tense verb and a future-tense verb, then Jesus probably meant that the Spirit as present with Jesus (then and there) was *with* the disciples and in the future would be *in* the disciples.

Jesus, the True Vine

JOHN 15:1–16:4

EXPOSITION

John 15 follows John 14 thematically in that it continues the theme of God and the believers living and abiding in each other. Chapter 15 advances the image from an inorganic dwelling to an organic one: "house" and "rooms" become "vine" and "branches." In chapter 15 the imagery of vine and branches speaks of a living union between Christ and his believers, as well as a spiritual union among all those attached to him. Each believer's union with Christ is the basis of his or her union with all other believers. This illustration of vine and branches corresponds to the Pauline image of the head and many members comprising the one body of Christ; both show the relationship between Christ and the church as a living, organic entity. Finally, this chapter provides further explanation about how the disciples, with the help of the Comforter, would continue Jesus' work of glorifying the Father in the midst of a hostile world.

The reader should be cautioned that no illustration or parable is complete in and of itself with respect to purporting theology. Theology should be based on plain statements, not parables. Hence, we should be careful not to formulate a theology based on Jesus' illustration of the vine and the branches. Most of Jesus' illustrations, taken as a whole, portray his observations about certain spiritual realities. For example, the parable of the sower in the synoptic Gospels is an illustration of how different people respond to the message of the gospel. We go beyond the intent of the parable if we ask questions such as, "Were the people represented by the rocky soil and those choked by weeds ever regenerated? Were they true Christians who then lost their salvation?" Likewise, we go beyond the intent of Jesus' illustration about the vine and the branches when we ask, "Were the branches that didn't bear fruit true Christians who lost their salvation?" To ask these questions is to read our theology into the text. Rather, we should take the text for what it portrays of the relationship of Christ and believers.

15:1-16/*Fertility of Spirit*

Jesus used timeless and universal word pictures to graphically illustrate spiritual concepts. In chapter 14 he used the image of a house with many rooms to picture believers' eternal dwelling with God. Now he uses another illustration of how believers are a part of Christ as a branch is part of a vine. Because some Bible teachers have minutely stretched aspects of Christ's parables beyond their intent, we need to be reminded that every illustration has its limitations. Or as one homiletician said, "No illustration will walk on all fours." We must be careful not to build a theology or construct a doctrine on each word in the particulars of a parable or illustration. Parables, stories, and illustrations are used to elucidate or illuminate a certain truth. Rather than dissect the illustration, we should look at the illustration as a whole. From this vantage point, we look at Jesus' words in chapter 15 and conclude he is instructing his disciples about relationships.

Our relationship to the Savior. As Jesus spoke of the true vine, the disciples may have thought of Psalm 80, where Israel is pictured as the vine that brought forth wild grapes rather than the intended fruit of God's desire. When Jesus came, he was the True Vine of God's planting. This created the opportunity for God to display to the whole world the results of lives vitally related to himself. Jesus says he is the Vine and all believers are branches tended by the Father. The spiritual graces or fruit that adorn believers reflect the work of God. It is not something *we do* that produces fruit; it is something *God does* because of our existence in Christ Jesus. The fruit Jesus speaks of here is God expressing himself through the believer. Elsewhere in the Scriptures fruit can signify converts, or in some cases the effects of one's conduct, but here Jesus is talking of character. The words of Jesus are words of comfort and assurance, not commands. He certainly is not demanding that we do something. He is saying, "You are a part of me; we are together, united in the same way as branches to the vine. As you remain steadfast in your trust of me, your 'remaining' will naturally, spontaneously reveal God's fruit."

Even in our abiding, it is Christ who sustains that union. If we are apart from him, there simply is no fruit of God's producing. The beauty of this relationship is that there is no striving, no works, no pressure to perform, no wearing of sack-cloth and attention-getting self-denials. Jesus did not say, "I am the room; find the secret key and we'll be together." There is no spiritual elitism, no secrets to the "deeper life," no complicated, burdensome, stressful, demanding discipline initiating one into an exclusive type of Christianity. We must simply recognize whose we are and where we are—in him. Jesus puts it as simply as possible: You are a branch; abide in me. What can a branch do except abide? Our abiding is absorbing Christ, dwelling in his words, recognizing that he is with us, and enjoying the pleasure of his company.

We are to remain in him, unlike Judas, who never really was a part of him and so was purged. Professing religious people, having never had the life of God, having never received his sustenance, are finally severed from their superficial connection with Christ, like withered, dead branches removed by the gardener who cares for his vineyard. Anyone and everyone outside of Christ is dead and totally incapable of producing God's fruit. If there is no fruit, it's evident that the profession of abiding in Christ is spurious. But every branch truly connected to the Vine will have fruit.

Our relationship to one another. It is possible that fruit bearing, if not understood properly, could produce competition among Christians. Knowing human nature as he does, and recognizing that religious snobbishness could develop among believers, Jesus makes it abundantly clear that our abiding in him should produce love for the other branches, which represent believers. If we try to produce on our own a love for fellow believers, it will most likely prove to be hypocrisy in action. How can we possibly "pump up" something of divine origin? The love of which Jesus speaks is of God and comes to us, to be expressed naturally, as part of the life we have in the Vine. Having experienced God's love, we must continue in that love and demonstrate that love to other believers. Jesus said for us to love each other "as I have loved you." If we consciously, continually abide in his love, that love will express itself to those of the household of faith. Such a command is not intended to heap guilt upon us but to liberate us and give us great joy as we abide in Christ.

In an attempt to describe life's relationships, Steven Covey said in *The Seven Habits of Highly Effective People* that we are born dependent, strive to become independent, and if we ever reach full maturity, it is because we have learned to be interdependent. In the Christian life we need to be very much aware of our interrelatedness in the household of faith. We are to be lovers, not loners, allowing the acceptance we are experiencing in Christ to be expressed to all believers. This love for fellow believers is critically important since we will experience the animosity of the world.

Our relationship to the world. The antagonism of the world is to be counteracted or repelled by love for one another. Believers need to be united by the bonds of brotherly love because the world hates them, and the devil will endeavor to stir up bitterness, dissension, and strife among them. Jesus tells his disciples what the rest of the New Testament reminds us—that believers are aliens in this world. Aliens must always expect to experience a degree of prejudice against them. *World* in the sense Jesus is using the term is society organized without God, a culture or system of living that does not recognize God and is, in fact, at enmity with God. Today in some places of the world, mostly in America and Western Europe, Christians live in an environment somewhat shaped by the Christians who preceded them, so that they are protected by law from persecution. But today in many parts of the world, Christians daily face what the disciples faced after Christ's ascension. The Jewish world hated Christ because he claimed to be God. The Roman world hated him because he claimed to be King. Literally without a cause, they hated Christ. Such hatred seems so irrational, but we fail to grasp this reality: Apart from Christ's love in our heart, we (all mankind) are enemies of God.

It shouldn't surprise us that what happens to the Vine happens to the branches. Because of our union with Christ we may face the violent animosity of the world before our life's journey is complete. What a comfort these words of Jesus must be for all those who do experience persecution. He identified himself with his own. Saul of Tarsus was wreaking havoc on the church in his persecution of the believers when Jesus appeared to him on the road to Damascus, asking, "Why do you persecute me?" (Acts 9:4). Experiencing persecution may tempt us to think that we are forgotten or forsaken by the Lord, but he told his disciples that he loved them as he loved the Father. Can we doubt for even an instant that Jesus loves the Father? Never! We are sustained in the hour of persecution by the reality of Christ's love and the mutual support we give each other as believers.

We shouldn't be surprised if we face persecution. Since we have declared our trust in Christ as the most important relationship in life, we antagonize those who regard God as totally irrelevant. Godly living (abiding in Christ) exposes evil and brings antagonism. Rejectors of God prefer darkness to light and so oppose anyone who exposes their evil situation. The disciples had witnessed the excommunication of the man born blind and healed by Jesus. They themselves would soon experience similar banishment, worse persecution, and even martyrdom. We who follow in their train should not be surprised at the world's hatred. We, like those before us, must bear it patiently, supporting each other in love, for ours is the victory in Christ Jesus, who gives us the Holy Spirit. We should always keep in mind that we are indissolubly connected to Jesus—as a branch is to the vine. As such, we enjoy a sense of fellowship and communion, going to the Father in Jesus' name and offering our petitions, having the Father delight in hearing and answering those prayers, and bringing forth eternal fruit.

Verse 16 has a unique phrase, "fruit that will last." Hardly anything corrupts faster than fruit. But the fruit of God is permanent and incorruptible. The only fruit that outlasts life and this world is the fruit of the person who abides in Christ. To abide in him is to let God produce in us rich, luscious, beautiful, eternal fruit to his glory.

KEY WORDS AND PHRASES

Vineyard imagery saturates this chapter; some of the more important terms are as follows:

- » The Father is *the vinegrower.*
- » Jesus is *the vine.*
- » The believers are *the branches.*
- » Branches connected to the vine *bear fruit.*
- » The same branches are *pruned* to bring forth *more fruit.*
- » Unconnected branches *wither* and *are burned.*

NOTES

15:1 I am the true vine (NRSV). Israel was the vine of God's planting, but it failed to bear the proper fruit (Isa 5:1-7; Jer 2:19-21). Jesus, with his believers incorporate in him, is the True Vine—the true fulfillment and actualization of the vine. As the entire race of Israel sprang from the patriarch Israel, the new generation of God's people is here viewed as originating from Christ, organically united to him, as branches growing from a vine. This then becomes the fulfillment of Psalm 80, in which "the son of man" is said to be the Vine planted by God.

my Father is the vinegrower (NRSV). Or gardener, cultivator. The vine and the branches, God's New Testament economy, are under the care of the Father. According to certain lexical studies, it is possible to translate the Greek words for "vine" (*ampelos*) and "branch" (*klēma*) as "vineyard" and "vine." This would mean that Christ is the vineyard, and each believer a vine planted in him, all under the care of the Father. However, most commentators prefer to see this chapter as speaking of a single vine with many branches (see Barrett, Morris).

15:2 every branch in me. The union between the Vine and the branches is characterized by the expression "in me." But this union can be broken. The Father **cuts off every branch . . . that bears no fruit.** The **branch that does bear fruit** God **prunes so that it will be even more fruitful.** The combination of the Greek words *airei* (takes) and *kathairei* (cleanses, purges, or prunes)—a definite wordplay that cannot be matched in English—is interesting. Most commentators understand the first word to designate the action of taking away or cutting off, and the second word to describe pruning to increase fruit bearing (see 15:6). This is a principle that Jesus repeatedly taught: Life comes from death. As it was with Jesus, the Vine, so it is with all the believers, the branches.

15:3 You are already clean. The Greek word for "clean" (*katharoi*) means "cleansed," "purged," or "pruned." (It is the participle form of the verb *kathairei* appearing in 15:2.) Jesus' illustration here shifts to a different level of abstraction. Purging, like pruning, is a spiritual cleansing, a taking away of the filth. This verse indicates that the disciples were already clean on account of the word Christ had spoken to them. According to 13:10ff, Jesus made it clear that his betrayer, Judas, was not clean; he was one of those branches that was cut off. But the other eleven disciples, now with Jesus, were all clean and ready for fruit bearing.

15:4 Abide in me as I abide in you (NRSV). This verse presents an important theme in this passage. Once each branch, each believer, has been positioned in the Vine, he is charged to remain in union with the Vine. The Greek word for "abide" is an aorist verb in the imperative mood. The verb here is constative; it encompasses the entire act of abiding and views it as a single event. Then, in the following sentences, Jesus uses present-tense verbs to describe the continual activity involved in maintaining oneness with him.

Just as the branch cannot bear fruit by itself unless it abides in the vine,

neither can you unless you abide in me (NRSV). As Jesus had a living dependence on the Father (see 6:57), so Jesus' believers need to have a living dependence on him. It is impossible to live the Christian life apart from Christ!

15:5 *he will bear much fruit.* Each branch that continues to remain in the vine will continually produce fruit. Some commentators say the fruit refers to new converts (cf. 15:6), and others, "the fruit of the Spirit" (see Gal 5:22-23). Andrew Murray says, "The essential idea of fruit is that it is the silent natural restful produce of our inner life" (*Abide in Me*). The fruit is the practical expression of the indwelling divine life. This expression in our lives should attract people to Jesus and thereby cause them to want to become new members of God's vine.

15:6 *Whoever does not abide in me is thrown away like a branch and withers; such branches are gathered, thrown into the fire, and burned* (NRSV). There are two basic ways to understand this verse. (1) It could speak of a branch that had union with the Vine and then lost the living connection. Each branch that does not continue to abide in the Vine is expelled by natural consequence. Having lost its union with the Vine, it dries up and falls off as a dead branch. (2) It could speak of one who appeared to be united to the Vine but never was and, therefore, dropped off. This condition is described in 1 John 2:19: "They went out from us, but they did not belong to us; for if they had belonged to us, they would have remained with us. But by going out they made it plain that none of them belongs to us" (NRSV). The consequence of never being united to Christ is that such ones are thrown away into the fire. Readers adopt different interpretations based on their theology. Whatever one's interpretation, the reader should note that the text speaks of being thrown out, of drying up, and then being gathered for burning. If the first interpretation (above) was the one closest to the original intent, one would think that Jesus would have spoken of drying up first, and then being expelled from the Vine. But the opposite order suggests that these branches never had a living union with Christ—they had been rejected and expelled (aorist tense in Greek).

Seen within its context, the verse is probably more parabolic and illustrative than doctrinal—unless, of course, the words apply to ones such as Judas Iscariot (see comments on 15:3). On the whole, the verse speaks of the vital necessity of abiding in the Vine and the consequences of not doing so. (See Ps 80:8-16; Isa 5:5-7; Ezek 15:2-7; 19:10-14; and the introduction to this section.)

15:7-8 *If you abide in me, and my words abide in you* (NRSV). The whole notion of abiding in Christ could be understood so subjectively that each believer could determine for himself what it entails, so Jesus equated abiding in the Vine with abiding in his Word. When a believer is abiding in Christ and Christ's words are abiding in him, his prayers will be answered. This does not mean that all requests are granted, however. The context suggests that the prayers should pertain to fruit bearing and glorifying the Father.

so you will be My disciples (NKJV). This reading is supported by some early manuscripts, while others read, "that you may become my disciples." The difference in meaning is scarcely perceptible. Whichever reading is original, John sees fruit bearing as "the outward and visible sign of being a disciple" (Barrett). In the midst of an unbelieving, Christ-rejecting world, those who abide in Christ bring glory to God.

15:9-13 *As the Father has loved me, so I have loved you; abide in my love* (NRSV). An incredible promise! We do not doubt that God loved the Son, but it may seem incredible that Christ loves us in the same manner. It is not based on words or on the believer earning such love. Let us cherish this love and remain in it. One of the practical ways to *abide* in this *love* is to keep Jesus' commands—just as he kept his *Father's commandments*. If we do so, we will experience the daily joy of obedience to our Lord (15:9-11). Jesus' commands are summed up in one command: *"love one another"* (NRSV). And the highest expression of love for another is that a person *lay down his life for his friends*—just as Jesus did for those he loved.

15:14-16 *You are my friends if you do what I command. I no longer call you servants, because a servant does not know his master's business. Instead, I have called you friends, for everything that I learned from my Father I have made known to you.* In Jesus' day the disciples of a rabbi were the servants of the rabbi. Jesus now reveals the new level of relationship he was initiating with his disciples—no longer as rabbi to servant, but now as friend to friend. How wonderful to be friends of Jesus! Once we were enemies, but now Jesus considered his disciples to be his friends because he had told them everything he had heard from the Father. He trusted that they would receive these communications and then pass them on to others as the gospel. In fact, he *chose* them and *appointed* them to go forth with the gospel. Again it is most evident that God was in charge. He did the choosing. He has appointed us to bring forth fruit. This is not an ordination but a placing, a positioning. This, of course, recalls the image of vine and branches at the opening of this chapter. Each believer is chosen by the Lord to be a branch in the Vine, bearing *fruit that will last*. The remaining, lasting fruit could signify new believers or the fruit of the Spirit—especially brotherly love (see 15:17). Then Jesus speaks of making requests to the Father: *the Father will give you whatever you ask in my name*. As in 15:7-8, the request making is linked with the fruit bearing. "It is not possible for the disciples to bear lasting fruit if their requests are not granted by the Father" (Schnackenburg).

15:17 *This is my command: Love each other.* This is a pivotal verse in this section, for it recapitulates the theme Jesus introduced in 15:12 and yet also serves as a contrast for what follows. The disciples are to love one another because they will take Jesus' message to a world that despises them. The external hatred should intensify, not diminish, the internal love of the Christian community. And so it has been—history has shown that persecution serves to increase love among believers.

15:18 *If the world hates you, be aware that it hated me before it hated you* (NRSV). The world of which John spoke is that mass of humanity under Satan's domain that opposed Christ. It was on the verge of totally rejecting its God and Savior, Jesus Christ, by assenting to his crucifixion. The same world would surely hate those who proclaim their allegiance to this crucified Lord. Today those believers who live in the West, or at least in North America, live in an environment somewhat shaped by Christians who preceded them, so that by law they are protected. But in many places of the world it is not so: Those who reject Christ persecute those who follow him.

15:19 *If you belonged to the world, it would love you as its own. As it is, you do not belong to the world, but I have chosen you out of the world. That is why the world hates you.* A Christian's distinction and separation from the world constitute his sanctification, a sanctification not of his own choosing, but of the Lord's. This holy separation arouses the animosity of those from whom we are separate and distinct. The world would prefer that we were like them; since we are not, they hate us (see 1 Pet 4:3-4). Any professing Christian who is warmly embraced by the world at large should reexamine the reality of his claim to discipleship (2 Tim 3:10-12; Jas 4:4; 1 Jn 2:15-17; 3:1; 4:5-6).

15:20-21 *Remember the word that I said to you, "Servants are not greater than their master"* (NRSV). Jesus had told them this earlier that evening (see 13:16; cf. Matt 10:24).

If they persecuted me, they will persecute you; if they kept my word, they will keep yours also (NRSV). This proclamation points to the practical unity of the Vine with the branches. The life of the believers is intrinsically joined with Christ's; his experience will be theirs, both negatively through persecution and positively through acceptance. When Saul of Tarsus was confronted by the risen Christ on the road to Damascus, Jesus took Saul's persecution of the Christians to be a persecution of himself: "Why do you persecute me?" (Acts 9:4). To persecute the body of Christ is to persecute Christ. On the positive side, the disciples' message was often received, not as the word of men, but as the word of God (see 1 Thes 2:13). This is the portion of those who bear Jesus' *name*.

15:22-25 *If I had not come and spoken to them, they would not be guilty of sin. Now, however, they have no excuse for their sin.* "Jesus does not mean, of course, that the Jews would have been sinless had he not appeared. But he does mean that the sin of rejecting God as he really is would not have been imputed to them had they not had the revelation of God that was made through him" (Morris). But since they rejected the Word, the very revelation of God the Father to men, they had no way to cover up their sin. Their rejection of Jesus caused their sin of unbelief to be fully exposed. They hated the Son and the Father—even after seeing the marvelous works Jesus performed and seeing the Son of God himself with God the Father manifest in him: *"But now they have seen these* *miracles, and yet they have hated both me and my Father."* The Scriptures predicted this rejection and hatred. Citing **their Law** (i.e., the Scriptures), Jesus quoted Psalm 69:4 (a messianic psalm): *"They hated me without reason"* (see also Ps 35:19). Ultimately, this sin is the worst kind because it is an irrational rejection of Christ.

15:26 But I will send you the Comforter—the Holy Spirit, the source of all truth. He will come to you from the Father and will tell you all about me (TLB). In 14:26 Jesus said that the Father would send the Comforter in the name of his Son. Just as the Son had come in the Father's name (i.e., the Son, as the very embodiment of the Father, came to express the Father), so the Spirit would come in the Son's name, as the embodiment of the Son, to make the Son real in the believers' experience. However, in 15:26 it is stated that the Son would send the Comforter, the Spirit of truth, from the Father. There is actually no contradiction, for Jesus said that he would send the Spirit "from the Father." (In fact, Jesus emphasized that the Spirit proceeds out from the Father.) Therefore, both 14:26 and 15:26 identify the Father as the one from whom the Spirit would be sent. John 15:26 adds an extra detail: The Son would also send the Spirit. Thus the Father and Son together would send the Spirit. The function of the Spirit is to make Jesus real to the believers and to bear witness of Jesus (this function is described in 16:7-15).

15:27 You also are to testify because you have been with me from the beginning (NRSV). This statement refers especially to Jesus' original disciples, since only they had been with him from the beginning of his ministry (see Luke 1:2; Acts 1:21-22). But by application the verse could extend to all Christians as well.

16:1-4 The first four verses of the sixteenth chapter are a continuation of 15:18-27 in that they form the conclusion for Jesus' warning to his disciples concerning the persecution they will encounter after his departure. As such, they belong with chapter 15.

These things I have spoken to you, that you should not be made to stumble (NKJV). Jesus' words of 13:31–15:27 (and especially 15:18-27, which deal with the disciples' persecution) were given to the disciples as a safeguard against the trials that awaited them. Jesus did not want them to be caught off guard or ensnared in any way. (The Greek word translated "be made to stumble" [*skandalizō*] literally means "be ensnared.") This is really one of the most helpful things Jesus could have told these men. He made it clear that they were going to be hated and face trials. To be forewarned is to be forearmed.

They will put you out of the synagogue. In 9:22 and 12:42, it was said that anyone who confessed Jesus as the Messiah would be expelled from the synagogue (see comments on 9:22). Jesus now predicts the same for the disciples. Probably these disciples could not conceive of worship apart from the synagogue. But once they were thrust out, the church was born. At the time John wrote this

Gospel, there was a clear division between the church and the synagogue, since the synagogues had intensified their efforts throughout the first century to expel those who confessed Jesus as the Messiah.

an hour is coming when those who kill you will think that by doing so they are offering worship to God (NRSV). A prime example of such a one was Saul of Tarsus before his conversion. He thought he was serving God by killing those who proclaimed Jesus as their Messiah (see Acts 7:54–8:3; Gal 1:13-14; Phil 3:6). Saul had done this in ignorance because he was an unbeliever (1 Tim 1:13). This is just as Jesus said, *"They will do such things because they have not known the Father or me."* Thus, the disciples were forewarned. When the persecutions would actually occur, the disciples would be better able to accept them because they would *remember* that Jesus had told them these things. He waited until the very last evening to tell them these things because he himself had been with them *from the beginning* (NRSV). As such, he was the object of persecution—not they. But in the future that would change.

Jesus and the Spirit

JOHN 16:5-33

EXPOSITION

This chapter opens with Jesus' promising the disciples that he would send them the Comforter, the Encourager, who is the Spirit of truth. The Spirit would convict the world concerning sin, righteousness, and judgment, and would lead the believers into all the realities of Christ. Following this discussion, Jesus explained to them that his departure would last only "a little while" (actually only three days), for he would see them again on the day of his resurrection, and then their sorrow would be turned to joy! Christ's resurrection would institute a new relationship between the disciples and Jesus' Father. His Father would become their Father also. They would then be able to approach him as his children and bring to him their requests through prayer.

16:5-33/A New Way to Pray

I once visited, for a few hours, the beautiful Butchart Gardens in Victoria, British Columbia. Magnificent roses were in abundance along with some tuberous begonias, but we missed the flowering quince, the lilac, rhododendrons, azaleas, and much, much more. Because of the constant change of time and weather, you can't see, in just one visit, all there is to see. So it is with God's Word. It may be that some Scriptures have produced their fruit for us already, so that at first glance we take in their beauty and assimilate their provision for spiritual growth and health. Other Scriptures may have just begun to yield some of their sweetness and their beauty. Some portions may be as unopened buds to us, which will unfold in all their beauty sometime in the future. Still other verses may be as the century plant and not unfold in our lifetime, for some of the prophecies of this Book are sealed until the time of the end.

So it is not surprising to note that Jesus spoke some words beyond the understanding of his disciples, as in this instance when his words baffled them as much as if he had spoken in a foreign tongue. They said, "We don't know what he is saying" (v. 17), for Jesus did not explain in detail what he meant by their seeing him "after a little while." The perplexed disciples tried to find out among themselves what he meant, but the bud of truth did not open to them until later. The important truth for us to grasp is that Jesus knew all about their perplexity. It was not as though he was totally oblivious to their lack of understanding; he knew perfectly well their confusion. Sometimes we fail to grasp the purposes of God in our lives, and his activity seems utterly incomprehensible to us. In those dark moments we shall be helped if we remember God knows perfectly the beginning from the end. He knows we "see through a glass darkly," and he *cares*. Where we seek explanations, the Lord gives promises. We say, "Lord, what does all this mean that has come upon me?" And he answers, "Never will I leave you; never will I forsake you" (Heb 13:5). We say, "Why me? Why this?" He says, "I am with you always" (Matt 28:20). In some cases the explanations will come at a later time. While we may not think so, it is nevertheless true that his promises are of far greater value than explanations.

It is quite natural that at this time, when he is trying to prepare his disciples for his immediate departure, one of his promises to them should involve prayer. He frankly tells them that a new order of things will be instituted. Believers will be able to go directly to the Father in prayer. Up until then, Jehovah was known as the God of Israel, but now believers could approach him just as children address their *father*. This is good news indeed—that we can take our requests directly to God because we have the assurance that he loves each one of us. The way to God is open for all—that is, all who love Christ—for they are loved by God.

Perhaps there is no other subject on which there is more confusion than that of prayer. A few misguided people have the idea that prayer is *our effort* to overcome God's unwillingness or reluctance to do something for us. That simply is not the case. We are not told to pray in order to overcome God's resistance. The Father *delights* to bless, and he takes great pleasure in meeting us at the place of prayer. Prayer is not an exercise humans have designed as necessary for saintly living, but prayer is the biblical method of demonstrating the reality of God and his definite interest in the affairs of his people. As Jesus explained this new order—this new way of praying, based upon a new relationship—he encouraged the disciples by the privileges that were soon to be theirs, and which are now ours.

A new practice for prayer. Jesus says, "I'll soon be gone [physically], but you may directly ask the Father." The word "ask" here implies seeking help. All believers are urged to make their needs known to God, and not just to make them known, but to do so with a settled confidence and assurance that he hears us and will answer. When I go to God in prayer, I find that speaking to him of the things that burden me has a purifying effect on my soul. Our needs send us to him, and when we talk things over with him, it pleases him to remove or ease our burdens. That is just one reason why the psalmist said, "It is good to be near God" (Ps 73:28). If we did not have some special needs to make us go to God, we would probably move from day to day forgetting the privilege of speaking with the Father. But having needs, we pour out our hearts to him, telling him of our financial worries, our family concerns, the desire for the salvation of loved ones, and the goals and aspirations of our hearts. As we unburden our hearts, he gives a peaceful spirit, a calm assurance, and a joyful heart. Then with lightened hearts and a sense of his blessing, we are able to go on to our tasks and responsibilities.

A new basis for prayer. The disciples could now approach God in the name of Jesus. Up to this time they had not prayed for anything through the mediation of Christ. They had followed him as Teacher, looked up to him as Master, loved him as a Friend, and believed him to be the Messiah predicted by the prophets, but they had not realized that he was the one Mediator between God and man. Through him alone God's mercy could come down to sinners, and only through him could sinful men draw near to God. Jesus tells them to approach God the Father in his name, the name above every name, the name God is pleased to honor. This is not a formula or a magic incantation to be automatically and unthinkingly appended to every prayer; it is a demonstration of our willingness to be united with the will of the Lord Jesus. We should ask ourselves, *Does this request really blend with the lifestyle, the desires, the spirit, and the attitude of Jesus Christ? Would Jesus pray this way to the Father?* Having passed such a test, we then can have great boldness and assurance as we speak with the Father.

A new certainty in prayer. Jesus makes it abundantly clear: "He will give . . . you shall receive." This matchless promise is reiterated in Hebrews 4:16: "Let us then approach the throne of grace with confidence, so that we may receive mercy and find grace to help us in our time of need." We do well to remind ourselves that there are no conditional clauses, limitations, or exceptions in this promise. We come to him; he gives; we receive. If this is not our regular experience, then we need to carefully evaluate whether we are praying in Jesus' name. Through him we have the right to boldly approach our heavenly Father, saying, in effect, "Your Son—my Savior, the Lord Jesus Christ—has told me to come to you and tell you all about my needs as they conform to the Lord's good pleasure. You will answer!" Such an understanding of prayer ought to do away with the uncertainties and doubts many have regarding the assurance of answered prayer.

A new result from prayer. Jesus promises that our joy may be full. As we bring our desires into harmony with God, we will know this promised joy. Viewing our communion with God in such a light gives a whole new atmosphere to prayer. It is not an empty exercise in which we approach God heavyhearted and con clude still heavyhearted. This marvelous promise is ours to experience. As we bring our requests into conformity and union with Christ's will, we shall, with all certainty, have the joy of the Lord. This joy is deep contentment—an inner satisfaction unrelated to laughter, gaiety, or mirth. The writer of many proverbs observed, "Even in laughter the heart may ache" (Prov 14:13). Solomon had in mind surface conditions that do not affect the deep issues of life. When we face the raging turmoils of life and commit them all to Jesus, we will know the gift of a God-given contentment ruling our spirit, not in some mediocre manner, but with full, complete joy. May the expectation of such a promise hasten us regularly to the place of prayer!

KEY WORDS AND PHRASES

The sentiment of this chapter—as it pertains to the disciples' sorrow about Jesus' departure—is best described by the short similitude Jesus told them: "A woman giving birth to a child has pain because her time has come; but when her baby is born she forgets the anguish because of her joy that a child is born into the world" (16:21).

   This similitude not only describes how quickly sorrow is turned to joy when that sorrow brings joy, it is also a depiction of God's people (represented by the disciples) being delivered from their sorrows and travails by virtue of Christ's victory over death (see comments on 16:21 below). Christ's journey into death and resurrection would produce the greatest joy this world has ever known.

NOTES

16:5-6 *Now I am going to him who sent me, yet none of you asks me, "Where are you going?"* It is important to note that the verb "asks" is present tense; otherwise, this statement would contradict 13:36 and 14:5. The disciples had asked (past tense) where Jesus was going. In this verse Jesus was asking for an immediate reaction to his words about his departure. Jesus knew that the disciples were very sad (*"you are filled with grief,"* he said) to hear about his departure. A gloomy scene: no one was talking—it was almost like a wake. "But if only they had asked where he was going, and grasped that it was to the Father, they would not have grieved but recognized that his departure was for their advantage" (Barrett).

16:7 *it is to your advantage that I go away, for if I do not go away, the Advocate* [the Comforter] *will not come to you* (NRSV). This verse connects with 7:39, which says that the Spirit would not be available until Jesus was glorified. Once Jesus was glorified—through the process of crucifixion, resurrection, and ascension—he could send the Spirit to the believers. Thus it was for their advantage that he had to go away. The absence of Jesus' physical presence would be compensated for by the presence of the Paraclete, through whom Jesus would also be spiritually present in each of his disciples. When Jesus was with his disciples in the flesh, he could only be *with* them, but after his glorification and the coming of the Paraclete, he could live *in* them through the Spirit. This was to their advantage. We think just the opposite—that if Jesus were here physically it would be better. But he made it clear that the spiritual relationship is better than the physical.

16:8-11 *When he comes, he will convict the world of guilt in regard to sin and righteousness and judgment.* Jesus here declares that the Spirit will convict the world (prove mankind guilty) concerning sin, righteousness, and judgment. This was Jesus' ministry while he was on earth. Now the Spirit would carry on this work primarily through the verbal witness of the apostles, for this is suggested by the Greek verb *elegxei*, which conveys the idea of "speaking to reprove." Thus in the book of Acts we see the Spirit working through the apostolic witness to convict the hearts of sinners. Peter's first gospel message in Acts 2 is a preeminent example. The Spirit will convict the world (1) of its sin *because men do not believe in me* [Jesus] (i.e., the world's unbelief is their sin); (2) concerning *righteousness, because I* [Jesus] *am going to the Father, where you can see me no longer* (i.e., it will now be the Spirit's function to show men that righteousness is in Christ); (3) concerning judgment *because the prince of this world now stands condemned* (i.e., the Spirit will show to mankind that Jesus judged Satan). Operating according to what Christ has accomplished, the Spirit convicts men concerning their sin of unbelief in Christ, concerning the righteousness that is found in Christ alone, and concerning the judgment over Satan that was accomplished by Christ on the cross (Morris).

The world was wrong in judging Jesus and taking him to the cross. But at the cross Jesus triumphed over the devil (Heb 2:14). This was a judgment against Satan and a triumph for Christ. The Holy Spirit would convict the world for having judged the wrong person—Jesus, not Satan. The irony is that the one who was seemingly judged on the cross (Jesus) was actually executing judgment on Satan.

16:12 Having indicated what the Spirit would be doing "in the world" (16:7-11), Jesus then relates (in 16:13-15) to the disciples what the Spirit would be doing in the believers (Morris). The Holy Spirit would lead them to truth that they could not handle right now. Jesus, having foreknowledge, could have told them all that was going to happen, but they would not have been able to bear it. In like manner, who among us really wants to know what the future holds? If God were to reveal to us our future, many of us would be aghast at what calamities and diseases await us.

16:13-15 These verses display a sublime picture of the interrelationship and inner workings of the three Persons of the Godhead. Particular details are given to describe the Spirit's function of conveying the Father and the Son to the believers, and of leading the believers into the Son and the Father.

he will guide you into all truth [or *reality*]. The prominent role of the Spirit of reality is to guide (lit., "lead the way"—the Greek verb shares the same root as the word for "way") the believers into (Gr., *eis*) all the reality of Christ. When the Spirit leads the believers into all the truth, he penetrates that sphere for them and guides them into a definite destiny—Christ.

He will not speak on his own; he will speak only what he hears. In addition to revealing Christ and guiding the believers into the experience of Christ, the Spirit's function is to continue the spoken ministry of Jesus. According to 14:26, the Spirit would come to carry on Jesus' speaking, both by way of teaching and by way of reminding the disciples of what Jesus had said during his ministry. The Spirit would also affirm Jesus' ministry by bearing witness to him (15:26). The Spirit's function throughout the church age has been to continue Jesus' spoken ministry. For example, in Revelation 2 and 3 *the Lord Jesus* addressed each of the seven local churches, and yet it is said that the churches should hear what *the Spirit* said to the churches (see Rev 2:1, 7-8, 11-12, 17-18, 29; 3:1, 6-7, 13-14, 22).

he will tell you what is yet to come. Most likely, this declarative function pertains to the Spirit's illumination of the events yet to happen in Jesus' life—i.e., his crucifixion, resurrection, ascension, etc. At the time these events happened, the disciples were unenlightened as to their significance. Afterwards, with the Spirit's guidance, they understood the meaning of all these events. The Spirit also reveals eschatological events (see 1 Tim 4:1; 2 Pet 3).

He will glorify me (NRSV). The Greek word for "he" indicates the personal identity of the Spirit. The Spirit does not glorify his own personality; rather he glorifies the Son's—*because he will take what is mine and declare it to you* (NRSV). The Spirit takes what the Son is and then reveals this to the believers.

All that the Father has is mine. For this reason I said that he will take what is mine and declare it to you (NRSV). Here the Spirit is seen in complete submission to and in harmony with the Son and the Father. He does not act or speak from himself. Nothing originates from him; all comes from the Son, and all is done to glorify the Son. Just as the Son did not do anything from himself, but only that which he heard and received from the Father, so the Spirit never acts independently from the Son. The Spirit's function is to reveal the Son (in all that he is) to the believers. Yet in revealing the Son, the Spirit is actually revealing the Father because all that the Son has comes from the Father. Thus the Spirit reveals the Son, who, in turn, expresses the Father. It is a clear revelation of the mutual interdependence of the Trinity.

16:16-19 *In a little while you will see me no more, and then after a little while you will see me.* Jesus knew something that his disciples didn't: he would be returning to them very soon. They were so filled with sorrow concerning his imminent departure (16:20) that Jesus had to assure them that the interim between his going and returning would be only for "a little while." The saying "In a little while you will see me no more, and then after a little while you will see me" was troublesome to the disciples. They were confused, even though earlier in the evening (ch 14) Jesus had spoken of his going to the Father and his imminent return to them on the day of the Resurrection. This "little while" would last only three days—during which time he would go to the cross, arise, ascend to the Father (20:17), and return to the disciples on the evening of the Resurrection (20:19-23).

16:20 Following his explanation of the interim between his departure and return, Jesus used a similitude (see 10:6; 16:25, 29) to depict how quickly the disciples' grief would turn to joy as well as to signify a spiritual truth about his death and resurrection: **You will grieve, but your grief will turn to joy.**

16:21 When a woman is in labor, she has pain, because her hour has come. But when her child is born, she no longer remembers the anguish because of the joy of having brought a human being [lit., "man"] **into the world** (NRSV). There may be more to this similitude than depicting grief turned to joy: (1) The woman's hour of labor corresponds to the "hour" the Lord constantly referred to throughout his ministry, which would be the hour of his glorification via crucifixion and resurrection (see 2:4; 7:30; 8:20; 12:23-24, 27; 13:1). (2) The man born into the world represents Christ, who was begotten from the dead (see Acts 13:33-34; Col 1:18). (3) The woman in labor, according to the context, probably depicts the grieving disciples who, in a greater sense, represent God's people who had the expectation of being delivered from their sorrows and travails by virtue of the Messiah's victory over death (see Isa 26:16-19; cf. Rev 12:1-5).

16:22 Now is your time of grief, but I will see you again and you will rejoice, and no one will take away your joy. Other manuscripts read, "You have sorrow now . . . and no one can take that joy from you." The reading with the present tense is more characteristically Johannine, for he has Jesus frequently using the present tense proleptically.[1] In any case, the joy of seeing the risen Christ would last a lifetime for each of the disciples. It is a joy that couldn't be snatched away by anyone or anything! Their joy would be rooted in the reality of the risen Christ.

16:23-24 In that day you will no longer ask me anything. This "day" is the day of Jesus' resurrection. When that day would come, their questions about his departure and return would be answered, for then they would understand. In the first "ask" of this verse the meaning is of inquiry, while the next "ask" involves petition, inaugurating the great invitation to pray in a new way—in the name of Jesus.

if you ask anything of the Father in my name, he will give it to you (NRSV). This reading is found in some manuscripts, while other ancient manuscripts read, "whatever you ask the Father he will give it to you in my name." The evidence for both readings is good.[2] Because Jesus usually spoke of making petitions to the Father in his own name (see 14:13, 14; 15:16; 16:24, 26), it would have been quite natural for scribes to conform the more unusual reading to the more usual order. In any case, this was another reminder that Jesus would not remain on earth indefinitely after he rose from the dead. Jesus encouraged them to **ask** so that they might **receive** and have full, complete **joy** (cf. 1 Jn 5:13-15).

16:25-27 I have said these things to you in figures of speech (NRSV). The Greek word for "figures of speech" (*paroimias*) could also be translated "similitudes" (see comments on 10:6; 16:21). Explicit predictions about future events would have overtaxed the disciples' weak faith at this point (cf. 16:12-13), so Jesus spoke to his disciples in figures of speech.

The hour is coming when I will no longer speak to you in figures, but will tell you plainly of the Father (NRSV). After Jesus arose and appeared to Mary Magdalene, he told her to tell his disciples: "I am ascending to my Father and your Father, to my God and your God" (20:17, NRSV). From that day forward, the disciples would enter into a new, revealed relationship with the Father by Jesus speaking to them about the Father through the Spirit (see comments on 16:13-15). And the disciples could make their requests known to the Father in Jesus' **name**. The Father would respond to the disciples because, as Jesus said, **"The Father himself loves you, because you have loved me and have believed that I came from God"** (NRSV). All who love Jesus and believe that he is God's Son are loved by the Father because they have loved him whom the Father dearly loves. The Greek word for "love" in this verse is *phileō*; it suggests fondness and intimate friendliness. Several early manuscripts read, "I came forth from God"; other ancient manuscripts read, "I came forth from the Father."[3] The first reading has earlier and more diverse support than the reading with "Father," which was probably assimilated from the next verse.

16:28-30 Then Jesus plainly said, **"I came from the Father and have come into the world; again, I am leaving the world and am going to the Father"** (NRSV). To which the disciples responded, **"Yes, now you are speaking plainly, not in any figure of speech!"** (NRSV). The disciples finally realized that Jesus had been speaking of his departure to the Father. Then they said, **"Now we know that you know all things, and do not need to have anyone question you; by this we believe that you came from God"** (NRSV). Now they were convinced that Jesus' impressive knowledge about future events marked him unquestionably as the Son of God come from God. To say that Jesus knew "all things" was tantamount to saying that he was omniscient and therefore divine. Nonetheless, it is amazing that it took them so long to realize his divine origin and divinity.

16:31-32 Though Jesus must have appreciated this acknowledgment of belief, incomplete as it was, he felt constrained to foretell the disciples' coming faithlessness in the face of adversity: **"The hour is coming, indeed it has come, when you will be scattered, each to his own home, and you will leave me alone"** (NRSV). This is an allusion to Zechariah 13:7, fully quoted in Matthew 26:31 and Mark 14:27. As predicted, all the disciples (except Peter and John—18:15) abandoned Jesus when he was arrested in the Garden of Gethsemane. Even though he was abandoned by his disciples, Jesus was not completely alone. As he said before (8:29), he now says again, **"Yet I am not alone because the Father is with me"** (NRSV).

16:33 Fortunately for the disciples' sake, Jesus did not end his discourse with the sad prediction in 16:32. He had a word of encouragement for them. He promised them **peace** through their union with him, the one who would **overcome** [or *conquer*] **the world** through his death and resurrection (cf. 1 Jn 5:4). By death, he would destroy the prince of this world, and in resurrection he would give the believers the ability to overcome the world by his life. *In this world* they would have *trouble*, but in Christ they would have peace.

ENDNOTES

[1]Some manuscripts ($\mathfrak{P}$22 $\aleph$ * B C W^C) read, "You have sorrow"; others ($\mathfrak{P}$66 $\aleph^C$ A D W) read, "You will have sorrow." The future tense verb appears to be an assimilation to the future tense in John 16:20. Some manuscripts ($\mathfrak{P}$22 $\mathfrak{P}$66^{vid} $\aleph$ A C) read, "takes"; others ($\mathfrak{P}$5 B D) read, "will take." Since the evidence among the earliest manuscripts is nearly divided, it is difficult to be dogmatic about one reading or the other. The reading with the present tense, however, is more characteristically Johannine. In the Gospel of John, Jesus frequently uses the present tense proleptically. Furthermore, the future tense could very well be an assimilation to 16:20.

[2]The reading "whatever you ask the Father in my name he will give it to you" is found in $\mathfrak{P}$22^{vid} A C^{3vid} D W. The reading "whatever you ask the Father he will give it to you in my name" is found in $\mathfrak{P}$5^{vid} $\aleph$ B C*.

[3]Several early manuscripts $\mathfrak{P}$5 $\mathfrak{P}$66^{vid} $\aleph$ *,2 A C^3 and W read, "I came forth from God." Other ancient manuscripts ($\aleph$ 1 B C D) read, "I came forth from the Father."

Jesus' Intercessory Prayer

JOHN 17:1-26

EXPOSITION

John 17 contains Jesus' intercessory prayer. This petition, which consummates his discourse begun in 13:31, expresses the deepest desires of Jesus' heart for his chosen ones. As such, this prayer is reminiscent of the prophetic blessings bestowed by such patriarchs as Abraham, Isaac, and Jacob on their sons just prior to death.

On the eve of his own death Jesus did not pray for the world, but for his own. He prayed for that group of men given to him as a gift from the Father, and he prayed for all who would believe in him through their message. He requested that all the believers would share with him in his glory and in his relationship with the Father. From eternity, the Father loved the Son, and the Son enjoyed coequal glory with the Father. The two (the Father and Son) with the Spirit are essentially and coinherently one. Jesus asked the Father to grant the believers a participation in this relationship by virtue of being in the triune God and the triune God being in them. Then, oneness among the believers was to issue from each believer's oneness with God.

17:6/The Real Lord's Prayer

It is universally felt that in some wonderful sense, the seventeenth chapter of John's Gospel is the sanctum sanctorum of Holy Scripture—the holy of holies. Here our Lord treats the Cross as behind him and permits us to hear him commune with the Father as from the other side of the torn veil. This chapter of twenty-six verses is a prayer—yet there is something so entirely beyond what constitutes prayer for us that we may call this communion.

This chapter is the Lord's Prayer. We generally use that term for the beautiful prayer he taught his disciples when he delivered the Sermon on the Mount: "Our Father in heaven, hallowed be your name, your kingdom come, your will be done on earth as it is in heaven. Give us today our daily bread. Forgive us our debts, as we also have forgiven our debtors. And lead us not into temptation, but deliver us from the evil one" (Matt 6:9-13). That is not really the Lord's Prayer, but a prayer outline or model given by the Lord, for he himself never prayed that prayer. He could never pray "forgive us our debts [sins]"—for he had none. What is generally designated the Lord's Prayer might more correctly be called the Disciples' Prayer. It is an outline given to the disciples for the petitions they might well bring to God, indicating the proper lines they should use in approaching God. John 17, on the other hand, gives us his own blessed utterances as he refers to his own glory, remembers his disciples, and thinks of all future believers. That is a three-point division for the entire prayer, but as we focus in on verse 6, three points emerge: what was revealed by the Son, what was a gift from the Father, and what was honored by the disciples.

The name, revealed by the Son. In reference to all of his followers, Jesus says to the Father, "I have made your name known" (NRSV). In the Old Testament, the expression "your name" is used in a special way. It does not refer simply to the name by which a person is addressed. It means the whole character and nature of the person, insofar as it can be known. In Psalm 9:10 we read, "Those who know your name will trust in you." This does not mean that those who know what God is *called* will trust him; it means that those who know what God is *like,* those who know the character and the nature of God, will be willing and glad to put their trust in him. Again the psalmist enlightens us at this point by saying, "Some trust in chariots and some in horses, but we trust in the name of the LORD our God" (Ps 20:7). The name of God signifies God himself—his perfections, his attributes, his character, his revealed self. In the Old Testament Jehovah manifested himself to his people by various names such as Jehovah-Jireh, "The LORD will provide" (Gen 22:14); Jehovah-Ropheka, "The LORD, who heals you" (Exod 15:26); and Jehovah-Tsidkenu, "The LORD our Righteousness" (Jer 33:16). By his name, God is made known. Through his revealed name we learn who God is. We also learn that he is jealous for his own holy name. How that name has been ignored, misrepresented, and blasphemed! So it was a glorious mission for Christ to come and manifest that name. Jesus counted it his highest glory to manifest that name to his own. Ignorance of that name is man's ruin, and knowledge of that name is man's salvation.

In Psalm 22:22 we read, "I will declare your name to my brothers." These words, taken from what we call a messianic Psalm, indicate that the Messiah would declare to his fellow man what God is like! This, of course, Christ wonderfully and perfectly did so that the promise of Isaiah 52:6 was fulfilled: "My people will know my name." Jesus has revealed the Father—his grace, his love, and his holiness.

The elect, a gift from the Father. In listening to the Savior pray, these disciples learned that it was not God's purpose to save the world en masse but to take out of the world a people for his name. There is humanity in its alienation from God, and from this estranged humanity God has given some to Christ. It was not that they were better than others. Indeed, they were children of wrath and enemies of God, with no love for him, no desire for him, no knowledge of him. Yet they were loved with an intensity that only God could be conscious of, and they were given to the Lord Jesus to be saved by him and to receive everlasting life. Had these disciples been the most faultless, perfect, constant, faithful, and loving of all those who do God's pleasure instead of a company of needy, weak, failing, unworthy sinners, our Lord could not have said more in their favor: "You gave them to me."

The more we discern the Father's interest in us, the greater our confidence when we come to him in prayer. What assurance we should have as we approach the throne of grace, realizing that the Father's heart has been set upon us from the beginning of all things! These words between the Father and the Son are registered for our sakes, that our faith may be increased and our hope established, and that we may love the Lord our God more fervently and continue on life's journey rejoicing.

In this intimate communion with the Father, Jesus does not speak of the heavens given to him, of the earth given to him, of thrones and dominions and principalities and powers and crowns given to him, but referring to his disciples, he says, "They were yours; you gave them to me." They are his flock, and he will gather them and watch over them. He will keep them, he will teach them, he will present them to the hosts of heaven without spot or wrinkle or any such thing some glorious day. They are his temple, and he will inhabit them. They are his inheritance, and he will protect them. No gift has ever been more cherished than the gift of believers from the Father to the Son. That is why he uttered this prayer—for our comfort and encouragement.

The Word, honored by the disciples. Our Lord commends his people to the Father in the highest possible way, for he says, "They have obeyed your word." Keeping, honoring, obeying the Word of God is the most acceptable action before God that believers can render. It is practical evidence of our love for God and our relationship to him. The world does not keep the Word of God; therefore it is impossible for God to be manifested to it. But as believers endeavor to keep his Word, he is ever increasingly manifested to them.

When Jesus prayed, "They have obeyed your word," he made no distinction between disciples. Some had more instruction than others. Some were much more faithful than others. Some walked much more closely with him than others. But making no distinction, Jesus spoke of them as one body and said to the Father, "They have obeyed your word."

Now there is a difference between our standing and our experience. In the case of the believers, God sees us only as he sees Christ—no spot, no stain; no possible accusation or condemnation can be brought against us, for we are complete in Christ. This is as true of one child of God as another. The least in the family, the feeblest believer in Christ, is as accepted as John or Paul or Simon Peter. "They have obeyed your word" is the way we are represented by Jesus before the Father. As to our experience, we sadly find our lives falling short of the high calling in Christ Jesus. We are often full of failure—our faith is quite feeble, our desires are often mingled with what is earthly and sensual, and we are disobedient to the commands of God. That is why we need to watch, to pray, to strive, to trust, to deny ourselves. But when Christ brings his own before the Father, it is with commendation: "They have obeyed your word."

Why should we keep his Word?

» It demonstrates our love—"If anyone loves me, he will obey my teaching" (John 14:23).

» It gives us joy and peace—"I have told you this so that my joy may be in you and that your joy may be complete" (John 15:11).

» It gives us comfort—Jesus sends the Comforter to teach us the Word (John 14:26), which is the foundation of our faith, our hope, the motive for our love, the lamp upon our path, our refuge in danger, our food in the wilderness, and our sword for the battle.

» It gives us assurance that our prayers are answered—"If you remain in me and my words remain in you, ask whatever you wish, and it will be given you" (John 15:7).

» It keeps us prepared in the time of temptation—"I have hidden your word in my heart that I might not sin against you" (Ps 119:11).

» It preserves us—"Since you have kept my command to endure patiently, I will also keep you from the hour of trial that is going to come upon the whole world" (Rev 3:10).

Since this is the case, we should let the Word of God be impressed upon our hearts, expressed in our daily living, confessed by our faith in Christ, and always professed in our conversation. When we keep his Word, we find that the Word steadies us, comforts us, enlightens us, strengthens us, and establishes us. What an incalculable joy it will be for us when we stand before the Father and hear the Son say, "They have obeyed your word."

KEY WORDS AND PHRASES

The key to understanding this prayer is that it is developed in three phrases. First, Jesus prayed for himself: he asked the Father to restore him to the relationship they had before the foundation of the world (17:1-5). Second, Jesus prayed for the eleven disciples: he asked the Father to protect them from the evil one and keep them sanctified by the Word (17:6-19). Third, Jesus prayed for all believers: he asked the Father to grant them all true, spiritual oneness so the world could see and believe the gospel (17:20-26).

NOTES

17:1-2 Jesus does not close his eyes to pray. Here is the greatest prayer recorded, and nothing is said about posture, etc., for the essence of prayer is communication with God. The hour had now come—the time of his final humiliation followed by his glorious resurrection. Jesus began his petition by asking the Father to **glorify your Son, that your Son may glorify** the Father. As was stated earlier (see 13:31), Jesus' glorification is the central theme of his discourse in 13:31 to 16:33. The glorifying of the Son involves a revealing of that which has been partially hidden. If the Father would glorify the Son in resurrection, the Son could in turn impart life to the believers (17:2) and so glorify the Father. Jesus made his requests known to the Father, realizing the Father **granted him authority over all people** and that he could **give eternal life to all those** (lit., "all which") the Father had **given him.** As was discussed earlier in connection with 6:37-39, Jesus used the neuter singular expression "all which" (Greek, *pan ho*) when referring to the one collective gift of all believers given to him by the Father. But in the same sentence he recognized the plurality and individuality of the members of that group by using a personal pronoun (Gr., *autois*—"them"). (See comments on 6:37-40 and 10:29-30.) Each believer is given to the Son as a gift from the Father. In turn, each believer is given the gift of eternal life.

17:3 And this is eternal life, that they may know you, the only true God, and Jesus Christ whom you have sent (NRSV). There may be an ellipsis in the first clause that could be filled in with the phrase "the result of receiving": "and this is the result of receiving eternal life." The reception of eternal life initiates a living relationship with God and his Son, Jesus Christ. The Greek verb *ginōskōsin* signifies the continual action of "getting to know." In colloquial English, we could render this verse: "And this is eternal life: that they may get to know you, the only true God, and Jesus Christ, whom you have sent."

17:4-5 I glorified you on earth (NRSV). In this statement, Jesus affirmed that he had glorified the Father on earth by accomplishing **the work** he was given **to do.** The last work, that of accomplishing redemption through his death on the cross, was about to be done. Looking beyond the Cross to his resurrection and ascension, Jesus asked the Father to glorify him with the glory he had with the Father **before the world existed** (NRSV). In saying this, Jesus lifted the veil to give us a glimpse of his relationship with the Father before the beginning of time. According to the Greek, Jesus was asking to be glorified alongside the Father (i.e., in the Father's presence) by means of (or with) the glory he had with the Father before the world was. In other words, Jesus was praying to enter into that pristine state of coequal glory with the Father, a position he possessed from eternity as God's Son (see 1:1, 18). He would enter into that glory in a new way—as the God-man, the crucified and risen Lord Jesus Christ. It is this glorified God-man we shall see in heaven.

17:6-10 After praying for his own glorification, Jesus turned the focus of his petition to his disciples. To these ones, whom the Father had given to him, Jesus had **revealed** the Father's **name** (NRSV; i.e., he had expressed the reality of the Father's person to them—see 1:18 and comments). They had received Jesus' words as messages sent from God; as a result, they had come to believe that Jesus *came from* the Father and was *sent* from the Father (see 16:28-30). These disciples were the object of Jesus' affection and prayer. He did not here pray for *the world*, but for the ones the Father had given him. They belonged to both him and the Father, and they were the ones in whom he would be glorified on earth after he returned to the Father. He was so confident of this glorification that he spoke of it as having been accomplished already: *"Glory has come to me through them."* This statement is a tremendous confirmation of their spiritual state; their reception of his words and their belief in him brought glory to Jesus.

17:11-12 Since Jesus would be leaving the world to rejoin the Father and since the disciples would be staying in the world, they needed to be kept from the evils in the world. *Holy Father, protect them in your name that you have given me, so that they may be one, as we are one* (NRSV).[1] Jesus was very much aware of the spirit world, and he prayed for the believers' protection from the evil one and their continued preservation by the Father. In our continued union with Christ, we are kept and separated.

Jesus asked that the holy (the adjective "holy" is appropriate for requests concerning sanctification) Father would keep them in the name that the Father had given him so that they would be one, even as the Son and Father are one. Jesus had kept them in his Father's name and *protected them* while he was with them. To be kept "in the Father's name" is tantamount to being kept by God's power (see Ps 20:1; 54:1; Prov 18:10). "By the Father's power, imparted to Jesus, Jesus himself guarded them as a treasure entrusted to him by the Father, and now he gives an account of his stewardship" (Bruce).

All of the disciples were guarded—*none of them is lost except the son of perdition* [or, "the man destined to be lost"—cf. 2 Thes 2:3], *that the Scripture might be fulfilled* (NKJV). The one who was lost was Judas Iscariot, who by his own volition betrayed Jesus, thus fulfilling what was predicted in Psalm 41:9 (quoted in John 13:18). Sometimes public prayer helps others who listen. Later on in Acts 1:17, Peter would refer to this very phrase in Christ's prayer.

17:13 *that they may have my joy made complete in themselves* (NRSV). Or this could be paraphrased, "may my joy be as fulfilling to them as it is to me." Jesus wanted his disciples to share in the joy he was about to experience in the presence of his Father. They couldn't leave the world with him, so he wanted to share his joy with them even while they were in the world. These words would have helped everyone present, for all were sad about the coming separation.

17:14-17 In this part of Jesus' intercessory prayer, he asked for the disciples' sanctification in the midst of a hostile world. Since he would be sending them forth into the world (even as the Father had sent him), they would need protection from *the evil one*, who controlled the world (see 12:31; cf. 1 Jn 5:18-19).

The two greatest sanctifying elements are God's **word** and **the truth**. Actually, both of these elements are inherent in one another—such that Jesus could say, **"Your word is truth"** (see also 8:31-32). God's word given to the disciples by Jesus is the absolute reality they had to cling to as they carried out their commission in the world. Belief in God's Word separates us from the world.

17:18-19 *As you sent me into the world, I have sent them into the world.* Once again Jesus spoke proleptically, for the disciples had not yet been commissioned by Jesus (see 20:21). But in view of their commission and their need for sanctification, Jesus proclaimed that he himself would fulfill his commission (i.e., die on the cross) and thereby sanctify himself: *And for their sakes I sanctify myself* (NRSV). This proclamation could also be translated, "On their behalf, I consecrate myself." Jesus consecrated himself to do the Father's will, to become a substitutionary offering (on the cross) made by the High Priest himself on behalf of his disciples. His consecration was for their sanctification (see Heb 10:5-10). Thus, the priest and the offering itself became one. "Here, then, the priest dedicates the sacrificial victim: it is because priest and victim are one that the sacrifice is not only completely voluntary but uniquely efficacious" (Bruce). As a result of Jesus' sacrificial death, the disciples would *be truly sanctified.*

17:20 After praying for his disciples, Jesus prayed for all those who would believe in him *through their message*. For the most part, the apostles' word became the New Testament Scriptures and the very foundation of the faith (see Eph 2:20). Indeed, John's Gospel itself is a fulfillment of Jesus' prayer, for his Gospel is the written message that went out to elicit faith (see 20:30-31). Furthermore, if it is fair to say that everyone who has become a Christian has done so through the apostles' words, then Jesus was praying for all the believers who would ever exist.

17:21 There are three requests in this verse, each beginning with "that" (Gr., *hina*): (1) *that they all may be one, as You, Father, are in Me, and I in You*; (2) *that they also may be one in Us*; (3) *that the world may believe that You sent Me* (NKJV). All the requests are subsequential: the second depends upon the first, and the third depends on both. In the first request, the Lord asked that *all* the believers may be one. This all-encompassing petition includes all the believers throughout time. The first request is qualified by an astounding fact: the oneness among the believers is to be *as* the coinherent oneness of the Father and the Son. In other words, as the Father and Son's oneness is that of mutual indwelling (10:30, 38; 14:9-11), so the believers are to have oneness with each other by virtue of the mutual indwelling between each believer and the triune God. This was illustrated by the Vine and the branches in chapter 15. Each and every branch in the Vine is one with all the other branches by virtue of their common participation of abiding in the Vine. Keep in mind that the branches may not be in close unity, but the unity is in the Son. We experience this whenever we meet true believers, no matter what their particular denominational preference.

17:22-23 Jesus further explained this oneness in terms of mutual indwelling: *that they may be one just as We are one: I in them, and You in Me; that they may be made perfect in one* (NKJV) or completed in their oneness. In 17:21 Jesus asked that the believers be *in* the Father and Son; in 17:22-23 he asked that the Father in the Son would together be in the believers. This is the completion and perfection of the mutual indwelling between the triune God and the believers. (See 1 Jn 4:13, which mentions the Spirit as the one who actualizes God's indwelling in the believers.) The reality and demonstration of this oneness will convince the world that the Father sent the Son. Again we should note that this occurs in the Spirit, not by man's ecumenical efforts.

17:24 *those you have given me.* Lit., "that which you have given me."[2] The term "that which" designates all the believers as the one collective entity given as a gift to him from the Father (see comments on John 6:37, 39; 10:29; 17:2). This is the same group referred to in 17:2; it includes all the ones who have received and will receive the gift of eternal life. This corporate whole is the universal church, the one body composed of many members. Jesus asked that each member could be with him *"where I am, and to see my glory."* Jesus' request concerns the believers' present experience and future hope. In the present, each believer is with Christ in God the Father (see 14:6; Col 3:3). Because of this relationship, the believer can see the glory of God in the face of Christ (2 Cor 3:18; 4:4-6). In the future, each believer will be with Christ in eternal glory, in the presence of the Father forever. The disciples had eternity to look forward to; Jesus could look back upon his eternal relationship with the Father and thus declare, *"You loved me before the creation of the world."* Again, Jesus lifted the veil to give us a glimpse of his eternal, preincarnate relationship with the Father. Even before the world existed, the Son enjoyed his Father's love.

17:25-26 In these last two verses, Jesus summarized the key themes of his intercessory prayer. Jesus addresses his Father as **Righteous Father** because "it is by God's righteous judgment that the world is shown to be wrong, and Jesus and the disciples right, in their knowledge of God" (Barrett). The world failed to recognize that Jesus was God's expression, God's communication to it. The world does not think of God in terms of righteousness. Unbelievers think of God as an old fuddy-duddy, a killjoy, or an angry disciplinarian. The disciples did recognize the truth, for they had come to believe that Jesus was the sent one from God. Jesus, who knew the Father personally and intimately, had revealed the Father to his disciples and would continue to do so. Thus, Jesus could say, *"I made your name known to them, and I will make it known"* (NRSV). Finally, Jesus asked the Father to love the disciples with the same love that he (the Father) had for his Son. This is a staggering thought! We are blessed beyond measure that the Father's love would be in us and that Jesus himself would be in us. At the end of Matthew's Gospel, Jesus promised his disciples that he would be *with* them all of their days (Matt 28:20). Here is an even greater promise: *I in them*

(NRSV, emphasis added). What a conclusion to this sublime prayer! It expresses the heart of the Father's desire, which is to have his Son (the "I") in a corporate people (the "them"): "I in them."

ENDNOTES

[1]In both 17:11 and 17:12 the best manuscripts ($\mathfrak{P}$66^{vid} ℵ B C W) read, "keep them in the name that you have given me." Other manuscripts (such as D, some later miniscules, and some early versions) read, "Keep in your name those whom you have given me." The original text indicates that Jesus had been given the Father's name. Westcott says, "These passages [17:11-12] suggest the idea that the 'giving of the Father's name' to Christ expresses the fullness of his commission as the Incarnate Word to reveal God. . . . And all spiritual truth is gathered up in the 'name' of God, the perfect expression (for men) of what God is, which 'name' the Father gave to the Son to declare when he took man's nature upon him."

[2]The best manuscript evidence ($\mathfrak{P}$60 ℵ B D W) supports the reading "that which you have given me," as opposed to the reading found in some manuscripts (A C L), "those whom you have given me."

Jesus' Arrest and Trials

JOHN 18:1-40

EXPOSITION

According to John's narrative, Jesus complied without any resistance to those who arrested him, tried him, and crucified him. Having complete foreknowledge of what was to come and being fully cognizant that all things would happen as they had been predetermined, Jesus unswervingly faced his own death. Unlike the other Gospels, there is no question in this account whether or not he would drink the cup the Father had given him (18:11). He would lay down his life voluntarily, and he would also take up his life again because he had received the authority to do so from the Father. This is not to say that Jesus did not pass through this time of trial without any human feelings. He indeed was troubled (see 13:21), and yet he did not agonize over his imminent death. Rather, he accepted his destiny with divine serenity and supernatural confidence in the outcome—his resurrection and ascension to the Father.

18:1-12/It Happened in a Garden

There are two famous gardens mentioned in the Scriptures, and though they are separated by thousands of years, something similar occurred in both places. In the Garden of Eden, God had walked with Adam in wonderful communion until Adam chose to hand himself over to the evil one and be at enmity with God. In the Garden of Gethsemane, where Christ had refreshing times with his disciples, one of them—having given himself to Satan—demonstrated his enmity against the Son of God and betrayed him into the hands of devil-controlled men. In Eden's garden the awful disease of sin first afflicted the human race. In Gethsemane we stand at the portal of that great and final work of Jesus in dealing with that sin.

Some believe that Gethsemane was a private garden, owned by a friend of Jesus. We can't be sure of that, but we do know that this garden was a favorite retreat where Jesus often refreshed himself, away from the commotion of the city and the pressures of the multitudes. Judas, knowing about the garden and how Jesus often went there to pray, went to this sacred place to betray the Son of God.

It is difficult to picture how this man who had been with Christ and the other disciples a few hours earlier could now be found among the Lord's enemies.

We wonder how he could do such a terrible deed. Because of such astounding duplicity, people usually take one of two extreme views in trying to portray Judas: Either he was a monster with a twisted, dark countenance or a misguided political enthusiast totally lacking perception into the real issues of what he was doing. He was neither monster nor misguided enthusiast. Rather, he is a supreme example of a person who yields to sin in the face of repeated warnings, entreaties, and divine opportunities, until at last he hates the light, refuses the proffered love, and takes his detestable place on the side of the enemies of Christ. Considering his enviable opportunity to be with Jesus for three years and his rejection of the truth, we can only think of Jeremiah 17:9: "The heart is deceitful above all things and beyond cure. Who can understand it?"

The events that took place when Jesus was betrayed are so common to most of us that we often read the record and miss some of the outstanding details. We read in verse 3 that Judas came with a "band" of soldiers. The Greek word for "band" means a tenth of a legion. A legion of Roman soldiers numbered six thousand men, so we are dealing with about six hundred men. Then there were officers of the chief priests, meaning Temple police, as well as representatives of the religious and political powers of that day. Another Gospel writer (Mark 14:43) tells us that a "great multitude" followed Judas to the Garden to capture Jesus. It is not far-fetched to think that six or seven hundred armed men were in that group to seize the Lord of Glory. The band of men brought swords, clubs, rope, and torches. They were about to arrest Jesus, who would make no attempt at flight or concealment. Think of it—they carried torches to search for the Light of the World. They were armed with swords and clubs and rope to subdue the Prince of Peace! The irony of it is almost laughable were it not so tragic.

A demonstration of Jesus' majesty. A great band of men was coming toward the Garden, holding torches, clanking armor, swinging ropes, grasping swords, and suddenly Jesus stepped forth from the shadows and faced the men. With calm and dignified composure he met the war party. Knowing all that was going to happen, he was not caught by surprise. In order for his death to have redeeming value, it had to be freely offered. His death was not merely a sacrifice, but a self-sacrifice. He freely gave himself for us all. He was no victim. He was no martyr. He was no resistant sin-bearer. Our Lord was taken not because he couldn't help it. Nor was he crucified because he could not prevent it. He set his face toward the Cross, willing to suffer unbelievable indignities and to die for sinners.

Facing that organized mob, he said, "Who is it you want?" They answered, "Jesus of Nazareth." Then Jesus replied, "I am he." When he said that, his personality and power must have streamed forth in a glory and majesty hitherto concealed from mankind. A burst of majesty halted them—something in his bearing caused them to shrink and fall; all strength left them. He did not strike them with his hand or rush at them, screaming ferociously, ready to do battle; he spoke but a few words, and they were completely overcome. They came to capture him, and then they were groveling in the dirt. They staggered and fell, and there stood Christ—regal, dignified, invincible, majestic. Someone Christ shall be seen in all his majesty and power by the whole world, and every knee shall bow and every tongue confess that he is Lord (Phil 2:10-11).

The power of his intrinsic glory that had flung his enemies to the ground could have held them there. Or the power that could heal the slashed ear could have destroyed with equal ease the entire band. Or a hundred thousand angels could have rushed to the scene and extinguished everyone in a moment. But he permitted them to rise and seize him, demonstrating the voluntary aspect of his death. Again he asked the question, "Who is it you want?" Visualize the scene. The great multitude of armed men smitten to the ground, and Jesus doing the interrogation! Jesus was asking the questions, and Jesus was stating who would be taken and who would be left alone! You can't help but ask yourself, "Just who is in command here?"

A demonstration of Jesus' mercy. Jesus regally faced these hostile, armed men—hundreds of them—and *he* issued orders to *them.* "Let these men [the disciples] go." It was not the purpose of this band to let Jesus' followers get away, for on their way back to the city, they tried to arrest a young man—probably John Mark—whom they took for one of his disciples, but he escaped with great difficulty (Mark 14:51-52). Jesus *commanded* the immunity of his disciples! He put forth a power over his own and secured their freedom from arrest. We should be encouraged by this action, for if he could so assure the safety of his helpless sheep in the hour of his own arrest, there can be no doubt of his ability, now that he is ascended and glorified, to preserve his weakest follower. If he can keep our souls safely for eternity, he can keep our lives safely in this world until he calls us home. In the hour of his humiliation, he protected and provided for those he loved. He did not lose one, not even Judas, for he never belonged. He was not saved and then lost. He was always under the dominion of Satan and was at last totally possessed by him.

Simon Peter wanted to save Jesus from this humiliation. But he was no expert swordsman, and what easily could have become a scene of immediate bloodshed was kept under control by the power of Christ. We know from the Synoptics that the wounded servant was healed as Jesus said to Peter, "Put away your sword; it is not needed. I must fulfill my purpose and the will of my Father." In other words, "Peter, you mean well, but you cannot keep me from the Cross."

A demonstration of Jesus' meekness. Behind the actions of sinful men the unalterable purposes of God were being accomplished. Jesus simply said, "Shall I not drink the cup the Father has given me?" It was not what Jesus suffered at the hands of men that made atonement for sin; it was what he suffered at the hands of God the Father. He was made to be sin! Death did not burden him, but death as the bearer of sin did make him sweat drops of blood. He dreaded and shrank from the coming separation from God, something he had never known. To be separated from God is the greatest tragedy in the world. To be forever separated from God is hell. In his humiliation, Jesus suffered greatly, and in drinking the cup he showed subservience, obedience, and meekness.

Verse 12 says, "They bound him." It is laughable. While it is a statement of fact, it could fittingly be read with a question mark, "*They* bound *him?*" The band, the council, the chief captain, and the Temple police rushed at him, knotted the ropes, and thought they bound him! What really bound him? His love for you and me. His love for the elect. *That* was what bound him—not the hemp cords of sinful, foolish, desperate men—but the eternal cords of divine love.

This scene affords an apt illustration of the doctrine of substitution. As the Good Shepherd steps to the front of the army and demands release for his flock, he is doing on a small scale what he did once for all at Calvary. He willingly submitted himself to the penalty due for sin—the shame of the Cross, the sharpness of death, the separation from God, the humiliation of the grave—all of this, that we might not be sin's captives.

KEY WORDS AND PHRASES

The earliest extant manuscript of the New Testament, 𝔓52, dated AD 110–125, contains seventeen words of John 18:31-33 on one side of a small papyrus fragment and fifteen words of 18:37-38 on the other side. This is the earliest record of any words Jesus spoke, and even though this manuscript is fragmentary, it preserves what Jesus said about why he came into this world: "For this I came into the world that I might testify to the truth. Everyone who is of the truth hears my voice." Jesus said these words during his trial, which was thoroughly unjust. Jesus was tried by judges who did not know the truth, for they rejected him who was and is truth. In the end, these judges would be judged by the truth they rejected.

NOTES

18:1 *After Jesus had spoken these words, he went out with his disciples across the Kidron valley to a place where there was a garden* (NRSV). Jesus could have gone to this garden directly from the house in which he celebrated the Last Supper with his disciples, or he could have gone there after walking with his disciples through the city. If the latter is true, all of John 15–17 could have been spoken as Jesus and his disciples walked from the upper room, somewhere in the heart of Jerusalem, to the garden of Gethsemane (specifically named in Matt 26:36 and Mark 14:32), located outside the eastern wall of the city, at the foot of the Mount of Olives. To get to the garden of Gethsemane, they had to cross the ravine of the Kidron. This ravine, filled with water torrents during the winter, was now dry. *Kidron* means "dark," not "cedars," as some suggest. Jesus, the Light of the World, passing though the "dark" was symbolic of what was to come.

18:2 Though *Judas* had left the group while they were still in the upper room (13:26-31), he probably surmised that Jesus would go to Gethsemane with his disciples *because Jesus had often met there with his disciples* (see Luke 21:37).

18:3 *Judas* acted as a guide to two groups: (1) *a detachment of soldiers* and (2) *some officials from the chief priests and Pharisees.* The Jewish leaders must have asked Pilate for a group of Roman soldiers to help them arrest Jesus. At this time, however, they did not reveal to Pilate that their ultimate intention was to procure Rome's assistance in executing Jesus. Perhaps the Jewish leaders had accused Jesus of being a rabble-rouser (see Luke 23:5), so the Romans would be inclined to cooperate in Jesus' arrest. Apparently they came prepared to meet violent resistance, for they carried *weapons.*

18:4 *Then Jesus, knowing all that was to happen to him, came forward and asked them, "Whom are you looking for?"* (NRSV). Jesus was in control. According to his prescience he knew all that was going to happen in connection with his betrayal, arrest, and crucifixion. No human could know his future in such detail. The time of his betrayal and arrest were predetermined; they could not happen after the Passover. One of the Twelve, Judas Iscariot, had been selected by Jesus. He knew from the beginning that Judas was a devil and would be his betrayer (see 6:64, 70). The method of execution, crucifixion, was predetermined, so Jesus knew that he would be lifted up on the cross (see 12:32-33). Thus it was clear that his executioners would be the Romans, for they were the unique administrators of this kind of capital punishment, and not the Jews, who executed by stoning (18:32). The Jews attempted to stone Jesus many times, but they never succeeded because it was not in accord with the divine plan. Now the time had come for Jesus to hand himself over to his executioners. The way he meets his enemies demonstrates his earlier words, "No one takes it [my life] from me, but I lay it down of my own accord" (10:18).

18:5-9 *"Jesus of Nazareth," they replied. "I am he," Jesus said.* Jesus' response is literally, "I am,"[1] which some commentators consider to be a declaration of deity, as in 8:58. The reaction this produced in these arresters indicates that Jesus' words must have been charged with a divine dynamo, for *they drew back and fell to the ground.* Ironically, those who had come to overpower Jesus were overpowered by him, and even lay before him prostrate. Perhaps for an instant their veiled eyes were opened, and they saw the glory of Christ. Before such majesty, they involuntarily fell to the ground. This display of power shows that Jesus could have exercised his power to thwart his arrest but chose not to. He was totally in charge; he was in control; he asked the questions. Nonetheless, he was willing to turn himself over to them, but he asked the soldiers to *let these men* [i.e., the eleven disciples] *go.* Two things are evident here. Jesus makes sure that he alone is taken, even to judgment. None of his disciples were to be included in his death, and it shows Jesus' protection of his disciples as he had promised them. John says that this *fulfilled* Jesus' previous words: *"I have not lost one of those you gave me"* (see 6:39; 17:12).

18:10-11 *Then Simon Peter, who had a sword, drew it, struck the high priest's slave, and cut off his right ear. The slave's name was Malchus* (NRSV). Peter squared off against Caiaphas's right-hand man, Malchus. Caiaphas, the mastermind behind the plot to seize and kill Jesus, must have instructed Malchus to take the lead in seizing Jesus. Peter must have stepped in front of Jesus and attempted to kill Malchus with his sword. At this point, Peter was demonstrating his willingness to die for Jesus (cf. 13:37). Later, we see a reversal. We may surmise that Caiaphas had told Malchus to make sure to get this fellow Jesus and not to let him escape; so Malchus was more aggressive than the others. Maybe he was attempting to push or shove Jesus, and Peter, our Lord's right-hand man, hastily came to Jesus' defense, even attempting to kill Malchus. Jesus quickly took control of the volatile situation, healing the man's ear (see Luke 22:51), and none from the arresting band retaliated. Peter demonstrated great courage (no doubt the adrenaline was pumping), but later on, under different circumstances, he denied he even knew Jesus.

Under orders from Jesus, Peter put his **sword back into its sheath** because Jesus would not avoid drinking **the cup that the Father** had given him (NRSV). He was determined to do his Father's will. This is the only mention of "the cup" in John's Gospel, whereas it is a central image in the synoptic accounts of the garden scene. "Taking the cup" is a biblical image and a Hebrew metaphor for receiving an event in life as coming directly from the hand of God (see Ps 75:8; Isa 51:17; Jer 25:15; Ezek 23:31-34). In this case, it symbolizes Jesus' drinking God's judgment for the sin of mankind. His death on the cross was a bitter cup.

18:12-14 The Jews and Roman **soldiers**, led by a **commander** (Gr., *chiliarch*) **arrested Jesus. They bound him and brought him first to Annas, who was the father-in-law of Caiaphas, the high priest that year.** Annas had been deposed as the Jewish high priest by the Romans in AD 15, but he still exerted great influence over the ruling high priest, his son-in-law, Caiaphas. He retained the title "high priest" as an emeritus title. Very likely, Annas had asked to interrogate Jesus and was given the first rights to do so (see 18:19-23). Caiaphas is further identified for John's readers as **the one who had advised the Jews that it would be good if one man died for the people** (see 11:49-50). Although Judas and Pilate have gone down in history as epitomizing depravity and moral cowardice, Caiaphas, who instigated the murderous plot of killing the Lord of glory, was more evil than both of them.

18:15 Two of the disciples followed Jesus to Annas's house: **Simon Peter** and **another disciple** who was **known to the high priest** (i.e., was an acquaintance of the high priest). Only this "other disciple" (the verb tense in Greek is singular) *went with Jesus into the high priest's courtyard.* This disciple is not identified by name. Many scholars logically believe that it was John, but other scholars conjecture that John, the son of Zebedee from Galilee, would not have been known by Annas. Some scholars have argued that the unnamed disciple was Joseph of Arimathea, who is called a "disciple of Jesus" (19:38). As a prominent member of the Sanhedrin (Mark 15:43; Luke 23:50), he would have had an "in" with Annas. However, the verb *followed* indicates that this disciple moved with Jesus from the Garden, and there is no indication that any other disciples besides the eleven were in the Garden with Jesus. If the disciple was John, the act of following Jesus all the way to his trial demonstrates his supreme devotion to Jesus. Furthermore, it validates the Gospel's authenticity by telling us that one of Jesus' very own disciples, who was close to Jesus in his public ministry from the very first and was near him at the Last Supper, who observed his death and took responsibility for his mother, was now here witnessing the events of the trial.

18:16-18 Whoever this disciple was, he secured permission for Peter to enter the courtyard. As he entered, *the girl at the door* asked Peter a question. *"You are not one of his disciples, are you?"* Since the girl's question anticipated a negative answer (according to the Greek), it provided an easy way for Peter to answer her query. Perhaps he thoughtlessly agreed with the girl so that he could stay in the outer courtyard. If so, his denial is not as blatant as is usually portrayed. But in any case his words *"I am not"* are a denial—just as Jesus had predicted (13:37-38; cf. Matt 26:33-35; Mark 14:29-31).

18:19-20 Annas *questioned Jesus about his disciples and about his teaching* (NRSV). Annas may have wanted to know how many disciples Jesus had gathered so as to assess the threat of possible retaliation from his followers. Jesus said nothing about his disciples, perhaps to divert attention from them and to protect them (as in 18:8). However, Jesus was very straightforward about his teaching, for he had *spoken openly to the world.* He said, *"I have always taught in synagogues and in the temple, where all the Jews come together. I have said nothing in secret"* (NRSV). There was a difference in Jesus' ministry to the public and his ministry in private to the disciples, as is evident by John 13–17. However, the substance of the ministry did not differ; so Jesus was correct in saying that he taught nothing in secret. Jesus had not started a mystery cult with clandestine meetings. Any Jew who heard Jesus' teaching at length could have related what he had taught, and any Jew could have become a believer.

18:21-23 *Why question me? Ask those who heard me. Surely they know what I said.* In saying this, Jesus may have been affirming the usual Jewish practice of having witnesses speak for the defendant, as opposed to the defendant speaking for himself (Carson). In any case, he was implying that the whole procedure was unwarranted. Nevertheless, his response incited anger. One of Annas's officers struck Jesus, saying, *"Is this the way you answer the high priest?"* Jesus defended himself, for he had received a blow unjustly: *"If I spoke the truth, why did you strike me?"* In contrast to the popular image of Jesus not saying anything before his accusers, this shows that Jesus did speak up for his rights. In this regard, he was not meek and mealymouthed, but righteously defensive. What Annas was doing was illegal and unwarranted. Jesus would not indulge Annas by providing him an apologetic (i.e., a legal defense).

18:24 Then Annas sent him bound to Caiaphas the high priest (NRSV). With Annas's interrogation over, Jesus was sent on to Caiaphas, the ruling high priest. John does not give us any record of the interview, but simply tells us in 18:28 that he was taken from Caiaphas's house to the Praetorium, where he was interrogated by Pilate. By taking into account the record of the synoptic Gospels, we can assume that the interview with Caiaphas was the same as that in which Jesus appeared before the Sanhedrin—for Caiaphas would have been presiding over the Sanhedrin (see comments on 18:28).

18:25-27 These verses are a continuation, narratively speaking, of 18:15-18. Peter is still in the courtyard of Annas's house and is still standing before a fire with several other people warming themselves on a cold evening (see 18:18). Whereas the synoptic Gospels indicate that Peter's three denials occurred in the courtyard outside Caiaphas's palace, John places the scene outside Annas's home. Perhaps this was the same courtyard and was shared by both Annas and Caiaphas, who lived near each other.

Again, Peter is asked a question that in the Greek expects a negative answer: *"You are not one of his disciples, are you?"* To which Peter responded, *"I am not."* Then came the third denial.

One of the high priest's servants, a relative of the man whose ear Peter had cut off [Malchus; see 18:10]*, challenged him, "Didn't I see you with him in the olive grove?"* According to Greek construction, this is a straightforward question anticipating a straightforward answer.

Again Peter denied it. This was the third time; *and at that moment a rooster began to crow.* This happened exactly as Jesus had predicted (see 13:38).

What do we make of Peter's actions at this time? He had followed Jesus right into the courtyard and was mingling among some of those servants who had come to arrest Jesus. This is not the behavior of a coward; rather, this behavior is consistent with Peter's boast to even die with Jesus. Then why did he deny him? Was it some sudden fear that overpowered him? Or paradoxically, did he deny knowing Jesus so that he could stay near Jesus and perhaps rescue him from his enemies? We cannot know his heart, but we do know his words, and in this testing moment he denied Jesus.

18:28 Meanwhile, Jesus was taken by the Jews *from Caiaphas to the Praetorium* (NKJV), which was the palace of the provincial Roman governor—in this case, Pilate. Pilate usually lived in Caesarea, but he came to Jerusalem during the

Jewish festivals in case he had to control any riots. Jesus' nighttime trial before Caiaphas and other Jewish leaders (cf. Matt 26:59-68) was apparently followed by an equally secret trial by the entire Sanhedrin (Luke 22:66–23:1) and then by Pilate's civil trial (John 18:28–19:16; cf. Matt 27:2, 11-26; Mark 15:1-15; Luke 23:1-25). (Jesus' trial before Pilate was interrupted by a brief appearance before Herod, the representative of Caesar; Luke 23:6-11.) Not one of these trials was carried out in accordance with justice and either Jewish or Roman law.

But they themselves did not go into the Praetorium, lest they should be defiled, but that they might eat the Passover (NKJV). There is obvious irony in this statement. Jesus' accusers were concerned about defiling themselves by entering a non-Jewish house, when in reality they were eternally defiling themselves by handing over the true Passover Lamb to be slain by Gentiles (Isa 53:4-7; 1 Pet 1:18-20). The Passover meal the Jews were intent on eating may have been the Feast of Unleavened Bread, which in Jesus' day was also called the Passover (see note on 13:1).

18:29-31 Pilate respected their Jewish custom and came out to them to determine if Jesus was guilty of a religious or civil crime. He demanded that they provide a bona fide legal charge against Jesus: "What accusation do you bring against this man?" To which the Jews replied, "If this man were not a criminal, we would not have handed him over to you" (NRSV). The vagueness of their answer prompted Pilate to dismiss the matter as one pertaining to religious law, not civil law. Pilate saw right through their subterfuge: they had no charges! They persisted, gaining Pilate's attention by insinuating that they had already found Jesus worthy of death by their own law but were not permitted to put anyone to death (NRSV). Being under Roman rule, the Jews were not permitted to carry out any execution without the Romans' sanction. (Stephen was killed illegally in a rage.) Thus, the Jews needed the Romans to execute Jesus for them.

18:32 This was to fulfill what Jesus had said when he indicated the kind of death he was to die (NRSV). The Jews executed capital punishment by stoning; the Romans, by crucifixion. Jesus had always foretold his death in terms of crucifixion. The Jewish leaders had attempted to stone him (8:59; 10:31) and throw him over a cliff (Luke 4:29), but in each case they had failed. Now they sought the Romans to kill Jesus for them by crucifying him. If Pilate assented, this would serve them well because it would give the appearance to the Jewish populace (who were enamored of Jesus at the moment) that the Roman leaders were responsible for his death.

18:33-36 Are you the king of the Jews? Since Jesus' enemies had accused him of sedition against the Roman Empire (Luke 23:1-2), Pilate asked Jesus if he really claimed to be a king. Pilate was concerned that Jesus' kingship might lead to an uprising, so he had an obligation to ascertain what kind of kingship Jesus possessed. Jesus then asked, *"Is that your own idea . . . or did others talk to you about me?"* In other words, "Do you, Pilate, personally want to know if I am a king, or are you simply carrying out an official interrogation?" With this question, Jesus was offering Pilate a chance to hear what this trial was *really* about. Pilate answers, in effect, "This is just business. I am not personally interested in you and your claims. I am no Jew. Your own people have delivered you to me for judgment. So what have you done? Why are they against you?" The Romans had *not* felt threatened by Jesus; the Jewish leaders had. Instead of answering Pilate's question, Jesus put Pilate at ease by explaining that his Kingdom was not an earthly kingdom for which he and his followers would fight. His Kingdom was not a threat to Pilate and Rome. Jesus' *kingdom is not from here* (NRSV); if it were, his servants would have violently resisted the Jews who came out to arrest Jesus. He is the king of a different realm, which is the Kingdom of God.

18:37-39 Pilate's words are treated as a question in most translations. The NIV, however, translates this, *"You are a king, then!"*[2] Jesus' response suggests that Pilate wasn't asking a question, but Pilate's declaration—whether sincere or sarcastic—elicited a bold response from Jesus: *"You are right in saying I am a king."* Jesus then went on to explain that his kingly mission was to witness to *the truth.* Truth, as presented in the Gospel of John, is that which has spiritual reality, that which is embodied in Jesus, and that which is conveyed by his words. Those who were inclined to receive spiritual reality heard Jesus' words: *"Everyone on the side of truth listens to me."* Pilate was not so inclined. He mused on the possibility of truly comprehending truth and then declared, *"I find no basis for a charge against him"*—that is, he was not guilty of any civil crime as far as Rome was concerned. Since Pilate knew that Jesus' accusers would reject this verdict, he attempted to resolve his thorny dilemma by declaring Jesus unofficially guilty and then pardoning him (see Mark 15:7-11), hoping to take advantage of the annual custom to release one prisoner at Passover. Pilate could have said, "According to your custom, I'm releasing this man, so don't touch him!" But he really dug at them: *"Do you want me to release 'the king of the Jews'?* Surely you want your 'king,' don't you?"

18:40 Pilate's offer enraged the screaming Jewish officials, and they demanded that **Barabbas**, a convicted **robber** (NKJV), be pardoned instead. The Greek word for "robber" (*lēstēs*) was "used by Josephus the historian to describe rebels against Roman authority" (Lindsell). Thus the rendering in the NIV: "Now Barabbas had taken part in a rebellion." He may have led the revolt mentioned in Luke 23:18-19, 25; according to Mark 15:7, he was imprisoned with others who took part in this revolt. Since Barabbas was a political criminal, the Jews' request for the release of Barabbas and not Jesus underscores the irony of the situation. The Jews, pretending to respect Roman authority, asked for the release of a revolutionary against Roman authority. Furthermore, they wanted to give life to a murderer and murder the one who had come to give them life!

ENDNOTES

[1] In many manuscripts (𝔑 A C L W 33) "Jesus" appears before "I am"; in one manuscript (B) "Jesus" appears after "I am." This addition seems to be the work of scribes attempting to clarify Jesus' self-identification: "I am Jesus." The bare statement "I am" is found in 𝔓60 D Origen.

[2] This rendering may be supported by one second-century manuscript, 𝔓90, which has *su ei* (the inversion suggesting an emphatic declaration—"you are!") instead of *ei su* (which is more suggestive of an interrogatory—"are you?").

Jesus' Crucifixion and Burial

JOHN 19:1-42

EXPOSITION

This chapter records not a tragedy but a victory. While it depicts Jesus' crucifixion at the hands of sinful men, we must keep in mind that ultimately God was in control here, not men. The Crucifixion was his plan, not theirs. All happened as it was supposed to happen. No one but Jesus, however, was aware of this. Since he knew his destiny (see 18:37), he walked into death boldly and calmly, carrying his own cross to Calvary (19:17). The Jews and the Romans were not taking his life from him; he was laying it down of his own accord. When he had accomplished salvation—when it was all "finished"—Jesus of his own volition gave up his spirit (19:30). As he had foretold, no one took his life from him; he had authority to give it up and then retake it in resurrection (10:18). From the cross, Jesus was exalted, as if it were his throne. On the cross was nailed the royal proclamation for all the world to read (written in the three major languages): "Jesus of Nazareth, the King of the Jews." A king went to the cross to conquer death. He did so, then rose to enjoy a glorious victory.

19:17-30/A Man Died for Me

At the beginning of our Lord's public ministry, when he cleaned the Temple, he was challenged for a sign demonstrating his authority. His reply was, "Destroy this temple, and I will raise it again in three days" (2:19). By that statement he meant to say that the ultimate, complete, final sign would be his death and resurrection. Jesus often referred to this time as his "hour," and the last chapters of John's record give us that final sign: the desolation of the temple—Jesus' death.

Viewing the death of Christ from only one vantage point is not sufficient. For instance, from the standpoint of God the Father, the death of Christ was a *propitiation,* where full satisfaction was made to his holiness and justice. From the standpoint of the Savior, his death was a *sacrifice,* an offering for sin, an act of obedience. From the standpoint of believers, it was a *substitution,* the Just for the unjust. From the standpoint of Satan, it was a *triumph,* but only momentarily, for then he realized it was for him certain defeat. From the standpoint of unbelievers, it must be considered *murder,* or a miscarriage of justice, or perhaps an unnecessary martyrdom. But however Jesus' death is viewed, we do well to follow the biblical restraint employed by the New Testament writers in describing the heinous crime of delivering up a just man unto death.

The Crucifixion. John records plainly and simply that Jesus, bearing his cross, went to a place called the Skull and was there crucified. It is utterly amazing that the supreme events of history are mentioned so simply. John used in his narrative one word for *scourging,* one word for *crucifixion,* and one word for *resurrection.* No awful details of the scourging, no gruesome description of the Crucifixion—just brief words and succinct sentences to relate tremendous events. The "place of the Skull" is the English form, "Golgotha" is the Hebrew (or Aramaic) form, and "Calvary" is the Latinized form. Calvary, Golgotha, Skull—grim names for a place where grim deeds were done. In spite of the colossal event that took place there, we do not know for sure the exact site of Golgotha. A few have suggested that it was the area where Adam was buried. Some believe that it was the very place where Abraham offered up Isaac. Others maintain that just as Israel is the center of the world's land mass, so Golgotha was the exact center of the world ("It was not done in a corner," Acts 26:26). Most Christians who have visited Jerusalem choose to believe that the spot was about three hundred yards outside the present-day Damascus Gate, on a slight hill, of which one side looks like a skull. But we do not know for certain; God has obliterated the record. Why? Because the place called Calvary is to us who believe not so much a geographical location as an experience. Calvary stands at the center of our spiritual world. The Holy Spirit brings Calvary right where we are, as we recognize what was done there. The spot is unimportant, but the transaction is all-important.

John spared us all the revolting details of this tragic story. Many have not followed the restraint of the divine record, and much has been said about the physical suffering of Jesus. That he suffered incredibly is undeniable, but we should properly note that the physical suffering was nothing compared to the fact that he suffered as the bearer of our sins. In fact, he was counted by his own people as something unclean—he had to die outside the city. In the book of Leviticus God gave the pattern to Israel that on the Day of Atonement the priest confessed his sins and the sins of the people over the head of the scapegoat. That goat was then taken outside the camp to die because it was henceforth unclean (Lev 16:10, 20-22). We read in Hebrews 13:12 that "Jesus also suffered outside the city gate to make the people holy through his own blood." Here we see the mob unconsciously perfecting the mightiest sin offering ever prepared. Our loving God "made him who had no sin to be sin for us, so that in him we might become the righteousness of God" (2 Cor 5:21).

John simply says, "They crucified him." Who are "they"? According to Acts 4:27, it was Herod, Pontius Pilate, the Gentiles, and the people of Israel. Government, religion, leaders, and rabble—all put him to death, for the world system at every level hates God. When Christ was crucified, he was placed between two criminals. Another Gospel record (Luke 23:42) tells us that one of them believed. That is the picture of how the world today is divided—for in God's sight the world is not divided among the rich and the poor, the great and the insignificant, the educated and the ignorant. There are just two groups: those who reject Jesus, and those who believe in his name.

The criminal charges. It was customary that when a criminal was crucified a list of his crimes was placed over his head on the cross for all to read. Pilate wrote the inscription, "Jesus of Nazareth, the King of the Jews." By it he meant that the only king or deliverer the conquered Jews could boast or need expect was a helpless sufferer, dying the death of a criminal. Pilate meant it to annoy the Jewish religious leaders. The priests hated the declaration and made their protest. But behind the writing hand of Pilate was the guiding hand of God, for what Pilate wrote was the truth John wished to establish, namely that Jesus was the Christ, the King of the Jews, the only Savior of the Jews, their only hope, both then and now.

Pilate wrote, "Jesus of Nazareth, the King of the Jews" in three languages: Hebrew, for the Jews going to the feast to see how pathetic was the case of the King of the Jews; Latin, representing Pilate's king and the language of law; and Greek, representing the language of culture and of the civilized world. So you have the language of the land, of military might, and of the arts. It is the language of Zion, the Forum, and the Acropolis. Of Jerusalem, Rome, and Athens. Of religion, power, and culture. Of the ancient Orient, a new empire, and the changing West. Of revelation, paganism, and worldly wisdom. In each of these realms—religion, law, and education—Christ is King. In religion, for he is the final and complete revelation from God. In jurisprudence, for he is the absolute Lawgiver and law administrator. In education, for he is the Creator and source of all knowledge. Yes, Pilate wrote, "King of the Jews," but he wrote far more than he realized. They tried to get Pilate's words changed, but he was unyielding, when earlier he had been so vacillating. Strange, isn't it, that we can be so stubborn about things that do not matter and weak about things that are of supreme importance.

The concluding conversation. It was the custom of that day that the executioner got the last personal effects of the criminal. It made no difference who was being executed. These soldiers in ignorance and blindness gambled within arm's length of what was at once the greatest tragedy and the greatest triumph of all history. But even the coarse, callous action of these ignorant soldiers in stripping Jesus naked and gambling for his seamless robe fulfilled the Scriptures.

In his wonderful selectivity, John recorded another incident in contrast to the four soldiers—that of the presence of four women. John never named himself in his writings, and he never named the mother of Jesus, nor did he name Mary's other children. Nevertheless, John made it very clear that Jesus, in the midst of providing redemption for mankind, had compassion for human sorrow, and he cared and provided for his mother. Mary has been so exalted by certain segments of the religious world that some have reacted by scarcely giving her the measure of honor due her. It will help us to keep a few facts in mind. There is no record that Jesus ever called Mary "mother." Here in this scene Jesus called her "woman" and bade her look to John, not to himself, as her son. She could not rely upon a human relationship. Jesus must be to her Savior, Lord, and God. As a result of Jesus' action, no human being is closer to the Savior than the penitent thief, or you or I—not even Mary.

On the Day of Pentecost, Mary took her place among the worshipers. It was not a special place of distinction or leadership, but it was with the 120 as a simple believer. She found that the salvation relationship transcends the family relationship. She found that it was more important to have Jesus as her Savior than to have him as her son. Mary, who had been honored by God, visited by an angel, and loved by a sinless son, found her hope not in the memory of these high and holy privileges, but in the mercy of a Savior who died for her. And a worthless, guilty thief discovered himself equal to blessed Mary in the opportunities of grace. Mary and the criminal—we must take our place with them and look to Christ alone for forgiveness of sins and full salvation.

Jesus, knowing that all was accomplished, said, "It is finished." John does not record it, but other Gospel accounts say that he cried with a *loud* voice. It was not the voice of the defeated; it was the shout of the victor. The Greek word for "it is finished" means far more than that something was over—it means that it was "rounded out to perfection." Those who have been exacting students of the prophetic Scriptures tell us that with this victorious shout—dismissing his Spirit—332 distinct prophecies in the Old Testament were literally and minutely fulfilled. All the types and prophecies, all the redemptive work, and all of the will of the Father were fulfilled. The purpose of his coming was complete.

None of the Gospel writers say he died. He yielded up his Spirit. Sin destroyed his temple. On the human level he was dead—the temple was dissolved. But on the divine level he finished the work he came to do. He *gave up* his Spirit—an act, voluntary and free. Redemption was complete. For those who are burdened by the guilt of sin, nothing remains to be done but to accept him as the Lamb of God, for in him alone is eternal life. The shedding of his blood covers my sin, gives me acceptance with God, releases me from bondage, delivers me from divine wrath, and makes me whiter than snow. To such a finished work we cannot add anything of personal merit, sacred rite, or carnal effort. We believe and receive. If the sacrifice of Jesus Christ on Calvary is not enough to save the soul, nothing that you or I can do or give will ever make up the supposed deficit. But there is no deficit! It is finished. My soul is eternally secure because the Son of God loved me and gave himself for me.

KEY WORDS AND PHRASES

Many of the events taking place during Jesus' crucifixion were destined to happen because they had been prophesied in Scripture:

» When Jesus was on the cross, the soldiers cast lots for his tunic without realizing that they were carrying out a part of prophecy (19:24, from Ps 22:18). But Jesus knew that what was transpiring was in accord with God's predestined will.

» Near the end of his crucifixion, Jesus, "knowing that all was now completed," said, "I am thirsty." This fulfilled Scripture (19:28, from Ps 69:21).

» After Jesus died, the soldiers refrained from breaking his legs. This also fulfilled Scripture: "Not one of his bones will be broken" (19:36, from Exod 12:46; Num 9:12; cf. Ps 34:20).

» Instead of breaking his bones, one of the soldiers used a spear to pierce his side, from which blood and water flowed out. This also fulfilled prophecy: "They will look upon the one they have pierced" (19:37, from Zech 12:10).

NOTES

19:1 *So then Pilate took Jesus and scourged Him* (NKJV). According to Mark 15:15, Jesus was given over to the soldiers to be scourged and crucified. This kind of scourging (Gr., *phragelloō*) would have been a torturous precursor to crucifixion. A man could die from this beating, for the Romans used whips reinforced with bone and metal to cut open the victim's body. But John's account accords with Luke's. According to Luke 23:16, 22, Pilate's intention was to teach Jesus a lesson by scourging him and then to release him. He thought the scourging would appease the Jews. This kind of scourging (Gr., *mastigoō*) would have been severe, but not fatal.

19:2 *And the soldiers wove a crown of thorns and put it on his head, and they dressed him in a purple robe* (NRSV). Adorning him with a crown and purple robe was done to mock royalty. According to Matthew 27:28, they first stripped him of his own outer garment. For other forms of mockery inflicted on Jesus, see Matthew 27:29.

19:3-4 *went up to him again and again, saying, "Hail, king of the Jews!" And they struck him in the face.* The Roman soldiers took devilish delight in mocking and pummeling their prisoner (cf. Matt 27:26-30). After Jesus' beating and the display of mockery, Pilate, for the second time (see 18:38), declared that he had found **no basis for a charge against** Jesus—i.e., not guilty of a crime warranting death.

19:5 *Then Jesus came out wearing the crown of thorns and the purple robe*, and Pilate uttered the now-famous words, **"Behold the Man!"** (NKJV; Latin, *Ecce homo*). Many have Christianized this statement and made it one of adoration for Jesus, the perfect man. But the words, as they came out of Pilate's mouth, were intended to draw the Jews' attention to the fact that Jesus had been beaten and humiliated. Wasn't that enough? Shouldn't this satisfy them? No, for the chief priests and Temple officials (who were those that arrested Jesus—see 18:3) shouted: *"Crucify! Crucify!"* (19:6). No one defended Jesus!

19:6-8 Pilate, holding his ground, responded, *"You take him and crucify him. As for me, I find no basis for a charge against him."* Thus Pilate dared the Jewish leaders to usurp the exclusive Roman authority of capital punishment by crucifying their "king" themselves. But the Jewish leaders were too shrewd to fall into this trap. (They did not want the guilt of this murder heaped on them.) So they said, *"We have a law, and according to that law he must die, because he claimed to be the Son of God."* The irony here is that the Jews appealed to Pilate to punish Jesus with Roman crucifixion for allegedly violating the Jewish sense of blasphemy. But when Pilate heard this, *he was even more afraid.* Since Romans were inclined to believe in human deities, Pilate took this statement seriously, and perhaps he intuitively sensed what the Jewish officials were too blind to see—that the man in his presence was more than just a human being. (According to Matt 27:19, Pilate's wife may have influenced Pilate's thoughts about Jesus, for she had a troublesome dream about "that innocent man.") Pilate was convinced that Jesus was not guilty of any civil crime, and Pilate's next question reveals that he wanted to know about Jesus' origin, not his actions. Pilate was afraid. He wondered if Jesus had really come down from the gods.

19:9-11 *"Where are you from?" But Jesus gave him no answer* (NRSV). Some ancient commentators (Augustine and Chrysostom) saw Jesus' silence as fulfilling Isaiah 53:7, but none of the Gospel writers made this connection. Pilate, astounded by Jesus' silence, reminded Jesus that he (Pilate) had the *power to release* him and *power to crucify* him. Pilate was vested with authority from Caesar to crucify or remit, but Jesus spoke of a higher authority that overruled Caesar's. Whatever Pilate was going to do was not because Caesar dictated it, but because God had dictated it. Pilate was claiming an authority he really did not have. God was in control!

You would have no power over me unless it had been given you from above (NRSV). To paraphrase Jesus: "What you are going to do, Pilate, is not because Caesar has given you power, but because God has given you authority to act in this case." In a court of law today we would consider a person insane who said this to the judge, but Pilate listened to these words, which further increased his fears.

the one who handed me over to you is guilty of a greater sin (NRSV). Jesus was referring to Caiaphas, the high priest who handed Jesus over to the Romans, not to Judas who had betrayed him to the Jews. For a Jewish high priest to deliver the Jews' King and Messiah over to the Romans for execution was a more heinous sin than for the Roman governor to sentence him to death. But both were sin, and as such Pilate was also guilty. Ironically, it turns out that Jesus became Pilate's judge while Pilate was trying to judge him.

19:12 *From then on, Pilate tried to set Jesus free.* By this time Pilate was apparently convinced that Jesus was some kind of extra-special, supernatural person, so he tried still another time to let him go. What is puzzling is, why did Pilate have to seek Jesus' release—couldn't he just mandate it? Apparently, the pressure from the Jewish leaders was too great. Notwithstanding, Pilate must have tried to negotiate with them, perhaps guaranteeing that he would convict him in the future if he committed a political crime. But the Jews were not about to let Jesus escape at this point in the trial, so in a final desperate ploy they appealed to Pilate's relationship with Caesar: ***"If you let this man go, you are no friend of Caesar. Anyone who claims to be a king opposes Caesar."*** This was sheer hypocrisy (since most Jews despised the Roman ruler), but their hatred for Jesus led them to this lie. At any rate, their ploy worked, for Pilate was very likely afraid that he would be reported to Caesar as having released a man who had been charged with sedition. There was so much political intrigue in the Roman Empire that Pilate dared not allow any incident to jeopardize his position with Caesar. He especially wanted to be considered a "friend of Caesar" (Gr., *philos tou Kaisaros,* a translation of the technical Roman term *amicus Caesaris*). Since the emperor awarded privileged status of "friend of Caesar" to loyal subjects, Pilate would not want a report to go to Caesar that criticized his ability to govern Israel.

19:13-15 *When Pilate heard this, he brought Jesus out and sat down on the judge's seat at a place known as the Stone Pavement (which in Aramaic is Gabbatha).* Although the text does not explicitly state that Pilate passed judgment on Jesus, Pilate's position on the judgment seat indicates that the judgment originated from him—thus he was responsible. The judgment seat (or *tribunal;* Gr., *bēma*) was located on the Stone Pavement, which was the courtyard of the Fortress of Antonia, located next to the northwest corner of the Temple area. This judgment came on ***the day of Preparation of Passover Week*** (i.e., on Friday) at ***about the sixth hour,*** which was some time before noon, indicating it had been a long trial. If this refers to the day before the Passover (the day in which people prepared for the Passover meal), then that would mean that Jesus was being crucified (as the Lamb of God) at the same time the Passover lambs were being slaughtered. That would also mean that the last meal Jesus had with his disciples was not the traditional Passover meal (see introduction to John 13).

Perhaps Pilate was too guilt-ridden to summarily condemn him, so in one last desperate effort he challenged Jesus' Jewish accusers to accept their king: ***"Here is your king."*** Or it is possible that this was a sarcastic statement intended to incense the Jewish leaders. Either way, the Jews continued with their plea: ***"Take him away! Take him away! Crucify him!"*** And then they added, ***"We have no king but Caesar."*** "Nothing could be more ludicrous than this protestation of loyalty on the lips of such men. It is another fine example of Johannine irony. They certainly claimed, in accordance with the Old Testament, to be God's people. They held that God was their King (Judg 8:23; 1 Sam 8:7). On this occasion they spoke in terms of cynical expediency. But they expressed the real truth. They showed in their lives that they gave no homage to God. They had no king but Caesar" (Morris).

19:16 *Finally Pilate handed him over to them to be crucified.* According to the grammatical structure of the Greek text, the pronoun "them" would refer to the "chief priests" in 19:15, but it was the Roman soldiers who actually carried out the crucifixion. The ambiguity was probably intentional. John wanted his readers to realize that it was the Jewish leaders who were ultimately responsible for Jesus' death, even though the Romans performed the execution. This idea is captured in the NEB: "Then at last, to satisfy them [the chief priests], he handed Jesus over to be crucified." (The same idea is expressed in Luke 23:25—"surrendered Jesus to their will.")

19:17-18 *Carrying his own cross.* According to John's account, Jesus carried his own cross. John is emphasizing his aloneness. The synoptic Gospels indicate that Simon, a Cyrenian, was forced to carry the cross for him (see Matt 27:32; Mark 15:21; Luke 23:26). Most likely, Jesus carried the cross (usually the horizontal cross beam) at first; but then, having become weak because of the flogging, Simon took over (Morris). Jesus went to **Golgotha**, meaning **the place of the Skull,** where he was crucified in between two robbers (cf. Matt 27:33-38; Mark 15:20-27; Luke 23:32-33). *Golgotha* is the Aramaic word for "skull." The familiar designation Calvary is derived from the Latin word *calvaria* (skull) and has come into Western European languages from its appearance in the Vulgate (Bruce). John simply says that **they crucified him**; he does not provide details about the execution process. The reader later discovers that his hands were nailed to the cross (see 20:25, 27). There is no effort here for the writer to play upon the readers' emotions, just the presentation of brief facts. We do well to follow the same principle and restrain ourselves in describing the awful torture Jesus suffered. In fact, not one of the Gospel writers provides any gruesome details about the crucifixion process; they all simply say, "They crucified him."

with two others. From the synoptic Gospels we know that these two were robbers or revolutionaries (see Matt 27:38; Mark 15:27; Luke 23:32). That Jesus was executed along with transgressors may have been predicted in Isaiah 53:12, but none of the Gospel writers notes this. The fact that these two men were crucified on that day suggests that this day was a "scheduled" day for execution, which would have made it all the more convenient for the Jews to convince Pilate to include Jesus in the execution. In other words, Jesus' execution would not have called for a special arrangement.

19:19-22 The chief priests would have wanted Jesus' crime posted as a false claim to kingship, but Pilate provided a tribute to Jesus' kingship in a trilingual placard that anyone in Jerusalem could read. He wrote, *"Jesus of Nazareth, the King of the Jews"* . . . *in Hebrew* [or Aramaic—the language of the Jews], *in Latin* [the Roman language, the official language], *and in Greek* [the lingua franca, the common tongue] (NRSV). There were people in Jerusalem from all over the Greco-Roman world at that time because they had come to celebrate Passover. Anyone could read that placard. The Jewish leaders tried to dissuade Pilate from writing *"The King of the Jews"* and into replacing it with *"This man said, I am King of the Jews"* (NRSV). Again, they were mistaken. Jesus had never said, "I am King of the Jews," though others had said it of him (see 1:49). In any case, Pilate refused to change the wording, declaring, *"What I have written, I have written."* By doing this, Pilate got the last word. The Jewish leaders wanted the populace to think that Rome had convicted and executed Jesus, but the words on the sign spelled the opposite: the Jews had killed their king.

19:23-24 *When the soldiers had crucified Jesus, they took his clothes and divided them into four parts, one for each soldier* (NRSV). The implication of this statement is that Jesus was crucified naked—what total humiliation! It was customary for Roman soldiers who performed the crucifixion to divide the victim's clothes among themselves. But one part of Jesus' clothes, his **tunic, was seamless, woven in one piece from the top** (NRSV). The soldiers decided that this tunic (the inner garment worn by a man) should not be split apart. Since a seamless tunic was an expensive article of clothing, they decided to cast lots (which is somewhat like rolling dice) for it. Little did they know that their actions had fulfilled Scripture: *"They divided my clothes among themselves, and for my clothing they cast lots"* (NRSV; see Ps 22:18). The Roman soldiers' participation in the specific fulfillment of prophecy refutes any notion that Jesus planned his death in an attempt to fulfill messianic prophecy by his own invention.

19:25-27 In contrast to the four unbelieving soldiers, near the cross stood four believing women: Jesus' **mother, his mother's sister, Mary the wife of Clopas, and Mary Magdalene.** The Greek signifies a contrast between the four soldiers and the four women. Jesus' mother is mentioned previously in the Gospel (2:1ff), but none of the other women. If "Salome" in Mark's list of women (see Mark 15:40) corresponds with "the mother of the sons of Zebedee" in Matthew's list (see Matt 27:55-56), then Mary's "sister" was very likely Salome. She was the mother of John (the Gospel writer) and James, called the sons of Zebedee. If this is true, Jesus, John, and James were cousins. Mary the wife of Clopas was the mother of James the younger and of Joses. Mary Magdalene is here mentioned for the first time in this Gospel; she will be a prominent figure in the next chapter because Jesus first appears to her after his resurrection.

When Jesus saw his mother there, and the disciple whom he loved [John the Gospel writer] *standing nearby, he* [Jesus] *said to his mother, "Dear woman, here is your son," and to the disciple, "Here is your mother." From that time on, this disciple took her into his home.* The last sentence helps the reader understand that Jesus was directing his disciple John to take care of Mary, his mother, in his absence. Mary had apparently been previously widowed through the death of Joseph and was being cared for by Jesus himself. Even while suffering in agony, Jesus demonstrated his care for his mother. That John was entrusted with the care of Mary shows what confidence Jesus had in him and reveals the intimacy of their relationship. This again affirms the fact, so often brought out in this Gospel, that John knew Jesus well.

19:28-30 *Later, knowing that all was now completed, and so that the Scripture would be fulfilled, Jesus said, "I am thirsty."* Jesus went to the cross to accomplish redemption and provide salvation for all who believe. Having accomplished this, he was now ready to die. All the verbal quotations of Scripture made by Jesus during his crucifixion came from David's Psalms of suffering (Pss 22:1; 31:5; 69:21). Here the quotation probably comes from Psalm 69:21: "They . . . gave me vinegar for my thirst." Thus, when he said, "I am thirsty," he was given some **wine vinegar** that was in *a jar* near the cross. Others say the Scripture is Psalm 42:2, "My soul thirsts for God, for the living God. When can I go and meet with God?" If so, this reveals Jesus' desire to be with the living God after his resurrection.

The soldiers (apparently) **soaked a sponge** with the wine and lifted it to his mouth on a **stalk of the hyssop plant**. The manuscript evidence, with one exception, supports "hyssop."[1] Perhaps Jesus took just enough wine to moisten his parched throat so as to shout the final proclamation: **"It is finished."** This glorious proclamation is pregnant with meaning. According to the Greek, the expression can also mean, "It is accomplished," "It is fulfilled," or even, "It is paid in full" (an expression that frequently appears in the nonliterary papyri with this meaning). His death accomplished redemption, and his death fulfilled all the Old Testament prophecies. Now it was time for Jesus to die. Thus, **he bowed his head and gave up his spirit.** This is not the normal way of speaking about one's death. The language describes a voluntary giving up of his spirit (cf. Luke 23:46, echoing Ps 31:5). Jesus' life was not taken from him (which would be indicated by the passive voice). He gave up his life of his own free will (see 10:11, 15, 17-18; 15:13). This was a display of Jesus' divinity, and yet it is mystifying—for how could God die? Thus as we deem Jesus' resurrection to be a miracle, so was his death.

19:31-34 *the Jews did not want the bodies left on the crosses during the Sabbath.* John noted that this was a **special Sabbath**. The Sabbath began on Friday evening after sunset and lasted until sunset on Saturday. This was a very special Sabbath, for it coincided that year with the Passover festival. "Such a conjunction of weekly Sabbath and annual Passover still occurs from time to time in the Jewish calendar" (Bruce). The Jews did not want to violate their law (Deut 21:22-23) by allowing three crucified Jews (Jesus and two robbers—who must have also been Jews) to remain hanging overnight on their crosses. Since the Romans usually left bodies hanging on crosses as a warning to the unlawful, the Jews had to request that the crucifixion be terminated early and the bodies removed. Again, the irony is blatant: the Jewish leaders had just crucified the Son of God, and all they cared about was fulfilling the law of God!

they asked Pilate to have the legs broken. Pilate agreed to this request, and his soldiers smashed the legs of the still-living robbers with clubs in order to speed up their death. A person being crucified could use his legs to lift up his body in an attempt to take more oxygen into his collapsing lungs. To break the legs of one being crucified would, therefore, quicken the death process, which was death by suffocation. When the soldiers came to Jesus and *found that he was already dead, they did not break his legs.* One of the soldiers, however, to make sure that he was really dead, pierced Jesus' side with a spear. This piercing caused *blood and water* to flow. Medical experts have attempted to diagnose what was punctured to create a flow of blood and water. Some consider that the pericardial sac was ruptured, but this is conjecture, for John does not say which side was pierced. John's testimony of this occurrence was important for him to affirm a major polemic in this Gospel against the Docetists who denied Jesus' humanity. Jesus was indeed a man composed of "blood and water," who actually experienced death as a human being (see 1 Jn 5:6-7). Beyond this, John probably saw the flow of blood and water from Jesus' side as symbolizing that Jesus' death (blood) is the means by which all believers can receive life and purification (water).

19:35 *The man who saw it has given testimony, and his testimony is true.* It is generally regarded that the expression "the man who saw it has given testimony" refers to the beloved disciple, John, who was an eyewitness of Jesus' crucifixion (see 19:26-27). The intent of this verse is to let the reader know that the written report of the details of Jesus' crucifixion can be trusted because it is an eyewitness account. The same kind of testimony is given in 20:30-31 and 21:24 (see comments).

He knows that he tells the truth. Commentators are divided as to whom "he" (lit., "that one"; Gr., *ekeinos*) refers to. This expression has been interpreted in a variety of ways: (1) That one (Christ) knows that he (John, the writer) tells the truth. Those who support this view say that *ekeinos* is used for "Christ" in 3:28, 30; 7:11; 9:28. (2) That one (God) knows that he (John, the writer) tells the truth. Those who support this view say that *ekeinos* is used for "God" in 5:19; 6:29; 8:42. But in those verses the context clarifies the identity, whereas in this verse it is not clear. (3) That one (John) knows that he (the writer) tells the truth. In order to accept this interpretation, one must believe that this verse was not written by John but by someone who published the Gospel in its final edited form. He is herein affirming that the eyewitness (John) knows that he (the writer) is telling the truth. In 21:24 it seems clear that John's companions (and perhaps editors and publishers of the Gospel) appended their own affirmation to John's testimony. Possibly, one of these men did the same in 19:35. "They could have added that that disciple himself vouched for the truth of what he said—if that disciple was still alive at the time of writing, as seems to be indicated" (Bruce).

(4) That one (John) knows that he (John) tells the truth. In this case, *ekeinos* (that one) is the same as "he who tells the truth." In other words, he used *ekeinos* to speak of himself. This was not unusual; for example, Josephus had done the same in his *Wars* (3.202). The one who saw the Crucifixion and witnessed the issue of blood and water was John the apostle. Whatever the interpretation, the intent of the verse is to affirm the veracity of the eyewitness account.

so that you also may [continue to] **believe.** Other manuscripts read, "that they may begin to believe."[2] Given John's tendency to use the present tense verb when speaking about a continual believing, a believing that extends beyond the initial act of faith, it seems more likely that John here wrote the present tense. In this verse John was certifying the trustworthiness of his testimony so that the readers, who were already believers, would continue to believe the veracity of the Gospel.

19:36-37 By not breaking Jesus' legs and instead piercing him with a lance, the Roman soldiers unwittingly fulfilled two biblical prophecies: (1) **None of his bones shall be broken** (NRSV; from Exod 12:46 and Num 9:12, which speak of the bones of the Paschal Lamb and are therefore more likely the biblical sources than Ps 34:20, which speaks of preserving life), and (2) **They will look on the one whom they have pierced** (NRSV; from Zech 12:10; cf. Rev 1:7). The text does not say, "They will look on one who was pierced," but "They will look at the one *they* pierced." This means that those who were responsible for Jesus' death would see that they had crucified their Messiah and would have to face the horridness of that heinous act. In other words, the passage is saying that the Jews couldn't get rid of Jesus by killing him. They would be confronted with what they had done. This was the stinging message the apostles preached again and again in Jerusalem. Peter told the Jews, "This man . . . you crucified and killed" (Acts 2:23, NRSV). And when Jesus returns in the Parousia, the Jews who crucified him will see their pierced Messiah—and not only the Jews, but all the world will gaze upon the pierced one (see Rev 1:7). Thus this prophecy had its immediate fulfillment when the Roman soldiers pierced Jesus' side with a spear, but it also looks to the future beyond the time of Jesus' resurrection (which is implicit by the future verb "they will look") to the day of his coming. He, the Lamb of God, bears the marks of death forever.

19:38-40 Two men (Joseph of Arimathea and Nicodemus), both secret disciples of Jesus, came forward to take care of Jesus' burial. They both had feared persecution from the Jewish religious leaders, so they had not openly followed Jesus (see 7:13; 12:42-43). But at last they came forward to show their devotion to their Lord. As a consequence, it is unlikely that they could remain secret believers any longer, nor could they remain accepted members of the Sanhedrin.

The first man was *Joseph of Arimathea*. A wealthy man from Arimathea and a prominent member of the Sanhedrin, he had not gone along with the council's decision to execute Jesus (Matt 27:57; Mark 15:43; Luke 23:50-51). It is likely that Joseph was known to Pilate. He *asked Pilate for the body of Jesus*, to give him a proper burial. Pilate assented. The other secret disciple was **Nicodemus** (see 3:1ff; 7:50-52); he joined Joseph of Arimathea (cf. Matt 27:57) in embalming and wrapping Jesus' body in regal style. This collaboration implies that they must have known of each other's belief in Jesus as the Messiah. Now that both of them were coming forward, they were in danger of being de-synagogued (see 9:22). The **mixture of myrrh and aloes,** weighing **about seventy-five pounds**, was an extraordinarily large amount of burial unguent, which must have cost Nicodemus a great sum. This shows that they considered Jesus worthy of a king's burial (cf. 2 Chr 16:14). They wrapped Jesus' body **with the spices, in strips of linen**, which was **in accordance with Jewish burial customs.** Unlike the Egyptians who used spices in the embalming process, Jews used spices as an aromatic to stifle the smell of putrification (Carson).

19:41-42 They brought Jesus' body to a garden *at the place where Jesus was crucified*, and they placed him in *a new tomb, in which no one had ever been laid.* According to Matthew 27:60, this was Joseph's own tomb that he now gave up for Jesus. Such tombs, hewn out of the solid rock and closed with heavy stones, were expensive (Morris). Soon this tomb would be empty again, and Joseph would be buried in it after he died. But for all Joseph knew, he was giving up his tomb for good. It was fortuitous that Joseph had a **tomb nearby** and that he wanted to put Jesus' body there because the burial had to happen quickly—prior to the coming of the Sabbath (which is what is meant by the expression *the Jewish day of Preparation*). Normally, touching a dead man's body made a person ceremonially unclean (Num 19:11). But Nicodemus and Joseph would still be able to eat the Passover, even after having touched a dead man's body, because there was a special provision for the Passover (Num 9:6-10). According to Luke 23:55, several women came with Nicodemus and Joseph to the tomb. Knowing its location, they planned to return there after the Sabbath was over.

ENDNOTES

[1]Instead of *hussōpō* (hyssop), one eleventh-century minuscule (476) reads *huss* (javelin); but the latter reading is very likely the result of haplography (see Metzger). Many commentators and translators (see NEB) have preferred "javelin" (or "pole," as in some ancient Latin manuscripts) over "hyssop."

[2]The earliest manuscripts read the present tense, "continue to believe": 𝔓66ᵛⁱᵈ (not cited in NA²⁶) ℵ * B; later manuscripts (ℵ² A D⁵ W) read the aorist tense, "believe."

Jesus' Resurrection

JOHN 20:1-31

This chapter contains the record of Jesus' resurrection and first appearances to his followers. The four Gospels provide different accounts of Jesus' resurrection appearances over a period of forty days (Acts 1:3). Jesus' first set of appearances (the first five listed in "Key Words and Phrases") occurred in Jerusalem; the second set (the last five in the same list) happened in Galilee. Jesus had instructed his disciples prior to his death to meet him after his resurrection in a designated place in Galilee (Mark 14:28), but because of their unbelief and fear, they remained in Jerusalem. After some time (maybe around two weeks), they returned to Galilee, where Jesus appeared to the eleven disciples and several others who, very likely, were among those who followed Jesus in his early ministry but did not go with him all the way to Jerusalem. The Gospel of John records three of Jesus' Jerusalem appearances in this chapter and one Galilean appearance in the final chapter.

20:1-19/The Day of Resurrection

During the course of human history, this world has witnessed some wonderful and significant events, but the most glorious day this world has known was the day Jesus of Nazareth rose from the dead. Now if Christ is not risen from the dead, we would have no Christianity, no Christian faith and hope, and no Christian church in any sense of the word. If this twentieth chapter is a lie, we have no Christ, no Redeemer, no Savior, and no Lord. The apostle Paul reminded the Corinthian believers that "if Christ has not been raised, our preaching is useless and so is your faith" (1 Cor 15:14).

The crux of the gospel is not only that Christ died for our sins but that he rose again the third day according to the Scriptures (1 Cor 15:3-4). He was delivered for our offenses and raised again for our justification. Had Christ remained in the tomb, it would have been the grave of all hope. But the Resurrection is true, and it proves many things. It proves that Jesus is the Son of God. It proves that his atonement for sin was complete, sufficient, and acceptable. It proves that Jesus' words are true and we can rely upon them. It proves that there is resurrection in store for us, as well. Today we worship a living Savior. It takes such a Savior to save us when we are lost, to comfort us when we grieve, to strengthen us when we are weak, and to take us to heaven when we die.

The guarded tomb. It was determined by Mary Magdalene and some other women that very early on the first day of the week, while it was still dark, they would go out to the garden tomb of Jesus. But before they arrived, the sublime event had occurred, and that event has filled the world with light and joy in all succeeding years. While the Roman sentries had been guarding the grave site, sometime before dawn there had been a slight earthquake, and the angel of the Lord had descended from heaven, torn away the Roman seal, and rolled the stone from its locked position—flinging it aside and sitting upon it. This was not done to let the Savior out but to let others see into an empty tomb. The terror of such events had caused the soldiers to leave in haste.

Meanwhile, the women hurried to the grave, wondering how they would roll that great stone from the entrance so they could enter the rock-hewn tomb and complete the entombment process. They had not heard of the seals and sentries the Sanhedrin had ordered to guard against any eventualities, for had they known, they would hardly have ventured near the garden. They were greatly startled, however, when, approaching the tomb, they saw at some distance that the stone was not in place. It was a great stone, the shape of a wheel and rolled on a slight track into a slot, which kept it solidly in place, securing the tomb. Mary Magdalene apparently detected this first. Without going closer, she assumed that grave robbers had taken Jesus' body, and she ran off to find the disciples. She broke in on their grief with the shocking report, "They have taken the Lord out of the tomb, and we don't know where they have put him!" (20:2).

The other women with Mary Magdalene did not leave with her but approached the tomb entrance, and there an angel told them that Jesus was gone: "Go quickly and tell his disciples: 'He has risen from the dead'" (Matt 28:7). Then they hastened to the city, perhaps to the upper room.

Now Peter and John headed for the tomb, perhaps to search for the body of Jesus. On the way, they met the returning women who told them of the angel's words. Then Peter and John started to run toward the tomb, but John outran Peter and reached the tomb first. Upon approaching it, John stopped and, stooping down, peered into the tomb. One look convinced him that no grave robbers had been there. He could plainly see what looked like the body of Jesus still wrapped and on the stone slab. Then Peter came running up to the place where John was, and he rushed right into the tomb with John following him, and they saw something that riveted them to the spot. The linen bands that had been wrapped around the body of Jesus had not been unwound, nor had they been cut or stripped off in some way. They lay just as they had been wound about the body of Jesus, only the body was no longer inside! Like a hand withdrawn from a glove and the glove still holding the shape, so the wrappings held the shape of a body, but the headpiece had been removed, and they could see there was no body in the cocoonlike wrappings. Peter and John stood there, looking and looking at those wrappings. They saw the truth and believed!

The gospel testimony. Peter and John left the garden, and Mary Magdalene came back to the tomb for a closer look. After standing outside the tomb weeping, finally she braved a look inside, and there on the stone shelf, where earlier had been the body of Jesus, there were now two sentry angels who sought in vain to comfort her. They said, in effect, "Woman, there is no need for tears." She replied, "They have taken my Lord away, and I don't know where they have put him." Then because of some slight movement behind her—or maybe because of the expression of love and adoration that came over the faces of the angels— Mary turned and saw Jesus standing there, but she didn't realize that it was Jesus. Supposing in her grief and confusion that the one standing near her was the gardener, she said that if he knew the whereabouts of the body she sought, she would gladly have it removed at her expense or even bear it away herself if necessary. Then Jesus spoke her name with his familiar intonation and emphasis: "Mary." And she answered in the country dialect they both knew so well, "Rabboni!" which means "Master." Of course she fell at his feet in worship and adoration. Jesus said, "Mary, you don't have to be afraid; I'm ascending to my Father, but you need not keep clinging to me, for I'll never really leave again." His ascension to the Father made it possible that he will never leave us or forsake us.

Mary hastened to tell the other disciples that she had seen the Lord and that he had *spoken* to her, but they did not believe her (Mark 16:9-11). She bore her testimony faithfully—she gave the first gospel witness—and yet those who should have happily believed did not. In close succession, the Lord appeared to others of the little group: to the women, as they ran to bring the disciples word; to Peter, alone; to the two who walked to Emmaus; and finally, that first day, he appeared to the assembled disciples (minus Thomas) in the upper room.

The glorious triumph. During Old Testament times, the Sabbath was the memorial of God's finished work in the creation of things. In New Testament times (or in this dispensation) the Lord's Day is the memorial of Christ's finished work, from which issues the new creation—salvation by grace. We, like those first Christians, keep the Lord's Day in memory of the Resurrection. On that first Lord's Day the disciples met behind carefully shut and locked doors. They feared the rumors of the morning's events would arouse the hate of the Pharisees. It may be they were startled by every passing footfall or voice in the street. Perhaps every movement or noise about the house (particularly a knock at the door) caused alarm. Then the two Emmaus travelers returned to tell how Jesus had opened the Scriptures to them. Suddenly, without announcement or preparation, the figure of their blessed Master stood in their midst with the old familiar greeting, "Peace be with you!"

Evidently he was clothed in the resurrected, spiritual body of which the apostle Paul wrote (1 Cor 15:42-45). He was not subject to all the laws that now govern our physical body. He could pass freely through unopened doors and at will could manifest himself, speak, stand, walk, eat, or appear in fleshlike body. Jesus appeared and stood in their midst. This was his rightful place, the place of preeminence. This was the first time since his resurrection that his disciples were gathered, and he was there with them. We can be sure because of his promise that he is present whenever two or three of his followers are gathered to worship him (Matt 18:20). So though we cannot see him with the mortal eye, we can be sure he is in our midst. We need not ask him or plead with him to meet with us—he is present. Perhaps what we need to ask for is a heart to discern him as we worship. For it is his presence in the midst of worshiping believers that gives Christian worship its unique character.

The first words Jesus spoke to his disciples were, "Peace be with you!" He had just been to Calvary, where he had made peace by the blood of his cross. Now he seemed to say, "It's all done; you have nothing to fear. I have made peace for all those who believe." Having put away their sins, he now removed their fears. True peace comes only through Christ's accepted work of death and resurrection. Of course this is the great need of all mankind—to have peace within. "Therefore, since we have been justified through faith, we have peace with God through our Lord Jesus Christ" (Rom 5:1). This is a peace *we* cannot manufacture, a peace *he* made for us and that we enter into and enjoy when we believe the truth of the gospel.

KEY WORDS AND PHRASES

Before teaching this chapter, it is helpful for students to get a clear picture of all the appearances Jesus made after his resurrection. According to a comparative study of the four Gospels, Acts 1, and 1 Corinthians 15:3-8, the following list shows Jesus' resurrection appearances in chronological order:

The first four appearances occurred on the day of Jesus' resurrection.

1. To Mary Magdalene and the other Mary (Matt 28:1, 9; Mark 16:9; John 20:14-18)
2. To Peter (Luke 24:34; 1 Cor 15:5)
3. To two disciples on the way to Emmaus (Mark 16:12; Luke 24:13-35)
4. To the disciples in Jerusalem (Luke 24:36-43; John 20:19-23)
5. To the disciples again in Jerusalem, for Thomas's sake, eight days later (John 20:26-29)
6. To seven disciples on the Sea of Tiberias in Galilee (John 21:1-23)
7. To the disciples on an appointed mountain in Galilee (Matt 28:16-20; Mark 16:15-18)
8. To five hundred believers; this may be the same as the seventh appearance (1 Cor 15:6)
9. To James, brother of Jesus (1 Cor 15:7)

10. To his apostles before his ascension from Bethany (Mark 16:19-20; Luke
24:44-53; Acts 1:1-12)

NOTES

20:1 *Early on the first day of the week.* The Jews had no names for the days of
the week except the Sabbath, the last day of the week. Our names for the days of
the week came to us from the Roman Empire.

Mary Magdalene. She was an early follower of Jesus (Luke 8:1-3) from
Magdala, a town near Capernaum. She had followed Jesus to Jerusalem and
then to the cross. She, with other women, watched his crucifixion (19:25) and
remained to see where he was buried (Matt 27:61).

went to the tomb. This tomb was apparently a rock-hewn, hillside burial vault
that was sealed by a massive circular stone rolled into place across the entrance
to the vault (Matt 27:59-60, 66; 28:2; Mark 15:46; 16:3-4; Luke 23:53; 24:1-2;
John 19:41-42). According to other Gospel accounts, she had come with some
other women (Salome and Mary the mother of James) to anoint the body of Jesus
with certain spices (Matt 28:1; Mark 16:1). Due to the short interim between
Jesus' death and the coming of the Sabbath on Friday evening, they did not have
time to properly anoint Jesus. When Mary arrived at the tomb, she saw that *the
stone had been removed* from the entrance. Mary assumed that Jesus' body had
been taken from the tomb.

20:2 *So she ran and went to Simon Peter and the other disciple, the one whom
Jesus loved* [John the Gospel writer], *and said to them, "They have taken the
Lord out of the tomb, and we do not know where they have laid him"* (NRSV).
The "we" here may indicate that Mary is speaking on behalf of others, especially
other women, since the synoptic Gospels mention that there were other women
who came to the tomb that morning. John's Gospel, however, focuses on just one
of these women, Mary Magdalene.

20:3-5 *The two were running together, but the other disciple outran Peter and
reached the tomb first* (NRSV). Two of the disciples who heard Mary's report,
Peter and John (here called the other disciple), ran to the tomb. John outran
Peter and arrived there first. John looked in and *saw the linen wrappings lying
there, but he did not go in* (NRSV).

20:6-7 *Simon Peter*, being bolder than John, *went into the tomb. He saw the
linen wrappings lying there, and the cloth that had been on Jesus' head, not
lying with the linen wrappings but rolled up in a place by itself* (NRSV). Peter
saw the cloth that had been wrapped around Jesus' head folded up in a place by
itself, separate from the linens that had covered his body. It is possible that the
glorified body of Jesus passed directly through the linen sheets, leaving them
in the same form as when they were wrapped around his body. It is not likely,

however, that the face cloth still retained the shape of Jesus' face (as some commentators have suggested). The purpose for providing this description, it seems, was to reveal that there was not a hasty removal of Jesus' body, as would have been done by grave robbers. Therefore, Mary's statement, "They have taken the Lord," was not accurate.

20:8-9 *the other disciple . . . also went inside. He saw and believed.* Since there is no direct object after "believed," the reader has to imagine what John believed. One explanation is that John believed Mary's story about the empty tomb. However, it is more likely that John believed in Jesus' resurrection. Whereas Peter just *observed* the situation (the Greek word *theōrei* suggests this), John *saw* (Gr., *eiden*) it for what it was: the position and condition of the graveclothes showed that a robbery had not occurred—a resurrection had! John perceived that Jesus had risen from the dead. As such, John was the first to believe in Jesus' resurrection.

Given that this is the meaning of the text, we must understand the next verse to indicate that, though John had come to believe in Jesus' resurrection, he **still did not understand from Scripture that Jesus had to rise from the dead** (cf. 2:22). He had faith but no understanding or knowledge; the knowledge would come later and affirm the faith. This knowledge would come as the disciples read the Old Testament Scriptures, such as Psalm 16:8-11, Isaiah 53:10-12, and Jonah 1:17ff (a passage used by Jesus himself pertaining to his resurrection—see Matt 12:39-40). As they read these things, they began to realize that Jesus' resurrection was predicted (see comments on 2:22).

20:10 *Then the disciples returned to their homes* (NRSV). The expression in Greek (*pros autous*—lit., "to them") is an idiomatic expression that could mean "to their own homes," "to their own place" (i.e., the same place where the disciples were gathered when Jesus first appeared to them; see 20:19), or "to their own people."

20:11 After John and Peter left, Mary (who must have followed them back to the tomb) remained **outside the tomb crying**, hoping that she would somehow discover where Jesus' body had been taken (see 20:13, 15).

20:12-13 *she saw two angels in white, sitting where the body of Jesus had been lying, one at the head and the other at the feet* (NRSV). The position of the angels indicates that Jesus' body had very likely been laid on a flat stone bench (as opposed to a *loculus,* a burial chamber hollowed out of an inner wall in a tomb). But Mary was so obsessed with finding Jesus' body that even the sight of two angels failed to lessen her desperation! When the angels asked her why she was crying, she told them, **"They have taken away my Lord, and I do not know where they have laid him"** (NRSV). The angels knew what Mary didn't: Jesus was risen from the dead, a cause for great joy! But Mary was weeping for the death of her beloved Master. Mary had not noticed what John had observed—the arrangement of the burial clothes indicated that Jesus' body had not been stolen away (see comments on 20:6-7, 8-9).

20:14-15 Then Mary **turned around** and looked behind her. There in the garden she saw **Jesus standing there, but she did not realize that it was Jesus.** He asked her the same thing the angels had asked: **"Why are you crying?"** Either because tears filled her eyes or because Jesus' appearance had drastically changed after the Resurrection, Mary did not recognize him. She imagined that he must have been **the gardener** and then said to him, **"Sir, if you have carried him away, tell me where you have put him, and I will get him."**

20:16 Jesus said to her, "Mary." She turned toward him and cried out in Aramaic, "Rabboni!" (which means Teacher). Mary had been looking for the body of her dead Lord; now, to her amazement, she stood face-to-face with her living Lord. Her immediate response was to touch him and cling to him.

20:17 But Jesus stopped her: **"Do not hold on to me,"** which could also be translated, "Stop clinging to me." The Greek verb underlying "clinging" is a present imperative. The action had already begun when Jesus spoke this to Mary. He was not preventing Mary from touching him (which would be the meaning if an aorist imperative had been used). Perhaps Mary wanted to hold Jesus and so recapture the former relationship with him or make sure he didn't leave her. But Jesus was indicating that he had entered into a new, spiritual realm as the result of his resurrection. Life was not as it had been before.

Jesus affirmed this change when he told Mary, **"Go to my brothers and say to them, 'I am ascending to my Father and your Father, to my God and your God'"** (NRSV). Because of Jesus' resurrection, his disciples had now become Jesus' brothers (see also Matt 28:10). His resurrection created this new relationship because it provides for the regeneration of every believer (see 1 Pet 1:3). After his resurrection, Jesus called his disciples "my brothers" (see Heb 2:11-14).

Furthermore, we should take note of the present tense in Jesus' statement, "I am ascending to my Father." The language gives no indication that this ascension would be in the future. According to John's chronology, Jesus would rise from the dead, ascend to the Father, and then come to the disciples—all within "a little while" (see 14:2-3, 18-20, 23; 16:16-22; and the comments on these verses). The Ascension spoken of in Luke 24:51 and Acts 1:9 is another ascension that occurred after the forty-day period of Jesus' resurrection appearances (Acts 1:3).

20:18 Mary Magdalene went to the disciples with the news: "I have seen the Lord!" Mary was the first person to see the risen Christ.

And she told them that he had said these things to her. Very likely this report was not believed (cf. Luke 24:10-11, where the women's report of the empty tomb was met with unbelief). Or if the report was believed and they had really heard what Jesus said about ascending to the Father, they may have thought they would never see Jesus again. But the words of Jesus' last discourse should have assured them that they would see him again after he had gone to the Father for "a little while."

20:19 *When it was evening on that day, the first day of the week, and the doors of the house where the disciples had met were locked for fear of the Jews, Jesus came and stood among them* (NRSV). On the evening of his resurrection Jesus made his first appearance to his disciples. This appearance is astounding because Jesus probably penetrated the locked room to enter into their midst. He could do this because resurrection and the subsequent glorification had altered his bodily form. In resurrection, he had become a life-giving spirit (1 Cor 15:42-45). At the same time, he still had a body, but a glorified one. In resurrection, he was the same person in a different form (see Mark 16:12). In this new spiritual form, he was able to transcend all physical barriers.

Peace be with you! This was a normal way Jews greeted one another. For Jesus to speak like this meant he wanted to put the disciples at ease. The deeper meaning of "peace" is that Jesus would give them the confidence to overcome fear and opposition (see 14:27; 16:33).

20:20-21 On the evening of his resurrection, Jesus appeared to his disciples and *showed them his hands and side.* Since they thought they were seeing a ghost or phantom (see Luke 24:37-39), Jesus needed to convince them that he himself in bodily form was present with them. When they realized who he was, they rejoiced. Jesus had predicted this three days earlier: "In a little while you will see me no more, and then after a little while you will see me. . . . You will grieve, but your grief will turn to joy" (16:16, 20). Mixed with their joy was tension and excitement, so Jesus again said to them, *"Peace be with you!"* Following this, Jesus commissioned them to be his emissaries, just as Jesus had been commissioned by the Father to be his emissary. The disciples were to be his testimony, even as he had been the Father's. But before they embarked on this wondrous task, Jesus gave them the Holy Spirit.

20:22 The impartation of the Holy Spirit was accomplished by Jesus' breathing the Holy Spirit into his disciples: *he breathed on* [or *into*] *them and said, "Receive the Holy Spirit."* Very likely, this verse consummates the Gospel of John because the Spirit who had been promised (7:37-39; 14:16-20, 26; 15:26; 16:7-15) was at last given to the disciples. After Jesus commissioned the disciples, he breathed (Gr., *enephusēsen*) into them and said, "Receive the Holy Spirit." Jesus' breathing into them recapitulated God's breathing into Adam (see Gen 2:7, LXX, where *enephusēsen* is used); Jesus was acting as God. This infusion inspired a new genesis, whereby Jesus regenerated the disciples (see 1 Pet 1:3). With this "in-breathing" came the actual impartation of the promised Holy Spirit.

This impartation was not a symbolic act or a foreshadowing of the Pentecostal outpouring. Some commentators (for example, see Bengel and Vincent) and translators, however, have asserted that since the Greek reads *pneuma hagion* (without a definite article before each word), it does not designate the personal Holy Spirit, but rather an earnest of that gift. But the expression *pneuma hagion*, appearing eighty-six times in the New Testament, is used thirty-seven times with an article and forty-nine times without an article. With or without an article, *pneuma hagion* indicates the Holy Spirit. The reason some insist on saying that the John 20:22 infusion was either a symbolic act or an earnest is that they believe that the Holy Spirit was given only at Pentecost and not until then. But the Gospel of John has its own chronology. According to the entire context of John's Gospel, Jesus would first ascend to the Father and then come to the disciples to give them the promised Spirit. That the timing in John does not coincide with the Luke/Acts sequence does not mean John is inaccurate (or needs reinterpretation). The two accounts do not contradict each other. The apostles received the Spirit into them on the evening of the Resurrection, and the Spirit came upon them on the Day of Pentecost. They were filled and empowered with the same Spirit.

Three of the Gospels (Matthew, Luke, John) connect the impartation of the Holy Spirit with the apostolic commission—in connection with the work of the Trinity. In Matthew, the disciples are charged with the great commission of discipling all nations and baptizing them in the name of the Father, Son, and Holy Spirit (28:19-20). In Luke/Acts, they are charged to be Jesus' witnesses after they have received the Holy Spirit promised by the Father (Luke 24:49; Acts 1:5-8). In John, the disciples are commissioned to be Jesus' sent ones, even as he had been sent by the Father, and are given the Holy Spirit to carry out this commission (20:21-22).

20:23 *If you forgive the sins of any, they are forgiven them; if you retain* [i.e., do not forgive] *the sins of any, they are retained* [i.e., they are not forgiven] (NRSV). Most commentators consider that this authority was given to the church and not to any one apostle or even group of apostles. This is affirmed by Matthew 16:18-19 and 18:18, where it is said that the church has authority to bind and loose. "The church is given authority to declare that certain sins are forgiven and certain sins are retained. This is not to be understood in any mechanical way. It is the result of the indwelling Spirit and takes place only as the Spirit directs" (Morris). It is also possible that the apostles were here commissioned not to do the work of forgiving or retaining but to preach the gospel of forgiveness and unforgiveness. For those who believe in Jesus, their sins are forgiven. To not believe is the greatest sin; it is unforgiveable.

20:24-25 *Now Thomas (called Didymus), one of the Twelve, was not with the disciples when Jesus came.* Thomas (whose nickname, Didymus, means "Twin"; see 11:16) was not with the other ten disciples when Jesus came (Judas Iscariot had committed suicide). When the disciples told him, *"We have seen the Lord!"* he did not believe. The disciples' first witnessing experience ended in failure. Here the sent ones were ready to tell the world about Jesus, but when they told one of their very own, he wouldn't believe! Thomas must have thought they had seen a phantom or a ghost, not the real flesh and blood of Jesus risen from the dead. Thomas insisted that he see the Jesus who had been crucified: *"Unless I* *see the nail marks in his hands and put my finger where the nails were, and put my hand into his side, I will not believe it."* By saying this, Thomas was insisting on physical proof before he would believe. For Thomas, seeing was believing.

20:26-28 At their next meeting *a week later*, Thomas was present when Jesus appeared again in a setting and fashion just like that recorded in 20:19. *"Put your finger here; see my hands. Reach out your hand and put it into my side. Stop doubting and believe."* Jesus used Thomas's own words about having to see the wounds in Jesus' hands and side before he would believe. How could Jesus have known what Thomas had said if he were still dead? Thomas was immediately enlightened. In an instant Thomas must have realized that Jesus, in his invisible presence, was there when he had voiced his doubts to the other disciples. In an instant, he must have realized that Jesus, as God, sees all, hears all, and knows all. Thus, he exclaimed to Jesus, *"My Lord and my God!"* Not only had Thomas come to believe that Jesus was risen; he had come to believe that Jesus was God. The greatest doubter became the greatest believer.

There is irony in all of this: Thomas wanted a vision of the physical Jesus and got it, but he also got the realization of Jesus' invisible omnipresence. This epiphany caused Thomas to say, "My Lord and my God!" This declaration is one of the clearest affirmations of Jesus' deity in the New Testament (cf. Rom 9:5; Phil 2:6; Col 2:9; Titus 2:13; 2 Pet 1:1; 1 Jn 5:20 in NASB or NIV). It is strategically placed by John at the very end of his Gospel (ch 20 was John's original ending; he later added ch 21 as an epilogue). It reaffirmed the declaration of Jesus' deity in the prologue (see 1:1, 18) and consequent chapters (see 8:58; 10:30).

20:29 Though Thomas proclaimed Jesus to be his Lord and God, Jesus did not congratulate him for this revelation (compare Jesus' similar response to Peter in 6:70). Rather, Jesus reproved Thomas for the way in which he believed, for he had to see before he could believe. The blessed ones are *those who have not seen and yet have believed.* This blessing has been realized by the millions of Christians who have never seen Jesus yet believe in him (see 2 Cor 5:7; 1 Pet 1:8). In this verse John shifts the focus from the original eleven disciples to all the believers. In so doing, John includes his readers, both past and present, for they are those who have never seen Jesus and yet believe in him. This verse, then, provides a natural bridge to the conclusion of this book (20:30-31), which encourages ongoing faith for those who believe in Jesus.

20:30-31 *Now Jesus did many other signs in the presence of his disciples, which are not written in this book* (NRSV). As in Luke's small preface (Luke 1:1-4), the purpose of these two verses is to tell us why John wrote this Gospel and to tell us something about his method of writing. Verse 30 indicates that John was very selective in recording the miraculous signs in this Gospel. From the Gospel itself, we know that Jesus performed several signs in his first visit to Jerusalem that are not specified (see 2:23; 3:2; 4:45). In each of the next three Jerusalem visits, John records one specific sign: the healing of the paralytic man (ch 5), the healing of the blind man (ch 9), and the raising of Lazarus from the dead (ch 11) prior to Jesus' final entry into Jerusalem. Besides these three recorded signs, there are three others, all having occurred in Galilee: the changing of water into wine (ch 2), the healing of the official's son (ch 4), and the feeding of the five thousand (ch 6). There are no other recorded signs beside these six. John was selective, probably because he knew that his readers were aware of the signs recorded in the other Gospels or knew of other miraculous events circulating in the oral tradition about Jesus' life and ministry. The six signs were enough for John to compose a convincing account of Jesus' claim to be the Christ, the Son of God.

But these are written so that you may come to believe that Jesus is the Messiah, the Son of God, and that through believing you may have life in his name (NRSV). This Gospel's *raison d'etre* is very clear: John wrote this Gospel to encourage belief in Jesus as the Christ and as the Son of God. All the "signs" in this Gospel point to Jesus as being the Christ and God's Son, who came to give life to all those who believe in his name (i.e., who trust him to be who he claimed to be—the Christ and the Son of God).

Most likely, John wrote this Gospel to encourage those who already believed to continue in their faith.[1] This can be inferred because John used the present tense for the subjunctive verb *pisteuō,* rather than the aorist (according to the best manuscript evidence). The present-tense verb suggests ongoing faith, a believing that extends beyond the initial act of faith. Indeed, the next expression "through believing you may have life in his name" also has two present-tense verbs: *believing* (a present participle) and *may have life* (a present subjunctive verb). John was emphasizing ongoing faith and continual appropriation of Jesus' life. We know that the early Christians were the recipients of the written Gospels; the apostles wrote the Gospels to affirm what they had believed via the oral teachings (see Luke 1:1-4). As such, John's Gospel was written to the community of believers. This does not mean, however, that the Gospel was not intended to go beyond this community. Indeed, history has shown that John's Gospel has been a powerful tool for evangelism. The gospel message not only sustains faith, it creates it anew.

ENDNOTES

[1] The earliest manuscripts ($\mathfrak{P}$66^{vid} $\aleph$ * B) read, "continue to believe," while later manuscripts ($\aleph^2$ A C D W) read, "believe."

The Epilogue: Jesus' Last Resurrection Appearance

JOHN 21:1-25

EXPOSITION

Most readers will recognize that chapter 21 is an epilogue or an appendix to John's narrative because the Gospel fittingly ends at 20:30-31. Nothing more needs to be said beyond what was said in chapter 20. The twentieth chapter recounts Jesus' resurrection and his resurrection appearances. It records Jesus' impartation of the Holy Spirit and commissioning of the apostles to continue his work; it affirms Jesus' deity through Thomas's confession; and it concludes with an excellent summary of why John wrote the Gospel, namely, to promote faith in Jesus as the Christ and Son of God, through whom the believer may receive life. Why then another chapter beyond the twentieth?

Very likely, John decided to add this chapter some time after he completed his Gospel[1] in order to clarify the misconception about the relationship between his own death and the Lord's return. Morris says, "When the Beloved Disciple was growing old and some thought that Jesus had said he would return before his beloved follower's death, it was necessary to correct the error. Harm could occur to the church if he died and still the Lord had not come" (see also Bruce and Westcott). In addition to explaining that Jesus had not said that John would not die before he returned (see 21:21-25), John used this chapter to show Peter's restoration after having denied the Lord three times. In none of the appearances recorded in chapter 20 had John mentioned any kind of special attention given to Peter by Jesus. And yet Peter needed this. And the Gospel needed this in order to be complete. Furthermore, John used this epilogue to show that Peter's death (by crucifixion) had been foretold by Jesus. At the time John wrote his Gospel and the epilogue (AD 85–90), Peter had already been dead for over twenty years (since AD 67).

Another reason John may have felt compelled to add an epilogue to his Gospel is that it would add a Galilean resurrection appearance to his account. Chapter 20 recounted only appearances in Jerusalem, when it is clear from all the Gospel accounts that Jesus appeared to his disciples first in Jerusalem and then in Galilee.

John 21:1-25/*The Heart of the Matter*

Men of action find it nearly impossible to wait. This is particularly true of those in leadership roles. King Saul found it to be unbearable mental and emotional anguish to wait for Samuel to appear (1 Sam 13:8-9). That was a case of unmistakable disobedience because Saul had been told to wait. But sometimes there isn't a divine message to wait. Many of God's children have agonized in their determination to discern the Lord's will in a matter. At times heaven seems unresponsive to earnest prayers for guidance. So we are most sympathetic with the bumper sticker that reads: "Do *something*, even if it's wrong." Waiting when you want to act requires great discipline.

From this perspective, perhaps we can better understand Simon Peter's action in this final chapter of John's record. Simon was definitely a man of action. He needed to be doing. Just sitting around got to him. Physical labor had been part and parcel of his life; inactivity was torture. So it was only natural that after a few days of "waiting for something to happen," he announced to some of the other disciples, "I'm going fishing." There are those who have found fault with the disciples' going fishing, implying by their criticism that these followers of Jesus officially forsook their spiritual calling and went back to the "old life" and former occupations. Such carping fails to understand that they, as yet, had not clearly perceived what the future held, and it improperly distinguishes too much between the secular and the sacred. If our work is neither unlawful, nor injurious to others, nor contrary to the general tenor of the Scriptures, we can then rejoice in honest labor. The Scriptures give us great peace of mind on this point, saying, "Whatever you do, do it all for the glory of God" (1 Cor 10:31). Perhaps we should reread *Practicing the Presence of God* and note again how Brother Lawrence washed pots and pans to the glory of God! Teacher, mechanic, salesperson, homemaker—it matters not; in all our dealings we should do our work to the glory of God. So fishing for fish or fishing for men can both be done apart from God's blessing or with his imprimatur. Before the day was over, Peter understood that the crux of the whole matter lay with one's heart attitude.

From disappointment to delight. The disciples fished all night and caught nothing. You don't have to be a fisherman to know how they felt. Have you ever worked very hard on something and had it come to nothing? You worked hard on a sales presentation, and no one bought it. You put in long, grueling hours on a project, and it was rejected. It is the common lot for us to experience emotionally what these men felt, having worked hard all night and gotten nothing. They were no doubt tired, hungry, and discouraged, but unknown to them, they were not alone. Jesus was about one hundred yards away, on the shore.

They didn't recognize him, and they certainly didn't expect him, but he was there and knew all about their situation. Jesus knew they had caught nothing. At his command they tossed the nets on the other side of the boat and began to haul in a record catch. This was the last recorded miracle ("sign") in John's Gospel showing clearly that Jesus is sovereign—over fish and nature and humans. Perhaps Jesus had directed the fish away from their nets all night, and now he directed a huge number into their nets.

Gradually, it began to dawn upon the disciples that the resurrected Jesus was always present, sometimes seen and recognized, and sometimes unseen. Admittedly, it must have been an unnerving experience to realize that Jesus was always present and could reveal himself at any moment! From John's perspective, Jesus had never left.

We do well to keep in mind that Jesus is not way off in heaven somewhere with his presence occasionally being sensed in a worship service, but he is with us, right now, today and every day. He is standing in the midst of scenes of beauty, though his foot leaves no impression on the sod and his form casts no shadow on the grass. He is standing amid the whir of deafening machinery, though he fills no space and utters no word audible to human ears. He is present in the Christian home, aware of the sickness, the good times, the needs, the disappointments, the laughter, and the tears, though none has ever heard the floors creak beneath his weight or seen any doors open to admit his person. He is "the silent listener to every conversation and the unseen guest at every meal."

Jesus provided a wonderful meal of grilled fish and fresh bread. Simon recognized that the Lord was present whatever his activity, and in this realization Simon's disappointment turned into great delight. It is not farfetched to note that Jesus' invitation to "come and dine" (21:12, KJV) is appropriate today. To the one lost in sin, he says, "Come and dine on my grace and forgiveness, for the gift of God is eternal life through me" (see Rom 6:23). To the needy and those weary of attempted good works, he says, "Come and dine on the good things I am ready to give you, for if you seek first the kingdom of God and his righteousness, all these things shall be added to you." To the unhappy and unsatisfied, he says, "Come and dine on the satisfying portion I alone can give you." And someday he will say to all those who belong to him, "Welcome to the marriage supper of the Lamb; come and dine!"

From failure to favor. After a wonderful meal, Jesus began talking to the disciples, specifically Simon Peter. But our Lord is not talking to just Peter, or even to just his disciples, for in his dialogue with Peter there is a message to all believers: the *form* of Christian service is not as important as the *nature* or *condition* of one's heart in Christian service. That all-important condition is declared to be love for Christ.

During the course of the conversation Jesus put a question to Simon three times. Probably he asked this same question over several hours, giving Peter time to ponder what Jesus was asking. "Simon son of John, do you truly love me more than these?" Didn't Jesus know if Peter loved him? Certainly he knew; he knows the depths of every heart. But Jesus needed to bring the relationship out in the open, to clear the air and get rid of the tension lingering from actions preceding the Crucifixion. Jesus helped Peter declare his love publicly so that he could assume apostolic leadership without shame. Jesus' question was a very simple one, but it was very searching. On the night of the betrayal, before they went to the Garden, Simon had said, "Even if all fall away on account of you, I never will" (Matt 26:33). He was saying in effect, "I love you more than the rest of the disciples!" How did he feel now, having cursed and denied Christ? Maybe he wasn't ready to boast of how much he loved, but he was ready to publicly declare, "Yes, Lord, you know that I love you."

Much has been made of the different words used in this exchange. Jesus used the most noble word for love, while Peter replied with a less intense word suggesting affection. If this is an accurate interpretation of the words used, Jesus accepted Peter's answer by responding, "Feed my lambs." That is, "We'll not talk about the intensity of your love; it is enough that you have affection for me. And since you do, I want you to tend my flock."

Three times Peter was asked the question, and finally he was deeply grieved at the persistence of Jesus and his own fear of hesitancy to declare publicly a superior, noble love for the Lord. But Jesus, knowing Simon's heart, knew that he would now give maximum attention to loving the Lord Jesus. The boasting and prayerlessness and denials and cursing were forgiven and forgotten, having been canceled by the shed blood of Christ and a public confession of Peter's love for Jesus. So Peter experienced favor in place of failure. It is almost as if we hear Jesus say to Peter, "I know your true devotion, and my grace will be sufficient for you, even to your martyrdom."

A little later Jesus began to walk along the shore—away from the dying embers, the boat, the fish, the other disciples—and said, "Come, Peter, travel with me. Your commercial fishing days are over; follow the way I lead, even to death." When Peter noticed that John was following at some distance, he said, "What about him? What is he going to do?" Jesus' illuminating response was, in effect, "Peter, it is not your responsibility what my other disciples do. I will order the path of each one. You are to die for me, but if I choose that John lives till I come back again, don't let that bother you—just follow me." Here is a great lesson for us. Our Lord deals with each of his own separately and in ways others cannot or may not understand. I dare not find fault with the way the Lord leads another believer. I must keep my eyes upon him and do what he asks *me* to do. My responsibility, like Joshua's, is, "As for me and my household, we will serve the LORD" (Josh 24:15).

In the last utterance of Christ recorded in this Gospel, he speaks of his coming again. The possibility is that he may come during our lifetime, perhaps even today. We should cherish such a truth and such a hope. John recorded only a few of the things that Jesus said and did. If everything our Lord did and said were recorded, the libraries of the world could not contain all the books that would be written (21:25). Books are inadequate to contain all there is to know about the innumerable triumphs, the inexhaustible power, and the limitless grace of our Lord Jesus Christ. But there is enough written to show every inquirer the way to God. There is enough written to satisfy the heart of every believer. And there is enough written to bring everlasting praise to Jesus Christ, our God and Savior.

KEY WORDS AND PHRASES

In this chapter, Jesus asked Peter three times if he loved him. When Peter responded affirmatively each time, the Lord directed him three times to take care of his sheep:

Jesus	Peter	Jesus
Do you love me?	Yes.	Feed my lambs.
Do you love me?	Yes.	Tend my sheep.
Do you love me?	Yes.	Feed my sheep.

After Peter's great failure of denying Jesus three times (13:38), Jesus would restore him and call upon him to become a leader and fortifier of his fellow disciples (see Luke 22:31-32). This chapter is devoted to showing how Peter, in the presence of the other disciples, was commissioned by Jesus to take care of the Lord's flock, motivated by his love for Jesus and Jesus' loving-kindness to him.

NOTES

21:1 *After these things Jesus showed himself again to the disciples* (NRSV). This opening statement tells the reader that the following narrative will lead to a resurrection appearance. As such, the suspense is lessened—quite unlike the other resurrection narratives (both in the Synoptics and John). Nonetheless, because chapter 21 is an epilogue, John needed to provide a good lead-in line.

by the Sea of Tiberias (NRSV). John 21 records Jesus' appearance to the disciples beside the Sea of Tiberias (another name for the Sea of Galilee; see 6:1 and note). Jesus had made at least six appearances in or around Jerusalem: to Mary Magdalene (Mark 16:9-11; John 20:11-18), to the other women (Matt 28:8-10; Mark 16:1-8; Luke 24:1-11), to Peter (Luke 24:34; 1 Cor 15:5), to two disciples on the road to Emmaus (Mark 16:12-13; Luke 24:13-35), to the disciples without Thomas present (John 20:19-25), and to the disciples with Thomas present (John 20:26-29). After the Jerusalem appearances, the disciples evidently returned to Galilee. Jesus made more appearances there: to the disciples on a mountain in Galilee (Matt 28:16-20; Mark 16:14-18); to five hundred believers (1 Cor 15:6); to James, Jesus' brother (1 Cor 15:7); and to the seven disciples who went fishing on the Sea of Tiberias (John 21:1-14). Prior to his resurrection, the Lord had told his disciples that he would meet them at an appointed place in Galilee after he arose (see Mark 14:28). But due to their unbelief and fear, they remained in Jerusalem. So Jesus first appeared to them in Jerusalem and then in Galilee. According to John's account, Jesus' appearance to the seven disciples by the Sea of Galilee was his third appearance to the disciples (see 21:14). Thus this appearance would very likely have been his first Galilean appearance.

21:2 Seven disciples were together at this time: (1) **Simon Peter** (who is mentioned first because he was the leader), (2) **Thomas (called Didymus)** (who was given special notice at the end of the previous chapter), (3) **Nathanael from Cana in Galilee** (who was first introduced in ch 1 and not mentioned again until the last chapter), (4 and 5) **the sons of Zebedee** (who are John and James), and (6 and 7) **two other disciples** (who are unnamed). This is the first time that James and John are mentioned as "the sons of Zebedee" in this Gospel. This helps identify the author as being John, the son of Zebedee, even though he is not specifically named as such.

21:3 Having gone back to Galilee, it was natural for some of the disciples to return to their occupation, fishing. Peter took the lead, and six other disciples went with him. That night, however, **they caught nothing**. This recalls Luke 5:1-11. In Luke 5, as well as in John 21, the scene shows Peter fishing, catching nothing, receiving a visitation from Jesus, and then witnessing a miraculous catch of fish. When Jesus appeared to Peter the first time, Peter fell on his knees before him and, realizing he was a sinful man, asked Jesus to depart from him. Jesus would not depart. He had come to Peter to make him his disciple. In this appearance, Jesus had come to restore Peter (after his having denied Jesus) and to encourage him to take care of the flock by asking him to feed his sheep.

21:4 Just after daybreak, Jesus stood on the beach; but the disciples did not know that it was Jesus (NRSV). Even though Jesus was only about a hundred yards away, Peter and the other six disciples did not know it was Jesus on the shore. Probably it was too dark to recognize him. The Greek text has the word *prōias*, indicating the time before sunrise while it is still dark (see 20:1, where the same word is used with the added descriptor "it was still dark").

21:5 "Children, you have no fish, have you?" They answered him, "No" (NRSV). The Greek construction expects a negative answer, as translated here. Jesus knew they had not caught even one fish. The sound of Jesus' voice should have given the disciples some inkling that it was Jesus speaking to them, but Jesus is not identified until after the catch of fish.

21:6 "Throw your net on the right side of the boat and you will find some." When they did, they were unable to haul the net in because of the large number of fish. Because the net was so laden with fish, the disciples had to drag the net behind the boat onto shore (21:8). This miraculous catch of fish was Jesus' last miraculous sign (see 20:30), revealing his power over nature. This miracle, at the end of Jesus' ministry, has many similarities to the miraculous catch of fish at the beginning of Jesus' ministry (Luke 5:5-9),[2] with the one notable exception being that in this miracle the net doesn't break.

21:7-8 That disciple whom Jesus loved said to Peter, "It is the Lord!" (NRSV). Again John the writer identified himself as "that disciple whom Jesus loved." Again he is given preeminence as the first to recognize the person on shore as Jesus.

As soon as Simon Peter heard him say, "It is the Lord," he wrapped his outer garment around him (for he had taken it off [for work]*) and jumped into the water.* Other translations speak of Peter "putting his outer garment on," but why would one put on a garment before swimming? It is more likely that Peter, who was probably dressed only in his undergarment, quickly tied his outer garment around his waist before plunging into the sea. But why did Peter jump into the sea? At first glance, the reader might think he did it to avoid embarrassment— this would especially be true if Peter was naked. However, it seems more likely that Peter jumped into the water and started swimming to shore so that he could be the first to greet Jesus (Bruce). If so, this shows that Peter did not feel alienated from Jesus; undoubtedly the restoration had already occurred in Jesus' special appearance to Peter on the day of resurrection (Luke 24:34; 1 Cor 15:5). Peter left his companions to do the work of *towing the net full of fish* behind the boat from *about a hundred yards* out.

21:9-10 *they saw a fire of burning coals there with fish on it, and some bread.* It is of note that a breakfast of fish and bread was already cooking before the disciples brought the fish they had miraculously caught. Evidently, some of the fish from the catch were added to those that were being cooked. This is implicit in what Jesus said, *"Bring some of the fish you have just caught."* Perhaps the symbolism of this is that, although Jesus could and does provide all, he wants the participation of his disciples. Nonetheless, there is irony in the words "the fish *you* have just caught," since the disciples hadn't really caught anything—all they did was let down the net at Jesus' command.

21:11 *Simon Peter climbed aboard and dragged the net ashore. It was full of large fish, 153, but even with so many the net was not torn.* Once the boat was near the shore, Peter got into the boat and single-handedly pulled the net full of fish ashore. This act reveals Peter's strength—to drag a net full of 153 large fish was no easy task! Though the number 153 could be symbolic, the context doesn't call for a symbolic interpretation; it is simply a detail that authenticates the eye-witness account. Likewise, the mention of the net not breaking serves to contrast this miraculous catch with that of Luke 5:1-11, wherein the nets were torn by the great catch. One of Peter's first encounters with Jesus involved a miraculous catch of fish, and his last encounter with the risen Jesus involved a miraculous catch. This must have affected Peter profoundly, reminding him of how the Lord had first appeared to him and called him to become a fisher of men. Jesus was now affirming that call and adding yet another commission—Peter was to catch men *and* shepherd them. From this dual commission came the expression "by hook and by crook" (i.e., the shepherd's staff).

21:12-13 *Jesus said to them, "Come and have breakfast." None of the disciples dared ask him, "Who are you?" They knew it was the Lord.* This participation in a meal with Jesus would have reminded the disciples of former experiences with their Master; even the wording **took the bread and gave it to them, and did the same with the fish** echoes the wording used in the Last Supper. However, it was not as before. "The disciples, it appears, were conscious of a certain uneasiness in the presence of their risen Lord. There was something quite familiar in having him with them by the lakeside, yet there was something quite unfamiliar in the company of one who had returned from the dead. Formerly they would not have thought of asking him 'Who are you?'—but they felt as if they ought to ask him; yet they could not bring themselves to do so, because, after all, they *knew* who it was" (Bruce).

The resurrection appearances where Jesus ate and drank with his disciples made a profound and lasting impact on them (see Luke 24:41-43). Peter later asserted his reliability as a witness of Jesus by saying, "He was not seen by all the people, but by witnesses whom God had already chosen—by us who ate and drank with him after he rose from the dead" (Acts 10:41).

21:14 This was now the third time that Jesus appeared to the disciples after he was raised from the dead (NRSV). In 21:1 the verb for "appeared" is active in both instances; here is it passive. The passive focuses on Jesus' self-disclosure. Between the lines, John might be telling his readers that Jesus was always present with his disciples after his resurrection, but then on certain occasions he chose to reveal himself to them. This kind of revelation is not a visitation (from heaven to earth) as much as it is an unveiling (from an invisible presence to a visible one). When Jesus was not seen by his disciples, it does not mean that he was not present; it only means that he could not be seen.

This was Jesus' third manifestation to his disciples (the first was recorded in 20:19-23, on the evening of the Resurrection, and the second in 20:24-29, a week later). In this third resurrection appearance Jesus had come to encourage them, especially Peter, concerning their future work. The text seems to imply that Jesus had come to remind them that they were not to return to their old life of fishing. He called them to be fishers of men, and he called them to start the church. Peter, the leader among them, needed to take the proper lead of the flock and feed it—not with physical food (which Jesus would provide), but with spiritual food. This is both implicit and explicit in this passage.

21:15-17 Jesus said to Simon Peter, "Simon son of John" (NRSV). This was Peter's natural name, the name Jesus had said when he first met this man (see 1:42). For Jesus to call him by his natural name was to remind him of his natural being prior to his conversion. In his denial of Jesus, this disciple had not lived up to his "Christian" name, Peter (meaning stone), but had reverted to his natural being.

do you love me more than these? (NRSV). According to the Greek, Jesus' first question to Peter could be rendered in three ways: (1) "Do you love me more than these men love me?" (2) "Do you love me more than you love these men?" (3) "Do you love me more than these things?" (i.e., all the things related to the fishing occupation). The first and the third renderings are more appropriate in this context than the second rendering, and the first seems the most appropriate because Peter had claimed, in the presence of all the disciples, that he would never forsake Jesus, even if all the others did (see Matt 26:33; Mark 14:29; John 13:37), implying that he had more love for Jesus than the others did. Of course, Peter's claims had not been realized; instead, he had denied Jesus three times.

Consequently, Jesus asked Peter three times, *"Do you love me?"* The first two times Jesus used the Greek word *agapaō* and the last time the word *phileō* to express two different kinds of love. In all three of his responses, Peter used the word *phileō*. (Some commentators make nothing of the lexical differences here and ascribe it to John's penchant for producing word variations. Perhaps this is true, but it seems that John—at least in this case—purposely used different Greek verbs for "love.") The Greek word *agapaō* designates volitional, responsible love that emanates not so much from emotion as from the soul and will. This is the sort of love one exercises in choosing to love those whom one would not naturally love. This is the kind of love God has for the world, a divine love. The Greek word *phileō*, designating the action of love that emanates from liking someone or something, conveys the idea of fondness. Peter, quite honestly, told Jesus that he was fond of him. Peter could not say that his love was an *agapē* love. When Jesus asked him the third time, he asked if he was fond of him. Peter told Jesus what he already knew: "I am fond of you."

Each time Peter told Jesus "I am fond of you," Jesus exhorted Peter to care for his sheep. This is expressed in three ways: (1) *"Feed my lambs,"* (2) *"Take care of my sheep,"* and (3) *"Feed my sheep."* Again, one could argue that the verbal variation does not produce meaning variation, but John used different terms for the sheep: *arnia* (lit., "young lambs" and "little sheep"—a term of endearment) and *probata* (the usual term for an adult sheep). Peter was charged to care for them by both feeding (*boske*) and shepherding (*poimaine*). Peter always remembered this commission; he became a dedicated shepherd of the flock (see 1 Pet 5:1-4), feeding the believers and leading them in the way of life.

21:18-19 *when you were younger, you dressed yourself and went where you wanted; but when you are old you will stretch out your hands, and someone else will dress you and lead you where you do not want to go.* On the surface, this seems to depict what happens to an older man who must become dependent upon others, but John's explanation (*Jesus said this to indicate the kind of death by which Peter would glorify God*) dispels this notion. The image depicts Peter's death by crucifixion. Tertullian (c. AD 212), referring to John 21:18, said that Peter was "dressed by another" when his arms were stretched out and fastened to the cross. Eusebius said that Peter, at his own insistence, was crucified head downwards, though most scholars consider this fantasy more than fact. At any rate, from this day onward, Peter knew what death lay before him. This prophecy remained with Peter all his days (see 2 Pet 1:14). Tertullian and other church fathers said that Peter was crucified in Rome under Nero around AD 65–67.

"Follow me!" With these words, Jesus reinstated Peter as his disciple. The verb is a present-tense imperative meaning "keep on following." Peter was called, as in the beginning, to once again follow Jesus and continue following until the end, even if that end meant martyrdom.

21:20-23 Having been told his destiny, Peter wanted to know what would happen to John (called *the disciple whom Jesus loved* and identified as the one who *had leaned back against Jesus at the* last *supper*). Jesus' response is somewhat mystifying: *"If I want him to remain alive until I return, what is that to you?"* Apparently, this statement could mean that John would remain alive on earth until the coming of the Lord (i.e., until the Parousia). Quite obviously, that is exactly how some of John's contemporaries understood the statement, as *the rumor spread among the brothers that this disciple would not die.* (If John remained alive until the Lord's coming, he would never have to experience death.)

But Jesus did not say that he would not die; he only said, *"If I want him to remain alive until I return, what is that to you?"* John insisted that they had misunderstood Jesus' words. What this means is that John *could* stay alive until Jesus' coming (if Jesus so desired), not that John *would* stay alive until his coming. Jesus' sovereignty over each man's life (Peter's and John's) was the issue, not the duration of John's life. What Jesus was communicating to Peter was that it was not for Peter to be concerned about what would become of John's life. He, Peter, was responsible to follow the Lord according to what the Lord had revealed to him. The same was true of John.

The Lord's command to Peter, *"You must follow me,"* applies to each and every believer. Each of us needs to respect the divine prerogative over other people's lives; each of us needs to respond to the Lord's call in our life, without comparing ourselves with others.

21:24 *This is the disciple who is testifying to these things and has written them* (NRSV). The last two verses of John's Gospel contain the conclusion (technically called a colophon), attesting to the veracity of the written testimony. Here the writer identifies himself with the disciple mentioned in the previous narrative (see 21:20). Since 21:20 refers back to 13:23-25 in identifying this disciple as one who sat next to Jesus at the Last Supper, this disciple is none other than John, the son of Zebedee (see discussion on authorship in the introduction to this book). John's testimony is trustworthy because he was an eyewitness of Jesus' life and ministry. He had known Jesus intimately and was very much loved by him. After many years of experience and reflection, during which time the Spirit of Jesus must have illumined John's mind concerning the meaning of Jesus' messages and the reality of Jesus' acts, John penned an account that reflects his spiritual insight into the life of Jesus Christ (cf. 1:14; 1 Jn 1:1-3).

and we know that his testimony is true (NRSV). This is probably the attestation of some of John's contemporaries (i.e., those in the Johannine community) who knew that what John wrote was true. Some of these men may have helped in the production of John's Gospel as amanuenses or publishers. Some scholars think these contemporaries were the Ephesian elders. (John resided in Ephesus in his later years.) Westcott writes, "The words were probably added by the Ephesian elders, to whom the preceding narrative had been given both orally and in writing."

21:25 But there are also many other things that Jesus did; if every one of them were written down [lit., one by one], **I suppose that the world itself could not contain the books that would be written** (NRSV). It is important to note the use of the first person singular "I" here, because this is the only time it is used in this Gospel. The one referred to as "I" here has to be the same as "the disciple" in the previous verse, whom we understand to be John, the son of Zebedee (see introduction). The only other place where a first person singular pronoun is used in a Gospel is Luke 1:3, where Luke used it in reference to himself. Luke clearly stated that he was not an eyewitness of Jesus (see Luke 1:2), but John was. Thus, this "I" in the conclusion to John is very significant, for it points to the personal signature of an eyewitness.

John's final statement is an expression of the writer's honest confession of his Gospel's limitations. The writer knew full well that he could have written so much more about Jesus' ministry. John selected only some of those events for his Gospel, and nearly every event was accompanied by a great amount of monologue and dialogue. If John had covered more events, how many more books would be required to contain all the material! Some of this material can be found in the other three Gospels, though there is so much more that could have been said by John and by the other Gospel writers. This, the fourth Gospel, completes the Gospel accounts of Jesus' life and ministry. In them enough is revealed to know Jesus and believe in him as the Messiah and Son of God.

ENDNOTES

[1]The epilogue may have been lacking from two early manuscripts, $\mathfrak{P}$5 and $\mathfrak{P}$75, thereby giving witness to the earliest edition of this Gospel, which lacked chapter 21. (This is fully explained in the appendix to Comfort's *The Quest for the Original Text of the New Testament*.) We do not know when this epilogue was added, but it seems certain that it was John—not another author—who compiled this chapter. The text itself suggests this, and some of John's associates affirmed this (see 21:24-25 and comments). Furthermore, the language of the chapter is thoroughly Johannine, and so is the style.

[2]A few scribes, noting the similarities between the two accounts, couldn't help but add a detail from Luke 5:5 after John 21:6. This was done by the scribe of $\mathfrak{P}$66—providing the earliest extant demonstration of Gospel harmonization. The addition was also made in $\aleph^c$.

The Woman Caught in Adultery

EXPOSITION

The story of the woman caught in adultery (often called the pericope of the adulteress) was taken into the Gospel text from an oral tradition. In its oral form, the story may have been in circulation since the early second century. Papias may have been speaking of this incident when he "expounded another story about a woman who was accused before the Lord of many sins, which the Gospel according to the Hebrews contains" (Eusebius *History* 3.39.17). However, in the pericope of the adulteress there is no mention of many "sins," only one—that of adultery (Bruce, pp. 417-418).

According to Ehrman ("Jesus and the Adulteress," *New Testament Studies* 34 [1988]: 24-44), this story was extant in written form as early as the fourth century in three different versions: (1) a story where the religious leaders were trying to trap Jesus as to whether or not he would uphold the Mosaic law, and he freely pardoned a sinful woman—a story known to Papias and the author of the *Didascalia*; (2) the story of Jesus' intervention in an execution—an episode preserved in the Gospel according to the Hebrews and retold by Didymus in his commentary on Ecclesiastes; and (3) the popular version found in most of the later manuscripts of John, "a version which represents a conflation of the two earlier stories."

This third version is the one printed in most translations of the Bible. When the Revised Standard Version was first printed (1952), this story was not included in the text; instead it was relegated to the margin. This caused such a furor among the reading public that the story was reinserted into the text in the next printing. Since then, no major translation has dared take the pericope of the adulteress out of the text! It is part of the fabric of the English Bible. Besides, most readers feel that this story has "the ring of truth" about it, to borrow a phrase from J. B. Phillips. As such, preachers love to expound on it and draw many practical applications from it. However, all such expounding must be done cautiously because this piece of writing cannot be put on the same level as the rest of the fourth Gospel, which was authored by John. It is in this light that we offer the following comments:

7:53–8:1 *Then each of them went home, while Jesus went to the Mount of Olives* (NRSV). This statement was intended to provide a bridge between the previous narrative and the pericope of the adulteress that follows. Since there is no record elsewhere in John of Jesus going to the Mount of Olives, it is safe to assume that the composer created this scenario based on Jesus' movements as recorded in the synoptic Gospels.

8:2 *All the people came to him and he sat down and began to teach them* (NRSV). Again, this detail is drawn from the Synoptics, which often picture Jesus sitting down to teach (a position assumed by rabbis). But in John, Jesus is said to have taught while walking, which was the peripatetic fashion of the Greek philosophers (see comments on 10:22-23).

8:3-5 *The scribes and Pharisees brought a woman who had been caught in adultery; . . . they said to him, ". . . Now in the law Moses commanded us to stone such women. Now what do you say?"* (NRSV). As is often the case in this Gospel, Jesus is pitted against Moses, the respected leader of the Jews (see comments on 1:17; 5:45-47; 6:32). However, these Jewish leaders did not accurately cite the law of Moses, for Leviticus 20:10 says that both the adulterer and the adulteress should be stoned. Why, then, did they bring only the woman? In their male-dominated society, all preference had been given to men, while women were treated as decidedly inferior.

8:6 *They said this to test him, so that they might have some charge to bring against him* (NRSV). Primarily, they were not testing Jesus to see whether or not he agreed with the law of Moses; he did, and they probably knew that. They were testing him to see if he would condone the stoning and thereby violate Roman law, which stipulated that all capital punishment was a Roman prerogative, not Jewish. If Jesus agreed, they could accuse him to the Roman authorities.

Jesus bent down and wrote with his finger on the ground (NRSV). To this day, the enigma remains: What was Jesus writing? The sins of all the people? (See comments on 8:8.) The Ten Commandments, or one of the commandments? (This is suggested by the fact that Jesus wrote "with his finger"—compare Exod 31:18, which says the Ten Commandments were written with the finger of God.) Or perhaps Jesus was writing, "I forgive the adulterous woman."

8:7 *If any one of you is without sin, let him be the first to throw a stone at her.* This statement sounds so much like what Jesus said on other occasions when the religious leaders were trying to trap him. His response avoids condoning or condemning the stoning. At the same time, he places the opprobrium of the stoning on their consciences. This statement is often used to support the maxim that one has to be perfect (i.e., without sin) before he or she can judge others. The upshot of this is that no one is qualified to judge anyone else because no one is perfect. In a sense, this is true because only God is qualified to judge us. But this must not be taken too far because Christians are called upon to judge those who disrupt the church with heresy or sin.

8:8 *Again he stooped down and wrote on the ground.* To this some manuscripts added "the sins of each of them." This, of course, is the interpretation of some scribe or scribes who could not resist supplying just exactly what Jesus was writing.

8:9 *they went away, one by one, beginning with the elders* (NRSV). The statement suggests that older people are more aware of their sins, while the younger are less inclined to admit guilt. Nonetheless, all had to admit that they were sinners.

Jesus was left alone with the woman standing before him (NRSV). The separation of the people from Jesus was not just physical; he was in a different category because he, as the divine one, was without sin.

8:10-11 *"Has no one condemned you? . . . Then neither do I condemn you,"* *Jesus declared. "Go now and leave your life of sin."* As we understand the use of "condemn," the Jewish leaders had condemned the woman. But the word is used technically here—they had not "brought judgment" against her by executing her. Jesus, the only one qualified to judge, did not condemn her, for he had not come into the world to condemn it, but to save it (3:17). However, this does not mean that Jesus condoned her sin. Therefore, he told her not to sin anymore, implying that she had been forgiven. Jesus said the same thing to the paralyzed man he had healed (see 5:14 and comments).

𝔓63: 3:14-18; 4:9-10

𝔓76: 4:9, 12

𝔓: 5:5; 17:3, 7-8

Bibliography

The works listed below are cited throughout the commentary by the author's last name (or authors' last names). These are excellent resources for teachers and preachers. Unless otherwise noted, each citation in this commentary corresponds with the same Scripture passage in the works listed below.

Abbott, Edwin A.
Johannine Grammar. London: Adam and Charles Black, 1906.

Aland, Black, Martini, Metzger, and Wikgren, eds.
The Greek New Testament. 3rd ed. New York: United Bible Societies, 1983. (Abbreviated as UBS³.)

Albright, W. F.
The Archaeology of Palestine. NY: Pelican Books, 1960.

Alford, Henry
The Greek Testament. 1852. Reprint. Grand Rapids: Guardian Press, 1976.

Barrett, C. K.
The Gospel According to St. John. Philadelphia: Westminster Press, 1978.

Bauer, Walter, William F. Arndt, and Wilbur F. Gingrich.
A Greek-English Lexicon of the New Testament and Other Early Christian Literature. Chicago: University of Chicago Press, 1979.

Beasley-Murray, George R.
John in Word Biblical Commentary. Waco: Word, 1987.

Bengel, J. A.
Gnomon on the New Testament. Translator, A. R. Fausset. Edinburgh: T & T Clark, 1877.

Braun, F. M.
Jean le theologien et son Evangile dans l'Eglise ancienne. 3 vols. Paris: Lecoffre, 1959.

Brown, Raymond E.
The Gospel According to John I–XII, XIII–XXI. New York: Doubleday, 1966.

Bruce, F. F.
The Gospel of John. Grand Rapids: Eerdmans, 1983.

Carson, D. A.
The Gospel According to John. Grand Rapids: Eerdmans, 1989.

Comfort, Philip W.
The Quest for the Original Text of the New Testament. Grand Rapids: Baker, 1992.

Dodd, C. H.
Historical Tradition in the Fourth Gospel. Cambridge: Cambridge University Press, 1963.

Gaebelein, Frank E., ed.
The Expositor's Bible Commentary. 12 vols. Winona Lake, IN: BMH Books, 1986.

Godet, Frédéric Louis
Commentary on the Gospel of John. Grand Rapids: Zondervan, 1969. (Orig. pub. 1893)

Gundry, R. H.
"In my Father's House are many *Monai*' (John 14,2)." *Zeitschrift für die Neutestamentliche Wissenschaft* 58:68–72, 1967

Hort, Fenton John Anthony
Two Dissertations. Cambridge: Macmillan, 1976.

Lindsell, Harold
People's Study Bible. Carol Stream, Ill: Tyndale, 1988.

MacGregor, G. H. C.
The Gospel of John. London: Hodder and Stoughton, 1928.

Metzger, Bruce
A Textual Commentary on the Greek New Testament. New York: United Bible Societies, 1971.

Moberly, R. C.
Atonement and Personality, Whitefish, MT: Kessinger Publishing, 2007.

Morris, Leon.
The Gospel According to John. Grand Rapids: Eerdmans, 1971.

Nee, Watchman
The Normal Christian Faith. Anaheim, CA: Living Stream Ministry, 1997.

Nestle-Aland
Novum Testamentum Graece. 26th ed. Stuttgart: Deutsche Bibelstiftung, 1979. (Abbreviated as NA[26].)

Newman, Barclay, and Eugene Nida
A Translator's Handbook on the Gospel of John. New York: United Bible Societies, 1980.

Robinson, J. A. T.
Redating the New Testament. London: SCM (Reprinted by Wipf and Stock, 2000), 1976.

Schnackenburg, Rudolph
The Gospel According to St. John. Translator, Kevin Smyth. New York: Crossroad Publishing Co., 1982.

Simpson, A. B.
When the Comforter Came. Camp Hill, PA: Christian Publications, 1991.

Vincent, Marvin R.
Word Studies in the New Testament. 1887. Reprint. Grand Rapids: Eerdmans, 1946.

Westcott, B. F.
Gospel According to St. John. 1881. Reprint. Grand Rapids: Zondervan, 1973.

Westcott, B. F., and F. J. A. Hort
Introduction to the New Testament in the Original Greek (with "Notes on Select Readings"). New York: Harper and Brothers, 1982.

1 John

Introduction[†]

After reading and studying John's Gospel, a person might wonder how the great truths presented in it were lived out in the church. Readers might also wonder how they themselves can better understand and experience the truths revealed by Jesus—ideas such as "living in the light" (John 8:12; 12:35-36), "remaining in Christ" (John 15:4-8), and "loving one another" (John 13:34; 15:12). John's first epistle answers both questions. It tells how Christians in the late first century were practicing (or not practicing) the profound truths proclaimed by Jesus, and it provides key insights into how we today can live in the Spirit of Jesus to experience spiritual transformation and love for the members of Christ's community, the church.

AUTHOR

Since the author does not name himself, the key to determining the authorship of this epistle (as well as that of 2 John and 3 John) is its similarity to the Gospel of John. The similarities between John's Gospel and John's epistles are so remarkable that it would be difficult to argue that these writings were done by two different people. The syntax, vocabulary, and thematic developments are so strikingly similar that most readers can tell that the epistles were penned by the writer of the Gospel of John. Therefore, the way to establish the authorship of the three epistles is to establish the authorship of the fourth Gospel.

Whoever wrote the Gospel of John was an eyewitness of Jesus and among the very first followers of Jesus. The writer of this Gospel calls himself "the disciple Jesus loved" (John 13:23; 19:26; 20:2; 21:7, 20); he was one of the twelve disciples, and among them he was one of those who was very close to Jesus (e.g., see John 13:23-25, where "the disciple Jesus loved" is said to have been leaning on Jesus' breast during the Last Supper). From the synoptic Gospels we realize that three disciples were very close to Jesus: Peter, James, and John. Peter could not have been the author of this Gospel because the one who called himself "the disciple Jesus loved" communicated with Peter at the last supper (John 13:23-25), outran Peter to the empty the tomb on the morning of the resurrection (John 20:2-4), and walked with Jesus and Peter along the shore of Galilee after Jesus' resurrection appearance to them (John 21:20-23). Thus someone other than Peter authored this Gospel. And that someone could not have been James, for he was martyred many years before this Gospel was written (AD 44; cf. Acts 12:2). This leaves us with John, the son of Zebedee, who, like Peter and James, shared an intimate relationship with Jesus. Most likely, John is also the "other disciple" mentioned in the fourth Gospel (e.g., John 18:15). He and Andrew (Peter's brother) were the first to follow Jesus (John 1:35-40), and he was the one who was known to the high priest and therefore gained access for himself and Peter into the courtyard of the place where Jesus was on trial (John 18:15-16). This one, "the disciple [Jesus] loved," stood by Jesus during his crucifixion (John 19:25-26) and walked with Jesus after his resurrection (John 21:20). And this same disciple wrote the Gospel that today bears his name (John 21:24-25).

The author's claim to have been an eyewitness is just as pronounced in 1 John as it is in the Gospel of John. The author of 1 John claims to be among those who heard, saw, and even touched the eternal Word made flesh (1:1-4). In other words, John lived with Jesus, the God-man. As such, his testimony is firsthand; he was an eyewitness of the greatest person ever to enter human history. As Smith (1979:151) put it, "The author of [1 John] claims to have been an eye-witness of the Word of Life (1:1-3) and speaks throughout in a tone of apostolic authority, and there is abundance of primitive and credible testimony that he was St. John, 'the disciple whom Jesus loved,' and the last survivor of the Apostle-company."

But some scholars have thought that some other John (not the apostle) was the author. They make this judgment on the basis of a quotation from Papias, who was bishop of Hierapolis in the Roman province of Asia Minor (c. AD 100–130). His comment, transmitted through Irenaeus and recorded by Eusebius, is as follows: "If anywhere one came my way who had been a follower of the elders, I would inquire about the words of the elders—what Andrew and Peter had said, or what Thomas or James or John or Matthew or any other of the Lord's disciples say; and I would inquire about the things which Aristion and the elder John, the Lord's disciples, say" (Eusebius *History* 3.39.4-5).

Since two different people named "John" are referred to in this quotation, some scholars have surmised that the first "John" mentioned was John the apostle and the second "John" was an elder but not one of the original twelve disciples. (This was Eusebius's opinion, contra Irenaeus, who considered both mentions to refer to the same person, the apostle John—see House 1992:530.) Since the writer of 2 John and 3 John calls himself "the elder," many have thought that the author of the three Johannine epistles was this "John the elder," not John the apostle. Although this could be true, it is not likely. First of all, according to Eusebius's quote, Papias did not say that John the elder was the writer of the three epistles of John. Second, it seems that Papias was speaking of two different categories of sources for his learning. The first was teachings passed down from those who *had been* eyewitnesses of Jesus, his original disciples—namely Andrew, Peter, Thomas, James, John, Matthew, and the other disciples of the Lord. The second source was the ongoing teaching of disciples who were still alive when Papias made this statement—those such as Aristion and John the elder (who was literally much older at this time). Note that Papias spoke of what the first group had "said" (past tense), and what those in the second group "say" (present tense; cf. Stott 2000:39-40). John the apostle was in both groups. Furthermore, John is lumped together with the other "elders" in the first group (who were also Jesus' apostles), and he is specifically called an elder in the second group.

Later in life, John the apostle called himself an elder. After all, Peter and Paul, both apostles, each called themselves "elder" (Phlm 1:9, "old man," NLT; cf. 1 Pet 5:1). The title "elder" probably points to John's position at that time; he was the oldest living apostle and chief leader among the churches in the Roman province of Asia Minor. This is made clear in the first epistle by the way he addresses the believers as his "dear children" (2:1, 18, 28; 3:7; 5:21).

In any event, whichever John wrote these epistles, he must have been an eyewitness of Jesus. We know for certain that John the son of Zebedee was an eyewitness. If there had been another John, called John the elder—he would have probably been one of Jesus' 72 disciples (Luke 10:1) in order to claim "eyewitness" status. (This would also apply to Aristion.) But then, given the identical style between the epistles and the Gospel, this other "John" would also be the author of the fourth Gospel, and that can't be so, for we know that the disciple who wrote the fourth Gospel was among the inner circle of the Twelve (see the discussion above). Once again, the facts presented in the fourth Gospel and the similarities of 1–3 John to the Gospel press us to conclude that the author of the epistles and the author of the Gospel must be one and the same: John the apostle, the son of Zebedee. The earliest identification of John the apostle as the author of 1 John comes from the late second century, when both Irenaeus (*Heresies* 3.15.5, 8) and the Muratorian Fragment identified 1 John as his work.

Instead of dictating the epistle to an amanuensis, it appears that John himself penned it (1 Jn 2:12-14), as was his habit—as explicitly expressed in 2 John 1:12 and 3 John 1:13, and implicitly expressed in the Gospel (John 21:24-25).

DATE AND OCCASION OF WRITING

We really do not know when 1 John was written. For one thing, it could have been written before he wrote the Gospel or after it. In 3 John 1:9, the apostle says, "I wrote to the church about this." This could refer to 1 John or the Gospel, but the reference (in context) is more likely to 1 John (see note on 3 Jn 1:9). Nonetheless, the dating of John's Gospel does bear on the dating of 1 John because the two are written in so similar a style and concern so many of the same issues. Extant manuscript evidence, particularly the papyrus manuscript known as $\mathfrak{P}$52 (P. Rylands 457, dated c. AD 100–120; for details of dating, see Comfort 2005:139-143), shows that the original Gospel had to have been composed before AD 100. The question is, how long before AD 100?

J. A. T. Robinson has placed the composition of the Gospel of John and 1–3 John before AD 70. In fact, Robinson has dated all the New Testament writings to pre-AD 70—primarily on the grounds that not one New Testament writer comments on the destruction of Jerusalem as having already occurred. This significant point, coupled with the fact that John speaks of a certain portico at the Sheep Gate in Jerusalem that was *still* standing at the time of writing (see John 5:2, where John uses the present tense verb in the Greek) suggests a pre-AD 70 date for John's Gospel. Based on their relationship to his Gospel, 1–3 John would be dated similarly in Robinson's perspective (see Robinson 1976:277-278).

However, we agree with most other scholars who tend to date the Gospel of John to the AD 80s, placing it in the following chronology: John and the other apostles were probably forced to leave Jerusalem by AD 70, if not earlier, due to mounting persecution. It is possible that John gathered with some of the Samaritan converts (see John 4:1-45; Acts 8:9-17) and with some of John the Baptist's followers in Palestine, where they continued to preach the Word. Sometime thereafter (but probably no earlier than AD 70), they migrated to Asia Minor and began a successful ministry among the Gentiles (see Barker 1981:300-301).

John wrote a Gospel for these Gentiles somewhere around AD 80. Sometime thereafter, some of the members of the community left to form a rival group. John, therefore, wrote 1 John in order to deal with the crisis by encouraging the believers to remain in Christ and in the apostolic fellowship and by denouncing those who had not remained. Thus, the first epistle was probably written around AD 85–90.

We have early historical records indicating that John wrote his Gospel while living in Ephesus. For example, Irenaeus wrote, "John, the disciple of the Lord, he who had leaned on his breast, also published the Gospel, while living at Ephesus in Asia" (*Heresies* 3.1.1). Irenaeus (who lived AD 130–200) received this information from Polycarp, who in his younger years was personally instructed by John. Thus, it stands to reason that John wrote his three epistles to certain local churches in Asia—especially to those around Ephesus, the church in which John functioned as an elder in his latter days. (The same churches probably include those mentioned in Rev 1:11.)

One of the circumstances that prompted his first epistle was that a heretical faction had developed within the church, one that promoted false teachings concerning the person of Christ. Scholars have identified this heresy as Docetism in a general sense and have pointed specifically to Cerinthus as the perpetrator of the specific brand of Docetism that 1 John addresses. Our knowledge of Cerinthus comes from Irenaeus, who cited Polycarp (a disciple of John) as saying that there was an incident once when John discovered that Cerinthus was in the same bathhouse in Ephesus—John cried out, "Let us save ourselves; the bath house may fall down, for inside is Cerinthus, the enemy of the truth." Irenaeus continued by saying that John proclaimed his gospel to refute the errors of Cerinthus (*Heresies* 3.3.4; 3.11.1; see Brown 1982:766-771 for a full record of the historical evidence concerning Cerinthus). The Docetists denied that Jesus had actually partaken of flesh and blood; they denied that God had come in the flesh (see 4:1-3). They did not deny Jesus Christ's deity; they denied his true humanity (see discussion below under "Major Themes"). John specifically refuted the Cerinthian heresy in 5:5-8. This setting undermines Robinson's dating of John's writings (both Gospel and epistles) to pre-AD 70; instead, it points to a date in John's later life, in which he was probably in his 70s or 80s.

AUDIENCE

In recent years various scholars have tried to identify the original Johannine community—the group of believers for whom John wrote his Gospel and the epistles. That there was a Johannine community seems evident from the way John speaks to them and of them in his three epistles. The apostle John and the believers knew each other well, and the believers accepted the teachings of the apostle as "the truth." John encouraged them to stay in fellowship with him (and the other apostles); if they did so, they would enjoy true fellowship with the Father and the Son (1:1-4).

In the Gospel this linking of the believers, John, and Jesus is also made evident. Throughout the Gospel John lets his readers know that he had a special relationship with Jesus. As the Son, who was "near to the Father's heart," was the one qualified to explain the Father to mankind because of his special relationship with the Father (John 1:18), so John, who reclined on Jesus' chest, was qualified to explain Jesus and his message to his readers because of his intimate relationship with Jesus. In John's Gospel "the beloved disciple" or "the other disciple" is given a certain kind of preeminence: He is one of the two first followers of Jesus (John 1:35-37); he is the closest to Jesus during the Last Supper (John 13:22-25); he follows Jesus to his trial (John 18:15); and then he alone of the Twelve goes to Jesus' cross and is given a direct command from Jesus to care for Jesus' mother (John 19:26-27). He outruns Peter to the empty tomb and is the first to believe in Jesus' resurrection (John 20:1-8), and he is the first to recognize that it was Jesus appearing to them in the Galilean visitation (John 21:7). Because of his relationship to Jesus, John's testimony to his community could be trusted.

Culpepper (1975:261-290) attempts to reconstruct some of the distinctives of this Johannine community. He conjectures that this community was a kind of school (*scholē* [TH4981, ZH5391]) that claimed Jesus as its founder and John as its master teacher. This school studied the Old Testament and was reared on the teachings of John about Jesus, therein absorbing John's esoteric language about mystical experiences with Jesus. This school was also responsible in collaborating with John to produce his written Gospel. As a community, they were detached from Judaism (perhaps several of the members were ex-synagogue members who were expelled for their faith in Jesus), and they struggled with false teachers who denied Jesus as the God-man.

Then Culpepper does another study of John's Gospel based on theories of reader reception. Adopting Iser's model of the implied reader (see Comfort's evaluation [1997:27-28]), Culpepper sketches the general character of John's intended readers by what information (or lack thereof) the author supplies in the narrative concerning characters, events, language, cultural practices, and so forth. According to Culpepper's study (1983:206-223), John's intended readers were expected to already know most of the characters in the Gospel of John (with the exception of the beloved disciple, Lazarus, Nicodemus, Caiaphas, and Annas). The readers should know the general regions where the stories take place but be unfamiliar with the specific locations—for which the author supplies some details. Thus, the readers were not from Palestine. As would be expected, the readers knew Greek but not Hebrew or Aramaic. The author assumed that his readers used a Roman (not a Jewish) system of keeping time and that the readers had little knowledge of Jewish festivals and rituals. However, the readers were expected to know the Old Testament Scriptures and to understand messianic expectations. On the whole, it seems that the readers were not Jewish but Hellenistic Christians who would already have been familiar with many parts of the gospel story.

If the Gospel and epistles were directed to the same audience, then it stands to reason that the readers of John's epistles were primarily Hellenistic Christians. This accords with the tradition that John devoted his last years to ministry in Ephesus, where he was an elder. As such, the recipients of his epistles would have been those in the church in Ephesus and those in the nearby churches. (The same churches probably include those mentioned in Rev 1:11.)

By doing a close study of the epistles, one can surmise that the readers of John's epistles were close to John, so as to be considered his spiritual family. His readers were believers of all ages (children, young men, and fathers; 2:12-14), who needed to be affirmed as a community in love, life, and truth. They depended on John for his eyewitness account about Jesus and for his insights about his personal relationship with Jesus. They must have been accustomed to his rambling style, and they must have understood certain references that are vague and perplexing to modern readers. For example, we assume that they understood John's words about "he who came by water and blood" (5:6, NLT mg) and about the sin that "leads to death" and the sin that doesn't (5:16-17). We modern readers, however, are forced to conjecture.

It must also be said that the readers of John's first epistle must have known John's Gospel well, especially the upper-room discourse of John 13–17, because there are so many close connections between the two writings (Burge 1996:39; Stott 2000:20-22). John's first epistle is, in effect, a commentary on his Gospel, particularly John 13–17—even more so, an application commentary. John wanted to make sure his readers, whether among the heterodox group or orthodox, were properly understanding Jesus' teachings and applying them in their Christian lives.

CANONICITY AND TEXTUAL HISTORY

Records of the early church indicate that the First Epistle of John was readily received and recognized as John's writing. Polycarp, the disciple of John, quoted 1 John 4:3 (*To the Philippians* 7). Eusebius said of Papias, a disciple of John and a friend of Polycarp, "He used testimonies from the First Epistle of John" (*History* 3.39.17). Irenaeus often quoted this epistle (cf. Eusebius *History* 5.8); in his work *Heresies* (3.15.5, 8), he quoted from John by name (1 Jn 2:18, etc.), and in *Heresies* 3.16.7, he quoted 1 John 4:1-3; 5:1; and 2 John 1:7-8. Clement of Alexandria referred to 1 John 5:16 (*Stromata* 2.66). Tertullian in *Against Marcion* 5.16 refers to 1 John 4:1, and in *Against Praxeas* 15, to 1 John 1:1.

The Muratorian Fragment shows the church's acceptance of two of John's epistles (probably the first and second) by around AD 200. Origen (according to Eusebius *History* 6.25) spoke of the first epistle as genuine and "probably the second and third, though all [churches] do not recognize the latter two." Eusebius (*History* 3.24) said that John's first epistle and Gospel were acknowledged without question by those of his day, as well as by the ancients. Jerome said the same thing in his *Catalogue of Scriptures*. The second and third epistles took longer to be accepted into the canon because they were brief, personal letters. As such, they would not have been in general circulation among the churches. But once they were generally known, they were accepted into the canon.

The most reliable manuscript for John's epistles is Codex Vaticanus (B), followed by Codex Sinaiticus (ℵ). Other good manuscripts are 𝔓74 and 1739. Codex Alexandrinus (A) tends to be expansive and erratic in John's epistles. Several Western witnesses, especially in the Vulgate manuscripts, have extended interpolations (see notes on 4:3; 5:7b-8a, 10, 20). First John also has one early-third-century witness, 𝔓9, but it is scant and its textual character is unreliable.

LITERARY STYLE

It is not evident that 1 John is an epistle. It does not contain the name of a sender or addressee in the prescript, and there is no greeting in the conclusion (Schnackenburg 1979:1-3). It is more like a treatise in epistolary format—akin to Romans and Ephesians. However, even those two Pauline epistles have the kind of beginnings and endings (with introductions and greetings respectively) that are typical of other letters from the time period. First John stands alone among all the New Testament letters (Romans—Jude) in its format. It has a brief poetic prologue and an abrupt ending, lacking any kind of doxology. The whole of the book contains John's full explanation of Christian life and doctrine as a model for all orthodox believers to emulate. The audience is universal in scope—the same audience intended for the fourth Gospel. Thus when 1 John was published and circulated, it probably went to all the churches in the Roman province of Asia Minor and beyond.

John's first epistle has a very unusual thematic structure. Tenney (1985:377) says, "First John is symphonic rather than logical in plan; it is constructed like a piece of music rather than like a brief for a debate. Instead of proceeding step by step in unfolding a subject, as Paul does in Romans, John selects a theme, maintains it throughout the book, and introduces a series of variations, any one of which may be a theme in itself." Moving in and out of this thematic development is a constant presentation of antithetical proclamations, posed in pairs, such as light versus darkness, love versus hate, truth versus falsehood, righteousness versus sin, Christ versus Antichrist, and so forth. With John, there is no compromise, no blurring of the distinctions; it is all black and white. One who doesn't love, hates, and a hater is a murderer. This kind of extreme posturing is startling and effective in getting the reader's attention. In this regard, John followed his teacher quite well, for Jesus was a master at making bold and startling statements.

MAJOR THEMES

The Believers' Experience of the Triune God. John's epistles are an extension of John's Gospel (especially John 13–17) in that both present details about the relationship between the triune God and the believer. John shows how it was Jesus' primary aim to reveal the Father to those who believe and bring them to truly know the Father and participate in Christ's own enjoyment of the Father—as well as to enjoy their union with the Son through the Spirit.

God the Father and God the Son have always shared the same divine, eternal life and enjoyed each other's love. They created human beings so that they could share this life and love with them. God is glad to give the divine, eternal life to each believer and so beget many lovely and loving children. And God's desire has always been to include these children in the fellowship he had always enjoyed with his one and only Son. Thus when the Son was sent to earth, he was commissioned by the Father to explain and express him to mankind. His mission was also to bring all the believers into a life relationship with the Father. But believers could never participate in living fellowship with the Father and the Son without experiencing the Holy Spirit. With the reception of the Spirit comes the reception of life (cf. John 6:63; 7:39) and the ability to experience Jesus in and as the Spirit.

Jesus had told the disciples that he would give them another Comforter (John 14:16-18). Then he told them that they should know who this Comforter was because he was, then and there, abiding with them and would, in the near future, be in them. Who else but Jesus was abiding with them at that time? Then after telling the disciples that the Comforter would come to them, he said, "I will come to you." First he said that the Comforter would come to them and abide in them, and then in the same breath he said that he would come to them and abide in them (see John 14:20). In short, the coming of the Spirit-Comforter to the disciples was one and the same with the coming of Jesus to the disciples.

On the evening of the Resurrection, the Lord Jesus appeared to the disciples and then breathed into them the Holy Spirit (John 20:22). This inbreathing, reminiscent of God's breathing into Adam the breath of life (Gen 2:7), became the fulfillment of all that had been promised and anticipated earlier in John's Gospel. Through this impartation, the disciples became regenerated and indwelt by the Spirit of Jesus Christ. This historical event marked the genesis of the new creation. The believers now possessed Jesus' divine, eternal, risen life. From that time forward, Christ, as spirit, indwelt his believers. Thus in his first epistle, John could say, "We know he lives in us because the Spirit he gave us lives in us" (3:24), and again, "God has given us his Spirit as proof that we live in him and he in us" (4:13). Christ is in us because his Spirit is in us.

John's emphasis on the Spirit in his Gospel is carried over into his first epistle in the form of practical teaching concerning what is called the discernment of the Spirit. Since all Christians had the Spirit, any Christian could claim to be led by the Spirit or receive revelations from the Spirit. In the first century, most Christians did not have a New Testament to affirm or denounce any such leadings or revelations. Thus, all Christians had to test the spirits of the prophets (i.e., the proclamations of those claiming to be led by the Spirit) as to whether their proclamations were true or false. John said that every Christian has the anointing (the working of the Spirit) and can make such discernments (2:20-21; 3:24–4:6; and see Burge 1996:24-30).

John's epistles are an extension of his Gospel's focus on the triune God, but with an added emphasis—the practical, tangible experience of the triune God in the life of the believer as tested by the believer's relationship to the other members of the church community. For example, the Gospel speaks much of the mutual abiding of the triune God and the believers (cf. John 14–17), but there it is spoken of as a nascent revelation. In the epistles, all talk of one's living in God must be tested by how one lives with his or her companions in Christ.

This leads to one of the primary themes in these epistles: love for God must be exhibited in love for another. If we could ask John what is the one message he wanted us to get from these epistles, he would probably say, "Love one another." This command did not originate from John; it came straight from the lips of Jesus (John 13:34; 15:17). John repeated this command often (2:7; 3:11, 23; 2 Jn 1:5-6), reinforcing it with the logic that since "God is love," all who claim to love God must exhibit that nature in their relationship with others.

Christological Orthodoxy versus Heresy. One of the reasons that prompted the writing of John's epistles was that a heretical faction had developed within the church, one that promoted false teachings concerning the person of Christ. Scholars have identified this heresy as Docetism generally and pointed specifically to Cerinthus as the perpetrator of the specific brand of Docetism. The Docetists denied that Jesus had actually partaken of flesh and blood; they denied that God had come in the flesh (cf. 4:1-3). According to Irenaeus, Cerinthus "represented Jesus as having not been born of a virgin, but as being the son of Joseph and Mary according to the ordinary course of human generation, while he nevertheless was more righteous, prudent, and wise than other men. Moreover, after his baptism, Christ descended upon him [viz., upon Jesus, the mere human] in the form of a dove from the Supreme Ruler, and that then he proclaimed the unknown Father, and performed miracles. But at last Christ departed from Jesus, and that then Jesus suffered and rose again, while Christ remained impassible, inasmuch as he was a spiritual being" (*Heresies* 3.3.4). John refuted the Cerinthian heresy in 5:5-8 (see comments there).

The heretical faction within the church (or churches) that John was addressing eventually left the fellowship, and in so doing, they exposed themselves as not genuinely belonging to God's family (2:18-19). But their false teachings still lingered in the minds of the faithful; so John wrote to clear the air of all the falsehoods and bring the believers back to apostolic orthodoxy and to the basics of the Christian life.

Warnings about the Antichrist. According to 1 John, anyone who denies that Jesus is the Christ, that he is the unique Son of God, or that he has come in the flesh, is an antichrist. The biblical term, however, principally refers to a particular person in whom that denial reaches its consummate expression and who will play a key role in the final stage of history.

The word "antichrist" occurs only four times in the New Testament, all in John's epistles (2:18, 22; 4:3; 2 Jn 1:7). In 2:18, John refers also to "many such antichrists." John assumed that his Christian readers knew about the Antichrist and had been taught to expect his coming (2:18-27). The presence of many antichrists, in fact, indicated that the end time had arrived. But John warned that a final Antichrist (who, like the others, would deny that Jesus is the Christ) would yet make an appearance.

John further described any person or message that did not "acknowledge the truth about Jesus" as being of the spirit of the antichrist (4:3). In his brief second epistle, John referred to "many deceivers" who would not acknowledge the coming of Jesus Christ in the flesh (2 Jn 1:7). Such a person, he wrote, was "a deceiver and an antichrist."

In the book of Revelation, John's symbol for the Antichrist is probably "the beast" (Rev 13:1-18; 17:3, 7-17). The Beast is described not only as one who opposes Christ, but more specifically as a satanically inspired Christ-counterfeit. Although the Beast (Antichrist) is clearly distinguishable from the Lamb (Christ), he receives worship from everyone except God's elect. Another probable reference to the Antichrist is "the man of lawlessness" (2 Thes 2:3). The passage is difficult to interpret, but the person described seems to be the same person later designated by John as the Beast. Both the apostle Paul and John saw present events as leading up to the events of the future.

John's thoughts about the Antichrist probably came from the teaching of Jesus in the Gospels. A lengthy passage (Mark 13; paralleled in Matt 24; Luke 21) records the instruction Jesus gave his disciples about the tragic events and persecution to be expected before his return as the glorious Son of Man. His coming would be preceded by the appearance of many "deceivers" and "false messiahs." The term "false messiahs" is used only twice, both times by Jesus (Matt 24:24; Mark 13:22).

THEOLOGICAL CONCERNS

John's theological concerns are very practical in his first epistle. He urges his readers (1) to have fellowship with God in the light (1:7), (2) to confess their sins (1:9), (3) to love God (4:7-10), (4) to love their fellow Christians (4:11-12), (5) to abide in Christ (2:28), (6) to purify themselves from worldly lusts (3:3), (7) to know God personally and experientially (1:3), (8) to appreciate the gift of eternal life (5:11-12), (9) to follow the Spirit of truth (and the anointing) in discerning false teachings (2:20-27), and (10) to esteem Jesus Christ as the true God (5:20). Above all these items, John stresses how necessary it is for the early believers to maintain a proper relationship with those who had been with Jesus. In the prologue to this epistle (1:1-4), he invites all the believers to participate in the one apostolic fellowship. Fellowship is a two-way, simultaneous experience with fellow believers and with God. Fellowship serves to safeguard against pseudo-spirituality and extreme individualism. Throughout this epistle, it appears that John addresses his comments to those who were claiming to have a relationship with God and yet had left the fellowship of believers and did not love their brothers in Christ. Further, they had rejected the apostolic authority of John.

Throughout this epistle John calls into question all professed spirituality. This element is presented in a series of statements (usually phrased "if we say") that probably mimic what various Gnostic believers were claiming about their spiritual experiences (e.g., see 1:6; 1:8; 2:4; 2:6; 2:9). Talk is cheap; reality must be tested by one's relationship with the members of the church community. John urges the believers to know the truth and to live in it.

John's first epistle has much to say to those today who have Gnostic tendencies in the sense that they claim to have superior spiritual knowledge (or even experience) beyond that which ordinary Christians have. Indeed, some may even claim to have found the "secrets" to the deeper spiritual life, "secrets" which others can never know unless they become part of their special group. This superior knowledge often leads to an elitist attitude and disdain for other Christians. In short, the superior knowledge leads to rejection (a form of hatred) of other believers. John's epistle exposes this. If one truly knows Christ and lives in him, that person should love all fellow Christians. Love, not "superior" knowledge, is the proof that one has a genuine spiritual life.

THEMATIC OUTLINE

This book almost defies being outlined due to its symphonic thematic presentation (cf. "Literary Style," above). Among the many outlines offered by various scholars, some have organized it according to the three tests of life: righteousness, love, and belief. Others have used a simpler outline, generally framing 1 John according to the God proclamations: "God is light" (1:5) and "God is love" (4:8). (For discussions concerning the various outlines, see Brown 1982:764; Burge 1996:42-45.) But there is far too much overlapping material to make a clear-cut outline built around this thematic development. We have taken another approach: to organize the epistle around the theme of community fellowship, which is a fellowship that emanates from the triune God and should permeate the members of the believing community.

I. Experiencing Authentic Christian Fellowship (1:1–2:11)
  A. The Prologue (1:1-4)
  B. Living in God's Light with the Community of Believers (1:5-10)
  C. Experiencing the Ministry of Jesus, the Advocate (2:1-2)
  D. Living in the Light Means Loving Fellow Believers (2:3-11)

II. Maintaining the True Fellowship (2:12–3:10)
  A. The Community of Believers Affirmed as a Spiritual Family (2:12-17)
  B. Identifying the False Believers and the True (2:18-27)
  C. Being Prepared for Christ's Return (2:28–3:3)
  D. Recognizing What Kind of Life Prospers the Fellowship and What Contradicts It (3:4-10)

III. Loving One Another in the Community of Believers (3:11–4:21)
  A. Love for the Community Members, a Sign of Divine Life (3:11-18)
  B. Maintaining a Relationship with God by Being Faithful to Him and Living in Christ (3:19-24)
  C. Community Fellowship Protected by Watchfulness for Deceivers (4:1-6)
  D. God's Love Expressed in Community Love (4:7-21)

IV. Overcoming Hindrances to Community Fellowship (5:1-21)
  A. Overcoming the World (5:1-5)
  B. Discerning Truth from Falsehood and Keeping Eternal Life (5:6-12)
  C. Conclusion: Helping the Wayward Return to the Fellowship (5:13-21)

---

†This commentary on the epistles of John was previously published in a slightly altered form in the Cornerstone Biblical Commentary series.

The Prologue

1 JOHN 1:1-4

EXPOSITION

The prologue to John's first epistle is poetic, much in the same way the prologue to John's Gospel is poetic. In poetic format, the text of 1:1-3 could be rendered as follows:

> *As to what was from the beginning*
> *as to what we have heard*
> *as to what we have seen with our eyes*
> *and what we have gazed upon*
> *and as to what we have touched—*
> *this is the Word of Life,*
> *for the life was manifested*
> *and we are those who have seen*
> *and give you testimony*
> *as we proclaim to you*
> *the eternal Life that was with the Father*
> *and was manifested to us.*
> *What we have seen and heard*
> *we proclaim to you*
> *so that you may join our fellowship*
> *and have communion with the Father*
> *and with his Son, Jesus Christ.*

As poetry, the prologue presents abstractions that demand the reader's careful interpretation. For example, John did not identify "Jesus" as the subject in the first verse; rather, he called him "the Word of life." Furthermore, he did not use the personal pronoun, "he who was from the beginning," which would have made the simplest presentation. Rather, in the Greek he used the relative pronoun, "that which" or "what," so as to be more encompassing—and more compelling. John was speaking of the apostles' total experience of the incarnate God-man, wherein they heard his message, saw his miracles, gazed upon his glory, and even touched him.

John's first epistle opens in the same manner as his Gospel—both begin with a prologue. When John commenced his Gospel, he fondly recollected how he (and the other disciples, for whom he was a spokesman) beheld the Son's glory, the glory of a unique Son from the Father (John 1:14). And then John picturesquely described Jesus as the one who was both God and the Son of God living in the heart of the Father (John 1:18). In both the Gospel and the epistle, John reveals that he (along with the other apostles) has heard, seen, and even handled God in the flesh. In both books, he tells us that the one the apostles experienced is both "the Word" and "eternal life." The apostles had come to the realization that the Word of life, who had been in face-to-face fellowship with the Father for all eternity, had entered into time to be manifest in human flesh to them.

This experience was so life-changing and so memorable that John used the perfect tense verbs ("have seen" and "have heard"—1:1, 3) to convey the idea that the apostles' past experience of the God-man, the incarnate Son of God, was still vivid and present with them. (Such is the force of the perfect tense in Greek.) When the Son entered into time, the eternal fellowship of the father and Son also entered into time. Thus to have heard Jesus was to have heard the Father speaking in the Son (John 14:10, 24), to have seen Jesus was to have seen the Father (John 14:8-10), and to have known him was to have known him who was one with the Father (John 10:30, 38). The Son and the Father are so united that they are said to indwell each other (John 14:8-10). Christ perfectly expressed the Father because he lived in perfect union with him. Thus for the disciples, to know Jesus was to know the Father.

This is why the Son is called "the Word": he is the revealer, the communicator of God to humanity. As the Word, the Son of God fully conveys and communicates God. The Greek term translated "Word" is *logos* [TG3056, ZG3364]; it was primarily used in two ways: "The word might be thought of as remaining within a man, when it denoted his thought or reason. Or it might refer to the word going forth from the man, when it denoted the expression of his thought—i.e., his speech. The Logos, a philosophical term, depended on the former use" (Morris 1971:72-78). As a philosophical term, the *logos* denoted the principle of the universe, even the creative energy that generated the universe. The term *logos* may also have some connection with the Old Testament presentation of "Wisdom" as a personification or attribute of God (Prov 8). In both its Jewish and Greek conceptions, the *logos* was associated with the idea of beginnings—the world began through the origination and instrumentality of the Word (cf. Gen 1:3ff, where the expression "God said" is used repeatedly). John may have had these ideas in mind, but most likely he was originating a new use of this term to identify the Son of God as the divine expression. Paul had the same idea in mind when he said the Son is "the visible image of the invisible God" (Col 1:15). And the writer of Hebrews was thinking similarly when he said that the Son "expresses the very character of God" (Heb 1:3), which means that the Son is the exact representation (*charaktēr* [TG5481, ZG5917]) of God's nature and being (*hupostasis* [TG5287, ᶻᴳ5712]). In the Godhead, the Son functions as the revealer of God and the reality of God. He is God made tangible.

During the days of his ministry, Jesus was revealing the Father to the disciples and thereby initiating them into the divine fellowship. Once the disciples were regenerated by the Spirit and received God's eternal life, they actually entered into fellowship with the Father and the Son. Having been brought into this divine participation, the apostles became the new initiators, introducing this fellowship to others and encouraging them to enter into fellowship with them. Whoever would enter into the fellowship with the apostles would actually be entering into their fellowship with the Father and the Son.

In summary, the one, unique fellowship between the Father and the Son began in eternity, was manifest in time through the incarnation of the Son, was introduced to the apostles, and then through the apostles was extended to each and every believer. When a person becomes a child of God (through the new life given by the Holy Spirit), he or she enters into this one ageless, universal fellowship—a fellowship springing from the Godhead, coursing through the apostles, and flowing through every genuine believer who has ever been or will ever be.

How much greater is this view of fellowship than is the view commonly held! The true fellowship, having a divine origin, has been extended to people for human participation. How privileged we are to have been included! And we must never forget that this fellowship includes all the believers from the apostles to the present; it is not exclusive. How then can we continue to be so restricted and so sectarian? The Bible does not talk about "this fellowship" and "that fellowship." There is but one fellowship, as there is but one body of Christ. How good it is to come to the Lord's table to enjoy the communion of the believers—communion not just with those present at that particular meeting but communion with all of God's people who lived before us and who live now.

NOTES

1:1 *who existed from the beginning.* Lit., "what was from the beginning" (cf. NLT mg). There are two explanations for John's use of the relative pronoun ("what") instead of the personal pronoun ("who"): (1) John used the relative pronoun because it is more inclusive; it encompasses everything about "the Word of life" that the apostles had come to know and experience (so Westcott 1886:4-7). (2) John used the relative pronoun to point to "the message of life" (so Smalley 1984:5-6) as embodied in Christ, the Word. Since the prologue is a poem, John likely intended both meanings. In any event, this relative pronoun is resumed in the beginning of 1:3, where it is made clear the subject is "that which pertains to the Word of life" (1:1).

we have heard and seen. We saw him with our own eyes and touched him with our own hands. John made a point of saying that they had not only seen and heard the eternal One but they had also touched him. In other words, Jesus was truly physical. A certain group of Gnostics in John's day (and thereafter), called Docetists (derived from *dokeō* [TG1380, ZG1506], a Greek word meaning "it seems to be so"), claimed that the Son of God merely assumed the guise of humanity but was not truly human. Later in this epistle, John says that any person who does not confess that Jesus Christ has come in flesh is a person who does not belong to God (4:2-3).

the Word of life. This title describes the Son of God as the personal expression of the invisible God and the giver of divine, eternal life to believers. In the prologue to the fourth Gospel, John identified the Son of God as both "the Word" (*logos* [TG3056, ZG3364]) and "life" (*zōē* [TG2222, ZG2437]). The title "the Word of life" is a combination of the two. As "the Word," the Son expresses God; as "life," he imparts God's eternal life to believers.

1:2 was revealed to us. This phrase, which appears twice in this verse, accords with what John said in his prologue to the Gospel of John: "The Word was God . . . and the Word became human . . . and we have seen his glory, the glory of the Father's one and only Son" (John 1:1, 14).

eternal life. The Greek word translated "life" is *zōē* [TG2222, ZG2437]. In classical Greek, it was used for life in general. There are a few examples of this meaning in the NT (Acts 17:25; Jas 4:14; Rev 16:3), but in all other NT instances the word designates the divine, eternal life—the life of God (Eph 4:18). This life resided in Christ, and he made it available to all who believe in him.

with the Father. As in John 1:1, the wording (*pros* [TG4314, ZG4639] *ton patera*) suggests that the Word was "face to face with the Father." This connotes intimate fellowship (MM 554). By using this expression, John was implying that the Word (the Son) and God (the Father) enjoyed an intimate, personal relationship from the beginning. In Jesus' intercessory prayer of John 17, he revealed that the Father had loved him before the foundation of the world.

1:3 We proclaim to you. The "we" occurring throughout the prologue refers either to John and the apostles (for whom John is the spokesman) or to John and any other believers who saw Jesus Christ in the flesh.

1:4 that you may fully share our joy. Lit., "that our joy may be full." This is an attempt to render a variant reading found in ℵ B L 049, but it turns out to be a rendering of a conflated reading because it happens to accommodate another variant reading in other mss (A C P 33 1739), "that your joy may be complete" (as in the TR and KJV). This variant was created by some scribe(s) who thought it strange that John would have penned a letter for his own joy. However, the writer was thinking of their mutual happiness—his and his readers'. In other words, he wrote this letter to encourage the readers' participation in the fellowship that he (John) and the other believers were enjoying (cf. 2 Jn 1:12). Thus the NLT rendering gets at the heart of the meaning.

Living in God's Light with the Community of Believers

1 JOHN 1:5-10

EXPOSITION

Just as Christ shared the message he heard from the Father, so the apostles, in turn, shared the same message they heard from the Son. John did not use the term usually translated "gospel," but he did use similar words such as "witness" or "testimony," "word," "truth," and "message." The message is: God expresses himself as pure light (cf. John 1:4-5, 9; 3:19-21; 8:12; 9:5; 12:35-36, 46). Those who claim to know God must also be living in the light, for darkness and light are incompatible. We cannot live both in the darkness of sin and in the light of fellowship with God in whom is "no darkness at all." First John uses the Greek word for "darkness" seven times to refer to sin (1:5-6; 2:8-9, 11); one cannot live a sinful life and simultaneously claim to be living in the "light."

When Jesus was on earth, his divine life illuminated the inner lives of men. It penetrated people, illumining them to the divine truth and exposing their own sin to them. Everywhere Christ was present, he gave light—light to reveal his identity and light to expose sin (John 3:21; 8:12). No one could come into contact with Christ without being enlightened. His light would either expose or illumine, or both. So it is for the Christian who is indwelt by the Spirit of Christ. In his presence we see our sin and we see Christ's glory. Of course, a person can refuse to receive the light and remain in darkness. But whoever comes to the light will receive Christ's enlightenment.

Since God is pure light, the Son of God lives in pure light and is the light. Those who claim to live in the Son must also live in the light—that is, one must be illumined by the truth of who God is. To live in the light does not come from imitating God outwardly but from growing more like him in character; it involves transformation. As Paul put it, we are transformed into the image of the one we behold—the Lord, the Spirit (see 2 Cor 3:14-18).

The purpose of "living in the light" (1:7) is not to produce individual mystics but to arouse genuine fellowship among believers. This is important to John's overall argument. True spirituality is manifest in community fellowship. One cannot say he or she communes with God but then refuse to commune with

God's people. Such was the case with the Gnostics of John's day, and this is the situation with many people in our own times. They claim to get along well with God but can't get along with any of his children. John's point is that the natural result of living in the light (in fellowship with God) is a joyful relationship with other Christians.

Those who live in the light will be enlightened by God's Spirit concerning their sin. Jesus' "blood" (1:7, an expression used throughout the NT to encapsulate Jesus' redemptive death on the cross) cleansed us completely and brought us into fellowship with God; now the same blood of Jesus keeps us clean from every sin that would mar that fellowship. Confession of sin is a sign that truth, which is itself light, has already begun to illuminate our sin-darkened lives. If we refuse to admit that we have sin, we deceive ourselves. We certainly cannot fool God, but by refusing to admit our sin, we can cheat ourselves of fellowship with him.

So confession of sins is necessary for maintaining continual fellowship with God, which, in turn, will enable us to have good fellowship with the members of the church community. The Greek word translated "confess" (homologeō [TG3670, ZG3933]) basically means "to say the same thing" or "to acknowledge." Rather than denying our sin nature, we are to confess our sins. God says we are sinners in need of forgiveness. Therefore to "confess" means to agree with God concerning specific acts of sin we have committed; it is to admit we are sinners. When believers admit their sins, God cleanses them. Forgiveness and cleansing are guaranteed because God is faithful to his promises. God acts on the basis of his justice, not on the basis of how we think he feels about us. Christ has satisfied God's righteous demands on us so that now God is bound to forgive all who believe in his Son. We can depend on this.

Therefore it is foolish to claim that "we have not sinned" (1:10). However, various Christians throughout the ages have made this claim because they considered Jesus to have abolished their sins once and for all at the moment they believed, or were filled with the Spirit, or were sanctified. But experience teaches against this. Though Jesus condemned sin once and for all, we still sin when we live in the old nature. When we live in the Spirit, we live a sin-defeating life, but no one lives in the Spirit every moment of life. Even Paul struggled with this (see Rom 7).

We may admit to the presence of the sin nature while denying any personal sin and so deny any need for confession. If we do this, we are guilty of calling God a liar. The statement "we have not sinned" (1:10; ouch hēmartēkamen, perfect tense) speaks of a denial in the past that continues to the present. Unlike verse 8, which speaks of the guilt of sin or sinful nature, this verse speaks of the denial of particular sins. To make such a claim is to make God a liar because God's Word emphasizes the permeating and penetrating nature of sin. So to deny sin is in us indicates that God's "word has no place in our hearts" (1:10). John is not saying that if we make such a false claim, as given in verse 10, we do not have eternal life. He is saying that a person who makes such a denial of sinful acts does not have the Word of God permeating and changing his or her life.

NOTES

1:5 *the message.* This wording is based on the excellent testimony of ℵ A B. One variant (in C P 33 1739 cop) substitutes "the promise" for "the message." Another variant found in a few mss (ℵ ² Ψ) reads "the love of the promise." The idea of "promise" is difficult in this context because the statement that follows can hardly be construed as being a promise: "God is light and there is no darkness in him at all." Of course, "the promise" could be referring back to 1:3-4, wherein John promised the readers that they would be communing with the Father and the Son if they (the readers) maintained fellowship with the apostles—resulting in full joy for all. Nonetheless, "the message" has better documentary support as the original wording.

    God is light. This is a statement of the absolute nature and being of God, as are the statements that he is Spirit (John 4:24) and love (1 Jn 4:8). To say that "God is light" is to say that God symbolizes truth (compared to darkness that symbolizes error) and righteousness (compared to darkness that symbolizes evil). OT Scriptures speak of this: Pss 27:1; 119:130; Isa 5:20; Mic 7:8. In the Gospel of John, Jesus is this light (John 1:4; 8:12; 9:5; 11:9-10; 12:35-36).

    there is no darkness in him at all. The Gr. could be translated literally as "darkness is not in him never." God is untainted by any evil or sin (darkness). John speaks in absolutes, perhaps as no other writer in the NT. So here we have "God is light" and in him is no darkness whatsoever—that is, no change, no sin, no secrecy, no hiding in the shadows.

1:6 *if we say.* This is the first of several instances in which John challenges the claims of the Gnostic secessionists (see notes on 1:8; 2:6; 2:9; see also "Christological Orthodoxy versus Heresy" and "Theological Concerns" in the Introduction). They claimed to be living in God but failed to reflect his moral character. If we have fellowship with God, we should have some of his characteristics—something we share in common. Fellowship is another way of saying "commonality" with God.

1:7 *fellowship with each other.* This is the fellowship among believers that results from each believer having fellowship with the Triune God.

    the blood of Jesus, his Son. This reading has excellent documentary support: ℵ B C P 1739 syr^p cop^sa. A variant in the TR (supported by A 33 𝔐. it^{t,w,z} syr^{h**} cop^{bo}) reads, "the blood of Jesus Christ his Son" (so KJV and NKJV). Since divine names were often expanded by scribes, it is very likely that "Jesus" was expanded to "Jesus Christ" under the influence of John's usual wording (see 1:3; 2:1; 3:23; 4:2; 5:6, 20). The point of using just the human name "Jesus" is that it emphasizes the sacrifice he made in shedding his blood for our sins.

1:8 *If we claim we have no sin.* This is the second false claim of the secessionists (see note on 1:6).

    the truth. In order to clarify just what this "truth" is, some scribes expanded this expression to "the truth of God." When John speaks of "the truth" he is speaking of spiritual reality and veracity; it is a spiritual reality in the believer that could be verified by the apostles and other believers as being true (in both life and doctrine) to the teachings of Christ.

1:10 *If we claim we have not sinned, we are calling God a liar.* This verse parallels 1:8, except that here the focus is on the actual acts of sin emanating from the sinful nature. To claim we have no sin goes beyond self-delusion; it is charging that God is a liar! We must acknowledge that. God's Word emphasizes the permeating and penetrating nature of sin. So to deny that sin is in us indicates God's "word has no place in our hearts" (cf. 2:14; John 8:55; 17:6, 14, 17). John is not saying that if we make such a false claim we do not have eternal life. He is saying that a person who makes such a denial of sinful acts does not have the Word of God permeating and changing his or her life.

Experiencing the Ministry of Jesus, the Advocate

1 JOHN 2:1-2

EXPOSITION

In order to live in the light (1:5, 7), the first step is to confess sin (1:9), and the second is to forsake all sin (2:1). John emphasized our sinfulness in chapter 1 in order to make us despise our sin and try to stay free from it. God's gracious forgiveness is no license to sin. John would say: "Don't sin! Avoid it—flee from it." "It is possible to be either too lenient or too severe towards sin: too lenient encourages us to sin—too severe denies the possibility of sin or the possibility of forgiveness" (Stott 2000:84).

The fact is, we sin. And the righteous God has no choice but to hold us accountable for our sins. But Jesus acts as an intermediary between the Father and the confessing sinner to advocate that the sinner be considered righteous—not because the sinner is righteous but because the Advocate, Jesus Christ, is. Because Christ fulfilled the law and paid sin's penalty for us, he can plead for us on the basis of justice as well as mercy. When God raised Christ from the dead, he accepted once for all Christ's plea for our acquittal (cf. Rom 4:23-25).

The whole matter is best viewed in legal terms. That is why Christ is both our Advocate and the propitiatory sacrifice for our sins. First John 4:10 says that God demonstrated his love to us by sending his Son to become the "propitiation" (*hilasmos* [TG2434, ZG2662]) for our sins (cf. 2:2). Propitiation refers to Christ's satisfaction of God's justice, making it "propitious" (or "agreeable") for God to forgive us. As in the old covenant wherein God met his people when the blood of the sin offering was sprinkled on the altar, so in the new covenant Christ's sacrificial death has brought us into fellowship with God.

NOTES

2:1 *My dear children.* This expresses the tender affection of a father for his own children—the phrase could read, "My own dear children." The expression is patronizing in the best sense of the term.

if anyone does sin. We are all liable to occasional sins. We should not condone these sins, but while condemning them we should not fear to confess them to God.

an advocate who pleads our case. This is an expanded translation of the word *paraklētos* [TG3875, ZG4156] (transliterated in English as "Paraclete"). The word means "one who is called to our side." This could be a comforter, a consoler, or a defense attorney—an advocate. In John 14:26 and 15:26, the Holy Spirit is called our *paraklētos,* our comforter or encourager. Here, "advocate" is the best English equivalent because Jesus is here pictured as the one who represents the believers before the Father.

Jesus Christ, the one who is truly righteous. This is the title "the Righteous One," which was used of Jesus Christ from the earliest days of the church (Acts 3:14; 7:52) to describe him as the just and righteous Messiah who was unjustly killed by the Jewish leaders. This Righteous One was the perfect man, who fulfilled the law (Rom 10:4) and was the perfect sacrifice for sins. As such, he is the perfect Advocate for sinners.

2:2 *the sacrifice that atones.* Gr., *hilasmos* [TG2434, ZG2662], the noun form of the verb *hilaskomai* [TG2433, ZG2661]. Though the word meant "to appease" or "to pacify" in classical Gr., it is argued that as used in the NT, it means "to atone" or "to expiate" (that is, to make restitution or remove guilt). For example, Westcott (1886:85-87) says, "The scriptural conception of the verb is not that of appeasing one who is angry with a personal feeling against the offender, but of altering the character of that which, from without, occasions a necessary alienation, and interposes an inevitable obstacle to fellowship. Such phrases as 'propitiating God,' [i.e., pacifying him] and 'God being reconciled' [i.e., God being made agreeable] are foreign to the language of the New Testament." However, Stott (2000:87-88) cautions against excluding "appeasement" as being a possible meaning for this in the NT inasmuch as the NT writers did not use it in the sense of appeasing the capricious whims of a god, as was done in pagan societies, but rather of appeasing God's unwavering anger against sin. However the word is to be understood, it should not be lost on us that Jesus himself is the sacrifice for our sins.

and not only our sins but the sins of all the world. John was reminding all believers that Christ's atoning sacrifice is sufficient for the sins of every person in the world. Later in the epistle, John makes the point that Jesus is "the Savior of the world" (4:14).

Living in the Light Means Loving Fellow Believers

1 JOHN 2:3-11

EXPOSITION

The apostle John's emphasis on the conflict between darkness and light depicts the continuing struggle between the evil one (Satan) and Jesus. The light has come and the darkness has not overcome it (John 1:5). The world is a realm of darkness into which Jesus has brought light (John 3:19; 8:12; 12:46). God himself is light (1:5). True light comes only through Jesus (John 1:9). Anyone, therefore, who does not know God remains in darkness—that is, spiritual ignorance. Jesus had warned the Jewish leaders of his day that the light they thought they had was darkness (Matt 6:23), which meant that their religious truths had blinded them to the spiritual illumination they could have received from Christ. In like manner, certain Gnostics thought they were enlightened, but they were actually darkened by their so-called illuminations. They made wonderful claims—such as "I know God," "I abide in him," and "I am in the light"—probably all drawn from John's Gospel (see notes on 2:4, 6, 9), but their rejection of John and the other believers showed that they were lying. Ironically, their claims show that they knew Jesus' teachings as communicated by John and had even appropriated some of the most central ideas—knowing God, abiding in God, and living in the light.

However, all such claims are tested by adherence to one commandment, also put forth by Jesus and recorded by John in his Gospel: "I am giving you a new commandment: Love each other. Just as I have loved you, you should love each other" (John 13:34). But where is the newness of this command, since a command to love one another had already been mandated in the Old Testament (Lev 19:18, 33-34)? The newness of Jesus' command rests upon the reality that because our hearts have been changed by experiencing the love of Jesus, we reach out in reciprocal fashion to all those touched by that same love. It may not be easy to do, but grace helps us. Jesus commanded the disciples to love one another "as I have loved you." This love would be the mark of distinction: "Your love for one another will prove to the world that you are my disciples" (John 13:35). Tertullian said that the Gentiles saw this love and commented, "How they love one another!" (*Apology* 39.3.46).

The Christian rule of love is new because love to others is motivated by our love to Christ, who first loved us. He demonstrated what true love is by coming into our world and giving his life for each of us. As Christians, then, we should follow this supreme example by showing our love for fellow believers. Those who reject other Christians reject Christ's exemplary model. This rejection is the kind of hatred John was talking about. If we hate any of the brothers or sisters, then we are not in the light.

Those who left the community of fellowship did so out of spiritual pride. They disdained those "common" believers who had only "common" knowledge of God. Many people with this sort of Gnostic bent had infiltrated the churches and, in some form or another, disrupted the fellowship by their claims of having spiritual knowledge that was superior to that taught by the apostles. John pointed out that these people were deceived—living in the darkness, not in the light. In our own times, some leave the Christian community for a cult and think that, spiritually speaking, they are way ahead of those they left. But all the while they are in darkness. So darkened are their minds that they don't know where they are going. John's irony shows itself again—those who espouse superior knowledge are those who don't know! Such people are in darkness, not light; in sin and not in fellowship with God. They live there and do not know where they are going because they have lost their spiritual perspective and sense of direction (cf. 2 Pet 1:9).

NOTES

2:3 *we can be sure that we know him.* This could also be rendered, "By this we come to experientially know that we have experientially known him." The focus is on actual, experiential knowledge of God, contra the theoretical knowledge espoused by various Gnostics.

2:4 *If someone claims, "I know God," but doesn't obey God's commandments, that person is a liar and is not living in the truth.* John was likely quoting the claims of the secessionists or other spiritual elitists who espoused spiritual knowledge of God (see note on 1:6; cf. notes on 1:8; 2:6, 9). It is possible that they had attained this knowledge from reading John's Gospel. (Knowledge of God through Jesus is a constant theme in John.) This verse illustrates the principle set out in 2:3. John's answer to those who claim they "know God" but do not obey his commandments is that they are liars. John was very straightforward in his condemnation because he was dealing with Gnostics—those who claimed to have special, superior knowledge of God. But if they did not obey the divine command to love others, it was obvious that they did not belong to him.

2:5 *show how completely they love him.* Lit., "the love of God is perfected in these ones." There are three views on the meaning of the phrase "the love of God": (1) it refers to God's love for people (Westcott 1886:49); (2) it is a godly kind of love (Schnackenburg 1979:103); and (3) it is a person's love for God (Marshall 1978:125). All three meanings are acceptable. Behind the NLT's "completely" is *teleiōtai* [TG5048, ZG5457] ("has been perfected," has reached its goal—i.e., has matured). This can mean (1) the believer's love for God is matured in keeping God's Word, or (2) God's love for the believer is matured in the believer who is keeping God's Word. In this context, the point seems to be that as the believer pursues fellowship and obedience, God's love for him or her is more fully appreciated, and, in turn, the believer shows more mature love toward fellow believers. Perfection in the Greek mind did not mean flawlessness, but rather, more fully developed, matured. Smalley (1984:49) sees the perfect tense here as having the force of the present tense in the sense that the process of fulfillment had already begun and was continuing.

That is how we know we are living in him. By our progress toward this perfect love and obedience we will know that we are living in union with Christ. The idea of living "in him," first mentioned here in 1 John, is a carryover from John's Gospel, where Jesus spoke of the mutual indwelling of God and the believers— he living in them and they in him (cf. John 14:18-23; 15:4-5). John's epistle carries forward the practical implications of his Gospel.

2:6 *Those who say they live in God.* Lit., "The one saying [I] abide in him." John again refers to something that others were claiming (cf. note on 1:6). It is likely that such people were quoting the fourth Gospel (John 15:1-5) and were claiming that they were abiding in Christ.

should live their lives as Jesus did. The word translated "Jesus" is simply *ekeinos* [^TG1565, ^ZG1697] (that one); in 1 John it always refers to Jesus (3:3, 5, 7, 16; 4:17; cf. John 7:11; 9:12, 28; 19:21). Jesus' life on earth, demonstrating his obedience, is held up as the model and example.

2:7 *I am not writing a new commandment for you; rather it is an old one you have had.* This commandment is to love one another (3:11). One of the major themes in 1 John is that of brotherly love (cf. chs 3–4). It is a distinguishing mark of a Christian to serve others rather than oneself.

from the very beginning. For John, the beginning has two meanings: (1) It means from the time the disciples first heard Jesus' command to love one another (John 13:33-34); (2) it also means from the time these same teachings were passed on to the believers, to whom he was writing (see 2:24; 3:11; 2 Jn 1:5-6). In other words, the apostles had been faithful to teach others what they had heard from Jesus from the very beginning of his ministry so that their beginning could be as close to the apostles' as possible. Since a lot of new and strange doctrines were circulating in those days, John was encouraging the believers to stay with the primary, fundamental teachings of the apostles.

This old commandment . . . is the same message you heard before. At the end of this clause the majority of late mss repeat the expression "from the beginning," from the first part of the verse (so TR, KJV, and NKJV).

2:8 *Yet it is also new.* The commandment of love is new and different from the old system of the law. The word "new" (*kainēn* [^TG2537, ^ZG2785]) connotes what is new in quality more than what is new in time.

Jesus lived the truth of this commandment, and you also are living it. Vine (1970:27) put it well when he said, "Not only had the commandment been given by him but it had also been exhibited in his example. It is also true in the children of God because it is to be received and fulfilled by them. The new commandment of love finds concrete expression in the daily life of the believer in union with Christ. This love was first shown by Christ in his life on earth, and it is only because he first fulfilled the commandment of love that we can now fulfill it."

the darkness is disappearing, and the true light is already shining. F. F. Bruce's (1970:54) expansion on this is elucidating: "Although 'the true light' is already shining, the darkness has not passed completely away; it is in process of 'passing away.' It is diminishing as the gospel is preached worldwide and the light now shining is from Jesus Christ, the Light of the World. Thanks to the victory of Christ, the outcome of the conflict between light and darkness is a foregone conclusion, but the conflict is still going on. Hence, the tension of the Christian life in the present world is a tension reflected throughout this epistle, not to say throughout the whole New Testament."

2:9 *If anyone claims, "I am living in the light."* Again, John cites what others were claiming—namely, that they were living in the light (see note on 1:6). It is quite possible that such people were saying that they were experiencing the reality of Jesus' words about him being the light of men, as recorded in John's Gospel (John 8:12; 12:35-36).

but hates a Christian brother or sister, that person is still living in darkness. The hatred mentioned here is probably a form of rejection. For example, when God said, "I have loved Jacob, but Esau I have hated" (Mal 1:2-3, NIV), he was not speaking of his emotions toward the two but of his election of one and subsequent rejection of the other (so NLT). In the context of 1 John, "hatred" is tantamount to rejection of other Christians. The secessionists were rejecting John and the community of believers associated with him, while claiming to live an enlightened life—something John makes clear is an impossibility.

2:10 *Anyone who loves another brother or sister is living in the light and does not cause others to stumble.* Or as it says in the TEV: "There is nothing in him that will cause someone else to sin." Those who hate (i.e., reject) their brothers and sisters are both a stumbling block to themselves and also cause others to stumble. The word John uses here, *skandalon* [TG4625, ZG4998] (stumbling block), indicated the trigger to a trap. Thus causing one to stumble means to cause them to be ensnared or entrapped.

2:11 *anyone who hates another brother or sister is still living and walking in darkness.* In the context of this epistle, John was probably referring to those secessionists who had left the fellowship of the church and thereby rejected John and those with him. They claimed to love God, but they hated the other children of God. As such, John perceived that they were living in spiritual darkness.

The Community of Believers
Affirmed as a Spiritual Family

1 JOHN 2:12-17

EXPOSITION

These verses contain a pair of triplets that describe John's readers as "children," those who are "mature in the faith" (or *fathers*), and those who are "young in the faith" (or *young men*). (Accordingly most translations, including the NLT, set 2:12-14 as poetry.) These three classifications are not physical age groups (John calls all his readers "dear children"—see 2:1) and their order is not chronological. Therefore, it seems that each group is a reference to all John's readers. For example, viewed as children, they know their sins are forgiven. Viewed as fathers, they not only have a relationship with God, they have knowledge of God that has come from obedience to his commandments. Viewed as young men, they are strong. At the same time, John was being purposely ambiguous, as is inherent in poetry. Another understanding (which is secondary) is that these represent stages of spiritual maturity—for it is the children (the youngest believers) who would be most conscious of having their sins forgiven and of coming to know the Father; and it is the young, strong believers who would be engaged in spiritual warfare by means of God's Word; and it is the fathers who would have experientially known Christ, the one from the beginning (as this suggests antiquity). It is possible that the "fathers" were the ones who saw and heard Jesus while he was on earth.

The main thrust of the section is to encourage the believers in their pursuit of knowing God experientially. The young children are seen in relation to God as their Father, whom they could know only through the Son (cf. Matt 11:27). The fathers and the young men are said to have known God; this is experiential knowledge. No one can know God the Father apart from the Son. This knowledge, as well as knowledge of the Scriptures, gives them the strength to overcome the evil one (2:14). This strength is not the natural physical vigor of young men but the power of God's Word in them through the Holy Spirit (Isa 40:30-31). They can enjoy this power and this victory over Satan, John goes on to affirm, only by freeing themselves from the grasp of the evil things of the world.

John makes an unmistakable contrast: Those who love this world do so by pursuing the lust of their flesh, the lust of their eyes, and the pride of possessions (see notes on 2:15-16). They love a world that is passing away; whereas those who love the Father and obey him are those who live forever. Since Satan is in control of the world (5:19), believers must constantly guard against his assaults by becoming saturated with God's Word (cf. John 17:15-17). We are strong only because the Word of God abides in us.

NOTES

2:12 I am writing to you who are God's children. The term "children" has no reference to age here; rather, it is a term of endearment. Jesus used the same phrase when speaking to his disciples (cf. John 13:33).

2:13 you who are mature. Lit., "fathers." The various interpretations of this term are described in the next chapter.

Christ, who existed from the beginning. Lit., "the one from [the] beginning." The NLT correctly identifies this one as Christ, the eternal Word of life (1:1-2), but notice that John now speaks of "the one who is from the beginning," and not "that which was from the beginning" (as in 1:1). This signifies an emphasis on Jesus' person here.

you who are young. The various interpretations of this phrase are described in the next chapter.

2:14 I have written. This reading is strongly supported by 𝔓74ᵛⁱᵈ ℵ A B C L P 33. The Majority text reads, "I write"—the result of harmonization to 2:12 and 2:13. John's shift to the aorist tense is stylistic. It is called the epistolary aorist; it represents the idea that by the time the readers read what is written in the epistle, the writing will be a past event.

Christ, who existed from the beginning. Lit., "the one from [the] beginning." This is the reading in several mss (𝔓74 ℵ A C). A few other mss, including B, read, "that which was from the beginning," as in 1:1 (see comments there).

2:15 Do not love this world. In this verse, the "world" (*kosmos* [ᵀᴳ2889, ᶻᴳ3180]) is the morally evil system that is opposed to all that God is. In this sense, the world is the satanic system opposing Christ's Kingdom on this earth. It is the dominating order of things—a system and a people. It is activity apart from and against God. It is anything that arouses "the lust of the flesh, the lust of the eyes, and the pride of life" (2:16, lit. translation; 3:1; 4:4; 5:19; cf. John 12:31; 15:18; Eph 6:11-12; Jas 4:4).

nor the things it offers you. This statement would convict those who deny that they love the world but care keenly about some particular thing the world offers, such as wealth, honor, or pleasure.

for when you love the world, you do not have the love of the Father in you. God and the sinful world are such opposites that it is impossible to love both at once.

2:16 craving for physical pleasure. This refers to any kind of fleshly desire but especially "the craze for sex" (TLB) to which young people are particularly liable. We dare not excuse ourselves of lustful thoughts, because they are not from God.

craving for everything we see. Satan tempted Christ this way by showing him all the kingdoms of the world (Matt 4:8-9).

and pride in our achievements and possessions. Many commentators have noted that the three evils mentioned here were the elements in Satan's temptation of Eve (Gen 3:6) and of Jesus (Luke 4:1-12). Others see them as simply three categories of sin or three examples of sins characteristic of the world.

2:17 *anyone who does what pleases God will live forever.* In contrast to the three evil desires of the world, which are already "fading away," the one who does God's will remains forever united to God.

Identifying the False Believers and the True

1 JOHN 2:18-27

EXPOSITION

This section gives us the reason behind John's appeal in the opening verses of the epistle (1:1-4). John had invited all the believers to remain in fellowship with him and his fellow eyewitnesses as the means of guaranteeing their genuine fellowship with God the Father and his Son. For people to purposely cut themselves off from having fellowship with the apostles was tantamount to cutting themselves off from God. Since the apostles *were* in fellowship with God, one could not leave their fellowship and still claim to be in fellowship with God. Thus their departure was a sign that they never really knew God in the first place.

According to John's statement in 2:19, some had, in fact, already left the fellowship of the apostles and the churches established by them. These were the secessionists. At one point, they had been part of the church community, in fellowship with John and the other eyewitnesses. Then they left that fellowship and evidently became promoters of false teachings about Jesus (cf. 4:1; 2 Jn 1:7). But just who were these people that left the fellowship? In 2:19, John speaks of "us" and "they" (lit., "they departed from us"). The plural pronoun "us" refers either to the apostolic circle or to both John and his readers. In other places in the epistle, the "us" is the apostolic community, with John's readers being the "you" of the epistle (see especially 1:1-4). If this is so here, John may be saying that the false teachers were among those individuals still alive late in the first century who had been eyewitnesses of Jesus. Yet at some point they broke away from John and his coworkers. If the "us" refers to the entire church community (i.e., John and his readers), then the false teachers would not necessarily have been part of the apostles' early contemporaries. Either way, these people had once been part of the church community and then left. Their departure was a clear indication that they never really belonged.

But those who departed weren't just secessionists; they were antichrists (2:18, 22). This means that they were deceptive teachers and false prophets (cf. 4:1; Mark 13:22—Jesus predicted such false Christs and false prophets). These antichrists must have tried to seduce various church members to believe their heretical teachings about Jesus. In John's day, one such antichrist was Cerinthus, who was an avowed enemy of John the apostle. Polycarp, a disciple of John, said that

John once left a bathhouse when he heard that the heretic Cerinthus was inside, for fear that the house would fall in ruins since "the enemy of truth" was there. (This story comes from Irenaeus's *Heresies* 3.3.4.) Cerinthus denied that Jesus was the Christ. He spoke of "Jesus" and "the Christ" as two separate beings who were united only from the time of Jesus' baptism to the time he was crucified—at which point, so Cerinthus taught, "the Christ" left Jesus (see comments on 5:6-12 and "Christological Orthodoxy versus Heresy" in the Introduction). According to John's epistles, any denial that Jesus is the Christ includes a denial that he has come in the flesh (1:1-3; 4:3; 2 Jn 1:7). Cerinthus had clearly departed from the apostolic truths and fellowship, and there were others who had done likewise.

It is a relief to the church when members who have already left the truth and cut themselves off from spiritual fellowship finally leave publicly. But not until the resurrection will the church be completely free of such people. One should not get upset over false believers within the church. They will always be present, but God knows those who are truly his (cf. Matt 13:24-30, 36-43). In the meantime, we should not quickly judge everyone who leaves the church. There are those who love Jesus and are truly saved but leave the church because they have been hurt or "burned out," but they still belong to God's family. Then there are those who leave the church and deny its teachings about Christ. Furthermore, they parade their contempt for the people of God. They remain agnostic or perhaps join a cult. These are the kinds of people John wrote about. They should be refuted and opposed, while the discouraged ones should be encouraged and restored.

The anointing that each and every one of the believers has received helps them to discern the false from the true. Thus the emphasis is on shared, communal knowledge. There is nothing "secret" that is kept from most Christians and revealed to only a select few. The false believers claimed to have special knowledge and probably a special anointing from God. But all the true Christians share the same anointing (see note on 2:20). As Christians, now indwelt by the Holy Spirit, we are joined to Christ, "the Anointed One," and share in his anointing (2 Cor 1:21-22). This anointing from the Holy Spirit enables believers to know everything that pertains to false and true teaching. Furthermore, it enables us to discern who the antichrists might be. Jesus promised that he would send the believers his Spirit, who would teach them of the truth (John 16:12-15).

The second part of the antichrist heresy that John was dealing with was the false teaching that denied the Father and the Son (2:22-23). To do so meant that one would claim to know God the Father apart from the Son and thereby reject the Son as the Father's revelation to mankind. Many of the Jewish religious leaders of Jesus' day rejected him as the Father's "Word," the Father's revealer to mankind (see John 5; 8). Most Jews have persisted in this disbelief. Denying any notion of the Trinity, especially the Father-Son relationship, they claim that only Yahweh is true God. In other words, they believe that only the Father is deity.

Other notable antichrists throughout history espousing this same heresy are Muslims and Jehovah's Witnesses. Muhammad explicitly denied that Jesus was the divine Son of God, stripping him of his deity and labeling him with the title "prophet"—albeit a prophetic forerunner to Muhammad himself, the culmination of all prophets. The Koran espouses the one true God as Allah and denounces the Trinity. As such, Muhammad denied God's revelation to humanity in the incarnation of the Son of God, Jesus. While the Koran does speak of Jesus as Messiah (Suras 3:45-47; 5:72) this is patent heresy—John would have labeled Muhammad an antichrist.

Jehovah's Witnesses posit a similar heresy. They believe that only Yahweh (Jehovah) is true God, not Jesus, the Son of God. They deny Jesus' deity. Church historians point to Arius (died AD 336) as the earliest example of this heresy (consequently known as the Arian heresy). Arius taught the following: "The Father existed before the Son. There was a time when the Son did not exist. Therefore the Son was created by the Father. Therefore, although the Son was the highest of all creatures, he is not the essence of God" (Douglas, Comfort, and Mitchell 1992:35-36).

The Nicene Creed (AD 325) rejected Arius's heresy and upheld the apostolic teaching that the Father and the Son are coeternal and share the same essence (*homoousios*). Both the Father and Son are eternal God. All who deviate from this teaching—especially in the direction of diminishing the Son's deity—would be considered by John to be antichrists promoting heresy.

By the power of the anointing, Christians can discern lying antichrists. We do not need another teacher, because the Holy Spirit, the Spirit of truth, is our teacher; so we will remain in Christ and in what he has taught us (cf. Jer 31:34; John 6:45; 16:13). This does not mean that a Christian has no use for teachings from others; it means that a believer is able to discern and reject what is false (2:21). The better we know the truth, the more easily will we be able to identify a lie.

NOTES

2:18 *the last hour.* John and other NT writers called the period that began with Christ's first coming "the last days" (cf. Acts 2:17; Heb 1:2; 1 Pet 1:20). They understood this to be the final era in world history because neither the former prophecy of the OT nor any new revelation predicted the coming of another era before Christ's second coming.

You have heard. They had heard from the apostles (e.g., see 2 Thess 2:3-10).

the Antichrist. This is the reading in some mss (‭א‬² A 33 𝔐); others do not include the definite article (‭א‬* B C 1739), which could be rendered in English, "an antichrist." The absence of the article points to character—"one who is antichrist"; the inclusion of the article points to identity—the specific Antichrist. Either way, an antichrist is one who is "instead of Christ"; he claims to himself what belongs to Christ and poses as a substitute for Christ. The person called "Antichrist" is probably the same as "the man of lawlessness" in 2 Thes 2:3 and "the beast" in Rev 13:1-10.

already many such antichrists have appeared. As precursors to the one Anti-christ, these many antichrists are the false teachers who deny (1) that Jesus is the Christ (2:22); (2) that Jesus is God's Son (2:23); and (3) that Jesus was God manifest in the flesh (4:2; 2 Jn 1:7). They are deceivers and liars.

2:19 *These people left our churches.* Lit., "they departed from us." This describes the secessionists. See discussion in the exposition section above.

2:20 *the Holy One has given you his Spirit.* Lit., "you have an anointing (*chrisma* [^TG^5545, ^ZG^59]) from the Holy One" (cf. NLT mg). As "Christ" means "the anointed one," the one on whom the Spirit was poured out (cf. Luke 4:18), so Christians are anointed ones in that they partake of the Spirit of Christ (2 Cor 1:21-22).

all of you know. This is the reading according to some ancient Gr. mss (א B). Other mss read "you know everything" (A C 33 1739 𝔐 it syr cop^bo^). According to the first reading, John was affirming that all the members of the church community know who is a genuine believer and who isn't (see 2:19). The emphasis of the second reading is on the anointing and how it enables believers to know everything.

2:22 *And who is a liar? Anyone who says that Jesus is not the Christ.* The great central reality of all Christian truth is that Jesus is the Christ. To deny this is blatant heresy. The heretic Cerinthus taught that "Jesus" and "the Christ" were two separate beings who were united only from the time of Jesus' baptism until the time he was crucified—at which point, Cerinthus taught, "the Christ" left Jesus.

Anyone who denies the Father and the Son is an antichrist. The wordplay is interesting here: Anyone denying that Jesus is the "Christ" (2:22a) is "an antichrist" (2:22b). Those who reject the Son cannot know the Father, since the Father is known only through the Son (John 14:6-9). The Son is the expression of the Father—God made visible, God made known. To see the Son is to see the Father (John 14:8-10). He is the image of the invisible God (Col 1:15), the express image of God's substance and the radiance of his glory (Heb 1:2-3). Thus the claim of any religious person to worship God the Father while denying that Jesus is his Son is simply a false claim.

2:23 *Anyone who denies the Son doesn't have the Father, either. But anyone who acknowledges the Son has the Father also.* In both this epistle and his Gospel, John makes it very clear that the Father can be known only through the Son (cf. John 14:6-10).

2:24 *So you must remain faithful to what you have been taught from the beginning.* If John's readers would let the truth that they had learned from their initiation into the Christian faith and the truth that was proclaimed by John *remain* in them, then they would *remain* in the Son and in the Father. The message is that Jesus is the Christ (2:22), the Son of God come in the flesh (1:1-4). If the believers resisted the lies of the antichrists and remained in the truth they had begun in, they would also "remain in fellowship with the Son and with the Father." By clinging to the truth about God the Father and Christ his Son, we can be sure we will never be separated from fellowship with God.

2:25 And in this fellowship we enjoy the eternal life he promised us. See John 3:15, 36; 6:40, 47, 57; 17:2-3 for examples of promises related to eternal life. The expression "eternal life" is both quantitative (illimitable time) and qualitative (eternal in nature, as in the nature of God).

2:26 I am writing these things to warn you about those who want to lead you astray. As in 2:12-14, 21, John took pains to make it clear that his purpose in writing was to combat the seduction of the believers by false teachers and to affirm the practical import of his teachings.

2:27 But you have received the Holy Spirit. Lit., "you have received the anointing" (chrisma [TG5545, ZG59]); see note on 2:20. One ancient ms (B) reads, "you have received the charisma" [TG5486, ZG5922] (spiritual gift). This was probably a transcriptional mistake (with a one-letter difference in the two words) because the scribe did not make the same change in the next occurrence of the same word later in the verse.

   the Spirit teaches you. Lit., "the anointing teaches you." One ancient ms (ℵ *) reads, "his Spirit teaches you."

Being Prepared for Christ's Return

1 JOHN 2:28–3:3

EXPOSITION

Although we already have fellowship with Christ through his indwelling Spirit, a time is coming when we will see him face-to-face, in all his glory (3:2). Just as he could be seen, heard, and touched in his first manifestation, so it will be true at his second appearing. John's statement implies that Christ may come at any time, so we must always be ready. Though guaranteed eternal life (5:11-12), true believers will nonetheless give account to God (Heb 13:17) and be judged by their works (Matt 16:27; 2 Cor 5:10).

At this time in our lives, the world may not fully recognize us as the children of God, but it will when we are fully glorified with Christ. Nonetheless, our lives should display the fact that we are God's children now. Contrary to the belief of the Pelagians, we do not become children of God by doing right. Rather, doing right is a sign that we have already become God's children—because we cannot do right on our own.

In this section, John declares that something inconceivably wonderful is waiting for us—even more glorious than what we now have as God's children. And of this prospect we can be sure: In eternity we will be with Christ and be like Christ. We already have a hint of what this future glory will be like, though the world is completely ignorant of it. Christ will be revealed to us and in us, in all his glory (2 Cor 4:4). In the same way, believers will be revealed to the world as God's children, sharing in Christ's glory and honor. This is the hope of every believer, even of all creation itself. As the apostle Paul said, the whole creation is waiting for the day when the children of God will be revealed in all their glory, reflecting the image of Christ (cf. Rom 8:18-30).

But seeing Christ is something that begins in the earthly life of the believer. The idea is not that we see him physically but that by constantly gazing at Christ, we will become like him and reflect his glory (2 Cor 3:17-18). As John said it, "we will see him as he really is" (1 Jn 3:2). This means more than a merely physiological occurrence; it means "perceiving," "recognizing," even "appreciating." In order to know someone—to see them as they really are—you have to pass through similar experiences. Therefore, in order to see Jesus as he really is, we must experience the power of his resurrection and the fellowship of his sufferings. This was Paul's aspiration, and it should be ours (Phil 3:7-14). Of course, this was also John's aspiration, as expressed in the following verse: "All who have this eager expectation will keep themselves pure, just as he is pure" (3:3). Everyone who has the hope of seeing Christ and being like him realizes that Christ is morally pure and therefore pursues purity now. We can do this only through Christ's Spirit in us—as Jesus said, "Apart from me you can do nothing" (John 15:5). This is an ongoing purification process, which begins at rebirth and continues until the day we see Jesus. The purer we become, the clearer our view will be of Jesus, who is pure through and through.

NOTES

2:28 *dear children, remain in fellowship with Christ.* John repeated this command (cf. 2:27); the term of endearment ("dear children") reveals how deep his loving concern was for these Christians. He was so anxious for their spiritual lives that he said over and over, "Remain in him; don't let anyone lead you away from him."

2:29 *Since we know that Christ is righteous, we also know that all who do what is right are God's children.* John's reasoning is that God is righteous, and therefore he is the source of righteousness. If a person's actions demonstrate righteousness, we know he or she acquired this righteousness from God by being given a new nature.

3:1 *See how very much our Father loves us.* The word behind the English expression "how very much" is *potapēn* [TG4217, ZG4534], a term that speaks of something that has come from another country. In other words, it is "exotic, extraordinary." The translation could read, "Behold, what extraordinary love the Father has poured on us."

his children. The Greek word translated "children" (*tekna* [TG5043, ZG5451]) emphasizes birth rather than infancy. John is here calling attention to the wonderful fact, carried over from the last verse (2:29), that God has spiritually begotten us as his children.

and that is what we are! God gives us both the title and the reality. This clause was dropped from several late mss (K L 049 69 𝔐), probably because it was perceived as being redundant with the next clause, which says, "we already are." But the clause is present in 𝔓74vid ℵ A B C 33 1739, an excellent array of witnesses.

Recognizing What Kind of Life Prospers the Fellowship and What Contradicts It

1 JOHN 3:4-10

EXPOSITION

Early in his first epistle, John not only exposes the false teaching of the Gnostics but offers corrective instruction to true believers regarding the nature of sin. His main point in 3:4-10 is that a life of sin is incompatible with the new life in Christ.

Sin is rebellion against God; it is the recurring, irrational impulse to do anything rather than obey God. This aspect of sin is incompatible with being born of God. Sin is the Christian's enemy. It removes the believer from the light. It must be resisted; it cannot be tolerated. Where failure occurs, sin must be confessed to the Lord and then abandoned. The purpose and intent of the believer always remains the same—to commit no sin. But if any believer should fail and commit sin, they should neither deceive themselves about it, nor lie about their actions, nor give up walking in the light. The response to a lapse into sin is not to deny it but to seek the forgiveness of God, made available through Jesus Christ.

No one born of God can continue in sin or practice a life of sin. In fact, a life of sin (that is, active rebellion against God's known will) is evidence that one is not really God's child. The continual practice of sin is incompatible with the new nature derived from the new birth. Those who continue in sin are lawbreakers; they live unrighteous lives because they live in sin. Living in sin and living in God are mutually exclusive, like darkness and light. The way to be free from sin is to live in Christ. When believers commit sins (1:8-10; 2:1-2), these sins do not come from, or belong to, their life in Christ because they cannot sin as long as they are living in Christ. Complete union with Christ, which brings complete separation from sin, is the ideal for each and every Christian. This ideal, while never perfectly attained in this life, differs from that claimed by the Gnostics, who professed sinlessness by denying sin's existence. According to John's perspective, the degree to which one sins is the degree to which one is still in darkness and therefore still exhibits the characteristics of evil. John believed in transformation—from darkness to light, from sin to sinlessness, from hate to love.

The devil sinned even before the creation of the world; and ever since, as the prince of this world, he has been both sinning and causing people to sin. John's words here are very similar to what Jesus told the Jewish leaders who refused to accept his message. In John 8:44, Jesus told them, "You are the children of your father the devil, and you love to do the evil things he does." This statement, which is developed in 3:7-15, indicates that a person's actions are a manifestation of his true source of being. The intent to murder comes from the father of murder, the devil. The devil was the instigator of Jesus' murder and the perpetrator of the lies the Jews believed about Jesus. The devil, Jesus said, "was a murderer from the beginning. He has always hated the truth, because there is no truth in him. When he lies, it is consistent with his character; for he is a liar and the father of lies" (John 8:44). The devil, through his lies to Eve (Gen 3:4-5), paved the way for death to enter into the world, causing Adam and Eve and all their posterity to be alienated from God. In this sense, the devil was a murderer and a sinner from the beginning.

Though we might have hoped that Christ would have obliterated Satan, he didn't; rather, Christ came to undo Satan's work and thereby free people from sin and all its awful consequences. John is therefore arguing that Christians cannot be involved in what Christ came to destroy—that is, lies and unrighteousness.

When we were "born again," a new life was born within us. The new life, or nature, which is "born of God" does not habitually practice sin and is entirely incompatible with sin. It gives us a hatred for sin, and though at times we may give in to sin, we are continually fighting against it. Sin is still active, but it no longer has complete control over us. The normal direction of a Christian's life is against sin and toward God. The Holy Spirit works, through the Word of God, to sanctify us or to make us holy and pure, as Christ is (3:3; cf. 5:18).

Some teachers have wrongly affirmed that 3:9 teaches that the Christian does not sin in the new nature, although the physical body may sin. This is Gnostic dualism: a division of the physical from the spiritual. The text does not say that the new nature does not sin but that the person himself does not sin. Other teachers—especially in the holiness movement—have used this verse to say that a person, once regenerated, can never sin. If he or she does, they have lost their salvation and must get saved and be regenerated all over again. To avoid this dilemma, many in this movement will never confess to having sinned; instead, they will call their sins "errors" or "mistakes." Both of these views misunderstand this passage. Each person lives only one life, and it is ultimately characterized by either abiding in Christ or practicing sin. One must look at the habitual, volitional characteristics of those who profess the new birth; if they can be characterized as rebellious, then they are not born of God.

In the end, we all must admit that one of the greatest tensions in the Christian's life is the presence of sin. Various theological answers have been purported—all the way from total eradication, on one hand, to acquiescent cohabitation on the other. Both are extreme positions, unsatisfactory to the sincere believer. Though believers are absolutely and totally forgiven for sin, the marks of sin are still on them. Christ died to deliver the redeemed from sin's guilt, and he now lives to save the believers from sin's power. Regenerated people are new creations in Christ, and as such, a new principle of life has been implanted in them. They have an awareness of God, a desire for God, and a responsiveness to God. At the same time, the Holy Spirit is constantly at work in believers' lives, purifying and cleansing their nature from the pollution and uncleanness of sin, renewing in them the image of God. This is a lifelong renovation of our natures by the Holy Spirit, as we yield to God. Such a cooperative effort between the believer and the Holy Spirit is called "sanctification" and is defined in the Westminster Shorter Catechism (Question 35) as "the work of God's free grace, whereby we are renewed in the whole man after the image of God, and are enabled more and more to die unto sin, and live unto righteousness."

John was well aware of the difficulties involved in living the purified life and of the power of opposition from the evil one. Nevertheless, the evil one need not prevail. One must negate the innate, carnal self-will and the rebellious, egocentric behavior patterns that develop from birth. We need to keep the Word of God, value it, obey it, and live by it. As we do so, Christ promises to keep us (Rev 3:10) and preserve us (Ps 25:21). It is not the quality of strength in the life of the believer that gives one hope of prevailing against sin, but the mighty presence and power of God.

NOTES

3:4 *Everyone who sins is breaking God's law.* This statement is probably aimed at the Gnostic secessionists who considered themselves to be free from sin (see 1:8, 10 and notes).

for all sin is contrary to the law of God. Lit., "sin is lawlessness"; grammatically, this could also be inverted to read "lawlessness is sin." Here is a basic definition of sin and lawlessness. The word *hamartia* [TG266, ZG281] (sin) was used by Homer and other ancient Greek writers in reference to "missing the mark" (BDAG 49). One picture of sin, then, is that God's law is this mark or standard that we aim at and miss. The term *anomos* [TG459, ZG491] (lawlessness) in this context signifies reckless disregard of God's principles for righteousness.

3:5 *you know that Jesus came to take away our sins.* The term translated "came" (*ephanerōthē* [TG5319, ZG5746]) more precisely means "was manifested." The coming of the Son of God was his manifestation in human form among humans. He became flesh so as to express God to humanity (1:1-4; John 1:1, 4, 18; 14:9). He also became flesh in order to take away the sins of the world (John 1:29, 36). As such, he fulfilled the OT picture of both the sacrificial lamb and the scapegoat by taking away our sins once for all.

3:6 *Anyone who continues to live in him will not sin.* John's argument here is that those who are joined to Christ should live as Christ lived—pure, without sin. The word rendered as "continues to live" (*menōn* [TG3306, ZG3531]) indicates "abiding" and "remaining." This is the same verb John used in his Gospel when Jesus illustrated the believers' dependence on him by speaking about branches remaining in the Vine. As a branch lives in the Vine, it draws its life from the Vine.

anyone who keeps on sinning does not know him or understand who he is. John is again presenting the ideal. In this verse, John purposely used the present-tense verb to denote the sin he speaks of as an ongoing, repeated action. He was not saying that a person who sins even once has never known God, but he insists that as far as we continue in sin, to that degree we do not know God.

3:7 *don't let anyone deceive you about this.* Many scholars think this is a concluding statement for vv. 4-6, with the rest of v. 7 being a summary statement. Apparently, the false teachers who were denying the doctrine of Christ (2:22) were also claiming that they knew God, yet they were living unrighteous lives (cf. 1:6). The believers should not be deceived by such people.

When people do what is right, it shows that they are righteous, even as Christ is righteous. It is not doing righteousness that makes us righteous, but rather our righteousness given to us by Christ that naturally leads to doing righteous acts. This principle can function as a tool for discernment: a tree that bears good fruit is a good tree; it is not that the fruit makes the tree good, but it shows that the tree is good (cf. Matt 7:15-20).

3:8 *But when people keep on sinning, it shows that they belong to the devil.* "The Devil is the source of sin, and therefore the one who leads a sinful life is spiritually connected with him" (Vine 1970:56). It is in this sense that the person who continually sins belongs to the devil. The devil cannot create or produce children, but people become children of the devil by imitating him. This was Jesus' argument against the Jewish religious leaders who wanted to kill him; these evil intentions showed that they were children of the devil, a murderer (cf. John 8:39-44).

who has been sinning since the beginning. Since the beginning of creation—and probably before—the devil has lived a life in opposition to God.

But the Son of God came to destroy the works of the devil. As in 3:5, the word translated "came" is *ephanerōthē* [TG5319, ZG5746] (was manifested). The repetition of the verb here suggests that the Son of God's appearance on earth was to die for sins and, in so doing, to overthrow the power of the devil. The word behind "destroy" (*lusē* [TG3089, ZG3395]) does not mean to annihilate; rather, it means "to break down" (cf. Eph 2:14), "to undo," "to render ineffective." In other words, the works of the devil have been deprived of force, rendered inoperative, conquered, and overthrown (Stott 2000:129).

3:9 *Those who have been born into God's family do not make a practice of sinning, because God's life is in them. So they can't keep on sinning, because they are children of God.* At first glance, this appears to completely contradict what

John said earlier: "If we claim we have no sin, we are only fooling ourselves and not living in the truth" (1:8). Here he is saying that "we do not sin." Do we sin or don't we? Experience tells us that we do, but our spirits tell us that we aspire not to sin. This aspiration comes from "God's life" within each believer. The Gr. term here is *sperma autou* [TH4690, ZH5065] (his seed); it signifies God's life and God's nature. Since we have God's nature in us, we can become partakers of the divine nature and thereby live a sin-free life (see 2 Pet 1:3-4). This is also called *regeneration* (Titus 3:4-5, NLT mg).

3:10 *Anyone who does not live righteously.* Living righteously means living in a right relationship with God. This does not mean that we live perfect lives but that we keep ourselves in a good relationship with God. When we sin, we confess our sins. Then we continue to live in fellowship with God.

Love for the Community Members, a Sign of Divine Life

1 JOHN 3:11-18

EXPOSITION

This section thematically follows the previous one in its message that the presence or absence of brotherly love is a sure way to tell a true child of God from a pretender. Our nature has consequences; eventually we act the way we really are. To love the brothers and sisters in the believing community demonstrates that we belong to God; to reject the brothers and sisters demonstrates that we don't really belong to God.

Our love for one another is a constant manifestation that we are living in Christ. John never tired of telling the brothers and sisters to love one another. In his *Commentary on Galatians* (6.10), Jerome said that even when the apostle John was very old and had to be carried to the church meetings, he continued to remind the believers of Christ's command: "My little children, love one another." The brothers and sisters may have grown tired of always hearing the same instruction, but John insisted that this was the command of the Lord Jesus (see John 13:34) and that if we could attain just this one thing, it would be enough.

Hatred toward other Christians is a clear indication of a person's alignment (perhaps unwitting) with the devil. Those who hate (that is, reject) other Christians belong to their father, the devil (3:10, 12, 15). This statement accords with Jesus' indictment made against the Jewish leaders who wanted to kill him. Jesus told them that they were children of the devil for wanting to murder him because the devil was a murderer from the beginning (John 8:43-44). John cited Cain as an exemplary brother-hater and murderer (3:12). Cain, Abel's brother, was jealous of Abel's receiving approval from God. This jealousy led to murder (Gen 4:8). If we hate someone, we wish he or she were dead, and the Lord sees the inner desire as equal to the outward act that would result from it (cf. Matt 5:21-22). Therefore, those who hate are murderers. Perhaps the foothold the devil used in Cain's case was Cain's intense desire to outdo Abel, to show himself better than Abel. The devil always uses some foothold to get us to sin. It is possible that the secessionists from the Johannine community left because they were jealous of John. After departing, their goal was to poison others against John. Diotrephes was likely such a poisoner (see comments on 3 Jn 1:9).

It is notable that Jesus, after telling his disciples to love one another, reminded them that the world would hate them (John 15:17-18). The world hates us because it can see the difference between our godly lives and its own evil. The world would prefer that we were like them; since we are not, they hate us (see 1 Pet 4:3-4). Any professing Christian who is warmly embraced by the world at large should reexamine the reality of his claim to discipleship (2:15-17; 3:1; 4:5-6; 2 Tim 3:10-12; Jas 4:4). The world's hatred for the believers should increase believers' love for one another. This love does not cause us to have eternal life, but it is evidence that we already have it. We must each ask ourselves if we have this love. If we do, then we can be sure that we have eternal life and that this will be publicly revealed when Christ comes. Those who do not love do not abide in light but in darkness (2:11); they are not abiding in life but in death (3:14). Their source is not God but the devil (3:8). Thus it is clear that eternal life is not living inside them because it is not the controlling factor in their lives.

To summarize: Hatred characterizes the world, whose prototype is Cain. Hatred originates in the devil, issues in murder, and is evidence of spiritual death. Love characterizes the church, whose prototype is Christ. It originates in God, issues in self-sacrifice, and is evidence of eternal life (Stott 2000:146-147). Interestingly and significantly, John uses three different Greek words meaning "life" in 3:15-17. The three words are *zōē, psuchē, bios*. The word *zōē* [TG2222, ZG2437] is used in the New Testament to designate divine, eternal life—the life of God. This life resided in Christ, and he made it available to all who believe in him (cf. 3:15). In 3:16, *psuchē* [TG5590, ZG6034] (soul, personality, life) designates the natural life that all human beings are born with; as a human, Jesus had a *psuchē* or "soul." He gave up his soul (*psuchē*) in death so that we might have *zōē*, eternal life of God. In 3:16-17, John states that believers should likewise sacrifice their *psuchē* (life, soul) by giving their *bios* [TG979, ZG1050] (life, livelihood) to those in need. The word *bios* refers to one's "livelihood" or "that which is necessary to sustain physical life" (cf. NLT, "enough money to live well"; 3:17). John shows these three aspects of life to be inextricably intertwined: Believers demonstrate that they have eternal life (*zōē*) by imitating Christ in surrendering their earthly life (*psuchē*), specifically in the giving of their livelihood (*bios*) to sustain the life (*psuchē*) of other believers. This is the true and best manifestation of love. Our actions of taking care of others in need are true demonstrations of our love.

NOTES

3:11 *This is the message.* This is the reading according to A B 049 33 𝔐. Several other mss (ℵ C P 1739 cop) read, "This is the promise." The same textual variant in nearly the same mss occurs in 1:5.

you have heard from the beginning. This "beginning" does not refer to the time Jesus first told his disciples to love one another (see John 13:34-35; 15:17);

it refers to the time when John's audience first became believers and heard the message of the gospel (see note on 2:7).

We should love one another. This is the central theme of this section.

3:12 We must not be like Cain, who belonged to the evil one and killed his brother. John returns to the thought of 3:8, and he gives an example of the works of the devil—the actions of Cain.

And why did he kill him? Because Cain had been doing what was evil. "Cain, who murdered his brother (Gen 4:8), showed by that act that he hated him, and his hatred indicated quite clearly to which spiritual family he belonged" (Bruce 1970:94).

and his brother had been doing what was righteous. Abel made sacrifices to God that God approved because Abel acted in faith (Heb 11:4).

3:13 So don't be surprised, dear brothers and sisters, if the world hates you. Jesus told his disciples the same thing—and in the same context (John 15:18; 17:14). Hatred from the outside world should serve to increase the believers' love for one another.

3:14 If we love our Christian brothers and sisters, it proves that we have passed from death to life. John now reduces the world to two spheres, that of death and that of life. Love for fellow believers is experiential evidence that one has passed from the realm of death to the sphere of life. "Passed" is a perfect-tense verb indicating that something experienced in the past has continuing and abiding results in the present. Christians experience a permanent passage from death to life at the time of regeneration.

But a person who has no love is still dead. This translation has the excellent ms backing of א A B 33 1739 it cop. Other mss supply "the brother," (C 044 𝔐) or "his brother" (P syr) so as to qualify the idea: ". . . has no love for [his] brother." To have no love speaks of the spiritual condition of the unregenerate—that is, such people are spiritually dead. If a person does not have any love for other Christians, it shows that the person does not share the same life as the others—it reveals that the person has not migrated from death to life.

3:15 Anyone who hates another brother or sister is really a murderer at heart. The dark image of Cain still lingers. To not love (3:14) is to hate—there is no middle ground (cf. Matt 5:21-22).

3:16 We know what real love is because Jesus gave up his life for us. Christ's example shows us that real love involves self-sacrifice, which, as 3:17-19 points out, must result in self-sacrificial actions. Reduced to the absolute minimum, love gives and hate takes.

So we also ought to give up our lives for our brothers and sisters. We do this by becoming truly concerned about the needs of our Christian brothers, and by unselfishly giving time, effort, prayer, and possessions to supply those needs.

Such an attitude would result in actually dying for a brother or sister if this were ever necessary. Our lives should not be more precious to us than God's own Son was to him.

3:17 If someone has enough money to live well and sees a brother or sister in need but shows no compassion—how can God's love be in that person? If we are to give our very lives for our brothers and sisters, we certainly should not hold back money or anything we own from Christians who are in need.

Maintaining a Relationship with God by Being Faithful to Him and Living in Christ

1 JOHN 3:19-24

EXPOSITION

In this section, John continues to affirm that life must match doctrine. One can claim to be in the truth, but one's deeds prove or disclaim that profession. We can be assured that we are practicing what we preach if we have active love toward other Christians. The person who loves in truth (3:18) knows that his behavior has its source in truth and has confidence before God (3:21). If we are demonstrating love by our actions, we will not constantly wonder whether God condemns us or condones us. John could speak this way because he was not speaking to people whose consciences were deadened by continual, deliberate sin (1 Tim 4:2); he was speaking to Christians who knew Christ's commands and were testing themselves by them.

God's knowledge of our thoughts and motives should relieve us, not terrify us (see note on 3:20). This is the interpretation favored by the NLT rendering. As written, this passage functions to console the believer whose heart (or conscience) accuses him or her of sin because God, in his greatness, assures the believer of his love. But it is also possible to read this passage in another way: "And by this we know that we are of the truth, and shall assure our hearts before Him. For if our heart condemns us, God is greater than our heart, and knows all things" (3:19-20, NKJV). In this rendering, the phrase "God is greater than our heart" intensifies John's warning. The condemning voice of our conscience merely echoes the judgment of God, who knows our lives better than we do. Thus we cannot gloss over or excuse our sin as insignificant. No matter which interpretation we are convinced of, we can come confidently to God when we recognize that his grace and mercy are greater than our guilt.

Furthermore, when believers live (abide) in Christ, their prayers will be answered. This does not mean that all requests are granted; the context of a parallel passage, John 15, suggests that the prayers should pertain to fruit-bearing and glorifying the Father. The same holds true for John's statement, "We will receive from him whatever we ask." Our requests will be honored by God when they are focused on accomplishing God's will. This accords with how Jesus taught his disciples to pray: "May your will be done on earth, as it is in heaven" (Matt 6:10).

Continual abiding engenders continual faith (see note on 3:23). Our faith in Christ must be ongoing. To believe in the name of Jesus Christ is to believe in his person—who he is and what he represents. We must believe in Jesus as the Son of God; we must be careful not to believe in him according to our own conceptions but according to the biblical presentation of his person. The result of believing in Jesus is that we love all others who also believe. This comes not only from Jesus' command (John 13:34; 15:17) but from Jesus' new life imparted into us by the Spirit.

John concludes this section of his epistle with an affirmation of what theologians call "mutual indwelling." Mutual indwelling means that God and the believers live in one another. This is made possible by the presence of the Spirit in the believer's life. The Christian lives in the Spirit, and the Spirit lives in the Christian (3:24). An appropriate—albeit limited—analogy is a human being's relationship to air: We must live in the air so that the air can come into us and live in us.

The indwelling Spirit provides us with the presence of the indwelling Christ. For the Spirit to live in us is to have Christ live in us (see Rom 8:9-11). When Christ gave us his Spirit to live in us, he gave us himself to live in us (cf. John 14:16-20; 1 Cor 15:45; 2 Cor 3:17-18). The Holy Spirit manifests himself in our lives and conduct. It is he who inspires us to confess Jesus as the Christ. It is he who empowers us to obey God's commandment, which is to love our brothers and sisters.

In summary, this section is John's reiteration and application of Jesus' upper room discourse, wherein Jesus first gave the disciples the commandment to love one another (John 13), then revealed to them that he would indwell them by his Spirit (John 14), and finally encouraged the disciples to practice abiding (living) in him so that he could live in them and their prayers could be answered (John 15–16).

NOTES

3:19 *Our actions will show that we belong to the truth.* Lit., "By this we will know that we are of the truth." The best mss (‭א‬ A B C 33 1739) support the verb tense as being future. In inferior mss (K L 049 𝔐—so TR), the tense is present, "we know"; this displays assimilation to the present-tense verb, "we know," used predominately in this epistle (see 2:3, 5, 18; 3:24; 4:6, 13; 5:2). John deviated from the present tense in this instance because he wanted to include a notion of future accountability, as well as ongoing accountability.

3:20 *Even if we feel guilty, God is greater than our feelings, and he knows everything.* As is discussed in the exposition section above, this statement has two possible interpretations—one positive and one negative, each depending on how the expression "God is greater than our feelings [lit., hearts]" is understood. The positive interpretation is that the believer can take consolation in God's beneficent greatness (cf. Brooke 1912:100; Stott 2000:150-152). The negative interpretation is that the believer should recognize that God, who is greater than us, would echo any condemnation and do so in greater fashion (cf. Alford 1976:4.479-481). The context would seem to support the positive interpretation inasmuch as John was trying to encourage the believers, not discourage them. Certain scholars would repunctuate 3:19-20 to make it even clearer that John intended a positive interpretation. Burge (1996:164), following Marshall (1978:198), suggests this format:

> 19a: "In this [the love and obedience we exhibit, vv. 11-18] we will know that we are of the truth."

> 19b-20: "We will reassure our hearts in his presence whenever our hearts condemn us, because (1) God is greater than our hearts, and (2) God knows all things."

3:22 *And we will receive from him whatever we ask because we obey him and do the things that please him.* This statement follows what Jesus uttered in his final discourse to his disciples, as recorded in John 15:7—"If you abide in me and my words abide in you, ask for whatever you wish, and it will be done for you" (NRSV).

3:23 *We must believe.* This reading is based on the aorist verb, *pisteusōmen* [TG4100, ZG4409], found in B 𝔐. The more likely reading is a present subjunctive, *pisteuōmen* (we should continue to believe), found in ℵ A C 044 0245 33 1739. The variant reading has better support and suits the context. John was not asking his readers to begin to believe (which is the force of the aorist); he was asking them to continue in their faith.

3:24 *remain in fellowship with him, and he with them.* Lit., "abides in him [Christ] and he [Christ] in him [the believer]." This is the first time in this epistle that John mentions the mutual indwelling of Christ and the believer. This was a major theme in Jesus' last discourse, as recorded in John's Gospel (John 14:20; 15:5; 17:21-26).

And we know he lives in us because the Spirit he gave us lives in us. The way in which Christ lives in the believer is by his indwelling Spirit. In Jesus' last discourse, he told the disciples that he would give them the Spirit of truth to live in them. In the same breath, he told them that he would come to them (John 14:16-20). The coming of the Spirit to indwell the believers is none other than the coming of Christ in his invisible, spiritual presence to live in the believers. John's mention of the Spirit in this verse prepares the way for 4:1-3, which deals with the spirit of truth versus the spirit of error.

Community Fellowship Protected by Watchfulness for Deceivers

1 JOHN 4:1-6

EXPOSITION

The statement "And we know he lives in us because the Spirit he gave us lives in us" (3:24) serves as a transition to chapter 4. Those who are indwelt by the Spirit have the ability to discern the Spirit of truth from the spirit of error because the anointing of the Spirit teaches them about these things (see comments on 2:20, 27). In John's day, the secessionists may have claimed to speak Spirit-inspired messages. Those messages had to be tested. The same holds true throughout all church history.

Those who have the Spirit of God confess that Jesus is God's Son come in the flesh. In other words, they acknowledge the full reality of the Incarnation. This is John's "litmus test" for distinguishing heresy from orthodoxy. This doctrinal test of orthodoxy is spelled out clearly: a person must confess that "Jesus Christ has come in the flesh." This means that a person must acknowledge Jesus' divinity and preexistence as the Son of God (that he "has come"; cf. 4:15), as well as Jesus' incarnation and true humanity (that he has come "in the flesh"). This truth is made explicit in John 1:1 and 1:14—"the Word was God . . . [and] the Word became human." It is also affirmed in John's prologue to this epistle (1:1-4).

Jesus did not merely appear to be a man; he actually became a man, with a human body. John's "statement is directed against the gnostic error promulgated by Cerinthus, that 'the Christ' descended into an already existing man" (Vine 1970:75). John was also speaking against this heresy in his Gospel when he said, "the Word *became* human" (John 1:14, emphasis added). "The verb is in the perfect tense in the Greek ('has come'); it represents an abiding effect. From his incarnation onward, Christ was, and ever is, possessed of true Manhood" (Vine 1970:76). God the Son is forever fully God and fully man, though in immortal, incorruptible flesh. A prophet's denial of Jesus' full and true humanity proves that the prophet is not "of God." The church has fought the battle for this truth concerning Christ's person ever since John's day—the late first century. Indeed, the earliest extant quote of 1 John comes from Polycarp (*To the Philippians* 7.1), who quotes 1 John 4:2-3: "Everyone who does not confess that Jesus Christ has come in the flesh is antichrist."

The responsibility for testing the spirits does not rest solely on scholars or church leaders but on every Christian. Whenever we hear someone teaching about Jesus, our spiritual "antenna" ought to be operating so that we can sense whether truth or falsehood is being spoken. The church does not now have any of the apostles present to correct error, but we do have the Holy Spirit and the Scriptures written by the apostles. All those who are indwelt by the Spirit of truth and anointed by the Spirit can know the truth; it is not reserved for a special few. The greater the number of believers who know the truth and can discern error, the stronger the church will be against deception. Those who have the Spirit should be able to discern true prophets from the false. Whereas a true prophet is one who receives direct revelation from God (cf. Deut 13, 18), a false prophet is one who claims to have received direct revelation from God but actually has not.

False teachers and false prophets, being a part of the world system, will be accepted by the world. This is why so many cults are readily accepted in the world; they offer something new and distinctive to a world that is looking for novelty and speciality. The presence, even in our own times, of false prophets, false teachers, and antichrists should not surprise us. Jesus warned his disciples of their coming (Matt 24:15, 24-26), and the apostles, in turn, warned the believers (cf. 2 Thes 2:3-12; 2 Pet 3:3ff). They will enter our churches, speak on our radios, and appear on our televisions. We can discern them and reject them if we know the truth and pay attention to the inward teaching of the Spirit. If something they say doesn't "sit right" with our spirit, we should compare their teachings against the apostolic truths as presented in Scripture. We should be especially sensitive to remarks made about the person and work of Jesus Christ. In John's day, many rejected Jesus' humanity; in our day, many reject Jesus' deity.

NOTES

4:1 *do not believe everyone who claims to speak by the Spirit.* The literal expression here is "do not believe every spirit" (used also in 4:2 and 4:3); "every spirit" is a metonymy for "every prophet" in the sense that the prophet is an instrument for the spirit's utterance (cf. Acts 4:25). First Timothy 4:1 has a parallel expression inasmuch as the words "the Holy Spirit tells us clearly" is tantamount to saying "prophecy indicates." Paul conveys nearly the same idea in 1 Cor 14:29-32, where he conjoins "the prophet" exercising his or her gift with "the spirit."

You must test them. Lit., "test the spirits." The plural "spirits" does "not refer to a multiplicity of divine spirits or even of evil spirits but to a multiplicity of human beings who may be inspired in their spirits by the Spirit of God or the spirit of falsehood" (Marshall 1978:204). The test question is made explicit in 4:2-3.

many false prophets. This is probably another name for the many antichrists (see comments on 2:18-19).

4:2 *If a person claiming to be a prophet.* Lit., "Every spirit that" (cf. also NLT mg). The NLT understands this correctly; the reference is to the spirit of the speaker, the spirit of the prophet.

acknowledges that Jesus Christ came in a real body. There are three parts to this confession: (1) Christ had an existence prior to becoming flesh; (2) Jesus is the Christ; and (3) he became a man. In other words, Jesus was the Christ come in the flesh (Stott 2000:154-156). The verb "came" (a perfect active participle in Gr.: *elēluthota* [TG2064A, ZG2262]) implies the coming of Jesus Christ from God, as well as the preexistence of Christ before the Incarnation (Marshall 1978:205).

4:3 *if someone claims to be a prophet.* Lit., "every spirit that." The reference is to the spirit of the prophet.

does not acknowledge . . . Jesus. In this context, refusing to "acknowledge Jesus" or "confess Jesus" means denial of Jesus' true person as both God and man. This is the true reading according to the best ms support (א A B C 33 1739* 𝔐). A few other witnesses, however, read, "annuls Jesus" (1739ᵐᵍ Vulgate [which reads *solvit* = "severs"] Irenaeus, Clement, Origen [per 1739ᵐᵍ], Augustineᵐˢˢ [per Socrates]). This variant, which is noted in NRSV mg and NJB mg, is an antignostic statement. Those "annulling Jesus" or "severing Jesus" destroy the orthodox teaching about Jesus' incarnation. Some church fathers thought the severing would be to divide "Jesus" from "the Christ," as was done by Cerinthus and later by Nestorius (cf. discussion in Smalley 1984:214-215).

Such a person has the spirit of the Antichrist. In the Greek, there is no word for "spirit" here; rather, just the neuter article *to* [TG3588, ZG3836] (the), which is used substantively to refer back to *pneuma* [TG4151, ZG4460] (spirit) in the first part of the verse. The spirit operating in the false prophets is the spirit of the antichrist (2:18), the spirit of error (4:6).

which . . . is already here. The relative pronoun "which" is neuter in the Gr., again referring to *pneuma* [TG4151, ZG4460] (spirit). John says "it [the spirit] is already here" because the spirit of the Antichrist is already present, while the appearing of the Antichrist himself is yet impending.

4:4 *you belong to God.* This is said in emphatic contrast to the false teachers who were enemies of Christ.

You have already won a victory over those people. Christians don't have to overpower false prophets to conquer them; rather, they can overcome them and their teachings by recognizing them and then refusing to follow them. The believers in the churches John was writing to had already done this; they had not succumbed to the false prophets.

the Spirit who lives in you is greater than the spirit who lives in the world. The NLT specifically identifies what the Gr. text leaves unclear: "the one who is in you is greater than the one in the world." This one could be God the Father, Jesus, or the Spirit—or all three, the Triune God (Smalley 1984:227).

4:5 *Those people belong to this world.* In John's Gospel and epistles, the term *kosmos* [ᵀᴳ2889, ᶻᴳ3180] (world) describes the world system in which every human being lives, and it refers to this system as it stands in opposition to God and the people in the system. This system is opposed to God's realm because Satan exerts his influence over it.

4:6 *we belong to God.* John was primarily speaking of himself and those with him, who were the true teachers of Christ, but his statement also includes all those who speak from God and therefore speak the truth.

those who know God listen to us. John was following Jesus in this proclamation, for Jesus declared, "Anyone who belongs to God listens gladly to the words of God" (John 8:47).

they do not belong to God. "They" refers to the false prophets (4:5); since they do not know God, they cannot speak for him.

the Spirit of truth. According to the Gospel of John (John 14:17, 26; 15:26; 16:13-15), the "Spirit of truth" is the Holy Spirit, who proceeds from God and teaches the truth about Christ (cf. 1 Jn 2:20, 27).

the spirit of deception. This expression is unique in the NT; the closest parallel is found in 1 Tim 4:1 (deceptive spirits). The spirit of deception is the spirit of the antichrist present in the false prophets; it is the spirit that leads people away from the truth about Christ.

God's Love Expressed in Community Love

1 JOHN 4:7-21

EXPOSITION

From 3:11 through 3:23 John's major theme was love. At 3:24 he mentioned the Spirit and went into a brief excursus in 4:1-6 concerning the discernment of false spirits. At 4:7 John resumes and elaborates on a major theme in this epistle: Love among Christians demonstrates love for God and love from God, for God is love. And that love was demonstrated unmistakably in Jesus in order to solve the problem of sin.

Our recognition of Jesus as the Son of God and the Savior of the world leads believers to know the love of God. This love flows through us to others and is evidence of our relationship to God. This love also gives us the assurance of being accepted by God, to the extent that even our fears of the final judgment are overcome.

"God is love" (4:8) is one of the three great Johannine expressions of the nature of God. The other two are "God is light" (1:5) and "God is Spirit" (John 4:24). The statement "God is love" is certainly one of the most profound divine revelations. Our inability to fully grasp its import lies in our defective use and understanding of the term "love." We tend to think of love as an emotion, a feeling, or maybe a fluctuating attribute. However, "God is love" is properly interpreted as meaning that God, self-conscious and moral, creates, sustains, and orders all things in love. Love is the very essence of God. Of no other person could it possibly be said, "he is love" or "she is love." Only God is completely loving, because love is his very entity, nature, and character. When John writes, "God is love," he is giving the reader the clearest, briefest, most comprehensive expression possible of the nature of God.

Nothing in God is in the slightest way incompatible with love; in him there is no malice, no malignity, no coldness, no indifference, no malevolence, no spite, no rancor. Rather, his nature demonstrates consistency in fidelity, tenderness, compassion, active favor, loyalty, covenant keeping, longsuffering, and gracious giving. God's love is ever abounding, ever present, ever beneficial, and can never be diminished in the slightest way. God's love is so boundless that it is impossible either by experience or by definition to scale its heights or fathom its depths (cf. Eph 3:17-19).

"God is love" manifested itself singularly in his gracious act of sending his only Son, Jesus Christ, into the world to take upon himself the consequences of people's sins, thereby to absolve them of their guilt and to free them to live eternally in his love. In other words, God loved in a way that resulted in a gift. The Word made flesh is Love Incarnate. Love moved to action so efficaciously that it has reached the darkest, most dismal, most unheavenly people. "God is love" is basic to the gospel message. God loves and thus gives—his Son, forgiveness, salvation, fellowship, eternal life. It is in the crucifixion and resurrection of Jesus Christ that we see most clearly the love of God. Love is written all over the cross. It is the gospel. There would be no gospel—no good news—without love.

True fellowship with God is based on love. The Son showed love for the Father by obeying his commands. The believer shows love for the Son by obeying his command to love one another (4:11). Love is a divine reality coming to believers from the Father, through the Son, returning from them through Christ to the Father, marking them as true believers and proving the authenticity of Christ's mission.

In all of this it must be remembered that John's exposé on love (*agapē* [TG26, ZG27]) is not primarily to encourage individuals to love God privately but to motivate the brothers and sisters in God's community to love one another. This love proves the reality of one's personal love for God. Those who have received God's gift of life are endowed with the nature of God and thereby become partakers of the divine love. Our love for fellow Christians provides proof of our spiritual birth and relationship with God (4:20). Anyone in whom God lives will naturally reflect his character. To claim to know God while failing to love is a false claim. It is just as false as claiming to know God, who is light, while still living in darkness (1:5-6).

God's supreme love for us is the motive of our love for one another (4:11). Remember, God's great initiating love is an expression of true and real love, and in our appreciation and gratitude of such love, we should be the initiators of loving fellow believers. It is in loving one another that we really demonstrate our love for God.

The apostles had the privilege of seeing God manifest in the flesh (1:1-3; 4:14; John 1:14), a privilege that later believers do not have in this life. Nonetheless, having never seen Jesus, we still love him, even as Peter said (1 Pet 1:8). But we cannot claim to love someone we have never seen and at the same time despise those who belong to him. Evidently, John made this point to expose the secessionists to the Johannine community (see "Date and Occasion of Writing" in the Introduction; and comments on 2:19). They must have talked about their great "love for God." So John said to them, "How do you measure your love for God?" The evidence of one's love for God is one's love for fellow believers. That is measurable, evidential, and observable. If we do not love our Christian brothers and sisters, who are God's visible representatives, how can we love the invisible God?

All believers need to reach maturity in love for God and love for each other. As we mature in love, we will be motivated by love to please God. Until we mature, we will motivated by fear—fear of God's punishment. But John affirms that it is love, not fear, that should motivate us (4:17-18). We are in a new era—of the new covenant—where God is the initiator and supplier. As he supplies the love, we receive, and in that receiving, fear is cast out. Eventually, we will have "perfect" love—that is, our love will have reached maturity. We must not think of "perfect" as meaning flawless. A fully developed apple is mature (or "perfect"), even if it has bumps, scabs, and bruises. None of us will be flawless and faultless in this lifetime, but we can become mature in our love for God and his people.

John's words are challenging, especially those in 4:17-18, because he himself could not have said these things if they were not real to him. Thus we gather that he probably considered himself to have matured to the extent that (1) he was a living representative of Jesus Christ on earth, and (2) he was motivated by pure love, not fear, to please the Lord. Because he knew that he was motivated by love, he did not fear the day of judgment. The extent to which we fear the day of judgment is a converse measure of how truly we are living in God's love. Let us take John as our example to live in God, who is love, and thereby love one another. May this love be perfected in us.

NOTES

4:7 *for love comes from God.* God is love (4:8) and the source of all love.

Anyone who loves is a child of God. In Greek, the present-tense verb here indicates ongoing action: "Everyone loving has been born of God." This verse is not saying that every person who experiences any kind of love has, therefore, been regenerated by God. Even the worst people can have loving moments. What this is saying is that like begets like. Those born of God, who is love, will also love and be characterized by love.

and knows God. The verb indicates an ongoing knowledge, as in "getting to know God" (*ginōskei* [TG1097, ZG1182] *ton theon*). This is a continual, growing, spiritual knowledge based on actual experience of God in our lives.

4:8 *anyone who does not love does not know God.* A person who does not love Christians has never known the God whom Christians love. The verb translated "know" in this verse is in the aorist tense, thereby indicating that such a person not only doesn't know God now but has never known him.

God is love. We cannot turn this around to say, "Love is God," or weaken it by saying, "God is loving," as if this were just one of God's attributes. Rather, God is love in his very essence. Those who do not love other children of God do not know God. "God is love" is the second description of God's absolute nature in 1 John; the first is "God is light" (1:5).

4:9 This verse nearly replicates the well-known statement in John 3:16, thereby showing that John wrote both the fourth Gospel and this epistle. The main thrust of this verse, as well as of John 3:16, is that God was motivated by love for humanity when he sent his only Son to give eternal life to all who will believe. **his one and only Son.** The Greek is *ton huion* [ᵀᴳ5207, ᶻᴳ5626] *autou ton monogenē* [ᵀᴳ3439, ᶻᴳ3666]). The term *monogenē* is a title for Christ found only in John's writings (John 1:14, 18; 3:16, 18; cf. 1 Jn 5:18 and note); this title expresses the Son's unique position as the Father's beloved Son (cf. Smalley 1984:241-242). The NLT rightly avoids the old KJV rendering, "only begotten Son," because the term *monogenē* does not emphasize birth ("begotten") as such but speciality (the "one and only"). Jesus Christ is God's uniquely favored Son.

4:10 This is real love. In the ancient Greek language there were four words for love that generally focused on four different aspects of love: (1) *eraō* for fervent longings, esp. sexual passion; (2) *phileō* [ᵀᴳ5368, ᶻᴳ5797] for friendship; (3) *stergō* for benevolent devotion, esp. among family members; and (4) *agapaō* [ᵀᴳ25, ᶻᴳ26] for loving-kindness. The fourth word is the term used by John to characterize God's love.

not that we loved God, but that he loved us. Initiating love is greater than responding love (cf. Rom 5:8).

and sent his Son as a sacrifice to take away our sins. The supreme manifestation of God's love was demonstrated in sending his Son to die for us to take away our sins. By removing our sins, God removed the barrier between himself and us (Rom 5:1-2; Eph 2:18) so that he could live within us and we could live within him. The word *hilasmos* [ᵀᴳ2434, ᶻᴳ2662] (sacrifice), is the noun form of the verb *hilaskomai* [ᵀᴳ2433, ᶻᴳ2661], which in classical Gr. meant "to appease" but in the NT means "to atone" or "to expiate" (see note on 2:2).

4:12 No one has ever seen God. This statement reiterates what John said in the prologue to his Gospel (John 1:18), which recalls what God said to Moses in Exodus 33:20. Moses wanted to see God's glory, but he was not allowed to gaze directly upon God; God told him that no man could see God's face and live. In John 6:46, Jesus said that no one has seen the Father except he who is of God— this one has seen the Father. This means that only the Son, who is himself God, has seen God and can communicate his glory to people.

his love is brought to full expression in us. This means that the believers' love for each other, finding its source in God's love, has ripened and matured so as to find expression in self-sacrifice.

4:13 God has given us his Spirit as proof that we live in him and he in us. Lit., "He has given us . . ." The subject of this sentence could also be "Jesus" because the mutual abiding is often spoken of as a spiritual reality between Jesus Christ and the believers. If so, it could be rendered "Jesus gave us of his own Spirit." This means that the Spirit is not some anonymous source of inspiration but the representative of Christ himself. After Jesus' resurrection, his Spirit could live in the believers and the believers could live in his Spirit. According to John 14:16-20, the disciples would begin to experience what it meant to live in God and have God live in them once Christ sent them the Paraclete, the Spirit of truth. Thereafter they would know that the Son is in the Father, and they are in the Son, and the Son is in them (John 14:20). See comments on 3:24.

4:14 *we have seen with our own eyes and now testify that the Father sent his Son.* The "we" refers to the apostles and other eyewitnesses of Christ's life on earth (see comments on 1:1-4). They were appointed by Christ to testify to others about their firsthand, eyewitness experiences (1:3). Therefore Christians have two proofs of God's love for us: (1) the indwelling presence of God's Spirit and (2) the testimony of the apostles and other eyewitnesses of Jesus.

    to be the Savior of the world. The expression "Savior of the world" occurs only one other time in the NT—in John's Gospel in the passage where the Samaritans recognize that Jesus is the Messiah (John 4:42). John made it clear that Jesus was not just the Jews' Messiah but the world's Savior, the Deliverer of all those who put their trust in him.

4:15 *All who confess that Jesus is the Son of God.* The verb translated "confess" is an aorist subjunctive (*homologēsē* [^{TG}3670, ^{ZG}3933]). This *could* imply that this confession is done once for all; however the aorist does not always signal once-for-all action. When a person confesses that Jesus is the Son of God, he or she is declaring that Jesus is God's unique Son.

    have God living in them, and they live in God. The person who believes in Christ is indwelt by God and simultaneously dwells in God. This mutual indwelling, experienced by the Father and Son (John 10:38; 14:10; 17:21), is a special privilege for the believers (cf. John 14:20; 15:5; 17:21-24).

4:16 *We.* This pronoun refers to John and his readers, rather than just the apostles and/or John's coworkers.

    know how much God loves us. John is not so much speaking of the degree ("how much") of love but of the specific quality of love God has for us.

    God is love. Only three times in the NT is such a short definition of God given, all in the writings of John. According to John, "God is Spirit" (John 4:24), "God is light" (1 Jn 1:5), and "God is love" (1 Jn 4:8, 16).

4:17 *as we live in God, our love grows more perfect.* The word "perfect" here does not mean "flawless" but "mature and complete." This perfection develops our relationship with God, who is love.

    So we will not be afraid on the day of judgment, but we can face him with confidence. Confidence is the opposite of "fear" (4:18). The result of living with Christ and growing more perfect in love is confidence in the day of judgment, which is terrifying to other people (Acts 24:25; Rom 2:16).

    because we live like Jesus here in this world. Lit., "because as that One [Jesus] is, so are we in this world." This causal explanation is astounding because it says that Christians are like Jesus in the sense that they bear his likeness in this world. This, of course, is the ideal of Christlikeness, which exists to one degree or another in various believers. But John did not qualify his statement, so it could be read to mean that all Christians—regardless of maturation—are now even as Christ is, when experience tells us that this is not so. Noting this difficulty, several scribes tried to fix it in various ways. One eleventh-century ms (2138) exhibits, in one way or another, all the changes found in several other mss (including ℵ). Ms 2138 reads, "We may have confidence in the day of judgment, because just as that One was blameless and pure in the world, so we, who [also] have human nature, will be in this world" (Comfort 2007:781-782). This fix allows for the believers to be like Christ with respect to his humanity and also allows for a maturation process (note the future tense: "will be").

4:19 We love each other. Cf. NLT mg: "Greek *We love.* Other manuscripts read *We love God;* still others read *We love him.*" These three variant readings are supported by different Greek mss: (1) "We love" (A B 1739); (2) "We love God" (ℵ 048 33); (3) "We love him" (Ψ 𝔐—so TR). Textual criticism favors the simple expression, "We love." Ancient scribes felt compelled to provide a direct object, and chose "God" or "him." The NLT translators supplied "each other" because the context of 1 John 4 speaks about community love. However, it is best to omit any direct object—John was emphasizing that we are now able to truly *love* because God demonstrated what love is when he sent his Son to die for our sins (Comfort 2007:782).

because he loved us first. God is always the initiator (see comments on 4:9-10).

4:20 If someone says, "I love God." This is a very rare statement, found only here in the NT. Once again, John was probably quoting those spiritual elitists who made boasts about their relationship with God. This boast—"I love God"— can be tested by one's love for the community of God. If such a person rejects other believers or refuses to fellowship with them, his or her love for God should be questioned. Such was the case with Diotrephes who refused to have fellowship with John and his coworkers (cf. 3 Jn 1:9-10).

4:21 he has given us this command: Those who love God must also love their Christian brothers and sisters. This is a powerful summary statement. Not only is it logical to love God's children if we love God (4:20), it is also God's command.

Overcoming the World

1 JOHN 5:1-5

EXPOSITION

In this section, John encourages faith in Jesus as the Christ and as the Son of God. John concluded his Gospel (at the end of ch 20, before adding an epilogue) in the same way. In the Gospel he wrote, "These are written so that you may continue to believe that Jesus is the Messiah, the Son of God, and that by believing in him you will have life by the power of his name" (John 20:31). When John speaks of believing in Jesus as the Christ, he means that people must believe that Jesus of Nazareth was God's one and only Anointed One. He was anointed by God's Spirit to preach the gospel, heal the sick, raise the dead, die on the cross for our sins, and rise from the dead to become our life. When John speaks of believing in Jesus as the Son of God, he means that people must believe that Jesus of Nazareth was God become human, God come from heaven to earth in human flesh. They must believe that he has always been the Son of God, coeternal with the Father, sharing the Father's glory from everlasting. And they must believe that he and he alone is the unique Son of God. No one else can legitimately make that claim because no one else has proven to be deity by rising from the dead (cf. Rom 1:3-4).

The belief John speaks of is not a one-time event. According to him, both in his Gospel and this epistle, faith in Christ must be ongoing and perpetual. This is indicated by his habitual use of the present tense for "believe" (the present participle *pisteuōn* [TG4100, ZG4409] is used both in 5:1 and 5:5). Though most Christians can point to a day when they first began to believe, they must continue to be believers every day.

We must always remember that all who believe that Jesus is the Christ, the Son of God, are our brothers and sisters—no matter what they think about other biblical matters, such as the Rapture, the millennial kingdom, speaking in tongues, baptism, eternal punishment, and so on. We should love all those who share the same faith we have in Jesus as the Christ, the Son of God, because we all have the same Father and the same divine life.

As noted below (see notes on 5:1 and 5:4), John calls upon the believers to love the collective community of believers. This love proves each believer's love for God. Furthermore, it is in this community that we have the power to overcome the evil forces of the world because the community of faith keeps encouraging each of us to continue believing, to remain faithful to Christ. It is by this kind of believing that we gain victory over the world system, which is permeated with false, anti-Christian teachings. By holding fast to our faith in Jesus as God's Son, we will not be steered away to false teachings. It is belief, not activity, that overcomes the world, and absolutely no one overcomes the world apart from believing that Jesus is the Son of God. And no one can do this alone. The collective body of regenerated believers—the community as a unit—has the power to conquer.

NOTES

5:1 *Everyone who believes that Jesus is the Christ.* Here, as in the Gospel of John, people are called upon to believe first that Jesus is the Christ, God's Anointed One, and then also to believe that he is the Son of God (cf. 5:5; John 20:31). It is possible that John was addressing the proto-Gnostics who denied the Incarnation (see note on 5:6).

And everyone who loves the Father loves his children, too. Lit., "Everyone loving the One who gives birth loves also the one born of him." This is the reading supported by A P 1739 𝔐 syr. Other mss (B 044 048^vid 33 cop) read "Everyone loving the One who gives birth loves also the one born." Two mss (ℵ 69) read, "Everyone loving the One who gives birth loves also that which is born." This last reading means that everyone who loves the Father (the One who has begotten) loves the collective community of believers (see note on 5:4 for a similar collective construction). All other mss have the masculine singular rather than this neuter construction.

5:2 *We know we love God's children if we love God and obey his commandments.* "Obey" is a synonym for "keep" (*tērōmen* [^TG5083, ^ZG5498]), a reading found in ℵ P (048) 𝔐. A reading found in other mss (B 044 81 1739) is "do" (*poiōmen* [^TG4160, ^ZG4472]). The first reading ("we keep") is probably the result of scribal assimilation to 5:3 (as well as to 2:3, 4, 5; 3:22, 24). The meaning of the verse, however, is not affected greatly.

Just as our love for our brothers and sisters is the sign and test of our love for God, so our love for God, tested by obedience, is the only basis of our love for our brothers and sisters. John was not contradicting what he said in 4:20-21; rather, he was insisting that love for God and love for our brothers and sisters cannot be separated.

5:3 *Loving God means keeping his commandments, and his commandments are not burdensome.* This is an extension of what Jesus said to his disciples, as recorded in the Gospel of John. He really had only one preeminent commandment for them: Love one another (John 13:34; 15:17).

5:4 *For every child of God defeats this evil world.* This is one way to interpret the text, but it misses a significant point. The Greek literally reads, "Whatever is born of God conquers the world" (as in NRSV). The Greek term for "whatever" is *pan to* [ᵀᴳ3956/3588, ᶻᴴ4246/3836]. John used this collective neuter construction to designate the collective unit of believers, not just a single believer. In other words, it refers to the whole body of those begotten by God (cf. Manson 1947:27). In the next verse he speaks of the individual. This same pattern—speaking first of the collective body of believers and then of each individual believer—is found in John 6:37, 39; 17:2, 24 (cf. Comfort 1994:191).

Discerning Truth from Falsehood and Keeping Eternal Life

1 JOHN 5:6-12

EXPOSITION

In our day, we hear people left and right denying that Jesus is God. In the days of the early church, there were just as many denying that Jesus was a true human being. They did this because they could not conceive of God, being a pure spirit, taking on actual human flesh, for that would mean that God had tarnished himself with sin. Therefore, they believed that Jesus had only the appearance of humanity—that is, he *seemed* to be human but wasn't really (hence the name "Docetists," from the Greek word *dokeō* [^{TG}1380, ^{ZG}1506], "appear, seem").

In John's day the Docetists (and specifically a man named Cerinthus, who was a Docetist) denied Christ's true and lasting humanity, saying that Christ could not have had real flesh and real blood. Refuting this heresy, John affirmed that he saw Jesus in the flesh (see 1:1-4 and comments), and he saw Jesus shed his blood and die (see comments on 4:2).

In order to accommodate his teachings, Cerinthus developed the heresy (later known as the adoptionist heresy) that Jesus of Nazareth became "the Christ" at his baptism and ceased being "the Christ" prior to his death. In other words, he taught that "the Christ" descended into the man Jesus after his baptism and then left him prior to his crucifixion. Cerinthus's heresy comes to us through the writings of Irenaeus:

> [Cerinthus] represented Jesus as having not been born of a virgin, but as being the son of Joseph and Mary according to the ordinary course of human generation, while he nevertheless was more righteous, prudent, and wise than other men. Moreover, after his baptism, Christ descended upon him in the form of a dove from the Supreme Ruler, and that then he proclaimed the unknown Father, and performed miracles. But at last Christ departed from Jesus, and that then Jesus suffered and rose again, while Christ remained impassible, inasmuch as he was a spiritual being." (*Heresies* 3.3.4)

In countering this heresy, John argued that Jesus was the Christ, the Son of God "through water" (prior to, during, and after his baptism), as well as "through blood" (prior to, during, and after his death on the cross). F. F. Bruce (1970:118-119) elaborates:

> The sequence "water and blood" is not accidental, but corresponds to the historical sequence of our Lord's baptism and passion. Cerinthus, we recall, taught that "the Christ" (a spiritual being) came down on the man Jesus when He was baptized but left Him before He died. The Christ, that is to say, came through water (baptism) but not through blood (death). To this misrepresentation of the truth John replies that the One whom believers acknowledge to be the Son of God (verse 5) came "not with the water only but with the water and with the blood."

The One who died on the cross was as truly the Christ, the Son of God, as the One who was baptized in the Jordan. In words that must have been clear to his original readers, John said, "And Jesus Christ was revealed as God's Son by his baptism in water and by shedding his blood on the cross—not by water only, but by water and blood. And the Spirit, who is truth, confirms it with his testimony" (5:6). What we can gather from this statement is that John was speaking of three critical phases in Jesus' life where he was manifested as God Incarnate, the Son of God in human form. This was made evident at his baptism (the water), his death (the blood), and his resurrection (the Spirit). At his baptism, the man Jesus was declared God's beloved Son (cf. Matt 3:16-17). At his crucifixion, a man shedding blood was recognized by others as "the Son of God" (cf. Mark 15:39). In resurrection, he was designated by the Spirit as the Son of God in power (Rom 1:3-4). This threefold testimony is unified in one aspect: Each event demonstrated that the man Jesus was the divine Son of God.

These divinely given witnesses should convince us that Jesus is the Son of God. According to Jewish law, the testimony of one man was not a valid witness. Truth or validity has to be established by two or three witnesses (Deut 17:6; 19:15). Therefore Jesus' self-witness would not validate his claims; he needed the witness of another. That other witness was his Father. Of course, he had more witnesses than just one. In the Gospel of John, Jesus defended his deity with a fivefold witness. In response to the Jewish leaders who had questioned his authority and assaulted his identity, Jesus indicated that he had five very reliable witnesses: (1) the Father himself (John 5:31-32, 37), (2) John the Baptist (John 5:33-35), (3) his own works (John 5:36), (4) the Scriptures (John 5:39-40), and (5) Moses (John 5:45-47). But of all these witnesses the greatest one comes from the Father. And his witness is transferred to us when we receive the Spirit. God's Spirit, alive in our spirit, gives witness to the fact that everything Jesus said and did is true. In fact, that is the primary function of the Spirit—to testify and reveal Jesus to each and every believer (cf. John 14:26; 15:26; 16:7-13).

Those who do not believe that Jesus is the Son of God should realize that by rejecting what God has so plainly told us, they are calling God a liar (5:10). This has two aspects: refusing to believe what God has said about his Son, and in consequence, refusing to believe in Christ, who, because he is God's Son, is the only one who can save people. What better reason can we have for believing something than that God says it is true?

Those who believe receive the greatest gift from God: eternal life. This is not something we have to wait to get. We have eternal life now; we possess a new nature and enjoy fellowship with God. Therefore, a believer need not be uncertain about whether he or she has eternal life. Those who have eternal life now (as a present reality and experience) are assured of everlasting life in the future.

NOTES

5:6 *Jesus Christ was revealed as God's Son by his baptism in water and by shedding his blood on the cross.* Lit., "This is the one coming by water and blood" (cf. NLT mg). As in 4:2 (see note), this points to Christ's incarnation, as well as to his entire life in the flesh. "John is not, of course, thinking narrowly of the mere moment when the Incarnation became a reality at the birth of Jesus; he is thinking of the total act of his coming into the world" (Marshall 1978:231).

The phrase "water and blood" can mean one of two things in this context: (1) The phrase may refer to Christ's death on the cross, at which time he was pierced and blood and water flowed out (John 19:34-35). John witnessed this, and asserted the importance of this occurrence. (2) The phrase "water and blood" could refer to Christ's baptism (water) and crucifixion (blood). This is more likely the correct interpretation (see exposition above for discussion).

And the Spirit, who is truth, confirms it with his testimony. The Spirit bears witness to the truth of Christ's life and work (cf. John 15:26; 16:13-15). This is why he is called "the Spirit of truth." The Spirit's primary role is to reveal Christ to the believers and to affirm Christ's message. This statement also affirms that the truth proclaimed by John is the truth proclaimed by the Spirit. Others could claim to have the Spirit and thereby speak certain truths, but all so-claimed "speaking from the Spirit" must accord with the apostolic truths (cf. 2:20, 27).

5:7-8 As is noted in the NLT mg, there is a substantially longer version of this passage, which appears in the KJV and NKJV as follows (the italic type shows the extra words):

And there are three that bear witness *in heaven: the Father, the Word, and the Holy Spirit, and these three are one. And there are three that bear witness on earth:* the Spirit, the water, and the blood, and the three agree as one.

This famous passage, called "the heavenly witness," has been the object of much discussion. The textual evidence against its inclusion is substantial: ℵ A B (044)

𝕸 syr cop arm eth. As such, it does not appear in any of earliest Greek mss nor in the majority of Greek mss; furthermore, it does not appear in any of the translations, except some of the Latin versions. The first time this passage appears in the longer form (with the heavenly witness) is in the treatise entitled *Liber Apologeticus* (ch 4), attributed to the Spanish heretic Priscillian (died c. 385) or his follower, Bishop Instantius. Metzger says, "Apparently the gloss arose when the original passage was understood to symbolize the Trinity (through the mention of the three witnesses; the Spirit, the water, and the blood), an interpretation which may have been written first as a marginal note that afterwards found its way into the text" (1994:648). The gloss showed up in the writings of Latin Fathers in North Africa and Italy (as part of the text of the epistle) from the fifth century onward, and it found its way into more and more copies of the Latin Vulgate. But "the heavenly witnesses" cannot be found in any Greek ms prior to the eleventh century, and it was never cited by any Greek father.

Erasmus did not include "the heavenly witnesses" in the first two editions of his Greek NT. He was criticized for this by defenders of the Latin Vulgate. Erasmus, in reply, said that he would include it if he could see it in any one Greek ms. In turn, a ms (most likely the Monfort Ms, 61) was especially produced to contain the passage. Erasmus kept his promise; he included it in the third edition of his Greek NT. From there it became incorporated into the TR and hence was translated in the KJV (as well as in the NKJV).

5:9 *Since we believe human testimony.* The law required two or three witnesses as adequate testimony to decide what was true (Deut 17:6; 19:15).

God has testified about his Son. This is fully developed in John 5:31-47, where Jesus affirms his Father's witness.

5:10 *All who believe in the Son of God know in their hearts that this testimony is true.* Lit., "Those who believe in the Son of God have the testimony in themselves." When a person becomes a child of God (by believing that Jesus is the Son of God), he or she knows it without any doubt because the Spirit who regenerated them gives them an inner witness to that reality (cf. Rom 8:16; Gal 4:6).

Those who don't believe this. Lit., "Those who do not believe God"; this is supported by ℵ B P 044 1739^{mg}. Other witnesses (A 1739* Vulgate), showing assimilation to the first clause, read, "Those who do not believe the Son of God."

5:11 *And this is what God has testified: He has given us eternal life, and this life is in his Son.* The divine, eternal life (Eph 4:18) resides in Christ, who makes it available to all who believe in him. Jesus Christ is life (John 1:4; 14:6)—life is available in him (2 Tim 1:10) and in no other (see note on 5:12). Those who do not have him remain in death.

5:12 *Whoever has the Son has life; whoever does not have God's Son does not have life.* Human beings do not have life in themselves; they receive their life from God's Son. The Son of God does not receive his life from any exterior source; he has life in himself and is life; he is the source of his very own life, a uniquely divine characteristic, unshared by any created being. Those who have the Son of God living in them have eternal life now—not life someday, not life later on, not conditional life, but life, eternal life, now.

Conclusion: Helping the Wayward Return to Fellowship

1 JOHN 5:13-21

EXPOSITION

The final nine verses of John's epistle comprise the epilogue. This particular epilogue has two functions: to summarize the main body of the writing and to prompt the believers to apply what they have heard.

First John 5:13 provides John's reason for writing the epistle. Remarkably, the wording is nearly identical to that found in John 20:31, John's purpose in writing his Gospel. But there is a difference. Whereas the Gospel encourages the continuance of faith in the Son of God as the means to enjoying the divine life, the verse in the epistle affirms the possession of divine life for all who believe in the Son of God. In both cases, John wanted his readers to be sure that they had eternal life. And this security is the basis for the other aim of John's letter: that they would be full of joy (1:4).

Because Christians possess and enjoy the life of God, we have the confidence that we are his children, which gives us confidence and boldness when we make our requests to God. When we choose to place our wills in line with God's will, the Holy Spirit in us will teach us to understand God's will more completely, and he will enable us to pray in line with God's will. This is the key to getting our prayers answered. Jesus himself was a model of this: He taught us to pray for God's will to be accomplished on earth (Matt 6:10). And he chose God's will over his own in accepting the bitter cup—death on the cross (Matt 26:39-42).

This much, as modern readers, we can understand quite clearly. But what John asked his readers to specifically pray for is somewhat beyond our ability to grasp because we are not told what the sin that "leads to death" is (5:17). Evidently his readers knew what he was saying, but we don't exactly know. F. F. Bruce said, "The distinction is one which John's readers were expected to recognize. But it is difficult to see how they could recognize the distinction except by the result. Elsewhere in the NT instances occur of sins which caused the death of the persons committing them, when these persons were church members" (1970:124). But the context of 1 John leads us to believe that John was not talking about physical death but spiritual death. The sin that led to this kind of death was the sin of leaving the apostolic truths concerning Jesus and pursuing Docetic Gnosticism. A brother in Christ could be deceived to follow this errant way, as indeed many early Christians did. Such brothers and sisters could see the errors of this way and return to the truth. Thus John encouraged the believers to pray for such people before these straying believers went all the way down the road that leads to death. Of course, some people had already gone that way. These were those who had left the community of true believers, thereby exposing the fact that they never really belonged among God's people (see 2:19 and comments). There was no point in praying for them because they had denied that Jesus is the Christ, the Son of God, thereby leaving themselves in a condition of spiritual death.

Only those who have faith in Jesus Christ as God's Son have eternal life. This life empowers all the children of God to overcome the evil in the world around us. This life also gives us a true understanding of God and his Son, Jesus Christ. There are two kinds of knowledge mentioned by John in 5:20, one that is absolute and the other that is ongoing. Using the Greek word *oidamen* [TG1492, ZG3857], John said that we absolutely know that the Son of God has come in the flesh. The purpose of his coming to earth was to reveal God the Father and to enable the believers to know him experientially (cf. John 17:3). Then John uses the Greek word *ginōskōmen* [TG1097, ZG1182]—that "we may get to know" the true one (i.e., God the Father). And how is it that we can know God? It is because we live in him by virtue of living in his Son (5:20b). This is one of the primary themes of John's Gospel and first epistle. The Son came to earth to bring the believers into God the Father by way of coming to live in him. The Son declared that he was the visible expression of the Father and the way for the believers to live in the Father (cf. John 14:1-18). To be in Jesus Christ is to be in God because Jesus Christ is "the true God" and he is "eternal life." Life is not a commodity. Life is a person— as Jesus said, "I am the way, the truth, and the life" (John 14:6). All three of these elements come together here at the end of John's epistle. Jesus is the way to the Father because he is the truth—the true One, the true God; and he gives eternal life to all who take this way!

Only God's life can truly be called "life" because all else that is called life eventually dies. God's life is eternal. The Greek New Testament has a special word for this eternal life; it is *zōē* [TG2222, ZG2437]. The word *zōē* in classical Greek was used for life in general. There are a few examples of this meaning in the New Testament (Acts 17:25; Jas 4:14; Rev 16:3), but in all other instances in the New Testament the word was used to designate the divine, eternal life—the life of God (Eph 4:18). The word *zōē* is used to describe the eternal life, the divine life—present in Jesus and available as a gift to all who believe in Jesus as the Son of God. To receive *zōē* is to have God's life now and to be guaranteed eternal life in the future. All those who have received this life are true members of God's family.

In closing, John tells his readers to keep themselves from idols (5:21, NLT mg). Though this ending is abrupt and lacks the kind of doxologies or conclusions found in other New Testament letters (see note on 5:21 and "Literary Style" in the

Introduction), it is a fitting conclusion. Given the context of this epistle, "idols" is probably a general reference to false teachings that present false images of Jesus Christ, who is "the only true God, and he is eternal life" (5:20). To replace Jesus with heresy is idolatry. Even today readers must take heed that they let nothing turn their faith from the Jesus of the apostles—the divine Messiah, both God and man.

NOTES

5:13 *I have written this to you who believe in the name of the Son of God, so that you may know you have eternal life.* This has excellent documentary support: ℵ * (A) B 0296. This is expanded in the TR (following P 𝔐) as follows: "and that you may continue to believe in the name of the Son of God" (NKJV; see also KJV). The expansion was intended to make this verse more closely follow John 20:31 (see exposition above). In its shorter form, this verse sufficiently concludes the previous section on eternal life and introduces the conclusion, which also pertains to eternal life (5:16, 20).

5:15 *And since we know he hears us when we make our requests, we also know that he will give us what we ask for.* We should not think that these requests are for our personal benefit. Prayer in line with God's will is prayer for the benefit of God's Kingdom, as the next verses (5:16-17) illustrate.

5:16 *sinning in a way that does not lead to death . . . a sin that leads to death.* What is the difference between the "sin that leads to death" and "the sin that does not lead to death"? Some commentators (Marshall 1978:274; Burge 1996:216) point out that these two kinds of sin are spoken of in the OT: (1) unconscious or accidental sins (Lev 4:2, 13, 22, 27; 5:15-18; Num 15:27-31); and (2) intentional sins, which could be punished by exile (Num 15:30-31) or death (Deut 17:12). But how this applies to Christians is not totally clear. (See exposition for further discussion.)

5:18 This verse appears in two ways in various translations because of a textual variant in the Greek mss: (1) Most modern versions (RSV, NRSV, NASB, NIV, NEB, NJB) read, "We know that any one born of God does not sin, but He who was born of God keeps *him,* and the evil one does not touch him." (This follows A* B it.) (2) The KJV and NKJV read, "We know that whoever is born of God does not sin; but he who has been born of God keeps *himself,* and the wicked one does not touch him." (This follows ℵ Aᶜ P 044 33 1739.) The difference between the two readings revolves around the pronouns "him" (*auton* [ᵀᴳ6, ᶻᴳ899]) and "himself" (*heauton* [ᵀᴳ1438, ᶻᴳ1571]). The difference in meanings also stems from the interpretation of the phrase "the one born of God" (*ho gennētheis* [ᵀᴳ1080, ᶻᴳ1164]), which could be a reference to Christ or to the Christian. The first reading affirms the interpretation that it is Christ; the second reading supports the interpretation that it is a Christian. The first reading indicates that the Son of God keeps the believer from sin. The second reading indicates that the believer, as a son of God, keeps himself from sin.

Many commentators (see Marshall 1978:252; Smalley 1984:293; Schnackenburg 1979:280; Metzger 1994:650) favor the first reading because (1) the first clause of this verse already mentions the believer who is born of God, (2) John consistently used the perfect tense to describe the believer who has become a son of God (2:29; 3:9; 4:7; 5:1, 4, 18a) whereas here the aorist is used (*ho gennētheis*), and (3) there is little or no security in the fact that the believer must keep himself. Rather, it is the One begotten of God, the Son of God, who keeps each believer from the evil one. This interpretation is made explicit in the NLT.

5:20 *we can know the true God.* This is based on the textual variant found in A Ψ 33 1739. The more likely reading, as found in ℵ^c B 81 syr^p cop^{bo}, is simply "We can know the true one."

we live in fellowship with the true God because we live in fellowship with his Son, Jesus Christ. To be in God is to be in God's Son; for when we are united to the Son, we are also united to the Father (cf. John 17:21-24).

Jesus Christ. He is the only true God. The word behind "he" is *houtos* [TG3778, ZG4047], meaning "this one" (the nearest one just mentioned); thus it refers to the person just named, "Jesus Christ." A large number of scholars are convinced that *houtos* refers to Jesus Christ and therefore think that John was unequivocally asserting that Jesus Christ is "the true God" (*ho alēthinos theos* [TG228/2316, ZG240/2536]). A full list with bibliography is supplied by Harris (1992:249). I also hold that John was saying that Jesus Christ is the true God. Jesus' deity is elsewhere affirmed in John's writings (John 1:1, 18; 8:58; 10:30; 20:28) as well as in other NT passages, such as Rom 9:5; Titus 2:13; 2 Pet 1:1. Harris (1992:250-252), however, thinks the wording here is saying that "God" (5:19) is the "true God" noted in 5:20. But what is the point of saying this? Of course God is the true God. John would not have needed to say this. Rather, he was affirming Jesus' deity, as he had earlier affirmed Jesus' humanity (4:1-6). This is the more natural reading of the Greek.

and he is eternal life. While the Father is the source of eternal life, Jesus Christ reveals that life and through his death makes that life available to the believers. He himself is the "eternal life" (John 14:6; cf. John 1:4).

5:21 *keep away from anything that might take God's place in your hearts.* Lit., "keep yourselves from idols" (cf. NLT mg). The thrust of the functionally equivalent translation is to help the modern reader understand that John was probably not talking about actual idols but about those things that rob Jesus of the worship due him as true God (5:20). It should also be noted that this ending is unlike all the other endings to NT epistles, which conclude either with a doxology or a personal greeting or both. The abruptness of the ending affirms the idea that 1 John was not ever written as a letter; rather, it was a kind of treatise or manifesto, like a pamphlet.

BIBLIOGRAPHY

See page 375, the bibliography for the Johannine epistles.

2 & 3 John

INTRODUCTION

The two shortest epistles in the New Testament, 2 and 3 John, are gems in their own right. Second John, a miniature version of 1 John, extols those who live in the truth and live in love, and warns against those who do not teach the apostolic truths about Jesus Christ—who, in some fashion, deny that he is the unique Son of the Father, the Son of God come in the flesh. Third John, giving us a window into the early church, presents us with two kinds of leaders: one who serves the Lord and others by living in the truth and practicing love, and another who refuses apostolic authority and loves himself more than the church.

AUTHOR

These two epistles were written by the same author, as is evident from their similarity of tone, style, and thematic development—all of which are also extremely similar to 1 John, which is undeniably similar to the fourth Gospel. The grammar, style, and vocabulary of 2 John compare very closely to 1 John. Five of the 13 verses of the second letter are almost identical with verses in 1 John (cf. 2 Jn 1:1 with 1 Jn 3:18; 2 Jn 1:2 with 1 Jn 2:4; 2 Jn 1:5 with 1 Jn 2:7; 5:3; 2 Jn 1:7 with 1 Jn 2:18; 4:2; 2 Jn 1:9 with 1 Jn 2:23-24). Third John has vocabulary and expressions that are distinctly similar, if not identical, to 2 John (cf. 3 Jn 1:4 with 2 Jn 1:4; 3 Jn 1:13-14 with 2 Jn 1:12), as well as to 1 John (cf. 3 Jn 1:11 with 1 Jn 3:6, 10). The style and voice are also markedly similar. Thus, we must conclude that the same writer who composed 2 John and 3 John also composed 1 John, the author of which was most likely John the apostle, the son of Zebedee (see "Author" in the Introduction to 1 John). In fact, it must be said that these two short letters would hardly have been included in the New Testament canon if their author was not the apostle John. Their authorship—by the beloved disciple—is what warranted their inclusion in the New Testament canon.

In both 2 John and 3 John, the writer calls himself an "elder" (2 Jn 1:1; 3 Jn 1:1). Quite literally, John was an old man at this point in his life. If he were 10 years (or so) younger than Jesus (who was born between 6 and 4 BC), then John would have been in his 80s (or thereabouts) when he wrote these two epistles (see below on date of writing).

DATE AND OCCASION OF WRITING

There is very little in the letters of 2 John or 3 John to point us to a date of writing. The similarities to 1 John strongly suggest a similar time period, around the late 80s or early 90s. The second epistle must have been written in the same time period as 1 John because it deals with the same issue—heresy regarding the human nature of Jesus Christ (2 Jn 1:7). It is a special warning for believers to not receive the traveling teachers who would be spreading the false teachings of the secessionists addressed in 1 John. The third epistle addresses related concerns: John cautioned Gaius about Diotrephes, who had evidently been affected by the secessionists to have a negative attitude about John and his coworkers.

The purpose of 2 John is manifold. In the first place, the recipient is urged to live in the truth and to continue practicing Christian love. The second and more compelling reason for the epistle is its warning against the deceivers who refused to acknowledge Jesus as the Christ and were actively recruiting others to join them. This same concern to prevent and correct false teaching prompted Paul to write Galatians (Gal 1:6), Colossians (Col 2:16-23), 2 Thessalonians (2 Thes 2:1-3), and 1 Timothy (1 Tim 4:1; 6:20-21). Other epistles were also written to deal with false teachers and their doctrines (cf. 2 Pet 2:1ff; Jude 1:3-4). John's first two epistles were written specifically as antidotes to the poisonous effects of Docetic Gnosticism, which was infecting many of the early churches. Third, the epistle was written to exhort the Christians to close their home meetings to false teachers (2 Jn 1:9-10).

The epistle of 3 John was written by John to commend Gaius and the other Christians in the same local church for living in the truth. He also commended Gaius for the hospitality he had given to those who were traveling "for the sake of the Name" (3 Jn 1:7, NIV). These traveling teachers had spoken well of Gaius's love for the church. In contrast to Gaius stood Diotrephes, whose love of power and authority motivated him not only to defy the authority of the elder John, but also to convince others to follow his defiance. He had refused to receive the coworkers sent by John. (Interestingly, Diotrephes was doing to John's emissaries the very thing John had told his churches to do to the false teachers in 2 John. He was treating John and his coworkers as false teachers.) Thus John indicated in this letter that he would come to the church and set things in order.

AUDIENCE

Second and Third John have been placed among the General Epistles (also known as the Catholic Epistles) by virtue of their association with 1 John. But they are not, by content, General Epistles. Second John was addressed to an individual or a specific local church, and Third John was addressed to a specific individual, Gaius.

Second John was written "to the chosen lady and to her children" (2 Jn 1:1). Some commentators think this refers to a specific woman and her actual, physical children (Smith 1979:162; Morris 1970:1271). Accordingly, some think that the Greek word for "lady" (*kuria* [^TG^2959, ^ZG^3257]) is a proper name, "Cyria"; this view was held by Athanasius (see note on 2 Jn 1:1). Clement of Alexandria in *Adumbrations* (see *Fragments of Clement of Alexandria* 1.4) said, "John's Second Epistle was written to a certain Babylonian lady named Electa," thus taking the word for "chosen" or "elect" as a proper name.

Most modern commentators think John was using this address as a surrogate for a particular local church, as perhaps Peter also did in 1 Peter 5:13 (cf. Smalley 1984:318; Marshall 1978:10; Burge 1996:232). They argue that the nature of the epistle points to a corporate personality, the local church (see comments on 2 Jn 1:5, 6, 8, 10, 12). As such, 2 John was probably sent to one of the churches in the Johannine community of churches, which was a cluster of churches in Asia Minor that were the recipients of John's apostolic ministry.

Another approach to identifying the addressee is to view this letter as being addressed to a specific woman *and* a local church that met in that woman's house. The New Testament gives us a picture of the early church wherein believers met in houses. This is the case in the book of Acts (cf. Acts 2:46; 5:42; 8:3; 12:5, 12), and it can be gathered from reading the New Testament epistles that there were similar situations elsewhere (cf. Rom 16:3-5, 14-15; 1 Cor 16:19-20; Col 4:15-16; Phlm 1:1-2). We know that some of these homes, where the church gathered, belonged to women—or at least were known by the name of the lady of the house. The church in Jerusalem gathered in the house of Mary (the mother of John Mark) to pray for Peter (Acts 12:5-12), and the natural conclusion is that the church habitually gathered there. The church in Corinth at one time assembled in the home of Priscilla and Aquila (Rom 16:3-5), and when Priscilla and Aquila lived in Ephesus, an assembly gathered in their home there (1 Cor 16:19-20). According to Colossians 4:15, the church in Laodicea assembled in the home of Nympha— indeed, Paul specifically calls it "the church that meets in her house." (For more discussion on house churches in the NT, see Comfort 1993:153-158). In light of this, the addressee in 2 John could very likely be a woman who housed an assembly of believers, who then are metaphorically and affectionately called "her children." This position is further reinforced by 2 John 1:10, where John makes a specific point of telling the woman and her children not to receive false teachers "into the house" (*eis oikian* [^TG^1519/3614, ^ZH^1650/3864]). In historical context, this would refer to the house wherein the believers assembled.

Third John was written to Gaius. Although the New Testament mentions several men with the name Gaius (Acts 19:29; 20:4ff; Rom 16:23; 1 Cor 1:14), it would be difficult to say that any one of these was the same as the Gaius in 3 John, especially since Gaius was a popular name in the first century. At any rate, Gaius was commended for his Christian life and hospitality and so was Demetrius (3 Jn 1:12), both of whom stand in sharp contrast to Diotrephes, who is literally called "the one loving to be first" (3 Jn 1:9).

Even though 2 John and 3 John were addressed to particular individuals or churches, John had his entire community of churches in mind. These churches had been infected by the false teachings of the Gnostics, particularly those who were propagating a heretical view about the nature of Jesus Christ, such as Cerinthus (see "Date and Occasion of Writing" and "Major Themes," both in the Introduction to 1 John). John sent out various coworkers to promote the apostolic truths and to reunite the community in Christian love. Diotrephes rejected these coworkers and was even cutting off those in his church who were receiving them. Though it is not stated explicitly, one can surmise that he was sympathetic to the secessionists and thereby was causing divisions among the Johannine community. Third John was written to announce John's intentions to go directly to that church and deal with this situation head on.

John's statement in 3 John 1:9, "I wrote to the church about this," indicates that 3 John builds upon a previous correspondence (likely 1 John). As such, both 1 John and 3 John were written to deal with the issue of teachers and leaders who opposed John and the apostolic teaching; Diotrephes was one of those leaders.

CANONICITY AND TEXTUAL HISTORY

In the early centuries of the church, 2 John and 3 John were not as well known as 1 John. Each epistle, written on only one sheet of papyrus, was a personal letter. As such, these writings would not have been circulated among the churches like 1 John was. Nonetheless, 2 and 3 John were recognized as John's epistles as early as the second century. Irenaeus quoted 2 John 1:7, 10-11 in his works (*Heresies* 1.16.3; 3.16.8), and Dionysius of Alexandria observed that John never named himself in his epistles, "not even in the second and third epistles, although they are short epistles, but simply calls himself the presbyter" (Eusebius *History* 7.25.11). Although their brevity and the personal nature of their contents caused 2 and 3 John to be less widely read and less likely to be quoted by the early church fathers, their personal nature also makes them less likely to be spurious, for they would serve no purpose as forgeries.

Eusebius (*History* 3.24.17) reckoned both epistles among the *Antilegomena* or controverted Scriptures, as distinguished from the *Homologoumena* or universally acknowledged Scriptures. Eusebius's personal opinion, however, was that the two short epistles were genuine. In *Demonstration of the Gospel* 3.5, Eusebius said that in John's "epistles" he does not mention his own name, nor call himself an apostle or evangelist, but an "elder" (2 Jn 1:1; 3 Jn 1:1). Origen (according to Eusebius's *History* 6.25.10) mentioned the second and third epistles, but added, "Not all admit their genuineness"—implying that most authorities did take them as genuine. These two epistles were eventually recognized as canonical soon after the Council of Nicea (AD 325). Thus Cyril of Jerusalem (AD 349) enumerated fourteen epistles of Paul, and seven Catholic (or General) Epistles, including 2 and 3 John. So did Gregory of Nazianzus in AD 389, the Council of Hippo (AD 393), and the Council of Carthage (AD 394).

The most reliable and earliest manuscript for 2 John and 3 John is Codex Vaticanus (B), followed by Codex Sinaiticus (ℵ), 𝔓74, and 1739. Codex Alexandrinus (A) tends to be expansive and erratic in these epistles. The earliest extant copy of 2 John is the uncial manuscript 0232, a miniature codex dated to the early fourth century. Its testimony is also reliable.

LITERARY STYLE

Of all the New Testament writings, these are the two shortest letters. We know that the author himself wrote these letters with "pen and ink" on papyrus (2 Jn 1:12; 3 Jn 1:13), as opposed to dictating the letters to an amanuensis. Both of these letters would have taken no more than one sheet of papyrus (averaging about 6" x 8"), written on both sides. Furthermore, these two letters have a format that is typical of letters written during the Hellenistic period. This is especially true of 3 John. It begins with an identification of the writer (the elder), then of the recipient (Gaius), followed by a statement of well-wishing: "I hope all is well with you and that you are as healthy in body as you are strong in spirit" (3 Jn 1:2). Examples of this abound in the extant papyri. For example, one second-century papyrus reads as follows:

> Antonius Maximus to Sabina his sister, many greetings. Before all things I pray that you are in health, for I myself also am in health . . . When I knew that you fared well, I rejoiced greatly. And I at every occasion delay not to write to you concerning the health of me and mine. Salute Maximus much, and Copres my lord. There salute my life's partner, Aufidia, and Maximus my son. (Deissmann 1978:1)

Other examples of ancient letters are provided in the commentary on 3 John 1:1-2.

In both 2 John and 3 John, John got to his point quickly and then concluded that he would rather communicate face-to-face than by letter, so he cut his writing short. Their vocabulary, syntax, and style completely accord with that found in 1 John.

MAJOR THEMES

John's second epistle can be described as a miniature version of 1 John. The same major themes that one finds in 1 John appear in 2 John. In both epistles John wants his readers to (1) live in the truth, (2) love one another, (3) be on guard against false teachers, and (4) adhere to the apostolic teachings—especially about Jesus, God's Son come in the flesh—in the face of Gnostic infiltration into the church. Marshall (1978:3) tells us that 2 John "presents us with a cameo of John's chief concerns; on one hand, the importance of adherence to the truth, especially believing the truth about Jesus as the Son of God, and of living in Christian love, and, on the other hand, the dangerous threat posed by heresy. Truth and love constitute the two main positive features of John's Christianity."

Third John focuses on a problem addressed in 1 John—namely, spiritual elitism bucking against apostolic authority. A certain man named Diotrephes (who probably sympathized with the false teachers who had left the church) was undermining the authority of the apostle John and was trying to frustrate his leadership by ousting all who were sent to the church by John and by excommunicating those in the church who did receive John's emissaries. So John wrote this letter to Gaius, who was still loyal to John, to encourage him to receive the teachers and workers sent by John, for they were, in fact, messengers of Christ.

THEOLOGICAL CONCERNS

The same theological motifs appear in 2 John that are in 1 John. In both epistles, heresies are denounced and the church is warned not to support the messengers of the heresy. Third John provides a window into first-century church leadership problems. The concerns it addresses have more to do with the practical administration of the church than with theological doctrines, but it nonetheless affirms the theology of 1 and 2 John—namely, that one cannot claim to know God and yet reject the people of God.

John's letters "contain theological, ethical, and practical truths which are fundamental to the Christian position in every age: that Jesus is one with God as well as one with us; that love and righteousness are indispensable to the believer who seeks as a child of God to walk in the light; and that unity, however flexible, is a demand laid upon the whole Church at all times" (Smalley 1984:xxxiv).

THEMATIC OUTLINE OF 2 JOHN

   I. Greetings (1:1-3)

   II. Live in the Truth (1:4-11)

   III. John's Final Words (1:12-13)

THEMATIC OUTLINE OF 3 JOHN (EXPOSITION BEGINS ON P. 365)

   I. Greetings (1:1-2)

   II. Caring for the Lord's Workers (1:3-12)

   III. John's Final Words (1:13-15)

Greetings

2 JOHN 1:1-3

EXPOSITION

The opening verses display the typical format used for letters in the Hellenistic period: identification of the writer, identification of the recipients, and a greeting and blessing. (The exposition of 3 John 1:1-2 gives two other examples of letters from the Hellenistic period.)

In this informal letter, John did not stand on his authority as an apostle, but instead identified himself as "the elder," one who watched over the believers with loving concern for their spiritual well-being. The word "elder" (*presbuteros* [TG4245A, ZG4565]) was also a reference to John's age; he must have been an old man at the time he wrote this epistle (perhaps in his 80s). As discussed in the notes following, the identification of the recipients as "the chosen lady and . . . her children" probably refers to a specific Christian woman in whose home a church assembled. The other two options are: (1) a specific woman and her actual children, or (2) a local church (see notes on vv. 6, 12, and 13). This chosen lady and her children were loved by all the believers who had come to know the truth. The "truth" John speaks of is the sum total of orthodox teachings concerning Jesus Christ, the Son of God, as defined by the apostles. All who have embraced the truth concerning Jesus' true deity and humanity are true members of the household of God.

Secular writers of the time often greeted their recipients with words of blessing such as these: "May good things be yours from the gods"; "May you have good health and absence of conflict." Contrast that with the richness of this greeting and blessing: "May you have grace, mercy, and peace from God the Father and from Jesus Christ, the Son of the Father." The apostle Paul often used "grace" and "peace" in his opening greetings; John also adds "mercy" here.

Though John does not speak of grace and peace as frequently as Paul does, he does mention them in his Gospel. The Greek text of John 1:16 indicates that grace is given to the believer as a continual supply—just when one measure of grace is used up, another replaces it. This grace keeps on giving, like a spring-fed well that never runs dry. Christ's dispensation of grace to every believer can never be exhausted because he is full of grace, which means he is full of God's kindness extended to us. God's mercy is seen in forgiving us and freeing us from sin, and peace is the result, providing cessation of turmoil and anxiety. These are gifts from God the Father and from the Father's Son, Jesus Christ. These blessings are transmitted to us from the Father through the Son. Some may claim to receive peace directly from God, apart from Jesus Christ, but no one can experience the Father apart from the Son. This is a consistent theme in John's Gospel (John 8:18; 14:6-10; 17:3) and John's epistles (see notes on 1:7-9).

"Truth" and "love" are appended to this blessing, as if they were afterthoughts, but this is not really the case because these words actually serve to introduce the next verses, where John emphasizes that it is necessary for all God's children to know the truth and live it out in their lives by practicing brotherly love.

NOTES

1:1 *John, the elder.* The Greek text does not include the word "John" (cf. NLT mg); it was added for clarification. In *Demonstration of the Gospel* 3.5, Eusebius said that in John's epistles, John did not mention his own name, nor call himself an apostle or evangelist, but an "elder" (2 Jn 1:1; 3 Jn 1:1). The title "elder" probably points to John's position at that time; he was the oldest living apostle and chief leader among the churches in the Roman province of Asia Minor. For further discussion concerning the title "elder," see "Author" in the Introduction to 1 John and in the Introduction to 2 and 3 John.

chosen lady. In ancient Greek, all words were written entirely in capital letters; thus one cannot tell from the ancient page whether the phrase *eklectē kuria* ("chosen lady") referred to a specific woman—either "Eclecta, a woman" or "elect Kyria"—or whether it denotes simply "an elect lady" or "chosen lady." Clement of Alexandria thought her name was "Electa" (*Adumbrations* 4 [i.e., *Fragments* 1.4]). Athanasius thought her name was the elect "Kyria." One modern English version (TLB) follows this, naming her "Cyria." It is likely that *kuria* [TG2959, ZG3257] should be understood as "lady" inasmuch as this was a common term used in the papyri of that time period when a writer was addressing a woman (cf. examples in Hunt and Edgar 1959:302-303).

Most commentators do not identify the recipient of the letter as an individual because the epistle does not speak of the woman with any particular details (in contrast to 3 John which speaks specifically of Gaius, Diotrephes, and Demetrius). Rather, they see this as a symbolic way of speaking about a local church (cf. Marshall 1978:60; Schnackenburg 1979:306-307). This interpretation is reinforced by John's conclusion of the letter with the salutation, "Greetings from the children of your sister, chosen by God" (1:13). However, it is possible that the "elect lady" receiving the letter could be a reference to a particular woman in whose home a local church met, and the elect sister sending greetings also to a particular woman in whose home a local church met (see "Audience" in the Introduction).

her children. If the recipient was a woman, these would have been her actual children; if the recipient was a local church, these would have been the members of the church. This understanding is reflected in the NLT mg: "Or *the church God has chosen and its members*." But it seems more plausible to consider that this "lady" was an actual woman and that her "children" were those who met in her home.

1:2 *the truth lives in us.* This language personifies "truth." Since Jesus Christ is the full expression and embodiment of truth (John 14:6; Eph 4:21), truth dwells in us because Christ dwells in us as the Spirit of truth (John 16:13). The word translated "lives" is *menousan* [^{TG}3306, ^{ZG}3531], which can also be translated "abiding" or "remaining"—a primary emphasis in this epistle is that believers should remain in the truth and not stray from it.

1:3 *Grace, mercy, and peace.* This is a unique constellation of blessings, found only here in the NT. The only other time John mentions "grace" is in John 1:16-17, which says "grace . . . came through Jesus Christ," so that "from his fullness we have all received, grace upon grace" (NRSV). John nowhere else mentions "mercy." "Peace" is found a few times in John's Gospel; each time Jesus appeared to the disciples after his resurrection, he blessed them with "peace" (John 20:19, 26).

Jesus Christ. Divine titles in the text of the NT were often subjected to scribal expansion. In this case, "Jesus Christ" (found in A B 048 0232 81 1739) was expanded to "Lord Jesus Christ" in Codex Sinaiticus and the majority of late mss. Then it was popularized by its inclusion in the TR and KJV.

the Son of the Father. This reading is based on the strong textual support of ℵ A B 048 0232 81 1739. The uniqueness of this expression (it occurs only here in the NT) prompted scribes to shorten it to "the Son" (found in a few late minuscules) or change it to "the Son of God" (1881 and some Vulgate mss). But the title "the Son of the Father" functions to show the unique relationship between the Son and the Father.

in truth and love. John speaks more directly about truth in 1:4 and about love in 1:5.

Live in the Truth

2 JOHN 1:4-11

EXPOSITION

By the time we have read the first four verses of this epistle, we should have noticed that the word "truth" is used five times: "whom I love in the truth," "everyone else who knows the truth" (1:1), "because the truth lives in us" (1:2), "in truth and love" (1:3), and "living according to the truth" (1:4). The threat of gnosticism infiltrating the church prompted John to counter their falsehoods with strong admonitions to the believers about knowing the truth concerning Jesus Christ and living in it.

Since there were many false teachings about Jesus Christ in the days of the early church, the apostles had to describe what teachings about Jesus were true and what teachings were false. The true teachings could be labeled as orthodox and apostolic; the false teachings were heretical. Those believers who adhered to the apostolic teachings—both in doctrine and in practice—were those who were living in the truth.

One of the prominent signs of living in the truth is that a believer loves the other members of God's family. The one command "to love one another" sums up all of God's commands. John repeatedly made the same proclamation in his first epistle (see comments on 1 Jn 3:11, 16-19). Since love is volitional, we can be *commanded* to love fellow believers. We don't have to *feel* like we love others; we need to *decide* to love others. This choice strengthens the unity of the church.

The believers needed to be encouraged to live in the truth because many false teachings were infiltrating the church. In John's day, the worst infection was coming from a specific group of Gnostics known as Docetists. These people denied Jesus Christ's real humanity; they promoted the falsehood that Christ only *seemed* to have a human body (see "Christological Orthodoxy versus Heresy" in the Introduction to 1 John). To deny Jesus' true humanity is to eradicate the fact that he actually shed real blood on the cross for the sins of the world. Thus denial of Jesus Christ's humanity is denial of his redemption.

One such false teacher in John's day was Cerinthus (who died c. 100). Probably born in Egypt and reared as a Jew, Cerinthus was leader of a group of

Christians that had Gnostic tendencies. He taught that Jesus was an ordinary man upon whom "the Christ" descended at his baptism. This divine power revealed the transcendent and unknown God. This "Christ" then abandoned Jesus before his crucifixion (cf. Hicks and Winter 1992:148).

False teachers such as Cerinthus proudly claimed to be offering "advanced" teaching—teaching that went beyond what Jesus and the apostles had taught. John drew a line in the sand, so to speak: Those who go beyond the apostolic teachings concerning Christ are deceivers and antichrists; those who stay with the apostles remain in the truth. This is why John could say, "Anyone who remains in the teaching of Christ has a relationship with both the Father and the Son" (1:9). The "teaching of Christ" is the true apostolic teaching concerning Christ, which was based on the teachings the apostles received from Christ. To remain in this teaching is to remain in the Son and the Father (see comments on 1 Jn 2:22-23). To depart from this teaching is a sign of apostasy, but it is more subtle than apostasy because these people claim to see more than what has been revealed in the New Testament. They claim to have special knowledge about spiritual things. The apostolic teachings concerning the person of Jesus Christ, however, are clear and simple: Jesus is God come in the flesh; he is God Incarnate, the God-man. A denial of either his full humanity or his full divinity is heresy.

John told his readers to be on guard against the deceivers. This was nothing new. Christ had previously warned his disciples, "Don't let anyone fool you. For many will come claiming to be the Messiah, and will lead many astray . . . so that if it were possible, even God's chosen ones would be deceived" (Matt. 24:4-5, 24, TLB). Paul had also previously warned the believers at Colosse (a church in the region where John ministered in his later days) about gnostic heresies:

> Don't let anyone capture you with empty philosophies and high-sounding nonsense that come from human thinking and from the spiritual powers of this world, rather than from Christ. For in Christ lives all the fullness of God in a human body. So you also are complete through your union with Christ, who is the head over every ruler and authority. (Col 2:8-10)

Paul was giving the same warnings that John later gave: Beware of anyone who denies the full deity or full humanity of Christ. We are complete in Christ Jesus; we need nothing beyond him. To be taken from Christ is to be robbed of our reward. It also robs the apostles of their reward (1:8), for they were the ones who brought the precious truths concerning Christ to the believers in the first place.

In John's day, the false teachers would infiltrate the church by entering into home meetings and spreading their deceptive teachings. In the early days of the church, the believers met in homes (cf. Rom 16:5; Col 4:15). These meetings could be corrupted and become spiritually detrimental due to the presence of false teachers and false prophets (cf. 2 Pet 2:1, 13; Jude 1:12). The only way to deal with such people was to not accept them into the fellowship (1:10). By helping them in any kind of way (such as providing housing or even a meal), the early Christians would have been promoting their cause. But John said it was worse than that—they would have actually been partners with them in their evil deeds (1:11). John practiced what he preached: Polycarp, a disciple of John, said that John once left a bathhouse when he heard that the heretic Cerinthus was inside, for fear the house would fall in ruins since "the enemy of truth" was there (Irenaeus *Heresies* 3.3.4).

In our own day, there are many aberrant and heretical groups that have deviated from basic Christianity. Most of these, in some fashion or another, have heretical and/or extremely unorthodox views about the person of Jesus Christ. Of course, these views will often be presented as "new light" or "special revelation." And those who hold these views will look down on other Christians for not being as "enlightened" as they are. We must not be deceived by such special "light" or special insights; rather, we must check to see if everything they say about Jesus Christ accords with Scripture. If it goes beyond what the apostles wrote, then we must judge it to be heretical. Our course of action is to refuse to participate in their movement so as not to promote error and falsehood.

NOTES

1:4 *How happy I was to meet some of your children and find them living according to the truth.* Though we do not know the individuals John was referring to, he was probably speaking of believers he met at some place other than the local church itself—or other than the home of the elect lady. His joy at meeting them and then discovering that they were living in the truth prompted him to write this epistle. In identifying only "some" of the children, he was not necessarily saying that others were not living in the truth. Rather, he was probably speaking only of those he met.

just as the Father commanded. The commandment to live in the truth came from the Father through the Son to the disciples (cf. John 15:15), who passed it on to the believers (cf. 1 Jn 3:23).

1:5 *I am writing to remind you.* This expression implies some degree of authority and shows John's deep concern. The pronoun "you" is singular here, which could designate a particular woman or refer to an individual church as a whole (see note on 1:1).

that we should love one another. This was Jesus' command to the apostles (John 13:34; 15:12), which John passed on to the believers (cf. 1 Jn 3:11-18). For the secessionists to reject the apostolic truths was tantamount to hating those who accepted these truths. By contrast, loving one another is a sign of accepting the truth and living by it.

This is not a new commandment, but one we have had from the beginning. In light of what John says in the next verse, the expression "we have had from the beginning" primarily refers to the time the apostles first heard Jesus give them this commandment of love (see John 13:34; 1 Jn 2:7).

1:6 *Love means doing what God has commanded us, and he has commanded us to love one another.* This virtually repeats what Jesus told his disciples (John 15:9). Those who really love God do what he says, and his command is that we love one another.

just as you heard. The Greek expression translated "you heard" is grammatically plural (*ēkousate* [TG191, ZG201]), indicating that John was speaking to several individuals. It should also be noted that the writer places himself among those who first proclaimed the gospel. Second-generation Christians (i.e., those not among Jesus' eyewitnesses), such as Luke and the writer of Hebrews, spoke of themselves as having heard the gospel from those who had heard and seen Jesus directly (cf. Luke 1:1-4; Heb 2:3).

from the beginning. Christians had been taught this commandment of love from the time they first heard the gospel preached by the apostles (cf. 1 Jn 2:7; 3:11 and notes).

1:7 *many deceivers have gone out into the world.* Jesus predicted that many false Christs would come (Matt 24:5). Some historically known deceivers were Theudas (Acts 5:36), Judas the Galilean (Acts 5:37), and one called "the Egyptian" (Acts 21:38). Another well-known Jewish messianic pretender was Bar Kochba, who led a second Jewish revolt against Rome, which ended in AD 135 with the banishing of all Jews from Jerusalem (Josephus *Antiquities* 20.97-99, 160-172, 188). Other unnamed false teachers are alluded to in 1 Timothy 4:1; 2 Timothy 3:8-9; 2 Peter 2:1; Jude 1:3-4. We do not know if these men were propagating teachings that denied Jesus Christ's true humanity. One man who did this was Cerinthus (see exposition above).

They deny that Jesus Christ came in a real body. John spoke of the same heresy in his first epistle (see comments on 1 Jn 4:2-3).

Such a person is a deceiver and an antichrist. These false teachers foreshadow the final personal Antichrist, who will embody all the evil of earlier anti-Christian systems and teachers (see comments on 1 Jn 2:18ff; 4:3).

1:8 There are three textual variants on this verse: (1) "Watch out that you do not lose the prize that we [the apostles] worked for, but that you receive a full reward" (B syr^hmg); (2) "Watch out that you do not lose the prize that you worked for, but that you receive a full reward" (ℵ A 044 0232 33 1739 it syr); (3) "Watch out that we do not lose the prize that we worked for, but that we receive a full prize" (𝔐; so also TR).

The shift from "you" (in the first clause) to "we" (in the next clause) is more likely due to the author than to copyists because scribes would have wanted to simplify matters, not complicate them. Thus the first reading is most likely original. As such, John was speaking of the labor that he, the apostles, and any other coworkers had done for the benefit of the believers. Since the apostles' work was to raise up churches, the loss of a church to heresy was a loss of the apostles' work. These laborers (the "we") proclaimed the truth, defined the truth, and defended the truth against heresy—all so that the church could get off to a good start and be built up. The believers, in turn, were admonished to exercise care in protecting that work from the destructive teachings of deceivers (1:7). John feared that the apostatized deceivers would disrupt the community of faithful believers.

Several modern versions have adopted the second reading (or at least noted it—so NLT mg). The point of this reading is that it admonishes the believers to hold fast to the truths they know to be real and effective in their spiritual lives and not to give in to any kind of deception that would rob them of their reward. The third reading, found in the TR, is the result of a scribal adjustment.

1:9 Anyone who wanders away from this teaching. Lit., "Everyone going beyond and not remaining in the teaching of Christ." This is the reading in the four earliest mss of 2 John (‫א‬ A B 0232). Later mss replace the participle *proagōn* [TG4254, ZG4575] ("going before" or "going beyond") with *parabainōn* [TG35, ZG4124] ("trespassing" or "transgressing"). This reading was adopted by the TR and so the KJV and NKJV. The word *proagōn* (NLT, "wanders away") literally means "leading forward"—hence, "to go before" or "to run ahead." This may be a sarcastic remark about the way in which the false teachers proudly claimed to be offering advanced teaching—so advanced that they went beyond the boundaries of true Christian belief.

1:10 don't invite that person into your home. This is very likely a reference to a house meeting of the church. Several such home meetings are mentioned in the NT. The church in Jerusalem must have had several groups at separate home meetings (cf. Acts 2:46; 5:42; 8:3; 12:5, 12), as did the church in Rome (cf. Rom 16:3-5, 14-15). A small local church may have had only one home gathering—as was probably the case with the church at Colosse (cf. Phlm 1:2). As mentioned in the Introduction, the house church to whom John was writing this epistle could have been one and the same as the one in Laodicea. (For a fuller discussion on house churches, see "Audience" in the Introduction; Comfort 1993:153-158.)

John's Final Words

2 JOHN 1:12-13

EXPOSITION

This letter closes almost as quickly as it began. John's desire to speak with the believers—rather than write more—accounts for the brevity of the entire letter. He concluded the letter with a promise of further communication in person; thus he and his recipients would complete each other's joy. John's love for the believers was not satisfied merely by writing a letter; he still longed (even in his advanced age) to visit them personally and discuss the truths of the gospel more fully.

As we all know, it is much better to be together in person with those we love than to only correspond by mail. Unfortunately for us, we don't get to read in this epistle as much as we might like, but there is enough here to give us a window into some important matters in the early church. By reading this short letter, we realize that the apostles were fighting for the basic truths concerning the person of Jesus Christ and that they were doing this on a house-by-house basis. Heretics and false teachers were prevalent and infectious. The only antidote was the apostles' living word. In our times, the antidote is the written word of the apostles. We should be thankful that we have their writings, even this one, though it is so short. From a theological perspective, 2 John is a condensed version of 1 John. To repeat what was said in the Introduction, 2 John is 1 John in a nutshell. In both epistles John calls his readers to (1) live in the truth, (2) love one another, (3) be on guard against false teachers, and (4) adhere to the apostolic teachings—especially about Jesus, God's Son come in the flesh—in the face of Gnostic infiltration into the church.

NOTES

1:12 *I have much more to say to you.* The word for "you" is plural in Greek, indicating a plural recipient—either a family of believers or the members of a particular local church.

but I don't want to do it with paper and ink. Lit., "not with a sheet of papyrus and ink." The modern idiom would be "sheet of paper" (BDAG 1081). This sheet (*chartēs* [TG5489, ZG5925]) would not have been paper, but a sheet of papyrus, onto which this entire short epistle could have been written (front and back).

The term was frequently used in Hellenistic times (cf. MM 685). For a similar expression, see 3 John 1:13.

talk with you face to face. Our English idiom "to speak face to face" parallels the Greek idiom here: "to speak mouth to mouth."

Then our joy will be complete. John made the same statement in his first epistle (1 Jn 1:4). John's joy was fulfilled by the fellowship he had with other believers.

1:13 Greetings from the children of your sister, chosen by God. Since the sister was not named, John was probably referring to the sister church where he was staying. This is why the NLT mg reads, "Or *from the members of your sister church*." This sort of reading also shows up in some mss of the Vulgate and in codex 307. A parallel greeting is found at the end of 1 Peter, where the apostle says, "She who is in Babylon, chosen together with you, sends you her greetings" (1 Pet 5:13, NIV). Convinced that this was speaking of a sister church, the translators of the TEV translated the clause, "Your sister church in Babylon, also chosen by God, sends you greetings."

The TR (followed by the KJV and NKJV) appends an "amen" to the end of the epistle, but this is completely out of character for this kind of personal letter.

Greetings

EXPOSITION

Of all the New Testament letters, this one has a format that is most typical of letters written during the Hellenistic age (325 BC–AD 325). The format for personal letters remained fairly constant for hundreds of years. Here is a letter dated 258/257 BC which came from a mummy's cartonnage (the plastered layers of linen or papyrus covering the body):

> Philotas to Epistratos, greeting. You do well if you are in health; we also are in health; Pleistarchos also is well and was gladly received by the king. You would please us if you take care of your health. Also remember us, just as we also remember you always. This will please us greatly. (Papyrus BGU XIV 2417)

Another papyrus manuscript (from the second century AD) demonstrates the continuation of the same style:

> Apollinarius to Taesis, his mother and lady, many greetings. Before all I pray for your health. I myself am well and make supplication for you before the gods of this place. (Hunt and Edgar 1959:302-303)

The opening of John's letter hardly differs from these in form. The writer is first identified; then the recipient. What usually follows is a "well-wishing" concerning one's health, which is usually followed by the writer asking the recipient to increase their mutual joy or pleasure in some way or another.

The writer of 3 John did not name himself; he simply identified himself as "the elder," just as he did in 2 John. The term "elder" (*presbuteros* [^{TG}4245A, ^{ZG}4565]) connotes that the writer was one who watched over the spiritual well-being of the believers. The word "elder" is also a reference to John's age; he must have been an old man at the time he wrote this letter (see "Author" in the Introduction). The recipient of the letter, Gaius, was probably an elder in a local church, because he was in the position of receiving the traveling teachers or coworkers (see 1:5 and comments). Three times in the first two verses John speaks of Gaius in very loving terms. He was loved by the congregation, loved by other believers, and loved by John.

John's personal greeting to Gaius indicates that they must have had a close relationship. John cared about Gaius's physical health and total well-being (1:2) and wished him well in regard to both. This is a good way for Christians to express their concern for each other. We should not care just for each other's souls but for each other's bodies, as well. This is linked with the principle of incarnation—God taking on a human body—which is a major theme in all of John's epistles. Our attitude toward the physical must reflect our relationship to the spiritual (1 Jn 3:14-18). We should not neglect the body under the pretense that we care only for that which is immaterial.

NOTES

1:1 *John, the elder.* The Greek text does not include the word "John" (see NLT mg). It was added for clarification. In *Demonstration of the Gospel* 3.5, Eusebius writes that John, in his epistles, does not mention his own name, nor call himself an apostle or evangelist, but an "elder" (2 Jn 1:1). The title "elder" probably points to John's position at that time; he was the oldest living apostle and chief leader among the churches in the Roman province of Asia Minor. For further discussion concerning the title "elder," see "Author" in the Introduction to 1 John and in the Introduction to 2 and 3 John.

Gaius. Several people with the name Gaius are mentioned in the NT: (1) a Macedonian traveling companion of Paul (Acts 19:29); (2) a native of Derbe in Lycaonia, who traveled with Paul from Ephesus to Macedonia (Acts 20:4); and (3) a prominent believer who hosted Paul and the whole church in Corinth (Rom 16:23; 1 Cor 1:14). The Gaius in 3 John was probably a different person than these three inasmuch as "Gaius" was a common name in those days.

1:2 *Dear friend, I hope all is well with you and that you are as healthy in body as you are strong in spirit.* The first part of this statement is a typical "well-wishing" found at the beginning of many letters written in the Hellenistic era. The second part, which literally reads, "as it is with your soul," is also found in many Hellenistic letters. The NLT rendering is a "Christianization" of it.

Caring for the Lord's Workers

3 JOHN 1:3-12

EXPOSITION

The main body of the letter has three purposes: (1) The first paragraph (1:3-4) commends Gaius and the other Christians meeting with him for living in the truth. (2) The second paragraph (1:5-8) commends Gaius for his hospitality given to those who were traveling "on behalf of the Name" (1:7, NLT mg). These traveling teachers had spoken well of Gaius's love for the church. (3) The third paragraph (1:9-12) condemns the deeds of Diotrephes. His love of power and authority led him to defy the authority of John, the elder, and he had even refused to receive the coworkers sent by John. It is quite likely that Demetrius was one of the coworkers sent by John because John commends him to Gaius. (He also may have been the carrier of this letter, 3 John.) After Gaius received him and gave him hospitality, Demetrius (representing John) could make a significant impact on the church by bringing apostolic truth to the members.

This short letter gives us a window into some interesting and significant features of the early church. What we can gather is that there were several traveling Christian workers going from church to church, teaching the apostolic truths of the gospel. Since these workers would not accept any support from the Gentiles (i.e., non-Christians), they needed to be helped financially by the churches. The coworkers' attitude about not receiving monetary help from unbelievers could have been motivated by Jesus' statement to his disciples: "Give as freely as you have received!" (Matt 10:8). The same principle is stated in the *Didache 11,* which instructs traveling preachers not to take anything but food from their hosts. If they asked for money they were considered to be false prophets. By way of example, Paul did not want to take money from those to whom he preached the gospel (1 Cor 9:11ff; 1 Thes 2:9). Because the pure and true Christian workers did not get money from unbelievers, John was calling upon the believers to care for them financially.

In this epistle specifically, it seems that the coworkers were part of John's community and therefore had been sent out by John. Their task was to carry his message to the churches in the Roman province of Asia. To receive them would be to complete the link between John and the churches, and thereby all would become co-laborers in advancing the cause of truth (and halting the spread of heresy). To reject these traveling teachers would be to reject John and the truth. Thus Diotrephes was not merely guilty of refusing to give hospitality to traveling teachers; he was guilty of separating himself (and members of his local church) from the apostle John.

It is quite possible that John had Diotrephes in mind when he was writing 1 John. Immediately after John said, "I wrote to the church about this" (v. 9; a possible reference to 1 John), he added, "but Diotrephes, who loves to be the leader, refuses to have anything to do with us" (3 Jn 1:9). In 1 John, the apostle urged the believers to continue in their fellowship with the apostles as a means to having true fellowship with God. These urgings may have been prompted by Diotrephes' attempts to keep the members of his church away from John and his coworkers. In 1 John, the apostle also condemned those who claimed to have fellowship with God while rejecting full fellowship with all the members of God's family. Diotrephes was thereby exposed. One cannot claim to love God while rejecting (the true meaning behind "hating") other members of God's family.

In one particular local church, Gaius had promoted church unity and solidarity with the apostle John by receiving the coworkers he sent. By contrast, Diotrephes was destroying the unity by rejecting those sent by John. As such, Diotrephes is a clear example of one who may have claimed to be spiritual but really was not because he did not love the brothers and because he rejected those who truly knew Jesus Christ. The lesson for us is that we cannot claim to love God if we don't love the church of God, the members of the Father's family.

Gaius stood in stark contrast to Diotrephes. He welcomed the brothers sent by John, and thereby promoted the cause of Christ and the propagation of the truth. Demetrius, one of John's coworkers and probably the carrier of the third epistle, also stood in contrast to Diotrephes because Demetrius had a good reputation among all the believers.

The situation described in 3 John has much to teach us about church leadership. It helps us to distinguish authoritarian leadership from the kind of leadership that arises from a spirit of servanthood. From the time of the apostles, the Christian church has always been served by leaders, however varied in status, title, or function. At the very onset of Christian gatherings, the believing community of the first century acknowledged some individuals as leaders. Sometimes these leaders emerged on the basis of their charisma; sometimes they were appointed by the apostles; and in some cases, they were elected by the church community. They certainly were not "clergy" in the modern sense. They were not rulers "over" the church, nor in charge of the church. Most often, they were gifted by the Holy Spirit to teach and edify the believers.

In 3 John we have a powerful example that juxtaposes two styles of church leadership: authoritarian self-promotion (Diotrephes) versus servanthood (Gaius). The first runs absolutely counter to the teaching of Christ and the apostles, while the second sets a pattern for all to emulate. An authoritarian leader exercises an undue influence on the decisions and lifestyle of other believers. This leads to manipulation and the dictating of a behavioral pattern that usurps the authority of the head of the church, Jesus Christ. A natural by-product of such dominance is that the word of the leader becomes more important than the Word of God. Often the ambitious leader degenerates into a petty tyrant. To guard against this, each local assembly must seek its direction and authority from the New Testament Scriptures, as historically interpreted by the collective body of Christ.

It seems to be an American obsession for church members to admire a strong and powerful church leader. His word is law. He acts swiftly and persuasively. He gets things done. Committees are for those minor details that do not concern him. He sets the program, and the program operates around him. Many are quite willing to meekly follow, giving modified support to this ecclesiastical superstar. One-man ministries abound for several reasons: tradition, lazy parishioners, and the attitude that "the pastor's paid to do it." Almost by default, some pastors become builders and defenders of their own little kingdoms.

Diotrephes knew nothing of the New Testament pattern of shared ministry. He loved to be first, to have preeminence. He actively engaged in a gossip campaign against the apostle John. In his arrogance he expelled some believers from the local congregation and was inhospitable to the visiting teachers. Diotrephes leads the way for those domineering, authoritarian leaders who blatantly violate the scriptural admonishment to servanthood.

Gaius, on the other hand, embodies the New Testament standard of servant leadership. He lived the truth, gave hospitality to the Lord's servants, and was known for his loving deeds. With a heart truly devoted to God, Gaius demonstrated that spiritual leadership is concerned more with the service one renders to God and fellow believers than with the benefits one can gain from a leadership role.

Those who lead would do well to bear in mind our Lord's words: "Whoever wants to be a leader among you must be your servant, and whoever wants to be first among you must be the slave of everyone else" (Mark 10:43-44), or as Luke records Jesus' words: "The leader should be like a servant" (Luke 22:26). Jesus provided his disciples an example of servanthood when he washed their feet (John 13:3-5); he was visibly demonstrating the spirit of servanthood. Such a model made an impact on Simon Peter, who, years later, would write in his epistle to the churches, "Care for the flock that God has entrusted to you. Watch over it willingly, not grudgingly—not for what you will get out of it, but because you are eager to serve God. Don't lord it over the people assigned to your care, but lead them by your own good example" (1 Pet 5:2-3).

NOTES

1:3 *traveling teachers.* Lit., "the brothers" (cf. NLT mg), but the context implies that these must have been the same ones who traveled from church to church, teaching the apostolic truths (see notes on 1:5 and 1:10).

   your faithfulness. Lit., "the truth in you." This truth was his "loyalty to Christ and the gospel by which his life was marked" (Bruce 1970:148). The NRSV reads "your faithfulness to the truth."

you are living according to the truth. Gaius conducted his life in the truth— he lived it, or as we might say today, "He was really into it." This is in clear contrast to Diotrephes, whose conduct was contrary to the truth.

1:4 *I could have no greater joy.* This reading has excellent textual support: A (C) L P (1739) syr cop^s. Another reading, "I could have no greater thanks," is supported by B (1243 2298) it cop^{bo}. Westcott and Hort, showing their preference for Codex Vaticanus (B), selected this reading for their text (see WH), but the textual evidence speaks against it.

my children. John was fond of calling the believers under his care "my children" (cf. 1 Jn 2:12-14). This use of the phrase supports the view that in 2 John the dear woman and her children, and the sister and her children, also refer to local churches.

1:5 *traveling teachers who pass through, even though they are strangers to you.* This is a justified interpretive translation of what is more literally "the brothers, especially [when] strangers." The context indicates that Gaius was caring for Christian workers, previously unknown to him, as they traveled from local church to local church.

1:6 *the church.* This is the first occurrence of the word "church" in all of John's writings (see also 1:9-10). This was most likely John's home church, perhaps the church in Ephesus. The context and wording point to a particular assembly of this local church (note the anarthrous expression *ekklēsias* [^{TG}1577, ^{ZG}1711]), during which some brothers told the believers about Gaius's kindness, which was then held up as an example for others.

Please continue providing for such teachers. Lit., "to send them on their way." This is an idiom for providing needed supplies for a journey. Since the traveling teachers were servants of the Lord Jesus, they were worthy of support.

1:7 *the Lord.* Lit., "the Name" (see NLT mg). The writer did not need to identify whose name he meant; every believer knew that "the Name" denoted "Jesus Christ." Other NT writers did the same; they simply said "the Name" and expected their readers to know whose name they meant—the name of Jesus Christ (cf. Heb 1:4; 6:10; 13:15; Jas 2:7; 1 Jn 2:12).

accept nothing from people who are not believers. Lit., ". . . from the Gentiles" (*ethnikos* [^{TG}1482, ^{ZG}1618]). At this time in church history (AD 80 at the earliest), non-Christians may very well have been considered to be "Gentiles"—just as previously all non-Jews were categorized as "Gentiles." Apparently these traveling missionaries had a self-imposed restriction to not take anything offered from unbelievers.

1:8 *we ourselves should support them.* This is the reading in ℵ A B C* 33 1739. A variant reading is "we ought to receive such men," found in C² P 𝔐 (so TR and

KJV, NKJV). A mere one-letter difference (upsilon/alpha) separates the two readings: (*[h]upolambanein* [^TG^5274, ^ZG^5696] versus *apolambanein* [^TG^618, ^ZG^655]). But there is a significant difference in meaning. The text, which has superior attestation, provides an encouragement for the believers to support traveling teachers by giving them hospitality (cf. BAGD 5) and an opportunity for ministry. The variant, which has inferior, late attestation, provides encouragement for the believers to welcome (cf. BAGD 94) the traveling teachers. The former speaks of a greater commitment on the part of the believers.

we can be their partners as they teach the truth. This reading is attested by only a few late mss (614 1505); it makes the people to be coworkers with one another, not with the truth. Better textual attestation (ℵ^c^ B C) supports the reading, "that we may become partners with the truth." Two mss (ℵ * A) read, "that we may become partners with the church." This last variant obfuscates the personification of the truth by substituting "the church" for "the truth." (The same change occurred in 1:12—see note.) The idea of the text is that the believers can promote and partner with the truth by supporting the traveling teachers who affirm the apostolic truths.

1:9 I wrote to the church about this. Lit., "I wrote something to the church." This reading has the support of ℵ* A B 048^vid^ 1739. Other mss read, "I wrote to the church" (C P Ψ 𝔐 [so TR]), and still others read, "I would have written to the church" (ℵ² 33 81 323 614 630 945 Vulgate syr). The first variant omits "something," probably so that readers won't think to trivialize any writings of the apostles. The second variant is probably an attempt to circumvent any queries about why John's previous letter to the church is not extant. Of course, if 1 John or 2 John were that letter, then there would be no perceived problem. But it is a matter of conjecture whether or not this correspondence "to the church" (the second use of *ekklēsia* [^TG^1577, ^ZG^1711] in all of John's writings; cf. 1:6) refers to one of John's previous epistles or to some lost epistle. Most scholars (e.g., Stott 2000:228-229; Marshall 1978:88) reject 1 John as an option because, though it is a letter to the church or churches in the Johannine community, it says nothing about the reception or rejection of traveling teachers (the subject at hand in 3 John). And though 2 John is probably a letter to a specific church, most scholars also reject it as an option because it, too, says nothing about traveling teachers (e.g., Smalley 1984:353-354). Most scholars, therefore, conclude that the letter John previously wrote got lost or was destroyed by Diotrephes.

However, John does not explicitly say that his previous letter dealt with the issue of receiving the traveling teachers. The text does not say, "I have written something to the church *about this*." Rather, it simply indicates that John wrote something to the church and that his letter to the church was not received by Diotrephes because he did not receive John and his coworkers. This situation coincides with a major theme in 1 John—namely, John's insistence that those who claim to have enlightened fellowship with God while disdaining fellowship with the children of God are liars. Such was Diotrephes. So 1 John could very well be the previous correspondence that John was referring to. With this as a possibility, the variant "I would have written to the church" could mean that John wrote to Gaius instead of to the church because he knew that Diotrephes would have interfered with his message to the church.

Diotrephes, who loves to be the leader. Lit., "Diotrephes loving to be first among them." Diotrephes apparently had an important position in the church. Maybe he was an elder or wanted to be; either way, he was blinded with pride and self-importance (cf. 1 Tim 3:6) and was acting against the apostle's teaching.

refuses to have anything to do with us. Given the context, this is a correct interpretation of "does not receive us."

1:10 when I come, I will report some of the things he is doing. John was prepared to publicly denounce Diotrephes before the whole church. (See 1:14 for John's anticipation of soon visiting the church Gaius belonged to.)

evil accusations he is making against us. The verb *phluareō* [TG5396, ZG5826], used only here in the NT, "has the meaning of making false accusations in a garrulous way" (Vine 1970:126).

1:11 those who do evil prove that they do not know God. As John made known in his first epistle (1 Jn 2:29), the works of evil done by men such as Diotrephes prove that they do not really know God.

1:12 Everyone speaks highly of Demetrius. The placement of Demetrius's name at the end of the letter suggests that he was the one who carried John's letter to Gaius. The fact that John commends Demetrius to Gaius seems to imply that he was better known to John than he was to Gaius. He may, in fact, have been one of the "traveling teachers" John had sent earlier.

as does the truth itself. This reading has excellent support (𝔓74c ℵ Ac B P 044 049 33 1739). The truth is depicted as a witness of the good works of Demetrius, for Demetrius had advanced the cause of truth. The scribes of two mss (𝔓74 A) changed "the truth" to "the church"; later, these mss were corrected to read "the truth."

you know we speak the truth. It was typical for John to use the plural "we" when affirming the veracity of his testimony (cf. John 21:24; 1 Jn 1:4-5).

John's Final Words

3 JOHN 1:13-15

EXPOSITION

This letter closes in a manner quite similar to what has been found in any number of letters from Hellenistic times. It was a letter from one friend to another. This shows that John and Gaius had a close relationship. John did not use his apostleship to command Gaius to do anything. Rather, he spoke to him as a friend. The same kind of spirit is exhibited in Paul's letter to Philemon.

Many Christians will testify of the same reality: Their closest friends are their brothers and sisters in Christ—even closer (in some ways) than their blood brothers and sisters. Jesus set the example. He called his disciples "friends." And because they were his friends, he expected that they would do whatever he commanded them (John 15:14-15). So it is true among Christian friends: We hear each other's requests and we respond, because we are friends.

NOTES

1:13 *I don't want to write it with pen and ink.* The pen would have been a stylus, shaped from a "reed" (*kalamos* [TG2563, ZG2812]). The "ink" (*melanos* [TG3188, ZG3506]) would have probably been a black or dark carbon-based ink. At the conclusion of 2 John, the writer also said he wanted to communicate further, but not with "paper and ink" (see note on 2 Jn 1:12).

1:14 *face to face.* The English idiom "face to face" parallels the Greek idiom here, which is, lit., "mouth to mouth."

1:15 *friends.* Gr., *philoi* [TG53, ZG5813]. The term "brothers" is usually used in the greetings found in NT epistles, but "friends" is appropriate in this friendly letter to Gaius.

Bibliography

Alford, Henry
The Greek Testament. Grand Rapids: Guardian, 1976. (Orig. pub. 1852.)

Aune, David
The New Testament in Its Literary Environment. Philadelphia: Westminster, 1987.

Barker, G. W.
1 John, 2 John, 3 John. Pp. 293-377 in *The Expositor's Bible Commentary,* vol. 12. Grand Rapids: Zondervan, 1981.

Barrett, C. K.
The Gospel according to St. John. 2nd ed. Philadelphia: Westminster, 1978.

Beasley-Murray, George R.
John. Word Biblical Commentary. Waco: Word, 1987.

Brooke, A. E.
A Critical and Exegetical Commentary on the Johannine Epistles. Edinburgh: T & T Clark, 1912.

Brown, Raymond E.
The Gospel According to John, vol. 1, chs. 1–12. Anchor Bible. New York: Doubleday, 1966.
The Gospel According to John, vol. 2, chs. 13–21. Anchor Bible. New York: Doubleday, 1970.
The Community of the Beloved Disciple. Toronto: Paulist, 1979.
The Epistles of John. New York: Doubleday, 1982.

Brown, Raymond, Joseph Fitzmyer, and Roland Murphy
The New Jerome Biblical Commentary. Upper Saddle River, NJ: Prentice Hall, 1990.

Bruce, F. F.
The Epistles of John. Old Tappan, NJ: Revell, 1970.
The Gospel of John. Grand Rapids: Eerdmans, 1983.

Bultmann, Rudolf
The Gospel of John: A Commentary. Translator, G. R. Beasley-Murray. Oxford: Blackwell, 1971.

Burge, Gary M.
The Anointed Community. Grand Rapids: Eerdmans, 1987.
Letters of John. NIV Application Commentary. Grand Rapids: Zondervan, 1996.

Carson, D. A.
The Gospel According to John. Grand Rapids: Eerdmans, 1989.

Comfort, Philip
The New Testament Ecclesia: The House Church and the Local Church. Pp. 153-158 in *The Topical Encyclopedia of Christian Worship,* vol. 1. Editor, Robert Webber. Nashville: Abbott Martyn, 1993.
I Am the Way: A Spiritual Journey through the Gospel of John. Grand Rapids: Baker Book House, 1994. (Reprinted by Wipf and Stock, 2001.)

"The Scribe as Reader: A New Look at New Testament Textual Criticism according to Reader Reception Theory." D. Litt. Dissertation, University of South Africa, 1997.
Encountering the Manuscripts: An Introduction to New Testament Paleography and Textual Criticism. Nashville: Broadman & Holman, 2005.
New Testament Text and Translation Commentary. Carol Stream, IL: Tyndale House, 2007.

Conway, C. M.
The Production of the Johannine Community: A New Historicist Perspective. *Journal of Biblical, Literature* 121:479-495, 2002.

Cullman, Oscar
The Johannine Circle. Translator, John Bowden. Philadelphia: Westminster, 1975.

Culpepper, R. Allen
The Johannine School. Missoula, MT: Scholars Press, 1975.
Anatomy of the Fourth Gospel: A Study in Literary Design. Philadelphia: Fortress, 1983.

Deissmann, Adolf
Light from the Ancient East: The New Testament Illustrated by Recently Discovered Texts of the Graeco-Roman World. Translator, Lionel R. M. Strachan. Grand Rapids: Baker, 1978. (Orig. Pub. 1922.)

DeYoung, James B.
1–3 John. Pp. 997-1079 in *Evangelical Commentary on the Bible.* Editor, Walter Elwell. Grand Rapids: Baker, 1989.

Dodd, C. H.
The Johannine Epistles. London: Hodder & Stoughton, 1946.
The Interpretation of the Fourth Gospel. Cambridge: Cambridge University Press, 1953.

Douglas, J. D. , Philip Comfort, and Donald Mitchell
Who's Who in Christian History. Wheaton: Tyndale House, 1992.

Dunn, J. D. G.
Jesus and the Spirit. Philadelphia: Westminster, 1975.

Elwell, Walter and Philip Comfort
Tyndale Bible Dictionary. Wheaton: Tyndale House, 2001.

Giles, Kevin
Prophecy, Prophets, False Prophets. Pp. 970-977 in *Dictionary of the Later New Testament and Its Developments.* Editors, Ralph P. Martin and Peter H. Davids. Downers Grove, IL: InterVarsity, 1997.

Gundry, R. H.
In My Father's House Are Many Monai (John 14:2). *Zeitschrift für die neutestamentliche Wissenschaft* 58:68-72, 1967
A Survey of the New Testament (3rd ed.). Grand Rapids: Zondervan, 1994.

Harris, M. J.
Jesus as God: The New Testament Use of Theos in Reference to Jesus. Grand Rapids: Baker, 1992.

Hicks, C. and M. Winter
Cerinthus. P. 148 in *Who's Who in Christian History.* Editors, J. D. Douglas, P. W. Comfort, D. Mitchell. Wheaton: Tyndale House, 1992.

House, W. H.
Papias. P. 530 in *Who's Who in Christian History.* Editors, J. D. Douglas, P. W. Comfort, D. Mitchell. Wheaton: Tyndale House, 1992.

Howard, W. F.
The Common Authorship of the Johannine Gospel and Epistles. *Journal of Theological Studies* 48:12-25, 1947.

Hunt, A. S. and C. C. Edgar
Select Papyri. Cambridge, MA: Harvard University Press, 1959.

Johnston, G.
The Spirit-Paraclete in the Gospel of John. Cambridge: Cambridge University Press, 1970.

Law, R.
The Tests of Life: A Study of the First Epistle of John. Edinburgh: T & T Clark, 1914.

Manson, T. W.
Entry into Membership in the Early Church. *Journal of Theological Studies* 48:25-33, 1947.

Marshall, I. H.
The Epistles of John. New International Commentary on the New Testament. Grand Rapids: Eerdmans, 1978.

Metzger, Bruce
A Textual Commentary on the Greek New Testament (2nd ed.). Stuttgart: German Bible Society, 1994.

Morris, Leon
1 John, 2 John, 3 John Pp. 1259-1273 in *The New Bible Commentary.* (Rev. ed.) Grand Rapids: Eerdmans, 1970.
The Gospel According to John. Grand Rapids: Eerdmans, 1971.

Oliver, W. H. and A. C. van Aarle
The Community of Faith as Dwelling Place of the Father. *Basileia tou theou* as Household of God. *Neotestimentica* 25:379-400, 1991.

Painter, J.
The Quest for the Messiah: The History, Literature and Theology of the Johannine Community. Edinburgh: T & T Clark, 1993.

Richards, W. L.
The Classification of the Greek Manuscripts of the Johannine Epistles. Society of Biblical Literature Dissertation Series. Missoula, MT: Scholars Press, 1971.

Roberts, C. H.
An Unpublished Fragment of the Fourth Gospel in the John Rylands Library. Manchester, 1935.

Robinson, J. A. T.
Redating the New Testament. London: SCM, 1976. (Reprinted by Wipf and Stock, 2000.)
The Priority of John. London: SCM, 1985.

Schnackenburg, Rudolph
Die Johannesbriefe. Freiburg: Herder, 1979.
The Gospel According to St. John. 3 vols. Translator, Kevin Smyth. New York: Crossroad, 1980, 1982.

Smalley, Stephen S.
1, 2, 3 John. Word Biblical Commentary. Waco: Word, 1984.

Smith, David
The Epistles of John. The Expositor's Greek Testament, vol. 5. Editor, W. R. Nicoll. Grand Rapids: Eerdmans, 1979. (Orig. pub. 1910.)

Stott, John
The Letters of John. Tyndale New Testament Commentaries (rev. ed.). Leicester: InterVarsity, 2000.

Stowers, Stanley K.
Letter Writing in Greco-Roman Antiquity. Philadelphia: Westminster, 1986.

Strecker, Georg
The Johannine Letters. Hermenia. Philadelphia: Fortress, 1995.

Talbert, C. H.
Reading John: A Literary and Theological Commentary on the Fourth Gospel and the Johannine Epistles. New York: Crossroad, 1992.

Tenney, Merril
New Testament Survey (rev. ed.). Grand Rapids: Zondervan, 1985.

Thompson, M. M.
1–3 John. IVP New Testament Commentary. Downers Grove. IL: InterVarsity, 1992.
The God of the Gospel of John. Grand Rapids: Eerdmans, 2001.

Vine, W. E.
The Epistles of John. Grand Rapids: Zondervan, 1970.

Westcott, B. F.
Gospel According to St. John. London: Macmillan, 1881.
The Epistles of St. John. London: Macmillan, 1886.

General Appendix: Manuscripts

John's Gospel is extant in many early manuscripts—dating from the early second century to the seventh century and coming from several geographical locations. These manuscripts, therefore, provide textual critics an excellent resource for their work in recovering the original wording of John's Gospel. The following list displays all the manuscripts cited in this commentary. Note that * after a manuscript refers to an original hand, c after a manuscript refers to a corrector, and vid is Latin for "it appears [to read as such]." Manuscripts referring to John's epistles are also included as indicated.

Significant Papyri (𝔓 = Papyrus)
𝔓2: 12:12-13
𝔓5: 1:23-31, 33-40; 16:14-30; 20:11-17, 19-20, 22-25
𝔓6: 10:1-2, 4-7, 9-10; 11:1-8, 45-52
𝔓9: 1 Jn 4:11-12, 14-17
𝔓22: 15:25–16:2, 21-32
𝔓28: 6:8-12, 17-22
𝔓36: 3:14-18, 31-32, 34-35
𝔓39: 8:14-22
𝔓44: 9:3-4; 10:8-14; 12:16-18
𝔓45: 10:7-25; 10:30–11:10, 18-36, 42-57
𝔓52: 18:31-34, 37-38
𝔓55: 1:31-33, 35-38
𝔓59: 1:26, 28, 51; 2:15-16; 11:40-52; 12:25, 29, 31, 35; 17:24-26; 18:1-2, 4-5, 7-16, 18-20, 23-29, 31-37, 39-40; 19:2-3, 5-8, 10-18, 20, 23-26
𝔓60: 16:29-30; 16:32–17:6, 8-9, 11-15, 18-25; 18:1-2, 4-5, 7-16, 18-20, 23-29, 31-37, 39-40; 19:2-3, 5-8, 10-18, 20, 23-26
𝔓63: 3:14-18; 4:9-10
𝔓66: 1:1–6:11; 6:35–14:26, 29-30; 15:2-26; 16:2-4, 6-7; 16:10–20:20, 22-23; 20:25–21:9
𝔓74: 1 Jn 1:1, 6; 2:1-2, 7, 13-14, 18-19, 25-26; 3:1-2, 8, 14, 19-20; 4:1, 6-7, 12, 16-17; 5:3-4, 9-10, 17; 2 Jn 1:1, 6-7, 13; 3 Jn 1:6, 12
𝔓75: 1:1–11:45, 48-57; 12:3–13:1, 8-9; 14:8-30; 15:7-8

𝔓76: 4:9, 12 and John's epistles
𝔓80: 3:34
𝔓84: 5:5; 17:3, 7-8
𝔓90: 18:36–19:7
𝔓93: 13:15-17
𝔓95: 5:26-29, 36-38

Significant Uncials

א (Codex Sinaiticus): all of John's Gospel
A (Codex Alexandrinus): all of John's Gospel
B (Codex Vaticanus): all of John's Gospel
C (Codex Ephraemi Rescriptus): 1:4-40; 3:34–5:16; 6:39–7:2; 8:35–9:10; 11:8-46; 13:8–14:7; 16:22–18:35; 20:26–21:25
D (Codex Bezae): all of John' Gospel except 1:16–3:26; 18:13-20
K (Codex Codex Cyprius): all of John's Gospel
L (Codex Regius): all of John's Gospel except 21:15-25
P (Codex Porphyrianus): 1 Jn 1:1–3:19; 5:2-21; 2 Jn; 3 Jn
Q (Codex Wolfenbuttel): 12:3-20; 14:3-22
T (Codex Borgianus): 1:24-32; 3:10-17; 4:52–5:7; 6:28-67; 7:6–8:31
W (Codex Washingtonianus): all of John (except 1:1–5:11 supplied by later hand, and 14:26–16:7 is missing)
044
048
049
323
614
630
945
0162: 2:11-22
0212: 19:38
0216: 8:51-53; 9:5-8
0217: 11:57–12:7
0218: 12:2-6, 9-11, 14-16
0232
02450264: 8:19-20, 23-24
1505

Significant Miniscules

33 John's Gospel
69 John's Gospel and epistles
81 John's epistles
1739 John's epistles

Significant Ancient Versions

Syriac (syr)
syr^h
syr^{h**}
syr^p

Old Latin (it)
it^{t,w,z}

Coptic (cop)
cop^{bo}
cop^{sa}

Other Versions
arm (Armenian)
eth (Ethiopic)